New GRE®
GRADUATE RECORD EXAMINATION

VERBAL WORKBOOK

Seventh Edition

KAPLAN

PUBLISHING

New York

For more GRE® prep, Kaplan offers a range of print and digital products, available in stores and online:

New GRE 2011–2012 Premier with CD-ROM

New GRE 2011–2012 Strategies, Practice, and Review

New GRE Math Workbook

New GRE Vocabulary Flashcards

Countdown to the New GRE app

Kaplan 101 New GRE Analytical Writing Practice Questions

Kaplan 101 New GRE Verbal Practice Questions

Kaplan 101 New GRE Math Practice Questions

New GRE® VERBAL WORKBOOK

GRADUATE RECORD EXAMINATION

PUBLISHING

New York

Published by Kaplan Publishing, a division of Kaplan, Inc.
395 Hudson Street
New York, NY 10014

Printed in the United States of America

10 9 8 7 6 5 4 3

ISBN-13: 978-1-4195-5001-0

Table of Contents

Acknowledgments.. ix

How to Use This Book xi

PART ONE: GETTING STARTED

CHAPTER 1 INTRODUCTION TO THE GRE VERBAL

Understanding the GRE Verbal Reasoning Section 3

MST Mechanics...3

Verbal Reasoning Question Types...4

Text Completion...5

Sentence Equivalence...5

Reading Comprehension 5

Analytical Writing...6

Analytical Writing Essay Types 6

PART TWO: VERBAL REASONING

CHAPTER 2 TEXT COMPLETION

Text Completion.. 11

Text Completion (One-Blank) Practice Set 15

Text Completion (One-Blank) Practice Set Answers and Explanations 17

Text Completion (Two-Blank and Three-Blank) Practice Set................. 24

Text Completion (Two-Blank and Three-Blank)
Practice Set Answers and Explanations................................... 26

Text Completion Practice Set 30

Text Completion Practice Set Answer Key 37

Text Completion Practice Set Answers and Explanations 38

CHAPTER 3 SENTENCE EQUIVALENCE

Sentence Equivalence 45

The Kaplan Method for Sentence Equivalence 46

Sentence Equivalence Practice Set 50

Sentence Equivalence Practice Set Answer Key 56

Sentence Equivalence Practice Set Answers and Explanations 57

CHAPTER 4 READING COMPREHENSION

Reading Comprehension 67

The Kaplan Method for Reading Comprehension 69

Reading Comprehension Practice Set 80

Reading Comprehension Practice Set Answer Key 96

Reading Comprehension Practice Set Answers and Explanations 98

CHAPTER 5 VERBAL REASONING PRACTICE SET

Verbal Reasoning Practice Set 1 107

Practice Set 1 Answer Key 116

Practice Set 1 Answers and Explanations 117

Diagnostic Tool 123

Verbal Reasoning Practice Set 2 124

Practice Set 2 Answer Key 132

Practice Set 2 Answers and Explanations 133

Diagnostic Tool 139

Verbal Reasoning Practice Set 3 140

Practice Set 3 Answers Key 149

Practice Set 3 Answers and Explanations 150

Diagnostic Tool 156

Verbal Reasoning Practice Set 4 157

Practice Set 4 Answer Key 165

Practice Set 4 Answers and Explanations 166

Diagnostic Tool 172

Verbal Reasoning Practice Set 5 173

Practice Set 5 Answer Key 181

Practice Set 5 Answers and Explanations 182

Diagnostic Tool 187

Verbal Reasoning Practice Set 6 188

Practice Set 6 Answer Key 196

Practice Set 6 Answers and Explanations 197

Diagnostic Tool 203

PART THREE: VERBAL CONTENT REVIEW

CHAPTER 6 VOCABULARY

Understanding Vocabulary 207

Word Groups 208

Word Groups Exercise 218

Answer Key for Word Groups Exercise 226

Answers and Explanations for Word Groups Exercise 227

Word Roots 230

Word Roots Exercises 248

Answer Key for Word Roots Exercise 251

Answers and Explanations for Word Roots Exercise 252

Words in Context 256

Words in Context Exercises 295

Answer Key for Words in Context Exercise 303

PART FOUR: ANALYTICAL WRITING

CHAPTER 7 THE ISSUE ESSAY

The Issue Essay 307

Pacing Strategy 313

Issue Essay Practice Prompts 315

Issue Essay Sample Essays and Explanations 319

CHAPTER 8 THE ARGUMENT ESSAY

The Argument Essay 329

Pacing Strategy 335

Argument Essay Practice Prompts 338

Argument Essay Sample Essays and Explanations 344

PART FIVE: ANALYTICAL WRITING CONTENT REVIEW

CHAPTER 9 WRITING FOUNDATIONS

Overview 355

Writing Style 355

Writing Style Exercises 356

Answers to Writing Style Exercises 360

Grammar.. 361

Grammar Exercises... 362

Answers to Grammar Exercises 366

Mechanics... 368

Mechanics Exercises 368

Answers to Mechanics Exercises 373

PART SIX: GRE RESOURCES

Appendix A: Kaplan's Word Groups 379

Appendix B: Kaplan's Root List... 387

Appendix C: Top GRE Words in Context 407

Acknowledgments

Special thanks to the team that made this book possible:

Arthur Ahn, Matthew Belinkie, Shannon Berning, Lauren T. Bernstein, Gerard Cortinez, Elisa Davis, Paula Fleming, Darcy Galane, Joanna Graham, Adam Grey, Adam Hinz, Gar Hong, Avi Lidgi, Kate Lopaze, Keith Lubeley, TJ Mancini, Jennifer Moore, Jason Moss, Walt Niedner, Robert Reiss, Derek Rusnak, Emily Sachar, Stephanie Schrauth, Sheryl Stebbins, Glen Stohr, Gene Suhir, Martha Torres, Liza Weale, Lee A. Weiss, and many others who have contributed materials and advice over the years.

How to Use This Book

Kaplan has prepared students to take standardized tests for more than 50 years. Our team of researchers knows more about preparation for the GRE than anyone else, and you'll find their accumulated knowledge and experience throughout this book. The GRE is a standardized test, so every administration covers the same content in roughly the same way. This is good news for you; it means that the best way to prepare is to focus on the sort of questions you are likely to see on Test Day. The main focus of this book is on strategic reviews, exercises, and practice tests with explanations that will help you brush up on your vocabulary, reading comprehension and writing skills. If possible, work through this book a little at a time over the course of several weeks. There is a lot of material to absorb, and it's hard to do all at once.

Getting Started

Part One of this book, "Getting Started," provides you with background information on the Verbal Reasoning section of the test, what it covers, and how it's organized.

Verbal Reasoning Section

The Verbal Reasoning section GRE contains three main question types: Text Completion, Sentence Equivalence, and Reading Comprehension. Part Three of this book covers these types with strategies and sample questions. Your focus here should be to familiarize yourself with the question types so you won't be trying to figure out how to approach them on Test Day.

Read the explanations to all the questions—even those you got right. Often the explanations will contain strategies that show you how you could have gotten to the answer more quickly and efficiently.

Analytical Writing Section

The Analytical Writing Content Review covers grammar, mechanics, and style, as well as strategies for writing effective paragraphs and essays. The final chapters of this workbook cover sample GRE prompts. Using these prompts, you can practice the skills you have learned to write strong essays. In addition to sample prompts, we've also included sample top-scoring essays so you can review the qualities that earn an essay a high score.

Verbal Content Review

Once you have the big picture, focus on the content. Part Two of this book, "Verbal Content Review," gives you a complete tour of the vocabulary that you will see on test day. The material in the Verbal Content review is divided into particular subjects. Each subject begins with a review, followed by practice questions. This structure makes it easy for you to pinpoint the vocabulary concepts you need to review and quickly get your skills up to speed.

Now you're ready to begin preparing for the Verbal Reasoning section of the GRE.

Good luck!

Getting Started

CHAPTER 1

Introduction to the GRE Verbal

UNDERSTANDING THE GRE VERBAL REASONING SECTION

The Graduate Record Exam's (GRE) Verbal Reasoning section emphasizes complex reasoning skills and rewards your ability to analyze the relationships among words and sentences as they are used in context. The exam tests vocabulary contextually, and the reading passages are both dense and written with a sophisticated level of diction. The goal of the test's content and emphasis on analytical skills is to provide an accurate indication of your ability to understand what you're reading and to apply reasoning skills to the text's premises and arguments. These are all skills you will need at the graduate level.

To perform well on the Verbal Reasoning section—to answer correctly as many questions as possible—you need to have a good grasp of vocabulary and the ability to apply reasoning skills. Part Two of this book explains the various question types in detail. Part Three reviews the foundations of vocabulary. Every chapter offers plenty of opportunities to practice and review your answers.

MST MECHANICS

The revised GRE is a multi-stage test (MST). While working within a section of the test, you may skip questions and return to them as long as time remains for the section. The test is computer based, presented in an interface with tools such as a Mark button (to indicate a question you want to examine later within the time allowed for that section), a Review button (to see your progress on the entire set of questions in a section), and an optional time display. As you prepare for test day, consider how these computer capabilities may help you manage your time for each section.

As best you can, approach the exam as you would a paper-based one. After all, the idea behind the MST is that it will feel more comfortable and familiar than some other computer-based or adaptive tests, on which you cannot move about freely within a section. Use the MST's design to your advantage. If a question looks too daunting, skip it. Use the Mark button to remind you to come back to the question when you have time at the end of that section. You can "Mark" a question whether or not you've answered it. By doing so, you can better organize your time by keeping track of which questions you are done with and which ones need a second look.

Finally, having an on-screen timer (which appears in the corner of the display) works to your advantage, helping you keep track of the time remaining in the section. But if you find yourself looking at it so frequently that it becomes a distraction, turn it off for a few minutes and refocus your attention on the test. Use the timer to help you make good decisions about how to spend your time within the section, but don't let it prevent you from concentrating on the questions.

VERBAL REASONING QUESTION TYPES

The GRE MST contains two Verbal Reasoning sections with 20 questions each. Each section lasts 30 minutes and contains a selection of the following question types:

- Text Completion
- Sentence Equivalence
- Reading Comprehension

The Verbal Reasoning portion of the GRE rewards a strong, university-level vocabulary and facility with understanding and analyzing written material. Specifically, it evaluates your ability to do the following:

- Accurately paraphrase sentences and paragraphs.
- Derive a word's meaning based on its context.
- Detect relationships among words.
- Understand the logic of sentences and paragraphs.
- Draw inferences.
- Recognize major, minor, and irrelevant points.
- Summarize ideas.
- Understand passage and paragraph structure.
- Recognize an author's tone, purpose, and perspective.

The GRE assesses those skills with an assortment of Text Completion, Sentence Equivalence, and Reading Comprehension items. The following chart shows how many questions of each type you can expect, as well as the average amount of time you should spend per question.

	Text Completion	**Sentence Equivalence**	**Reading Comprehension**
Number of Questions	Approx. 6	Approx. 4	Approx. 10
Time per Question	1 to 1.5 minutes	1 minute	1–3 depending on the length, to read the passage and 1 minute to answer each question

TEXT COMPLETION

You will find about six Text Completion questions in each Verbal Reasoning section. These questions are comprised of single sentences or short paragraphs of two or three sentences. The text has blanks replacing one, two, or three words. Your task is to select one word for each blank from a column of corresponding choices to complete the text logically. This question type tests your ability to read strategically—to recognize the point of a sentence and find the best word(s) to fit its meaning.

Chapter 2 presents the Kaplan Method for answering Text Completion questions and strategies to help you solve them efficiently.

SENTENCE EQUIVALENCE

Each Verbal Reasoning section features approximately four Sentence Equivalence questions. These questions provide a single sentence with one missing word. You must identify two correct words, either of which would complete the sentence. The correct answer choices, when inserted into the blank, will give the same meaning to *both* resulting sentences. These questions test your ability to determine a sentence's meaning and to use vocabulary in context.

You'll find the Kaplan Method for Sentence Equivalence questions and strategies to help solve them efficiently in Chapter 3.

READING COMPREHENSION

Reading Comprehension is the only question type that appears on all major standardized tests, and with good reason. No matter what academic discipline you pursue, you'll have to make sense of dense, complex written material. Being able to understand and assess such material is a crucial skill for every graduate student.

To make the test broadly relevant, and to better evaluate your ability to understand comparable material, the test maker, Educational Testing Service (ETS) adapts Reading Comprehension content from "real-world," graduate-level documents. GRE passages come from four disciplines: social sciences, biological sciences, physical sciences, and the arts and humanities.

The GRE includes roughly ten reading passages between the two Verbal Reasoning sections. Many of these passages are one paragraph in length, although a few are longer. Each passage is accompanied by one to six questions. These questions reward you for ascertaining the author's purpose and meaning, determining what can be validly inferred from the passage, researching details in the text, and understanding the meaning of words and the function of sentences in context.

Chapter 4 contains the Kaplan Method for answering Reading Comprehension questions and strategies to help solve them efficiently.

ANALYTICAL WRITING

The Analytical Writing section assesses not only how well you write, but also the thought processes you employ in formulating and articulating a position. In response to short, descriptive prompts, you produce two essays, one in which you evaluate an argument and one in which you make an argument of your own. Specifically, the Analytical Writing tasks measure your ability to do the following:

- Articulate and defend a position.
- Deconstruct and evaluate a complex argument.
- Develop a cogent argument.
- Assess the fundamental soundness of an argument.
- Recognize major, minor, and irrelevant points.
- Provide evidence and support for an argument.
- Detect the flaws in an unsound argument.
- Write articulately and effectively at a high level.

Regardless of your field, you will need these critical thinking skills to perform well in a graduate program.

ANALYTICAL WRITING ESSAY TYPES

The GRE's Analytical Writing section contains two different essay types. You'll be given 30 minutes for each essay. Here are your tasks:

- The Issue Essay Task provides a brief quotation on an issue of general interest and instructions on how to respond to the issue. You can discuss the issue from any perspective, making use of your own educational and personal background, examples from current or historical events, things you've read, or even relevant hypothetical situations. In this task, you develop your own argument in response to the prompt.
- The Argument Essay Task contains a short argument that may or may not be complete and specific instructions on how to evaluate the argument's strength. You will assess the argument's cogency, analyze the author's reasoning, and evaluate the use (or lack) of evidence. In this task, you critique the argument presented in the prompt.

You'll write the essays on the computer, using a simple word processing program with functions such as cut, paste, delete, and insert text but no spelling or grammar checker. Graders score the Analytical Writing essays based on your ability to plan and compose a logical, well-reasoned essay, one that's responsive to the test's instructions, under timed conditions. Only a score report is sent to the schools to which you apply.

Stay Updated

As ETS makes further announcements about the revised GRE, you can depend on Kaplan to provide the most accurate, up-to-date information. Get updates by visiting us at Kaptest.com/NEWGRE.

PART TWO

Verbal Reasoning

CHAPTER 2

Text Completion

TEXT COMPLETION

You will find about six Text Completion questions per Verbal Reasoning section on the GRE. In each Text Completion question, one, two, or three words from the sentence(s) will be missing. This question type tests your ability to recognize the point of the sentence and find the best word(s) to fit its meaning. Text Completion questions do not merely test vocabulary. By omitting a critical word (or two or three), they force you to read actively and strategically. In selecting the correct answer(s), you must consider the context into which they are inserted. For Text Completion questions with two or three blanks, all of the blanks must be filled in correctly to earn the point. *No partial credit is given.*

The directions for Text Completion questions will look like this:

> For this question, select one entry for each blank from the corresponding column of choices. Fill all blanks in the way that best completes the text.

A Text Completion question with one blank will look like this:

> Although the city's public mass transportation system has been _____ from active use, traces of its presence may be seen in the train stations that have been converted into shopping centers.
>
> (A) dilated
> (B) retired
> (C) metastasized
> (D) frozen
> (E) waxed

> ## The Kaplan Method for Text Completion (One-Blank)
>
> » **STEP 1**   Read the sentence, looking for clues.
>
> » **STEP 2**   Predict an answer.
>
> » **STEP 3**   Select the choice that most closely matches your prediction.
>
> » **STEP 4**   Check your answer.

How the Kaplan Method for Text Completion (One-Blank) Works

Here's how the Kaplan Method for Text Completion (One-Blank) works.

» **STEP 1**   **Read the sentence, looking for clues.**

There are always clues in the sentence that will point you to the right answer. The missing words in Text Completion questions will usually be similar or opposite to key words in the sentence.

On the GRE, a semicolon always connects two closely related independent clauses.

If a semicolon is followed by a "road sign," then that clue word indicates the sentence's direction. There are road signs in the GRE that tell you to go straight ahead and those that tell you to take a detour.

Straight-ahead road signs—*and, additionally, moreover, so*—are used when one part of the sentence supports or elaborates on the other part. They continue the sentence in the same direction. The positive or negative connotation of what follows is not changed by these clues.

Detour road signs—*but, however, on the other hand, to the contrary*—change the direction of the sentence. They indicate that one part of the sentence contradicts or qualifies the other part. The positive or negative connotation of an answer is changed by these clues.

Knowing and using the following road signs will help you to determine which way a Text Completion sentence is going and to predict what words will best fill in the blank(s):

Straight-ahead road signs:	Detour road signs:
And	*But*
Since	*Despite*
Also	*Yet*
Thus	*However*
Because	*Unless*
; (semicolon)	*Rather*
Likewise	*Although*
Moreover	*While*
Similarly	*On the other hand*
In addition	*Unfortunately*
Consequently	*Nonetheless*
	Conversely

Key words and key phrases are the descriptors that lead to the meaning of the missing words.

STEP 2 Predict an answer.

Once you've found the road sign and the key word(s) relevant to the blank, use them to predict an answer for the blank. Your prediction does not have to be a sophisticated or complex word or phrase, simply a paraphrase that fits logically into the sentence. By predicting, you avoid the temptation of trying every answer choice on its own, which can take up valuable time on test day.

STEP 3 Select the choice that most closely matches your prediction.

Quickly go through the choices and select the one that most closely matches your prediction of the correct answer. Eliminate choices that do not fit your prediction. If none of the choices match your prediction, reread the question and revisit steps 1 and 2.

STEP 4 Check your answer.

This step is simply double-checking that you did your work correctly and that your answer choice makes sense in context. If the sentence makes sense when read with your choice, confirm your answer and move on. If your choice does not make sense of the sentence, reread the question and revisit steps 1 through 3.

Apply the Kaplan Method for Text Completion (One-Blank)

Now, apply the Kaplan Method to a Text Completion (One-Blank) question:

Although the city's public mass transportation system has been _____ from active service, traces of its presence may be seen in the train stations that have been converted into shopping centers.

- (A) dilated
- (B) retired
- (C) metastasized
- (D) frozen
- (E) waxed

>> **STEP 1 Read the sentence, looking for clues.**

Begin by paraphrasing the sentence's main idea: The city's transportation system has not disappeared entirely, because traces of it may still be seen. The detour road sign "although" indicates that the verb that will fill the blank will contrast with the second half of the sentence.

>> **STEP 2 Predict an answer.**

Based on that paraphrase, you can predict that the correct answer will have a meaning similar to "removed" or "quit."

>> **STEP 3 Select the choice that most closely matches your prediction.**

Answer choice **(B)** *retired* matches the meaning of your prediction. The system has been "retired" from active service. Choices **(A)** *dilated* and **(E)** *waxed* mean "increased" or "widened"; they are the opposite of your prediction. Similarly, choice **(C)** *metastasized* means something has spread. Choice **(D)** *frozen* makes little sense in this context.

>> **STEP 4 Check your answer.**

To make sure your answer is right, simply plug it back into the original sentence:

"Although the city's public mass transportation system has been *retired* from active service, traces of its presence may be seen in the train stations that have been converted into shopping centers."

The sentence is logical, and the answer choice matches your prediction; it's the right answer.

TEXT COMPLETION (ONE-BLANK) PRACTICE SET

Try the following Text Completion questions using the Kaplan Method:

1. The director is normally lauded for his exciting science fiction films, but his latest effort is marred by its _____ special effects.

   (A) electrifying

   (B) piquant

   (C) bland

   (D) emotive

   (E) impenetrable

2. Despite her long battle with illness, the dancer displayed astonishing _____ of motion on stage.

   (A) indolence

   (B) hesitancy

   (C) extension

   (D) queasiness

   (E) fluency

3. Having established his competence as a playwright with his first play, the author went on to show greater _____ with his second.

   (A) characterization

   (B) mastery

   (C) understanding

   (D) perception

   (E) insufficiency

4. Such a _____ response to a client is not consistent with the high standards of customer service this company demands.

   (A) politic

   (B) cloying

   (C) meticulous

   (D) boastful

   (E) disrespectful

5. Difficult as it may sometimes be, in all our dealings with both clients and competitors, we must be seen to be above _____.

    (A) profit

    (B) integrity

    (C) question

    (D) reproach

    (E) scruples

TEXT COMPLETION (ONE-BLANK) PRACTICE SET ANSWERS AND EXPLANATIONS

1. C

Reading this sentence all the way through reveals that "normally" is a detour road sign, indicating that the sentence will change direction. So, while the director is normally "lauded," which means "praised," for his exciting films, his newest one is "marred" by its special effects. Therefore, the word that goes in the blank must be a negatively charged adjective that contrasts with "exciting." You can predict that the correct answer is a word that means "unexciting" or "dull." The answer that fits this prediction is choice **(C)** *bland.* Choices **(A)** *electrifying,* **(B)** *piquant,* and **(D)** *emotive* are related in meaning to "exciting" or "engaging." Choice **(E)** *impenetrable,* or incapable of being understood, is plausible. Impenetrable special effects would certainly mar a film, but *impenetrable* doesn't logically contrast with "exciting." *Bland,* on the other hand, is a direct opposite, and **(C)** is the correct answer.

2. E

"Despite" is a detour road sign indicating that the correct answer will contrast with the fact that the dancer has endured a long battle with illness. A reasonable prediction is *gracefulness,* which you would not expect from a dancer who has been seriously ill. The best choice is **(E)** *fluency.* "Fluency of motion" has a meaning similar to gracefulness, so it matches your prediction. Choice **(D)** *queasiness* does not fit the context of the sentence, as you would expect nausea from a dancer who has been ill. The same applies for **(B)** *hesitancy,* as you might expect the

dancer to be tentative in her movements. Choice **(A)** *indolence,* which means "laziness," doesn't fit because there would be nothing astonishing about that. Choice **(C)** *extension* doesn't make sense in this context.

3. B

The first clause in this sentence describes the playwright as "competent" in his first play, while the second clause asserts that he has progressed beyond mere competence in his second. *Prowess* is an excellent prediction. Choice **(B)** *mastery* fits perfectly; the playwright no longer is merely *competent,* he is now *masterful.* You can reject **(E)** *insufficiency* as the opposite of what the sentence needs. Choices **(A)** *characterization,* **(C)** *understanding,* and **(D)** *perception* are all elements of writing that the playwright may have improved upon, but you're looking for a more general word. Nothing in the sentence leads logically to a specific area of improvement.

4. E

The word "not" is a detour road sign indicating that the adjective in the blank (which describes the word "response") must be inconsistent with "high standards of customer service." This question requires close attention; all of the answer choices are, in at least one of their meanings, negatively charged. You need to distinguish the answer with the correct shade of meaning. High customer service standards imply proper etiquette, responsiveness, and professionalism. A simple, accurate prediction of the opposite of those is *rude*. Choice **(E)** *disrespectful* is the answer choice closest to that prediction. Choice **(A)** *politic* has a couple of meanings: "shrewd," not undesirable from someone working in customer service, and "tactful," just the opposite of what the correct answer must say here. Choice **(B)** *cloying* means "overly sweet," which some might find annoying but might be characteristic of someone overly enthusiastic in dealing with customers. Choice **(C)** *meticulous* means "attentive to detail," another trait not indicative of bad customer service. Choice **(D)** *boastful* means "full of excessive pride," which does not necessarily make someone rude or inhospitable.

5. D
To unlock this question, recognize that the term in the blank must be a negatively charged word with which a reputable business would not wish to be associated. *Suspicion* works nicely. Choices **(C)** *question* and **(D)** *reproach* could both work, but *reproach*, meaning "blame," is the much better fit for the context. It has a stronger charge than *question*, which is too neutral to work here. You can immediately eliminate **(B)** *integrity* and **(E)** *scruples,* which mean "adherence to ethical principles" and "moral considerations" respectively. These qualities are desirable in a business or company. In context, choice **(A)** *profit* makes little sense; it's not logical to say a company appears to be "above profit."

The Kaplan Method for Text Completion (Two-Blank And Three-Blank)

» **STEP 1** Read the sentence, looking for clues.

» **STEP 2** Predict the answer for the easier/easiest blank.

» **STEP 3** Select the answer choice that most closely matches your prediction.

» **STEP 4** Predict and select for the remaining blanks.

» **STEP 5** Check your answers.

A Text Completion question with two blanks will look like this:

Even when faced with continuing (i) _____, the recalcitrant graduate student persisted in his spendthrift ways; he abjured any thought of self-(ii) _____ and spent prodigally.

Blank (i)	Blank (ii)
Ⓐ lucre	Ⓓ adumbration
Ⓑ penury	Ⓔ aggrandizement
Ⓒ avarice	Ⓕ abnegation

A Text Completion question with three blanks will look like this:

Though scientific discoveries are often (i) _____ shortly after they've been accepted as fact, scientists still seem to leap to hasty conclusions, (ii) _____ that the (iii) _____ nature of what can be called "fact" has not eroded their confidence.

Blank (i)	Blank (ii)	Blank (iii)
Ⓐ validated	Ⓓ denying	Ⓖ predictable
Ⓑ published	Ⓔ refuting	Ⓗ volatile
Ⓒ disproved	Ⓕ demonstrating	Ⓘ illusory

How the Kaplan Method for Text Completion (Two-Blank and Three-Blank) Works

Here's how the Kaplan Method for Text Completion (Two-Blank and Three-Blank) works.

>> **STEP 1   Read the sentence, looking for clues.**

There are clues in the sentence(s) that point you to the right answer. The missing words in Text Completion questions usually have a relationship similar or opposite to other words or phrases in the sentence(s). Now that you have multiple blanks to contend with, it is even more important to watch the road signs. Different signs point different ways, leading to different relationships between the blanks and the key words and phrases. Remember, you must get the answer choices for *all* the blanks right for the question to be scored as correct.

Refer to the list of road signs in the previous section to help you to determine which way the sentence is going and to predict what words will best fill in the blanks and complete the sentence(s).

>> **STEP 2   Predict an answer for the easier/easiest blank.**

Identify the easier/easiest blank to work with. Once you've found the road sign and the key word(s) relevant to the easier/easiest blank, predict an answer for that blank.

The prediction does not have to be a sophisticated or complex word or phrase, but simply a paraphrase that logically fits into the sentence. By predicting, you avoid the temptation of trying every answer choice on its own, which can take up valuable time on test day. This is especially important on two- and three-blank sentences in which the answer choice for one blank affects what is acceptable in another.

>> **STEP 3   Select the answer choice that most closely matches your prediction.**

Quickly go through the choices and see which one matches your prediction.

Simultaneously, eliminate whichever answer choices do not fit your prediction. If none of the choices match your prediction, reread the question and revisit steps 1 and 2. If one does match, you should proceed to Step 4.

>> **STEP 4   Predict and select for the remaining blanks.**

Filling in the easier/easiest blank provides additional context for the remaining blanks.

For two-blank Text Completion questions, use the context to help you choose the answer for the remaining blank. If the answers for the second blank are not working out, you need to go back to Step 2.

For three-blank Text Completion questions, select the easier of the two remaining blanks and predict which choice will most logically complete the sentence. You now have two blanks to provide context for the last, most difficult blank. This approach to two- and three-blank questions is just a logical extension of the Kaplan Method as it applies to one-blank questions.

STEP 5 Check your answers.

This step is simply double-checking that you did your work correctly, and that your answer choices are correct in context. If the sentence makes sense when you read your choices back into it, you can confirm your answers and move on. If the sentence doesn't make sense when read with your choices, reread the question and revisit steps 1 through 4.

Apply the Kaplan Method for Text Completion (Two-Blank)

Now, apply the Kaplan Method to a Text Completion (Two-Blank) question:

Even when faced with continuing (i) _____, the recalcitrant graduate student persisted in his spendthrift ways; he abjured any thought of self-(ii) _____ and spent prodigally.

Blank (i)	Blank (ii)
Ⓐ lucre	Ⓓ adumbration
Ⓑ penury	Ⓔ aggrandizement
Ⓒ avarice	Ⓕ abnegation

STEP 1 Read the sentence, looking for clues.

This is a fairly straightforward question, once you wade through all the polysyllabic words. Look at the end of the second sentence; you'll notice that the student "spent prodigally," which means "wastefully." Even if you don't know the meaning of the word "prodigally," you can tell from words like "recalcitrant" and "spendthrift" that this is a student who isn't careful with the way he spends his money. If the student is poor at managing money, he's likely facing the specter of being in debt.

STEP 2 Predict the answer for the easier/easiest blank.

Start with the first blank. As noted above, the student is poor at managing money. That means whatever goes in the first blank has a meaning roughly synonymous with "poverty" or "debt."

STEP 3 **Select the answer choice that most closely matches your prediction.**

Look at the answer choices for the first blank. Choice **(B)** *penury*, which means "poverty," matches the prediction precisely. You can eliminate **(A)** *lucre* and **(C)** *avarice*, as those mean "wealth" and "greed," respectively.

STEP 4 **Predict and select for the remaining blanks.**

For the second blank, recall that the student is described as recalcitrant, which is a term for "stubborn." Therefore, he continued to waste money. To "abjure" is to "renounce or repudiate," so he repudiated spending wisely. Thus, "self-_____" must carry the meaning of restraint or self-denial, since he is renouncing any thought of restraint or temperance. That points to **(F)** *abnegation*, which means "denial." The root—"negate"— provides a helpful vocabulary clue. Choice **(D)** *adumbration* means a "foreshadowing," or "image of things to come," which makes no sense in this context. Choice **(E)** *aggrandizement* is wrong, as it means "an increase in wealth, power, or rank," and you know he did not shy from such things if he indulged in overspending.

STEP 5 **Check your answers.**

Putting both answers back into the sentence, you'll get:

Even when faced with continuing *penury*, the recalcitrant graduate student persisted in his spendthrift ways; he abjured any thought of self-*abnegation* and spent prodigally.

This sentence makes perfect sense.

Apply the Kaplan Method for Text Completion (Three-Blank)

Now, apply the Kaplan Method to a Text Completion (Three-Blank) question:

Though scientific discoveries are often (i) _____ shortly after they've been accepted as fact, scientists still seem to leap to hasty conclusions, (ii) _____ that the (iii) _____ nature of what can be called "fact" has not eroded their confidence.

Blank (i)	Blank (ii)	Blank (iii)
Ⓐ validated	Ⓓ denying	Ⓖ predictable
Ⓑ published	Ⓔ refuting	Ⓗ volatile
Ⓒ disproved	Ⓕ demonstrating	Ⓘ illusory

» STEP 1 Read the sentence, looking for clues.

Paraphrasing long sentences boils them down to their essentials. Here, you learn that something happens to discoveries shortly after they're accepted as fact; even so, scientists still jump to conclusions.

» STEP 2 Predict the answer for the easier/easiest blank.

Since the second clause refers to "what can be called 'fact,'" you can predict for the first blank that some discoveries are *invalidated* after their acceptance.

» STEP 3 Select the answer choice that most closely matches your prediction.

The best match for the prediction is choice **(C)** *disproved*. Choice **(A)** *validated* is the opposite of your prediction, and when these facts are *published*, choice **(B)**, is irrelevant to their validation.

» STEP 4 Predict and select for the remaining blanks.

Now, for the second blank, the only choice that works is **(F)** *demonstrating*. You can see from the sentence structure that the author intends for the scientists' continuing haste to *show* or *demonstrate* a further conclusion. Both choice **(D)** *denying* and choice **(E)** *refuting* are the opposite of what's needed.

Since the sentence posits that some "facts" turn out not to be facts at all, you can predict for the third blank that their nature is *changeable*.

Although it's not an exact match for your prediction, the best choice is **(I)** *illusory*. If the nature of facts was *predictable*, choice **(G)**, they wouldn't get disproven as often. And while **(H)** *volatile* does refer to changeability, it refers to extreme or explosive physical changes, not the type of change that's talked about here.

STEP 5   Check your answers.

Now, plug your choices into their respective blanks: "Though scientific discoveries are often *disproved* shortly after they've been accepted as fact, scientists still seem to leap to hasty conclusions, *demonstrating* that the *illusory* nature of what can be called "fact" has not eroded their confidence." These choices fit perfectly, creating a logical, sensible statement.

TEXT COMPLETION (TWO-BLANK AND THREE-BLANK) PRACTICE SET

Try the following Text Completion questions using the Kaplan Method:

1. Despite his insistence to the contrary, the author's (i) _____ hostility was evinced in the tone he used when describing the senator's qualifications; he did not (ii) _____ using words like "craven" and "ill-conceived" liberally when writing about the legislator's voting record.

Blank (i)	Blank (ii)
(A) manifest	(D) demur at
(B) dubious	(E) relish
(C) obscure	(F) hasten to

2. Given the (i) _____ nature of the evidence, the authorities are unlikely to present a (ii) _____ case against the accused.

Blank (i)	Blank (ii)
(A) abstract	(D) weak
(B) flimsy	(E) convincing
(C) rakish	(F) tepid

3. Every effort by the bank to determine the origin of the funds met with (i) _____ resulting from the web of (ii) _____ created by the account holder.

Blank (i)	Blank (ii)
(A) exuberance	(D) deceit
(B) apathy	(E) conviviality
(C) frustration	(F) temerity

4. The (i) _____ genius of the late Glenn Gould is (ii) _____ in his imaginative (iii) _____ for piano of Wagner's *Siegfried Idyll*, which the composer originally scored for full orchestra and presented to his wife Cosima on her birthday.

Blank (i)	Blank (ii)	Blank (iii)
Ⓐ unexceptional	Ⓓ apparent	Ⓖ diminution
Ⓑ overrated	Ⓔ ineluctable	Ⓗ homage
Ⓒ unmistakable	Ⓕ incommensurate	Ⓘ adaptation

5. Although the European Economic Community was established to (i) _____ the economic growth of all its member nations (ii) _____, some express (iii) _____ at what they claim is their unfair burden in maintaining the organization.

Blank (i)	Blank (ii)	Blank (iii)
Ⓐ retard	Ⓓ inequitably	Ⓖ enthusiasm
Ⓑ promote	Ⓔ vigorously	Ⓗ ennui
Ⓒ measure	Ⓕ equally	Ⓘ resentment

TEXT COMPLETION (TWO-BLANK AND THREE-BLANK) PRACTICE SET ANSWERS AND EXPLANATIONS

1. A, D

Take this question one blank at a time. "Despite" is a standard detour road sign, so you know the sentence will change direction. You know that the author's hostility was evinced (made evident) despite his insisting otherwise. So, whatever goes in the first blank will have a meaning similar to "obvious" or "evident." Choice **(A)** *manifest*, meaning "apparent," works perfectly. Choices **(B)** *dubious* and **(C)** *obscure*, meaning "doubtful" and "unclear," respectively, are the opposite of what you need. For the second blank, remember that if the author were openly hostile, he would be inclined to use negative terms like "craven" and "ill-conceived." Since "not" appears in front of the blank, you're looking for something that means "refrain from." Choice **(D)** *demur at* means to "shy away from." That fits perfectly; if the author was obviously hostile, he would *not* shy away from using strongly negative terms such as "craven" or "ill-conceived." You can rule out **(E)** *relish* and **(F)** *hasten to* straight away. To "relish" is to strongly like something, and to "hasten" is to hurry to do something; these terms produce the wrong meaning in the sentence following the qualifier "not."

2. B, E

This one may be more difficult than it appears at first glance. The word "unlikely" is a detour road sign, indicating that the two correct answers will be opposite in meaning to one another. Since the quality of evidence is directly related to the strength of the case the prosecutors can make against the accused, you can infer that "good" evidence will make them unlikely to present a "bad" case, and "poor" evidence will make them unlikely to present a "good" case. Thus, the correct answers must be oppositely charged. Start with the first blank. You'll notice that **(B)** *flimsy*, meaning "insubstantial," has a negative connotation, while **(A)** *abstract* is neutral and can therefore be ruled out. Choice **(C)** *rakish* means "jaunty" or "dashing"; it makes no sense to describe evidence this way. That leaves **(B)** *flimsy*; the evidence was, therefore, weak. Based on your initial reading of the sentence, you know that the second blank will have to mean "strong." With flimsy evidence, the prosecutors are unlikely to succeed. Choices **(D)** *weak* and **(F)** *tepid* are both negatively charged, while **(E)** *convincing* is positively charged and is a synonym for "strong" when describing a court case. "Given the *flimsy* nature of the evidence, the authorities are unlikely to present a *convincing* case against the accused."

3. C, D

Take this question apart by looking for contextual clues. The phrase "web of _____" in the second clause is always used in a negative fashion (you're unlikely to ever hear "caught in a web of virtue and delight!"). Start with the second blank, then. The best choice is **(D)** *deceit*, meaning "lies." That makes perfect sense in this context. A web of lies would make it very difficult to determine the origin of the funds. You can immediately rule out **(E)** *conviviality*, as this means "friendliness or agreeableness." Choice **(F)** *temerity* means "rashness" or "recklessness." This might, in some cases, be a negative attribute, but the problem in this sentence lies in determining the origin of the funds, which is unlikely to be obscured by the account holder's boldness.

Moving to the first blank, you're looking for a word to characterize the result of an effort that has met with a web of deceit. A good prediction would be *irritation*. Looking at the answer choices, **(C)** *frustration* is a perfect candidate, as it can be a synonym for irritation. Choice **(A)** *exuberance* has a strong positive charge, and it's therefore wrong. Choice **(B)** *apathy,* meaning "indifference," has a neutral charge, so it does not work in this context where you need a negatively charged answer.

4. C, D, I

There are several good clues to work with in this sentence, but the most important word is "imaginative," used to describe a work of Gould's. That helps you predict the first and second blanks. In such an imaginative piece, a *fertile* or *monumental* or *obvious* (blank i) genius would be *on display* or *revealed* (blank ii).

For the first blank the best match for your prediction is choice **(C)** *unmistakable*. Choice **(A)** *unexceptional* is inconsistent with the idea of genius, and nothing in the sentence supports the idea that Gould's genius was *overrated*, choice **(B)**.

For the second blank, choice **(D)** *apparent* matches your prediction best. Choice **(E)** *ineluctable* means "unavoidable," which is not the same as being *obvious*, and choice **(F)** *incommensurate* means "disproportionate."

Nothing in the sentence supports the idea of Gould's genius being too large or too small.

The third blank is a noun appropriate to the piece itself. The adjective that precedes the blank is no longer of help; presumably, any type of musical piece could be "imaginative." But, the GRE never creates a blank without clues. This is a piece for piano that was "originally" for full orchestra and is now "for piano". So, it must be a word meaning "reworking" or "rearrangement." Choice **(I)** *adaptation* works perfectly in this context. Choice **(G)** *diminution* does indicate a change, but it means "making physically smaller or decreasing stature or importance," which is not the same as reworking a piece of music for fewer instruments. Choice **(H)** *homage* means "reverence," which does not imply that a change was made to the composition. "The unmistakable genius of the late Glenn Gould is apparent in his imaginative adaptation for piano of Wagner's *Siegfried Idyll*, which the composer originally scored for full orchestra and presented to his wife Cosima on her birthday."

5. B, F, I

The word "Although" at the beginning of this sentence is a detour road sign. It signals a change in direction between the first and second clauses. In the first clause, you're told that the European Economic Community's goal is to do something to the growth of all of the member nations. No doubt this is a positive word; an organization would not be established to hinder the growth of the members of the group. Predict a word meaning "support" for the first blank.

The second clause tells you that some nations believe they unfairly bear a greater burden for running the organization and are expressing some type of feeling about this. Since the two clauses are in contrast, you can predict that this support was supposed to be provided to all members *fairly* or *evenly* and, for the third blank, predict that they "express *discontent*" about the fact that it is not.

For the first blank, the best match is choice **(B)** *promote*. Choice **(A)** *retard* means "delay," a negative action inconsistent with the context of the sentence. It's not illogical to imagine an organization founded simply to *measure* (choice **(C)**) countries' economic growth, but it doesn't make sense in contrast with a feeling that some countries bear an unfair share of the organization's maintenance.

For the second blank, the best match for your prediction is choice **(F)** *equally*. Choice **(D)** *inequitably*, or "unequally," is the opposite of your prediction. While members might have expected the commission to act **(E)** *vigorously*, or "with strength," this word doesn't create the necessary contrast with the second clause.

For the third blank, choice **(I)** *resentment* is closest to the prediction *discontent* and the best fit for the sentence as well. Neither choice **(G)** *enthusiasm* nor choice **(H)** *ennui*, which means "boredom," fits the logic of the sentence: "Although the European Economic Community was established to *promote* the economic growth of all its member nations *equally*, some express *resentment* at what they claim is their unfair burden in maintaining the organization."

KAPLAN'S ADDITIONAL TIPS FOR TEXT COMPLETION QUESTIONS

Look for What's Directly Implied and Not an Ambiguous Interpretation

The questions you'll encounter are written in sophisticated but still logical and straightforward prose. Therefore, the correct answer is the one most directly implied by the meanings of the words in the sentence. These sentences are constructed to allow you to identify the answer using the inferential strategies you just practiced.

Don't Be Too Creative

Read the sentence literally, not imaginatively. Pay attention to the meaning of the words instead of any associations or feelings that might come up for you.

Paraphrase Long or Complex Sentences

You may encounter a sentence that, because of its length or structure, is hard to get a handle on. When faced with a complex sentence, slow down and put it in your own words. Break long, complicated sentences into pieces and tackle one phrase at a time.

Use Word Roots

Use the Resources section of this book to learn the Latin and Greek roots of many common GRE words. If you don't know the meaning of a word, take a look at its root to get close to its meaning or understand what it must refer to. Etymology often provides clues to meaning, especially when you couple a root definition with the word in context.

TEXT COMPLETION PRACTICE SET

Try the following Text Completion questions using the Kaplan Method for Text Completion.

Basic

1. The diffident toddler was so uncomfortable at the birthday party that he constantly _____ his mother's side.

   (A) strayed from
   (B) fled
   (C) abjured
   (D) cleaved to
   (E) avoided

2. Having test-driven this car in a variety of realistic conditions and found its performance lackluster at best, I have to say that its maker's sanguine claims are _____.

   (A) understated
   (B) impeccable
   (C) unfounded
   (D) plausible
   (E) mediocre

3. In the world of professional team sports, individual prowess has its place, but ultimately the players are valued chiefly for their _____ qualities.

   (A) ethical
   (B) inspirational
   (C) dispersive
   (D) singular
   (E) collaborative

4. Although subjected to endless _____, he was unwavering in advocating his theory, claiming to be untroubled by the raillery.

   - (A) rebuttal
   - (B) approbation
   - (C) disavowal
   - (D) japery
   - (E) consent

5. After a destructive, summer-long drought, during which the crops _____, Midwestern farmers did not know whether to welcome or curse the heavy, late-August rains that finally swept through the region, washing away critical topsoil.

   - (A) acclimated
   - (B) persevered
   - (C) languished
   - (D) plundered
   - (E) retracted

6. The idea that the Internet is not a (i) _____ place has become ingrained in popular culture. Because of the increasing number of users, it has become more complicated for authorities to (ii) _____ the breaches of privacy that proliferate on a regular basis. The average user should remain (iii) _____ the exchange of personal data over the Internet.

Blank (i)	Blank (ii)	Blank (iii)
(A) sensible	(D) castigate	(G) indignant about
(B) secure	(E) relinquish	(H) skeptical toward
(C) reliable	(F) constrain	(I) prudent in

Intermediate

7. Now that the message of the underground, counterculture youth movement is being (i) _____ by the mass media, many of the movement's followers, once loyal to the cause, have (ii) _____.

Blank (i)	Blank (ii)
(A) reported on	(D) defected
(B) contradicted	(E) retaliated
(C) promulgated	(F) acquiesced

8. Although he founded an entire magazine about the art of the interview, Warhol was himself a (i) _____ interview subject, revealing little about his life and work and often supplying (ii) _____ answers to straightforward questions.

Blank (i)	Blank (ii)
(A) definitive	(D) ominous
(B) callow	(E) meticulous
(C) laconic	(F) enigmatic

9. Despite the widespread popularity of soy products among American consumers, discussion about the effects of soy on human health remains _____.

   (A) conclusive

   (B) contentious

   (C) preposterous

   (D) enlightening

   (E) fraudulent

10. Although the chairman's new policies cut costs at the time, his strategy was ultimately revealed to be _____, and his lack of foresight crippled the department in the long run.

    - (A) vacuous
    - (B) myopic
    - (C) prescient
    - (D) ingenuous
    - (E) ingenious

11. In conversation, people usually adjust the register, or (i) _____, of their speech according to the circumstances in which they find themselves. For example, they will be less (ii) _____ in their use of vocabulary and (iii) _____ when relaxing with friends than when they are speaking with clergy or legal officials.

Blank (i)	Blank (ii)	Blank (iii)
(A) meaning	(D) thoughtful	(G) lexicon
(B) significance	(E) interested	(H) grammar
(C) style	(F) formal	(I) verbiage

12. In the writer's view, now and then in the (i) _____ of politics, a person of observable integrity and moral strength appears in a way that draws public attention to the central rather than the (ii) _____ matters that affect our lives. Such a person is vital for a number of reasons: he or she cuts through the natural (iii) _____ of competing interests, focuses on key issues, posits realistic solutions, and brings together opponents who might otherwise never agree.

Blank (i)	Blank (ii)	Blank (iii)
(A) existence	(D) weaker	(G) usefulness
(B) hurly-burly	(E) confidential	(H) distractions
(C) practice	(F) peripheral	(I) succession

13. In the United Kingdom, a "stately home" is usually a large and impressive (i) _____, often centuries old, composed of many magnificent rooms worthy of noble occupation. Such houses are generally set in (ii) _____, well-tended grounds and are likely to look out over (iii) _____ of breathtaking beauty. Luckily, as a by-product of an ever-changing economy, stately homes are now often open to the public.

Blank (i)	Blank (ii)	Blank (iii)
(A) edifice	(D) confined	(G) fields
(B) architecture	(E) mown	(H) hills
(C) apartment	(F) expansive	(I) vistas

14. A dictionary that provides the (i) _____ of words—that is, the origin and development of their meanings—offers proof of a (ii) _____ language. Over time, words not only change but sometimes even (iii) _____ their meanings. "Nice," for example, is an instance of such a word. Today it means "agreeable" or "pleasant," whereas in Middle English it meant "stupid" or "ignorant."

Blank (i)	Blank (ii)	Blank (iii)
(A) toxicology	(D) nascent	(G) reverse
(B) etymology	(E) living	(H) amend
(C) taxonomy	(F) faltering	(I) exchange

15. The development of drama over the centuries has been a (i) _____ journey, from the open-air stylized performances of Greek and Roman tragedies and comedies to the more recent "three-walled" room of indoor theater. Yet, much has remained unchanged—actors in costume still (ii) _____ the stage before audiences who willingly suspend their (iii) _____ in order to enter into the "reality" of events created for them.

Blank (i)	Blank (ii)	Blank (iii)
(A) remarkable	(D) strut	(G) interest
(B) modest	(E) stalk	(H) concern
(C) implacable	(F) straddle	(I) disbelief

Advanced

16. In the workplace, it is important that employees (i) _____ the (ii) _____ of the company rather than the other way around.

Blank (i)	Blank (ii)
(A) object to	(D) standards
(B) conform to	(E) idiosyncrasies
(C) balk at	(F) peccadilloes

17. It is hard to believe that the highly (i) _____ game of soccer began many centuries ago as a rowdy (ii) _____ without rules, fought cross-country by entire villages determined to get possession of an inflated pig's bladder.

Blank (i)	Blank (ii)
(A) structured	(D) séance
(B) pell-mell	(E) massacre
(C) helter-skelter	(F) brawl

18. Although good writing is an art, it is also a (i) _____ skill that most people can master by following the principle that (ii) _____ and economy of language are good.

Blank (i)	Blank (ii)
(A) superfluous	(D) simplicity
(B) fundamental	(E) preponderance
(C) nugatory	(F) prolixity

19. Ambition is a useful (i) _____ that leads people to great achievement, but it can also be (ii) _____ force, as Shakespeare showed in his tragedy *Macbeth*.

Blank (i)	Blank (ii)
(A) tenet	(D) an ersatz
(B) indicator	(E) a pulsating
(C) motivator	(F) a destructive

20. Lacking members with a sound sense of (i) _____ knowledge, the explorers were almost certainly (ii) _____ to failure from the start.

Blank (i)	Blank (ii)
Ⓐ geographical	Ⓓ doomed
Ⓑ general	Ⓔ accustomed
Ⓒ abstruse	Ⓕ immune

TEXT COMPLETION PRACTICE SET
ANSWER KEY

1.	D	11.	C, F, H
2.	C	12.	B, F, H
3.	E	13.	A, F, I
4.	D	14.	B, E, G
5.	C	15.	A, D, I
6.	B, F, I	16.	B, D
7.	C, D	17.	A, F
8.	C, F	18.	B, D
9.	B	19.	C, F
10.	B	20.	A, D

TEXT COMPLETION PRACTICE SET ANSWERS AND EXPLANATIONS

1.   D

"Diffident" means shy or timid. Coupling that with the toddler's discomfort, you can reasonably infer that the child must have stayed near his mother's side. So, the answer choice must mean something like "clung to." *Cleaved* might strike you as having the opposite meaning, but the verb "to cleave" is interesting in that it can mean both to cut away and to adhere to. When the word "cleave" is followed by the preposition "to," it means "adhere to." In this context, **(D)** *cleaved to* is the right answer. Choices **(A)** *strayed from*, **(B)** *fled*, and **(E)** *avoided* can be eliminated, as they mean essentially the opposite. Choice **(C)** *abjured* means to shun or renounce, so that can't be right.

2.   C

The author characterizes the car's performance as "lackluster," so you know that the word that will go in the blank will say that the maker's "sanguine," or optimistic, claims about the car are groundless. A good, simple prediction is *untrue*. Looking at the answer choices, **(C)** *unfounded* means "baseless," and that's the answer. You can throw out **(A)** *understated,* **(B)** *impeccable,* and **(D)** *plausible. Understated* means "restrained," and that is not a negative characterization. *Impeccable* means "flawless," which is far too positive. *Plausible* means "possible," and the author is expressing doubt, not trust. Choice **(E)** *mediocre* does have a negative charge, but while the car in question is mediocre, the maker's claims need a word that speaks to their truthfulness, not their general quality.

3.   E

The word "but" is a detour road sign. So, start there. "Individual" is contrasted with whatever will go in the blank. A good prediction is *group*. The sentence would then mean something like "Individual prowess has its place, but players are chiefly valued for their group abilities." Looking at the answer choices, **(E)** *collaborative* means "working together." Collaborative qualities are a direct contrast to individual abilities. Perfect! You can reject **(A)** *ethical* and **(B)** *inspirational*; these are both admirable qualities but do not contrast with "individual" at all. Choice **(C)** *dispersive*, meaning "tending to disperse," makes little sense in context and is, at any rate, an undesirable quality in a teammate. Choice **(D)** *singular* means "unique" or "individual" and is not at all opposed to "individual."

4.   D

The key to this sentence is the word "raillery," meaning "good-natured mockery." The subject of the sentence is "untroubled by the raillery," so you can determine that what he has been subject to is a synonym for "raillery." Only **(D)** *japery*, also meaning "good-natured mockery," fits this description. Choices **(B)** *approbation* and **(E)** *consent* both mean "approval," so you can eliminate those immediately. Choice **(A)** *rebuttal* is a responding argument, and **(C)** *disavowal* is a rejection; while these terms might be related in idea to the sentence, they are not synonymous with "raillery."

5. C

"Destructive" is a key word that suggests a negative outcome. Since the farmers did not know whether to welcome or curse the rains, they had probably suffered a great deal under the dry spell. The correct answer is **(C)** *languished*, or "became weak." Choices **(A)** *acclimated* and **(B)** *persevered* suggest a more positive outcome than the sentence implies, so eliminate these choices. Choice **(E)** *retracted* doesn't make sense and can also be eliminated. The word *plundered*, choice **(D)**, means "to take something wrongfully," which doesn't fit the tone of the sentence.

6. B, F, I

Since all of the three answer choices fit the first blank, you must read the entire passage first, for context. The phrase "breaches of privacy" suggests that the Internet is a place where unauthorized third parties can obtain data. Choice **(C)** *reliable* doesn't quite fit this context, so you can rule it out. Although **(A)** *sensible* could work, the word **(B)** *secure* is more applicable to the issue at hand, so it is the best choice.

For the second blank choice **(F)** *constrain* means "to get under control," **(D)** *castigate* means "to criticize or punish," and **(E)** *relinquish* means "to surrender." *Relinquish* doesn't make sense, but either of the other two choices could work. The last sentence, however, does not suggest a tone of retaliation but more of personal responsibility. So, **(D)** *castigate* can be ruled out, and **(F)** is the correct answer.

Only one of the answer choices for the third blank, **(I)** *prudent in*, fits the tone of the passage. While the other two answer choices,

(G) *indignant about* and **(H)** *skeptical toward*, make sense in isolation, they suggest a more reactive attitude rather than the proactive one implied by the logic of the passage.

7. C, D

The detour road sign "now that" signals a change; something new and different is happening. The missing word in the first blank suggests a change in the youth movement's underground, counterculture status. Since the movement's followers were "once loyal," the detour road sign indicates that is no longer the case. Think about how the movement may have changed. Based on what's known, **(C)** *promulgated* is the best choice—something that was once underground is now being not only exposed but supported by the established media. It's unlikely that the fact the movement was being *reported on* would deter anyone; the whole reason for having a movement is to draw public attention to something. That eliminates choice **(A)**. The word *contradicted*, choice **(B)**, is plausible, but the context makes it more likely that this would reinforce the movement's oppositional stance. You can fill the second blank using a similar strategy—look for a word that suggests the opposite of "once loyal." When somebody defects, that person abandons something to go to the other side. Choice **(D)** *defected* is correct. If you *acquiesce*, you give in, which is not likely here since the sentence implies a reaction to being loyal. Throw out choice **(F)**. Choice **(E)** *retaliated* might seem tempting, but to infer that the movement's followers are now seeking revenge would require more information than the sentence gives; instead they are simply no longer loyal, and *defected* provides the best contrast.

8. C, F

For the first blank, you can use the clue words "revealing little" to narrow the choices. Given this context, choices **(B)** *callow*, a word that means "immature," and **(C)** *laconic*, which means "short and abrupt," are possible. Choice **(C)** is probably a better fit, but get a better sense of the whole sentence before deciding. Throw out choice **(A)** *definitive*, which means "final" and doesn't make sense here.

For the second blank, look for a word or phrase that means the opposite of "straightforward," something like *hard to read* or *evasive*. An *enigmatic* person says or does mysterious things, so **(F)** is a good fit. Choice **(E)** *meticulous*, which suggests great care and detail, is the opposite of what you want. Choice **(D)** *ominous* could work, but a word that means "threatening" is too negative here.

Now read the whole sentence, plugging both **(B)** *callow* and **(C)** *laconic* into the first blank. While "revealing little" could be seen as immature, the tone of the passage suggests Warhol was more sophisticated in his technique of evasion; **(C)** *laconic* and **(F)** *enigmatic* capture this tone.

9. B

"Despite" is a detour road sign that directs you to look for a contrast. If the popularity of soy is widespread, that means many people like to consume it. Because of the detour road sign, you can surmise that the effects of soy on health may be an issue people do not agree on. The correct answer is **(B)** *contentious*, which means "likely to cause disagreement." That choice is perfect for the context of describing a "discussion." Go ahead and rule out choices **(A)** *conclusive* and **(D)** *enlightening*, since they both suggest agreement. Choices **(C)** *preposterous* and **(E)** *fraudulent* are too extreme for the context.

10. B

The detour road sign "although" will help you with this sentence. You are told that the policies were initially effective at cutting costs, but that "his lack of foresight crippled the department in the long run." The straight-ahead road sign "and" connects this "lack of foresight" with the blank, so you can predict an answer meaning "short-sighted." Choice **(B)** *myopic* means "short-sighted," and it is the right answer. Choice **(A)** *vacuous* would mean the plans are empty or vain—and while you are told they are problematic, this is not the correct meaning. Choice **(C)** *prescient* means "farsighted," the opposite of what you are looking for. Choice **(D)** *ingenuous* means "sincere" or "guileless," and **(E)** *ingenious* means "brilliant," and neither of these fits the sentence.

11. C, F, H

Use the clues in these explanatory sentences to determine which words fit in the blanks. The word for the first blank must be an attribute of speech that could accompany "register." Speakers are unlikely to change the **(A)** *meaning* or **(B)** *significance* of their speech to fit the circumstances, but **(C)** *style* fits well as a partner for "register."

The second blank, preceded by "less," suggests a descriptive word in opposition to the phrase "when relaxing with friends." Neither **(D)** *thoughtful* nor **(E)** *interested* works here, because these qualities of speech do not necessarily change depending on whom one is with. In this case, the remaining word **(F)** *formal* matches the contrast between "friends" and "officials."

You may be able to identify quickly that both **(G)** *lexicon* and **(I)** *verbiage* refer to the specific words used, so both of these terms are redundant as a partner to "vocabulary." Instead, **(H)** *grammar* is the best choice.

12.   B, F, H
The choice of words in these two sentences depends mainly on sentence clues. The first choice here requires a word that contrasts with a good person who brings order and direction to a situation that lacks them. Only **(B)** *hurly-burly*, meaning "commotion" or "disorder," matches the sense of the sentence. The words **(A)** *existence* and **(C)** *practice* are too broad and general, and neither implies a chaotic situation.

The detour road sign "rather than" indicates that the adjective in the blank describing the "matters that affect our lives" is the opposite of "central." It might make sense to use **(D)** *weaker* here, but **(F)** *peripheral*, which means "at the edge of," is the exact opposite of the word "central." **(E)** *confidential* is not an appropriate choice.

The second sentence lists achievements of the good politician, so the "competing interests" that "he or she cuts through" would not have the characteristic of **(G)** *usefulness*. As the word "focuses" suggests, it is the **(H)** *distractions* of competing interests that prevent political progress, making this the best choice for the third blank. There might be

a **(I)** *succession* of competing interests, but "cutting through" it doesn't make sense.

13.   A, F, I
In these sentences, key words lead to the correct choices. The term "stately home" suggests that a word meaning "building" would fit best in the first blank. Choice **(A)** *edifice* is another word for "building" and has the connotation of size or importance. It is the correct choice here. Choice **(B)** *architecture* is a profession or an abstract quality, and **(C)** *apartment* is a portion of a building.

The grounds surrounding a "large and impressive" home are likely to be of great extent, which eliminates **(D)** *confined*. With its meaning of "abundant" or "sizeable," **(F)** *expansive* is the logical choice for the second blank. The grounds may or may not be **(E)** *mown*, but "well-tended" already covers this possibility.

Such a great house may or may not "look out over" **(G)** *fields* or **(H)** *hills*, but it would definitely look out over scenic "views," which is the meaning of **(I)** *vistas*, the correct choice.

14.   B, E, G
The word choice for the first blank is defined in the phrase "the origin and development" of word meanings. Each answer choice for this blank has its own specific meaning. The definition that determines the blank applies only to **(B)** *etymology*, the correct answer. The word **(A)** *toxicology* refers to the study of poisons and is therefore inappropriate. A **(C)** *taxonomy* is a system of scientific classifications.

The sense of the first sentence is that a dictionary showing the development of word meanings "offers proof" of a certain type of language. A language that is **(E)** *living* is one that changes and develops, which makes that the correct answer here. A **(D)** *nascent* language is one that has just been born, so rule that out. A language that is **(F)** *faltering* is "hesitant" or "unsteady," which makes no sense in the context.

The second sentence includes the construction "not only…but," which serves as a clue that you need a word that is more extreme than "change." The word **(G)** *reverse* is correct here because it carries the right weight and matches the example. The word **(H)** *amend* is synonymous with the word "change" and is therefore inappropriate. Choice **(I)** *exchange* makes some sense, since words might exchange meanings. However, this answer doesn't carry the idea of an extreme change, nor does it fit the example of "nice," used to illustrate it.

15. A, D, I

Key words are important in evaluating the answer choices in this passage. The first sentence suggests that the "journey" of drama over the centuries has been substantial. The word **(A)** *remarkable*, meaning "extraordinary" or "very noteworthy," is true to the nature of the journey and is the correct choice. **(B)** *modest* is the opposite of what's needed for the blank. The meaning of **(C)** *implacable*, "incapable of being appeased or changed," makes no sense in this context.

In the second blank, the word must describe the common movements of actors on the stage. To **(D)** *strut*, to "walk proudly or

pompously," is the best choice because it is more general and suggests the natural confidence of a performer. Actors may occasionally **(E)** *stalk* around the stage, but the word is too limited to fit the meaning here. The word **(F)** *straddle* has the specific meaning of standing with legs wide apart, which does not fit this situation.

The choice for the third blank is dictated by the phrase "in order to enter into the 'reality' of events created for them." Members of any audience know that a stage performance is not "real," but they put aside that knowledge in order to enjoy the play. Choice **(I)** *disbelief* is therefore correct; people often use the phrase "willing suspension of disbelief" to describe an audience's acceptance of the events in a play. Audiences do not put aside their **(G)** *interest*, which rules out that choice. The word **(H)** *concern*, which can also mean "interest" or "sense of unease," is also illogical in this context.

16. B, D

Reading this question through, you can see that it hinges on the relationship between the company and its employees. Employees are subservient to their employers, so for the first blank, you can reasonably predict that it will require a word with a meaning similar to "obey." Looking at the options, choice **(B)** *conform to* makes sense. Choices **(A)** *object to* and **(C)** *balk at* are wrong, as it is important that employees *not* do those things. For the second blank, you have to think about what would be ideal for employees to conform to. "Example" works well as a prediction. Choice **(D)** *standards* are practices to which companies would want their employees to conform, and it is the correct answer. Choice **(E)** *idiosyncrasies* means "quirks," and **(F)** *peccadilloes* means "minor faults," neither of which are to be imitated.

17. A, F

This question has a detour road sign that's a bit longer than usual. The phrase "It is hard to believe" indicates that the answer choices will contrast with one another. The second blank is a term described as "rowdy," so you can safely predict that the first blank will have the meaning of "calm" or "orderly" to describe early soccer.

The second blank is easier. With the context clue of "rowdy," **(F)** *brawl* works well. You can eliminate **(D)** *séance* because this is a ritual to speak with the dead. A séance would never be described as rowdy, nor would it describe a contest over an inflated pig's bladder. Choice **(E)** *massacre* does not fit because, while massacres are undoubtedly rowdy, it's bizarre to think of them having rules.

You can now answer the first blank with certainty. Choice **(A)** *structured* fits the prediction and contrasts with the rowdy brawl described in the second part of the sentence. Both **(B)** *pell-mell* and **(C)** *helter-skelter* describe unstructured situations, so they cannot be correct.

18. B, D

"Although" is a detour road sign, so you know that the first blank will detour in meaning from "art," as it is used to describe writing. Something less than "artistic" could be called *basic*. That's a good prediction for the first blank. Choice **(B)** *fundamental* fits perfectly. You can rule out **(A)** *superfluous*, as it

means "unnecessary," while you're looking for a term that describes writing at its bare essence. Similarly, you can reject choice **(C)** *nugatory*, which means "trifling." Moving to the second blank, the straight-ahead road sign "and" tells you that the blank will agree with "economy of language," or short, compact writing without ornamentation. Choice **(D)** *simplicity* is a perfect way to describe basic, fundamental writing. Choice **(E)** *preponderance* and **(F)** *prolixity* both have a meaning related to "excess" and thus are the opposite of what you need.

19. C, F

The conjunction "but" is a detour road sign, signaling a change in direction between the two blanks. For the first blank, ambition is described as being useful in leading people to achievement. A good prediction is *inducement*. Looking at the options, **(C)** *motivator* fits perfectly; ambition *motivates* people to great achievement. Choice **(B)** *indicator* is a passive word, not an agent that effects action. Choice **(A)** *tenet*, a component of a philosophy, does not work in this context because it does not "induce" action—it works more as a guide than as an impetus.

The second blank must contrast with "useful and achievement" and therefore has a negative charge. Choice **(F)** *destructive* fits perfectly; it's strongly negative, and "destructive force" contrasts perfectly with "useful motivator" as a description of ambition. Choice **(D)** *ersatz*, which means "artificial," is too neutral to contrast with "motivator." Choice **(E)** *pulsating*, meaning "throbbing," makes no sense in this context.

20. A, D

The phrase "almost certainly" is a straight-ahead road sign, indicating that the second clause in the sentence will continue the direction of the first. Reading the sentence, you can infer that the lack of a certain kind of knowledge affected the explorers' chances of success. A lack of knowledge would not prevent failure, so you can reasonably assume that it "led to" failure. This provides a good prediction for the second blank, so start there. Choice **(D)** *doomed* makes sense. A lack of knowledge *doomed* the explorers. A lack of knowledge would be unlikely to make an expedition **(F)** *immune* to, meaning unaffected by, failure, so **(F)** is wrong. You can also reject choice **(E)** *accustomed*; you have no idea whether the explorers have failed in the past. For the first blank, you're asked to find the word that characterizes this knowledge. Choice **(A)** *geographical* fits perfectly. It is precisely the type of knowledge an explorer would need and would be doomed without. Choice **(B)** *general* can be rejected; it's not specific enough to indicate why the explorers would be doomed. You can reject choice **(C)** *abstruse*, meaning "obscure" or "hard to understand," since this type of knowledge is not of importance to explorers per se.

CHAPTER 3

Sentence Equivalence

SENTENCE EQUIVALENCE

You will find about four Sentence Equivalence questions per Verbal Reasoning section on the revised GRE. Each consists of a single sentence with one word missing. They differ from Text Completion questions in that there will be six answer choices, two of which are correct. Your job is to identify the two answer choices that, when inserted into the sentence, correctly complete the sentence and produce sentences of similar meaning. These questions are similar to Text Completion questions, as both ask you to deduce the meaning of a missing word in a passage on the basis of incomplete information.

One very important thing to bear in mind when working out a Sentence Equivalence question is that the correct answer choices are often, *but are not necessarily*, synonyms. You must pay close attention to the differing shades of meaning that words have, and understand that the key to unlocking the correct answer is to look for choices that create sentences with similar meanings. You must select both correct choices in order to receive credit for the question; no partial credit is given for selecting one of the correct choices.

The directions for Sentence Equivalence questions will look like this:

> For each of the following questions, choose two of the answer choices that, when used to complete the sentence, produce two completed sentences that are similar in meaning.

A Sentence Equivalence question will look like this:

> Cora was not known for her reticence; regardless, she only _____ acquiesced to calls to join the conga line.
>
> ☑ A jejunely
>
> ☐ B exuberantly
>
> ☐ C willfully
>
> ☐ D grudgingly
>
> ☐ E candidly
>
> ☑ F timidly

THE KAPLAN METHOD FOR SENTENCE EQUIVALENCE

The Kaplan Method for Sentence Equivalence

» **STEP 1 Read the sentence, looking for clues.**

» **STEP 2 Predict the answer.**

» **STEP 3 Select the two choices that most closely match your prediction.**

» **STEP 4 Check your answers to see if the sentence retains the same meaning.**

How the Kaplan Method for Sentence Equivalence Works

Here's how the Kaplan Method for Sentence Equivalence works:

» **STEP 1 Read the sentence, looking for clues.**

As you read the sentence, pay attention to the part of speech that the answer choice will be, and compare it with the answer choices. Also look for specific words in the sentence that will help you understand its meaning. As mentioned in Chapter 2, these are descriptive phrases or contextual clues, called "key words" or "road signs," respectively, that determine the meaning of the missing word.

As a reminder, words that show that the second part of a sentence continues or builds on the meaning of the first—"straight-ahead" road signs—include:

And	*Because*
Also	*Consequently*
Similarly	*Likewise*
Thus	*Since*
In addition	*Moreover*

Words that show that one part of the sentence contradicts or contrasts with the other part—"detour" road signs—include:

But	*However*
Although	*Unfortunately*
Despite	*Unless*
While	*Nonetheless*
Yet	*Rather*
On the other hand	*Conversely*

Being aware of these road signs will help you to figure out the meaning of the sentence.

◈ STEP 2 Predict the answer.

Once you have read the sentence and identified clues to words that will complete the sentence, predict an answer. Your prediction should be a simple word that logically completes the sentence. Predict the right answer *before* you look at the answer choices.

◈ STEP 3 Select the two choices that most closely match your prediction.

Quickly review the six answer choices and choose the two words that, when plugged into the sentence, most closely match the intended meaning of the sentence, and thus, your prediction. Eliminate the answer choices that do not fit your prediction. Sometimes you will need to adjust your prediction in order to find two answer choices that match each other.

◈ STEP 4 Check your answers to see if the sentence retains the same meaning.

Read the sentence with each answer choice to check that you have selected the correct answers. Ensure that both answer choices make sense in the context of the sentence and produce resulting sentences with similar meanings. Pay close attention to the charge of a word's meaning. For example, *dislike* and *despise* both mean the same thing, but *despise* has a much *stronger* degree of charge to that meaning. Each sentence the correct answers produce will have the same meaning. If one or both of your answers do not make sense when you reread the sentence, revisit the question and repeat steps 1, 2, and 3.

Apply the Kaplan Method for Sentence Equivalence

Now let's apply the Kaplan Method to a Sentence Equivalence question:

> Cora was not known for her reticence; regardless, she only _____ acquiesced to calls to join the conga line.
>
> - [A] jejunely
> - [B] exuberantly
> - [C] willfully
> - [D] grudgingly
> - [E] candidly
> - [F] timidly

» STEP 1 Read the sentence, looking for clues.

The first thing you should notice is the structural road sign "regardless," which functions as a detour road sign. Therefore, the clause after the semicolon will depart from the meaning of the first clause. You're told in the first clause that Cora is "not known for her reticence," so the second will indicate hesitance or reluctance.

» STEP 2 Predict the answer.

The blank will be an adverb that describes "acquiesced," which means to "give in" or "relent." Since you're looking for a word that shows Cora being uncharacteristically reticent, a good prediction is *reluctantly*.

» STEP 3 Select the two choices that most closely match your prediction.

Evaluating the answer choices, you can immediately reject **(A)** *jejunely* "childishly," which doesn't make sense, and **(B)** *exuberantly* "gleefully," which implies Cora was anything but reluctant to join the conga line. You can eliminate **(C)** *willfully*, since it implies that she was headstrong, which does not harmonize with *reluctant*. Choice **(E)** *candidly* "openly" doesn't have a meaning close to *reluctant*. That leaves **(D)** *grudgingly*, meaning "resentfully unwilling," and **(F)** *timidly*, which means "in an easily frightened way." These two are the best matches.

STEP 4 Check your answers to see if the sentence retains the same meaning.

If you check your answers in the context of the original sentence, you'll arrive at two sentences that mean: "Cora was not known for being hesitant, but she only reluctantly joined the conga line." Notice that the two answer choices are not precise synonyms. Both connote reluctance, but with different shades of meaning. *Grudgingly* has an undertone of resentfulness, while *timidly* implies that one is fearfully shy. However, both produce sentences with similar meanings, and they're the correct answers.

KAPLAN'S ADDITIONAL TIPS FOR SENTENCE EQUIVALENCE QUESTIONS

Consider All Answer Choices

Make sure to read and check all answer choices in the sentence before making your final choice. An answer may fit well in the sentence and closely match your prediction, but if there is no other answer choice that also completes the sentence with the same meaning, it isn't correct.

Paraphrase the Question

If you rephrase a difficult or longer sentence into your own words, it will be easier to predict the right answer. Paraphrasing will also ensure that you understand the meaning of the sentence.

Look Beyond Synonyms

Simply finding a synonym pair in the answer choices will not always lead you to the correct answer. Answer choices may include a pair of synonyms that do not fit the context of the sentence. Both of those choices are incorrect. The meanings of both resultant sentences must be the same and correct. Be sure to try both words in the sentence, checking that each sentence has the same meaning, before making your final choice.

Use Prefixes, Suffixes, and Roots

Think about the meaning of the prefixes, suffixes, and roots in words that you know if you're struggling to figure out the definition of a word.

SENTENCE EQUIVALENCE PRACTICE SET

Try the following Sentence Equivalence questions using the Kaplan Method.

Basic

1. Although the report indicated a disturbing rise in obesity, many people, by choosing junk food over nutrition, continue to _____ the problem.

   A exacerbate

   B extort

   C abhor

   D compound

   E attenuate

   F mitigate

2. A notoriously private figure, the actor remained _____ when the paparazzi confronted him about recent rumors that his longtime marriage was on the brink of collapse.

   A ambivalent

   B reticent

   C gregarious

   D taciturn

   E pompous

   F imperious

3. Following up on a sizable lead in the polls, the gubernatorial candidate established _____ advantage over his incumbent opponent on election night and ultimately gained victory.

   A an inequitable

   B a negligible

   C a decisive

   D a disconcerting

   E a patent

   F an ignominious

4. Although the band received a glowing reception during its exhaustive world tour, the much-anticipated debut album met with uniformly _____ reviews.

   A deprecating

   B deferential

   C obsequious

   D unorthodox

   E eloquent

   F disparaging

5. The residents, who for many years relished the safe, idyllic surroundings of their suburban neighborhood, have in recent months faced _____ of vandalism.

   - [A] a deficiency
   - [B] an epidemic
   - [C] a backlash
   - [D] a scourge
   - [E] an abatement
   - [F] a revelry

6. In his laudatory _____, the food columnist captured the spirit of the hotel dining room.

   - [A] homage
   - [B] paean
   - [C] banter
   - [D] denunciation
   - [E] rebuff
   - [F] examination

7. After losing his entire fortune on Wall Street, the investor abandoned New York City and began a pilgrimage across Europe; in addition, he gave away most of his possessions and _____ materialism.

   - [A] espoused
   - [B] renounced
   - [C] disregarded
   - [D] initiated
   - [E] spurned
   - [F] aggrandized

8. The _____ entourage accompanied Elvis everywhere he went, and they fetched the singer anything he requested—however challenging or ridiculous—at a moment's notice.

   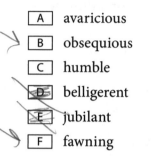

   - [A] avaricious
   - [B] obsequious
   - [C] humble
   - [D] belligerent
   - [E] jubilant
   - [F] fawning

9. The CEO felt he should keep the court case under cover so as not to cause alarm, but to do so would contradict his usually _____ management style.

   - [A] transparent
   - [B] pusillanimous
   - [C] aggressive
   - [D] forthright
   - [E] slipshod
   - [F] negligent

10. As a child, he was often lost in thought; consequently, as an adult, his contemporaries described him as _____.

    - [A] surly
    - [B] pensive
    - [C] meditative
    - [D] indigenous
    - [E] arcane
    - [F] livid

Intermediate

11. Although the suburban townhouse seemed decent enough, the buyer _____ when the real estate agent asked for a commitment.

    - [A] elaborated
    - [B] ambled
    - [C] vacillated
    - [D] groveled
    - [E] lamented
    - [F] dawdled

12. Despite the senator's blatant lies about her role in the scandal, many voters showed their _____ when it came time for reelection.

    - [A] resilience
    - [B] fortitude
    - [C] ignominy
    - [D] constancy
    - [E] ambivalence
    - [F] allegiance

13. Within hours the hurricane had weakened considerably, serving to _____ the fears of hundreds of residents who refused to evacuate.

    - [A] assuage
    - [B] emblazon
    - [C] ignite
    - [D] annihilate
    - [E] mediate
    - [F] allay

14. Despite being known by the moniker "the accidental president," Gerald Ford was _____ posthumously for actions he took to address both the Vietnam War and the Watergate scandal.

    - [A] emancipated
    - [B] extolled
    - [C] indemnified
    - [D] lauded
    - [E] denigrated
    - [F] belittled

15. The movie—adapted from a well-known story—was supposedly intended for all audiences, but many parents felt the content was too _____.

    - [A] ribald
    - [B] arcane
    - [C] superfluous
    - [D] pervasive
    - [E] lascivious
    - [F] esoteric

16. Not wanting to be caught _____, the graduate student spent hours frantically preparing for every possible question that might come at her during her thesis defense.

   - [A] unaware
   - [B] easily
   - [C] quickly
   - [D] unrehearsed
   - [E] early
   - [F] red-handed

17. One of the most _____ events of the transition from the Late Antiquity to the Early Middle Ages was the diaspora of Germanic tribes into lands that were once held securely by the Roman Empire, giving the time period the name "Migration Era."

   - [A] seminal
   - [B] abstract
   - [C] momentous
   - [D] gratuitous
   - [E] diluvial
   - [F] trifling

18. At the _____ of the ambassador, the magistrate relented and agreed to drop the charges.

   - [A] accession
   - [B] behest
   - [C] opposition
   - [D] delight
   - [E] interdiction
   - [F] urging

19. The singer was renowned for being _____; consequently, anecdotes about her tantrums grew to mythic proportions.

   - [A] captious
   - [B] dissolute
   - [C] irascible
   - [D] profligate
   - [E] smug
   - [F] nettlesome

20. The warriors didn't expect an assault on their olfactory senses; however, they were confronted with such a _____ group of opponents that they decided to beat a hasty retreat.

   - [A] cloying
   - [B] saccharine
   - [C] repulsive
   - [D] dejected
   - [E] fetid
   - [F] malodorous

Advanced

21. In contradistinction to the _____ cat, the dog is the quintessential pack animal.

   - [A] transparent
   - [B] supercilious
   - [C] solitary
   - [D] forthright
   - [E] maladroit
   - [F] aloof

22. Mozart manifested the signs of _____ genius when he began composing music at the precocious age of five.

    [A] refined
    [B] incipient
    [C] staggering
    [D] nascent
    [E] fathomless
    [F] piddling

23. Without more robust funding, the charity's goals will go unfulfilled; furthermore, thousands of _____ children will want for basic necessities.

    [A] prodigal
    [B] malnourished
    [C] vagrant
    [D] impecunious
    [E] indigent
    [F] overindulged

24. Jason hastened to _____ when he saw the boy trip over his untied shoelaces.

    [A] gasp in concern
    [B] assist with support
    [C] remedy the disaster
    [D] reprimand for negligence
    [E] prevent a spill
    [F] ease the pain

25. Not only was the author's prose _____, but also his well-known penchant for dissembling colored the way that reviewers read his texts.

    [A] fulsome
    [B] effulgent
    [C] effusive
    [D] unctuous
    [E] cryptic
    [F] vulgar

26. Nigel was usually a model of equanimity, so his _____ demeanor during the attorney's cross-examination left many surprised.

    [A] staid
    [B] equanimous
    [C] testy
    [D] placid
    [E] discomposed
    [F] jubilant

27. The unchecked _____ of state secrets is a source of great concern to intelligence agencies.

    [A] proliferation
    [B] retention
    [C] lassitude
    [D] acquisition
    [E] dissemination
    [F] quality

28. Although the celebrity _____ vociferously on political issues as a guest on several talk shows, her lack of experience in the area led many to ignore her.

   - [A] inveighed
   - [B] declaimed
   - [C] conceded
   - [D] demurred
   - [E] abstained
   - [F] acceded

29. Reginald's _____ aunt was spry for her age but nonetheless required help in ascending the staircase.

   - [A] acrobatic
   - [B] dexterous
   - [C] caustic
   - [D] genial
   - [E] septuagenarian
   - [F] hoary

30. _____, he decided to pass on the project, his professed support notwithstanding.

   - [A] Counterintuitively
   - [B] Unexpectedly
   - [C] Self-indulgently
   - [D] Obscurely
   - [E] Pusillanimously
   - [F] Punctiliously

SENTENCE EQUIVALENCE PRACTICE SET ANSWER KEY

1. A, D	11. C, F	21. C, F
2. B, D	12. D, F	22. B, D
3. C, E	13. A, F	23. D, E
4. A, F	14. B, D	24. B, E
5. B, D	15. A, E	25. A, D
6. A, B	16. A, D	26. C, E
7. B, E	17. A, C	27. A, E
8. B, F	18. B, F	28. A, B
9. A, D	19. A, C	29. E, F
10. B, C	20. E, F	30. A, B

SENTENCE EQUIVALENCE PRACTICE SET ANSWERS AND EXPLANATIONS

1. A, D

The word "although" is a detour road sign that suggests contrasting ideas. Try paraphrasing the sentence to clarify this relationship. "People _____ the obesity problem by eating junk food." So, although the problem is clear, people are making it worse. Make *to worsen* your prediction and look for two words that reflect this. Choices **(A)** *exacerbate* and **(D)** *compound* both mean "to make worse." These make sense in context. By eating junk food, people are doing the opposite of solving the problem. Choice **(B)** *extort* means "to take by force or threat." This doesn't make sense in the context of the sentence, so eliminate it. Choice **(C)** *abhor* means "to hate." The sentence suggests that people are ignoring the problem of obesity, not hating it. Choices **(E)** *attenuate* and **(F)** *mitigate* mean "to reduce." While these words have a similar meaning, it is the opposite of the meaning that fits the context, so you can rule out these answer choices.

2. B, D

The phrase "A notoriously private figure" provides the key description of the actor. An actor who is "private" probably doesn't share much information. Since he "remained" this way, you're looking for a word that suggests keeping to oneself or disclosing little about oneself. Choice **(B)** *reticent* means "silent" or "not revealing much." This is one of the correct answers. Choice **(D)** *taciturn* has a similar meaning to choice **(B)** *reticent*; both words mean "reserved in expression." These are the two correct answers. Review the

other choices to see why each is incorrect. *Ambivalent*, choice **(A)**, means "having mixed feelings"; that doesn't relate to the adjective "private." Choice **(C)** *gregarious* means "sociable." It is doubtful that a private person would be sociable with the press, so eliminate this word. A *pompous* (choice **(E)**) person is arrogant. Pomposity is unrelated to whether someone behaves as a private person, however. Choice **(F)** *imperious* has a meaning similar to *pompous*. Although these words would produce sentences with similar meanings, the synonyms *reticent* and *taciturn* fit the context and are the correct answers.

3. C, E

The straight-ahead road sign "following up on" indicates that the remainder of the sentence will match the first part. Since the candidate's advantage followed a sizable lead in the polls, it was likely as strong or stronger by election night. You want two words that complement the word "sizable." If something is *decisive*, there can be no doubt about it, so choice **(C)** is one of the correct answer choices. Choices **(D)** *disconcerting* and **(E)** *patent* both suggest something that is obvious. However, *disconcerting* is too opinionated a word; it implies that the candidate's victory caused alarm. Nothing in the sentence suggests that this is the case, so *decisive* and *patent* are the best fits. If something is *inequitable*, choice **(A)**, it is not equal, which you may deduce from the word parts *in-* and *equi-*. At first glance, this word may seem to fit. However, it suggests unfairness, and no clues in the sentence imply that the candidate acted unfairly. Choice **(B)** *negligible* means "slight" or "inconsequential in size," so that doesn't agree with the "sizable lead" described earlier. The prefix ig- in choice **(F)** *ignominious* tells you that, like "ignoble" or "ignorant," this is a negatively charged word. In fact, it means "shameful" and therefore doesn't fit the sentence.

4. A, F

"Although" suggests a contrast, so read the remainder of the opening clause to find out what will be contrasted in the second part of the sentence where the blank is located. The band received a "glowing reception" during its tour, so the album's reviews must have turned out to be quite negative. Choice **(A)** *deprecating* means "showing disapproval," so it is correct. You might have heard of people making "disparaging remarks" about each other. The word *disparaging* conveys a negative tone, so choice **(F)** completes the synonym pair. You may know the words *unorthodox*, meaning "odd," and *eloquent*, meaning "expressive." Neither word contrasts with "glowing," so eliminate choices **(D)** and **(E)**. Choice **(B)** *deferential* means "showing respect." This is the opposite of what you are looking for as is choice **(C)** *obsequious*, which means "fawning."

5. B, D

Read this sentence closely to uncover clues suggesting the direction the sentence is taking (whether the blank will continue or contradict the thoughts that come before). The phrases "for many years" and "in recent months" suggest a change of events. After many years of "safe, idyllic" life, people faced vandalism, which means there probably was

not much vandalism before. Look for words that suggest a spike in vandalism. *Epidemic*, choice **(B)**, is a word you have probably heard used to describe outbreaks of disease. It fits the context of a sudden increase in vandalism. The word *scourge*, choice **(D)**, is sometimes used as a synonym for *epidemic*. That's the other correct choice. Choice **(A)** *deficiency* does not fit. There is no shortage of vandalism. Choice **(C)** *backlash* seems like a possible fit, but it is not. A backlash, or sudden reaction, comes after an action or development, and there is nothing in the sentence to indicate that anything happened beforehand to prompt such a response. Eliminate it. *Abatement* is a reduction, the opposite of an increase, so rule out choice **(E)**. Choice **(F)** *revelry* suggests a party atmosphere. That makes no sense, so eliminate it.

6. A, B

This is a straightforward sentence, so you shouldn't overthink it. "Laudatory," which means "expressing praise," is your key word. You need to find two words that mean "positive review" and rule out any negative distracters. Choice **(A)** *homage* is an expression of respect and is correct. Choice **(B)** *paean* is a synonym of *homage*. If you didn't know the definition of *paean*, you could still eliminate the remaining choices. Either way, you should check all choices in each question before making a final decision. Choice **(C)** *banter* is idle chat; this doesn't make sense in context. Choices **(D)** *denunciation* (from *denounce*) and **(E)** *rebuff* both mean "to criticize." That is the opposite of the meaning you want. Choice **(F)** *examination* sounds formal and scientific, and it is netural in tone, not positive; you can rule out this answer.

7. B, E

Paraphrase this sentence to make the contrasting ideas more obvious: "He gave away his possessions and _____ materialism." Someone who gave away possessions would reject material things. Choice **(B)** renounced means "gave up," and choice **(E)** spurned means "scornfully rejected"; although not exact synonyms, both of these words function similarly in the context of the sentence. However, choice **(C)** *disregarded* means "ignored," which could also work. What separates **(B)** and **(E)**, the correct answers, from **(C)** is the intent; the first two suggest using a change in behavior to make a statement, which matches the mood of the passage. Just as importantly, the words match one another. Choice **(A)** *espoused* means "supported," the opposite of the meaning you need, so eliminate it. Choice **(F)** *aggrandized* means "made something look greater or stronger." Aggrandizing materialism is the last thing the investor was trying to do by getting rid of possessions. Even if you didn't know this word, it would make sense to choose **(B)** and **(E)** based on what you know.

8. B, F

You can tell by the straight-ahead road sign "and" that the second half will expand on or clarify the first part. Think about the type of person who would fetch anything another person wanted. In this case, you're looking for words that describe a "yes man" or "toady." Choice **(B)** *obsequious* describes somebody who will, as a form of flattery, do anything another person says. This is a correct answer choice. See if you can find another word like it. Choice **(C)** *humble* means "modest." At first glance, this seems

like a possible fit, but when compared to a word like *obsequious*, it is not extreme enough to convey the point being made. Choice **(F)** *fawning* means "showing extreme flattery," so it's the other correct answer. You might recall that avarice is greed; you can toss out **(A)** *avaricious*, which describes a greedy person, since the entourage is looking out for Elvis, not themselves. Choice **(D)** *belligerent* contains the root *belli-* (meaning "war"), like another more common word, *rebellion*. You can deduce that a *belligerent* person challenges others, which is not the case with those in the entourage. That rules out choice **(D)**. Choice **(E)** *jubilant* is used to describe somebody who is joyfully excited. This might describe Elvis's entourage, but it's not a synonym of *obsequious*, nor does it effectively describe the actions reported in the second half of the sentence.

9. A, D

The detour road sign "but" indicates a turning point in the sentence. You can predict that the words that fill the blank mean the opposite of keeping something under cover. Choice **(A)** *transparent* means "obvious, straightforward" and is correct. Choice **(D)** *forthright* means "straightforward" and appears to be another correct answer. Choice **(B)** *pusillanimous* means "timid, cowardly in nature," which doesn't fit the sentence. Eliminate it. Don't be tempted by choice **(C)** *aggressive*. Although you're familiar with the word and it sounds like it might fit the context, it's too strong. Remember, you need a word meaning "open" or "obvious" but not necessarily "forceful." Choices **(E)** and **(F)**, *slipshod* and *negligent*, mean virtually the same thing, "careless."

Neither makes sense in context. Stick with the correct pair, choices **(A)** and **(D)**.

10. B, C

The straight-ahead road sign "consequently" signals that the sentence will continue its direction. To understand this sentence, focus on the phrase "lost in thought." What feeling does this bring to mind? Typically, such a person is wistful, curious, or reflective. You want a word that continues this feeling. Choice **(B)** *pensive*, meaning "deep in thought," complements the phrase and is a correct answer. The next word, choice **(C)** *meditative*, is a synonym for *pensive* and is likely the other correct answer. Evaluate the remaining words just to be sure. Choices **(A)** and **(F)** are related words that differ in degree, *surly* being "irritable" and *livid* being "very angry." Neither works because they both carry a negative charge. Choice **(D)** *indigenous* means "native," which doesn't make sense in this sentence. The last choice, **(E)** *arcane*, means "difficult to understand." Although it's plausible, this word doesn't complement "lost in thought" as well as choices **(B)** or **(C)**, nor does it match either of them, so stick with those two.

11. C, F

The detour road sign "although" signifies a contrast. In the first clause, the homebuyer thinks a townhouse is "decent," so look for the opposite tone after the comma. Find a pair of words that suggest doubt or indecision on the part of the homebuyer. It's important to understand the subtle difference between choices **(B)** *ambled* and **(F)** *dawdled*. To *amble* is "to walk leisurely," while *dawdle* means "to waste time or delay in a decision." Both words suggest taking one's

time, but *dawdled* better fits the context and is one of the correct answers. Put *ambled* aside and try to find a better match for *dawdled*. Choice **(C)** *vacillated* also means "wavered." Check the other answers, but keep *dawdled* and *vacillated* for now. The word *elaborated* **(A)** means "expanded on a subject" and does not make sense in this context. Choice **(D)** *groveled* means "humbled oneself out of fear or service to another." While the homebuyer may have apologized for his behavior, this is too strong a word. It also does not align with *dawdled*. A person who **(E)** *lamented* mourned or expressed deep regret. Like *groveled*, the word *lamented* is inappropriate in this scenario. The correct answers are choices **(C)** *vacillated* and **(F)** *dawdled*.

12. D, F

You can use the detour road sign "despite" to conclude that one event happened despite another. Focus on the key words "lies" and "voters." How might voters act toward a candidate *despite* his lies? You're looking for a positive word, one meaning that the voters continued to support the untruthful legislator. You may know that choice **(A)** *resilience* means "toughness." This word could make sense, but there is likely a better fit. The voters don't need to remain tough. Set it aside and check the other words. Choice **(D)** *constancy* means "faithfulness" and is a correct answer. Choice **(F)** *allegiance* means something similar. Those two answers match your prediction. The word **(B)** *fortitude* is related to stamina and survival. It fits with *resilience* but not with the sentence, so eliminate it. Choice **(C)** *ignominy* means "disgrace" and, with its negative connotation, fits the senator but not her loyal voters. Finally, choice

(E) *ambivalence* suggests uncertainty about what to do. That would be a natural response to the senator's lying and therefore doesn't fit with the contrast signal "despite." The correct answers are **(D)** *constancy* and **(F)** *allegiance*.

13. A, F

Look at the key phrase "hurricane had weakened considerably." This phrase suggests a positive outcome for residents, so the correct answers will reflect this. Choice **(A)** *assuage* means "to lessen or relieve." It makes sense that people's fears were relieved. Choice **(F)** *allay* also means "to lessen or relieve." Only **(A)** and **(F)** are synonyms, so they're correct. Even if you didn't know the meaning of either correct answer, you could use the process of elimination to rule out the words you know don't fit. Choice **(D)** *annihilate*, meaning "destroy," is too strong to match either of the correct choices. Think about where you've seen the word; it's often used to describe war or acts of violence, which are not involved here. Choice **(B)** *emblazon* means "to display in a celebratory way." This doesn't work in the sentence. Choice **(C)** *ignite* means "to light a fire" or "to arouse one's passions." The residents may be excited by the good news, but this choice doesn't match the sense of relief in the two correct choices. Choice **(E)** *mediate* shares its root with the word *medium*, which means "in the middle." That doesn't make sense in the context of people who've just received news that a threatening storm is abating.

14. B, D

The thoughts in this sentence contrast with one another as evidenced by the detour road sign "Despite." Think about the connotation of the phrase "the accidental president." It's negative, so the sentence will shift to a positive tone; what was said about Ford after his death must have contrasted with how he was popularly regarded while in office. Look for adjectives that express praise for Ford's accomplishments. Choice **(B)** *extolled* means "praised" and is a correct answer. The root comes from the Latin for "lift up" or "raise." It's shared by the word *tolerate*, meaning "to bear or sustain." You may be familiar with the word **(D)** *lauded* from book or music reviews (and from the word "applause"); it also means "praised." *Lauded* must be correct, because no other word creates a sentence similar to the one produced by using *extolled*. Choice **(A)** *emancipated* or "liberated" is often used to describe freedom from slavery. While one could be emancipated from an image like "accidental president," it's not a common use of this word. Choice **(C)** *indemnified* means "gave security against future loss," which doesn't fit and can be eliminated. Choices **(E)** *denigrated* and **(F)** *belittled* are synonyms meaning "to attack one's reputation." This is the opposite of the meaning you need, so you can rule out this pair.

15. A, E

Despite the road sign "but," the contrast in this sentence may not be immediately apparent. The use of the words "story" and "parents" are clues that reveal the tone and the element of surprise in the sentence. Think about what kind of movie might concern parents, especially if children are in the audience. Choice **(A)** *ribald* is another word for "vulgar." This makes perfect sense in context, so hold on to it and find its match. Something *lascivious*, choice **(E)**, is obscene or vulgar, which matches closely the meaning of *ribald*. Don't be tempted to choose **(B)** and **(F)**, even though they are synonyms. *Arcane* means "mysterious" or "hard to understand." This doesn't fit the tone of the sentence. Something hard to understand might not appeal to all audiences, but it is unlikely to cause concern among parents in particular. Choice **(C)** *superfluous* means "more than needed." As with *arcane*, when you look at the sentence as a whole, this word is not the best fit. Something *pervasive*, choice **(D)**, covers a lot of space. This doesn't make sense in the sentence.

16. A, D

This question contains a subtle detour road sign, "not." The student spent hours preparing, so you're looking for something similar in meaning to "unprepared." Choice **(A)** *unaware* is pretty close, so hold on to that one. Choice **(D)** *unrehearsed* works perfectly, since it implies she hasn't prepared properly. Choice **(B)** *easily* could work; you wouldn't want to be tricked or confused easily, but no other answer choice creates a sentence with a similar meaning. The same reasoning applies to choice **(C)** *quickly*. Choice **(E)** *early* doesn't work in this context; it's unclear what "early" would relate to. Choice **(F)** *red-handed* is a distracter. The subject is a grad student, not a thief, so "caught red-handed" doesn't work in this context.

17. A, C

The blank describes an event that gave an era or epoch its name. So, the blank must be filled with words indicating "great importance." This one is a straight-up vocabulary test—there are no tricks or misleading answers. You must simply recognize that choice **(C)** *momentous* means "very significant," as does choice **(A)** *seminal*, in the sense of something's being influential or original. Choice **(B)** *abstract* means "theoretical" or "complex." Choice **(D)** *gratuitous* means "excessive." Choice **(E)** *diluvial* means "related to a flood." Choice **(F)** *trifling* means "insignificant." None of those fits the context of the sentence at all.

18. B, F

You're told that the magistrate "relented" (gave in) as a result of some action that the ambassador took. It's unclear whether the ambassador used power or persuasion, so consider words such as *insistence* or *plea*. Both are good predictions. But remember that the two words must result in equivalent sentences, so the correct pair will not blend the two potential meanings. Both correct choices will mean one or the other. Choice **(B)** *behest*, "a strongly worded request," works very well; a strongly worded request would induce someone to relent. Choice **(F)** *urging* creates a sentence similar to the one created by **(B)** *behest*. Those two are your answers. Choice **(A)** *accession* means "approval," which doesn't mesh with *insistence* and doesn't make much sense. (It would be an odd jurist who changed his mind due to someone's approval.) Choice **(C)** *opposition* seems to make sense, but no other answer choice creates a similar sentence. Choice **(D)** *delight* doesn't work in this context. Choice **(E)** *interdiction*, meaning "prohibition," does work, but it doesn't create a similar sentence to any other answer choice.

19. A, C

The hard part about this question is that all of the choices are undesirable traits that could lead to unflattering stories about a performer. However, only two of these answer choices will make sense given the context of the sentence. You're told that the anecdotes (stories) are about the singer's "tantrums," so the correct answers will relate to her irritability. A reasonable prediction for the correct answers is *irritable*. Choice **(A)** *captious* "easily displeased" is pretty close to your prediction, and it makes sense; if she's difficult to please, she's likely to throw tantrums. Choice **(C)** *irascible*, which means "easily angered," is also worth hanging on to. Someone who's easily angered will throw tantrums. Just as important, the sentence created with *irascible* has a meaning similar to the one created with *captious*. You can immediately reject choices **(B)** *dissolute* and **(D)** *profligate*. Both mean "morally corrupt"; that's negative, but it wouldn't incline someone toward tantrums. Choice **(E)** *smug* "haughty" is another unpleasant trait, but not one that describes someone who loses her temper. Choice **(F)** *nettlesome* "annoying" would mean that she is irritating, not that she's easily irritated. The correct answers are **(A)** and **(C)**.

20. E, F

The word "however" is a road sign indicating that the direction of the second clause will take a detour from that of the first. The first clause tells you that the warriors did not expect to encounter an "assault" on their olfactory senses (sense of smell). Since the road sign "however" signals a detour, you can infer that they did indeed encounter something quite smelly. *Smelly* is a simple, serviceable prediction; keep it in mind and scan the answer choices. Choices **(E)** *fetid* and **(F)** *malodorous* both specifically refer to disgusting aromas. They produce sentences with similar meanings and are the correct answers. You can reject **(A)** *cloying* and **(B)** *saccharine*; both mean "excessively sweet," which is the opposite of what you need. Choice **(D)** *dejected* is wrong because *dejected* means "sad" and has nothing to do with smell. Choice **(C)** *repulsive* is more difficult to eliminate (you might say, "That smells repulsive," after all), but the word has too broad a meaning to create a sentence equivalent to either *fetid* or *malodorous*.

21. C, F

Your first reaction here should be to notice the rather unusual word "contradistinction," which means "distinction by contrast." You can infer from the root *contra*, which means "in contrast to," that "contradistinction" is acting as a detour road sign in this situation. In this sentence, dogs are described as being "pack animals," which means they are social and communal. Because the blank, which describes cats, is in "contradistinction" to "pack animals," you need to predict something that is close in meaning to *isolated*. Choice **(C)** *solitary* certainly works well as a contrast to "pack animal." Keep that one. Choice **(F)** *aloof* "standoffish" fits just as well; those who are standoffish are solitary and dislike company. Choice **(A)** *transparent* is wrong; a characteristic in contradistinction to *transparent* would be "translucent" or "opaque." Choice **(B)** *supercilious* is tempting; it describes a popular view of cats (it means "haughty"), but it does not contrast with "pack animals." Choice **(D)** *forthright* (candid) is not necessarily characteristic of someone or something that prefers solitude. The same can be said for choice **(E)** *maladroit*, which means "awkward or clumsy."

22. B, D

You're told that Mozart's genius manifested itself at the "precocious" age of five. Precocious means "prematurely developed," an accurate description for a child prodigy. The blank describes such a genius, so the correct answer must mean "early" or "budding." Choice **(B)** *incipient* "at an early stage" works, since Mozart's genius was just beginning to blossom if he was five years old. Choice **(D)** *nascent* "beginning to exist or develop" creates a sentence nearly identical to the one created by *incipient*. Those two look like the answers, but check the remaining options to be sure. Reject choice **(A)** *refined*, since, by definition, refinement comes with time while this sentence describes Mozart's beginnings. Choice **(C)** *staggering* is harder to eliminate, since the genius of a five-year-old who composes symphonies is certainly staggering, but that doesn't dovetail with "precocious," and no other answer choice creates a sentence with similar meaning. Choice **(E)** *fathomless* (incomprehensible) can also describe genius, but it doesn't create a sentence similar to one created by another answer choice. Choice **(F)** *piddling* can be rejected outright, since it means "negligible" and certainly doesn't describe Mozart's genius.

23. D, E

In this question, "furthermore" is a straight-ahead road sign. The sentence will continue in the same direction in which it starts, connecting a lack of funding with the needs of children, who will go wanting without assistance. The blank describes the children. A simple, accurate prediction is *needy*. The sentence doesn't imply specifically what it is the children lack (food, shelter, education), and *needy* is broad enough to cover all contingencies. Choices **(D)** *impecunious* and **(E)** *indigent* both mean "impoverished" and thus create sentences with similar meanings. They both match your prediction, too. Reject choice **(A)** *prodigal* (wasteful) right off the bat; by definition, needy children can't be profligate. The same logic applies to choice **(F)** *overindulged* (spoiled); the children here are needy, not spoiled. While needy children could certainly be **(B)** *malnourished* "underfed" or **(C)** *vagrant* "homeless," these characterizations are too specific to create sentences similar to any others created by the answer choices. Choices **(D)** and **(E)** are the correct answers.

24. B, E

A typical reaction when someone sees a child tripping over his or her shoelaces is to help, so your first step is to look for words that relate to helping or taking care of someone. Choices **(B)**, **(C)**, **(E)**, and **(F)** all relate to helping in some way. Choice **(B)** *assist with support* is a good choice because Jason would step in to ensure that the boy does not harm himself, as does **(E)** *prevent a spill*. (In this case, the word *spill* means "fall" or "tumble.") Choice **(C)** *remedy the disaster* is overly exaggerated; although Jason would probably hope to prevent the fall, falling would not be a disaster within the context of the sentence. Finally, **(F)** seems like a strong choice, but there is no evidence in the sentence that the boy is in pain, nor is there any other answer choice that would create an equivalent meaning. While **(A)** *gasp in concern* is a natural reaction, Jason wouldn't "hasten to" gasp; it would be an unconscious reaction, so you can cross that one off the list. You can also cross off **(D)** *reprimand for negligence* because, while Jason could do such a thing, there is no other answer that would give roughly the same meaning in the sentence.

25. A, D

"Not only" is a straight-ahead road sign. Always paired with "but also," it indicates that the sentence will continue in its original direction. You're told that the author has a penchant for "dissembling," which means "to speak or act hypocritically." Since he dissembles when he writes, his prose can be described as "insincere." That's a good prediction, so start checking the answer choices. Choice **(A)** *fulsome* means "excessive" or "over-the-top." That's an excellent way to characterize insincere prose, so hang on to it. Choice **(D)** *unctuous* means "excessively smug," which is certainly insincere in its tenor. Those two choices match your prediction well, but check the other answer choices just in case. Choice **(B)** *effulgent* "radiant" doesn't make much sense here, especially if the author is insincere or dishonest. Choice **(C)** *effusive* "gushing" relates to the quantity of the prose, but not its truthfulness or sincerity. Choice **(E)** *cryptic* "mysterious" makes sense on its own, but no other answer choice creates a similar sentence. Choice **(F)** *vulgar* can be rejected for the same reason; it also has nothing to do with "dissembling."

26. C, E

The key to this question is the context key word "surprised." Since Nigel is typically a model of "equanimity" (calm), the correct answer choices, describing surprising behavior on his part, must mean something like "unsettled." Choices **(C)** *testy* "irritable" and **(E)** *discomposed* "out of sorts" create sentences that indicate that Nigel lost his cool and failed to remain calm. These are the correct answers. You can eliminate **(A)** *staid*, **(B)** *equanimous*, and **(D)** *placid*, as those are all synonyms for "calm," from which the sentence detours. Choice **(F)** *jubilant* "overjoyed" can also be rejected; although excessive joy does depart from "calm," no other word in the answer choices would create an equivalent sentence.

27. A, E

The blank in this sentence takes a verb that describes an action that would concern "intelligence agencies." Since the object of concern is state secrets, it's a good bet the agencies are alarmed with their "spread" or "leaking." Choices **(A)** *proliferation* and **(E)** *dissemination*, both of which are synonymous with "spreading," create similar sentences that make sense: intelligence agencies would be highly concerned about the spread of state secrets. Choices **(B)** *retention* and **(D)** *acquisition* can be ruled out, as intelligence agencies would be keen to both *retain* and *acquire* state secrets. Choice **(C)** *lassitude* "laziness" doesn't make sense in this context (state secrets can't be "lazy"). Choice **(F)** *quality* might be tempting, but no other answer choice produces a similar sentence.

28. A, B

The celebrity in the sentence has done something "vociferously." "Vociferously" means "clamorously" and describes speech, so you know she spoke ardently and loudly. She must also have been trying to convince her audience of something, since her action is contrasted with being ignored. A good prediction is *lectured* or *orated*. When you look at the answer choices, there's nothing that precisely matches your prediction, but **(A)** *inveighed* and **(B)** *declaimed* come close. Both have a connotation of oratory, typically arguing against something. That harmonizes very well with "vociferously." Choices **(C)** *conceded* "gave in," **(E)** *abstained* "declined to participate," and **(F)** *acceded* "agreed" can all be rejected as being too passive and therefore opposite of what you need. Choice **(D)** *demurred* "raised an objection" is wrong because its not strong enough.

29. E, F

This question obliges you to find an adjective to describe Reginald's aunt, who you are told is "spry" (nimble) for her age. However, "nonetheless" is a detour road sign, so the correct answers will both contrast with "spry." Choice **(E)** *septuagenarian*, which is a term for someone in her seventies, works well. Choice **(F)** *hoary* means "gray or white with age." These are the correct answers. You can reject choices **(A)** *acrobatic* and **(B)** *dexterous*, as these are both synonymous with "agile," in which case she would not need help getting up the stairs. Choices **(C)** *caustic* "sarcastic or corrosive" and **(D)** *genial* "pleasant" are also wrong, because they describe her personality, not her fitness.

30. A, B

The fact that the blank is the word that begins the sentence may make this question more challenging than a typical Sentence Equivalence question. The first clause is fairly direct; he passed on the project, and the blank will contain an adverb to describe this decision. The second clause contains the detour road sign "notwithstanding," which means "despite." "Professed," which describes his support, means "stated," so you know he passed on the project despite his vocal support. Therefore, you can predict the first blank to be something like *surprisingly* or *paradoxically*. Choices **(A)** *counterintuitively* "contrary to intuition" and **(B)** *unexpectedly* both match that prediction quite well. They both create sentences pointing out the subject's seeming inconsistency. Three of the other choices could work on their own in this context: **(C)** *self-indulgently* "to indulge one's own desires," **(D)** *obscurely* "vaguely," and **(E)** *pusillanimously* "cowardly" all characterize the way in which one could decline a project, but none logically contrast with "professed support." Choice **(F)** *punctiliously* "attentive to detail" does not make sense in this context. Only **(A)** and **(B)** logically complete similar sentences.

CHAPTER 4

Reading Comprehension

READING COMPREHENSION

Even though reading is a skill that you've been developing and practicing for most of your life, navigating the often verbose and detailed language of academia can be a challenge. While the revised GRE tests your ability to assess ideas and information, the greater test of the skills involved will come in the field of higher learning you pursue. Regardless of academic discipline, you will almost certainly be presented with written material at least as difficult to penetrate as the practice set questions to follow.

So that the GRE reflects the real-world nature of postgraduate reading, the passages are drawn from four standard disciplines of higher learning—social sciences, biological sciences, physical sciences, and arts and humanities.

The types of questions the GRE uses fall into three categories, distinguished by the answer choices: standard multiple-choice questions with one correct answer, multiple-choice questions in which one or more of the choices is correct, and questions that ask you to select the sentence from the passage that best answers the question. These different question formats reward a wide range of analytical skills, from determining the best definition of a specific word in context or identifying details that support a main idea to evaluating the author's perspective or drawing inferences from the evidence presented.

A Reading Comprehension passage and question will look like this:

> **Questions 1–3 are based on the following passage.**
>
> A pioneering figure in modern sociology, French social theorist Emile Durkheim examined the effect of societal cohesion on emotional well-being. Believing that scientific methods should be applied to the study of society, Durkheim studied the levels of integration in various social formations and the impact that such cohesion had on individuals within the group. He postulated that social groups with high levels of integration serve to buffer their members from frustrations and tragedies that could otherwise lead to desperation and self-destruction. Integration, in Durkheim's view, generally arises through shared activities and values. Durkheim distinguished between mechanical solidarity and organic solidarity in classifying integrated groups. *Mechanical solidarity* dominates in groups in which individual differences are minimized and group devotion to a common goal is high. Durkheim identified mechanical solidarity among groups with little division of labor and high degrees of cultural similarity, such as more traditional and geographically isolated groups. *Organic solidarity*, in contrast, prevails in groups with high levels of individual differences, such as those with a highly specialized division of labor. In such groups, individual differences are a powerful source of connection rather than of division. Because people engage in highly differentiated ways of life, they are by necessity interdependent. In these societies, there is greater freedom from some external controls, but such freedom occurs in concert with the interdependence of individuals, not in conflict with it. Durkheim realized that societies may take many forms and, consequently, that group allegiance can manifest itself in a variety of ways. In both types of societies outlined previously, however, Durkheim stressed that adherence to a common set of assumptions about the world was a necessary prerequisite for maintaining group integrity and avoiding social decay.
>
> 1   Which of the following is NOT a feature of an organic societal formation, according to Emile Durkheim?
>
> ⓐ   Members are buffered from individual frustration that would lead the individual to cease being a productive member of society.
>
> ⓑ   Citizens operate independently in their daily lives, but toward a common overall goal.
>
> ⓒ   Each person must come to accept a series of assumptions that form a collective worldview shared by the formation.
>
> ⓓ   Workers have an even division of labor and share the work of common tasks.
>
> ⓔ   Individual differences are celebrated, and have a strengthening effect on the society.

The GRE features three types of Reading Comprehension questions: Select One, Select One or More, and Select-in-Passage. You will review all three types in this chapter.

THE KAPLAN METHOD FOR READING COMPREHENSION

The Kaplan Method for Reading Comprehension

- o **STEP 1 Read the passage strategically.**
- o **STEP 2 Analyze the question stem.**
- o **STEP 3 Research the relevant text in the passage.**
- o **STEP 4 Make a prediction.**
- o **STEP 5 Evaluate the answer choices.**

How the Kaplan Method for Reading Comprehension Works

Here's how the Kaplan Method for Reading Comprehension works.

STEP 1 Read the passage strategically.

Reading strategically means identifying the topic, scope, and purpose of a passage, as well as noting the passage's structure and main points. The *topic* is the general subject matter, and the *scope* is the specific aspect of the topic that the author focuses on. In order to identify the topic, scope, and purpose, you should target the bones of the piece in the form of the passage's main ideas, primary arguments, secondary arguments, supporting statements or evidence, and conclusions. At this point you should start mapping the passage to, or take notes on scratch paper about, the points discussed above. For each paragraph, jot down a one- to two-line summary highlighting the main points. For any given passage, you should be able to both summarize the text and identify the main points in your own words before proceeding. It's also important to use the key words and phrases connected to the sentences to identify the important ideas and statements.

With each passage, you need to look for the purpose of the text: Why did the author write it? While there will be numerous facts provided in any given piece, not all passages are purely informative. There will be persuasive elements in each passage, even if designed only to convince you of the subject's importance. Identify early on whether the piece is primarily informative or argumentative, and to what degree. You do this by recognizing the author's tone, which reflects the author's attitude towards his or her subject. Tone is indispensible in identifying an author's purpose, especially if his or her purpose is not entirely explicit. If the author makes use of comparisons (*better, more effective*) or recommendations (*should, must, need to*), the author is trying to persuade. If the author writes in a more straightforward style with no persuasive or judgmental terminology, the piece is more purely informative. Pieces written in that tone are more likely to have the purpose of explanation or description. Purpose is important for Inference questions, which reward you for identifying the author's opinion on the subject matter.

In general, a social sciences piece is likely to argue a position because the complex nature of human behavior and interaction is open to wide interpretation. Likewise, a discussion of a piece of art or literature will likely contain arguments because the author asserts an interpretation of these art forms. Scientific articles, on the other hand, will be mainly informative, seeking primarily to explain a scientific concept or discovery. Still, there may be arguments or conclusions drawn about the importance of these discoveries or principles in daily application. Pay close attention to the author's tone; it is inseparable from his or her argument.

> **STEP 2   Analyze the question stem.**

Most GRE Reading Comprehension passages are accompanied by between one and three questions (or rarely, even more). Above the passage on the computer screen, you'll see a note that indicates the number of questions: "Question 11 . . ." or "Questions 4–6 . . . ." Not surprisingly, passages with only one question tend to be shorter (usually one paragraph), while those with several questions may be longer.

When a passage has only one question, it makes sense to read the question stem before reading the passage. You can target the text that answers the specific question. When multiple questions accompany a passage, however, you're better off reading the passage strategically before concerning yourself with the question stems.

When a passage has multiple questions, one stem may be concerned with the author's tone, another focused on a vocabulary term, and still another designed to reward your analytical reasoning skills. Reading with multiple questions in mind makes it difficult to discern the main ideas of the passage. It's usually more valuable to use the question stem to guide research for details in the passage than to try to read for several alternative details at the outset. Your passage map or notes will allow you to find the correct answer(s) quickly while still reading for the big points and main idea. You'll have the answers to general questions—"Which of the following best states the main idea/primary purpose of the passage?"—and the notes to research more specific questions. Likewise, by knowing the author's attitude and purpose, you'll be prepared for questions that ask what an author is most likely or least likely to agree with.

❖ STEP 3 Research the relevant text in the passage.

Notice that this step tells you to "research" the passage, not "reread" it. Once you have analyzed and understood the question stem, you should already have an idea of where in the passage you'll find the answer. Use your passage map or notes, the product of Step 1's strategic reading, to target this research step. Don't consider more text from the passage than is necessary to answer the question. If the question rewards your understanding of vocabulary in context, for example, you need not look further than the sentence in which it appears, and possibly the preceding sentence, to derive the answer.

❖ STEP 4 Make a prediction.

GRE questions will, by design, test your comprehension of what you have read and not just your ability to go into a passage and mine for details. As such, you will often have the ability to formulate a prediction as to the answers of many questions that deal with the main idea, conclusions, arguments, author's meaning, tone, and implications of the information provided. Before moving on to the answer choices, try to either form a response to the stem in your own mind or target the section of the passage that will contain the answer.

At times, you will have to infer an answer based on clues provided in the text, but the test will not ask you for outside information. In these Inference questions, research the relevant sections of the passage, those that provide evidence or details to support (or refute) the opinion or conclusion in question. When you find it difficult to make a specific, word-for-word prediction for the correct answer, remember that the correct answer will be supported by the passage. Use your research to evaluate the answer choices.

❖ STEP 5 Evaluate the answer choices.

You'll take this step a little differently depending on the Reading Comprehension question type you're answering. For a multiple-choice question with one correct answer, look to match your prediction and eliminate violators. When you find the unequivocally correct choice, select it. Time permitting, check the remaining choices and confirm that each is demonstrably incorrect. Eliminating incorrect answers not only helps narrow down options for questions that are hard to answer, it also validates the selection you are considering.

For a multiple-choice question in which multiple answer choices may be correct (a Select One or More question, indicated by "select all that apply"), you must check all of the choices. You receive credit only if you choose all of (and only) the applicable choices.

For a Select-in-Passage question, place your cursor over the correct sentence and click. Only one sentence from the passage will be credited as the correct answer.

When you're uncertain about the correct answer, begin by eliminating answers that are demonstrably wrong. Use the same steps as you would for finding the right answer: Weigh the choices against the passage text and eliminate choices that contradict, distort, or fall outside the scope of the passage. Determine the criteria for the correct answer and eliminate choices that violate them. Don't compare answer choices to one another; compare them to the standard of what the correct choice must contain.

Apply the Kaplan Method for Reading Comprehension

Now, apply the Kaplan Method to a Reading Comprehension (Select One) question:

Question 1 is based on the following passage.

A pioneering figure in modern sociology, French social theorist Emile Durkheim examined the effect of societal cohesion on emotional well-being. Believing that scientific methods should be applied to the study of society, Durkheim studied the levels of integration in various social formations and the impact that such cohesion had on individuals within the group. He postulated that social groups with high levels of integration serve to buffer their members from frustrations and tragedies that could otherwise lead to desperation and self-destruction. Integration, in Durkheim's view, generally arises through shared activities and values. Durkheim distinguished between mechanical solidarity and organic solidarity in classifying integrated groups. *Mechanical solidarity* dominates in groups in which individual differences are minimized and group devotion to a common goal is high. Durkheim identified mechanical solidarity among groups with little division of labor and high degrees of cultural similarity, such as among more traditional and geographically isolated groups. *Organic solidarity*, in contrast, prevails in groups with high levels of individual differences, such as those with a highly specialized division of labor. In such groups, individual differences are a powerful source of connection rather than of division. Because people engage in highly differentiated ways of life, they are by necessity interdependent. In these societies, there is greater freedom from some external controls, but such freedom occurs in concert with the interdependence of individuals, not in conflict with it. Durkheim realized that societies may take many forms and, consequently, that group allegiance can manifest itself in a variety of ways. In both types of societies outlined previously, however, Durkheim stressed that adherence to a common set of assumptions about the world was a necessary prerequisite for maintaining group integrity and avoiding social decay.

1. Which of the following is NOT a feature of an organic societal formation, according to Emile Durkheim?

   (A) Members are buffered from individual frustration that would lead the individual to cease being a productive member of society.

   (B) Citizens operate independently in their daily lives, but toward a common overall goal.

   (C) Each person must come to accept a series of assumptions that form a collective worldview shared by the formation.

   (D) Workers have an even division of labor and share the work of common tasks.

   (E) Individual differences are celebrated, and have a strengthening effect on the society.

The most common standardized test question—multiple-choice—has a strong presence on the GRE. Most often, the multiple-choice question asks you to select the best answer from a set of five choices. Only one choice is credited as the right answer; the other four options will either be incorrect or less complete than the correct selection.

STEP 1   Read the passage strategically.

As the author sets forth the criteria for Emile Durkheim's theory of social cohesion, he defines two models of social solidarity by introducing qualities that are common to both constructs before addressing the differences between the two. The passage concludes with a prerequisite for social cohesion common to both models. The two models have similarities, but note that the author is contrasting them with one another.

STEP 2   Analyze the question stem.

This question asks which choice is NOT a feature of the organic solidarity model. Normally, you would approach this question type by researching what the passage says *are* features of the organic solidarity model and eliminating answers that mention them. In this case, since the passage contrasts two models of societal formation, the correct answer will likely be a feature of the opposed mechanical solidarity model.

STEP 3   Research the relevant text in the passage.

The relevant text is the part of the passage that discusses the features of the two types of societal formation. Since the question asks you to find what is *not* common to the organic solidarity model, research the portion that defines the mechanical solidarity model as well. The author emphasizes one distinction between the models: the lack of a specialized labor force in the mechanical solidarity model versus the presence of a specialized division of labor in the organic solidarity model.

STEP 4 Make a prediction.

Apply your research to the "call" of the question stem. The correct answer here is a feature not found in organic solidarity groups. Since the author highlights the organic solidarity model's highly specialized division of labor, predict that the correct answer will describe a case in which labor is not differentiated. Now, check the answers to find the choice that matches this prediction.

STEP 5 Evaluate the answer choices.

Choice **(D)** *Workers have an even division of labor and share the work of common tasks* matches your prediction quite well. Societies that distribute labor evenly and parcel out common tasks among everyone are not using a specialized labor force. They fit the mechanical solidarity model, not the organic solidarity one. Choice **(A)** and choice **(C)** are found among the descriptions for both forms of Durkheim's societal formations, the first early in the paragraph and the other toward the end, so they are wrong. Within the section discussing organic solidarity societies, you can find, as part of the definition, differently worded forms of both choice **(B)** and choice **(E)**.

Apply the Kaplan Method for Reading Comprehension

Now, apply the Kaplan Method to a Reading Comprehension (Select One or More) question:

Question 2 is based on the following passage.

A pioneering figure in modern sociology, French social theorist Emile Durkheim examined the effect of societal cohesion on emotional well-being. Believing that scientific methods should be applied to the study of society, Durkheim studied the levels of integration in various social formations and the impact that such cohesion had on individuals within the group. He postulated that social groups with high levels of integration serve to buffer their members from frustrations and tragedies that could otherwise lead to desperation and self-destruction. Integration, in Durkheim's view, generally arises through shared activities and values. Durkheim distinguished between mechanical solidarity and organic solidarity in classifying integrated groups. *Mechanical solidarity* dominates in groups in which individual differences are minimized and group devotion to a common goal is high. Durkheim identified mechanical solidarity among groups with little division of labor and high degrees of cultural similarity, such as among more traditional and geographically isolated groups. *Organic solidarity*, in contrast, prevails in groups with high levels of individual differences, such as those with a highly specialized division of labor. In such groups, individual differences are a powerful source of connection rather than of division. Because people engage in highly differentiated ways of life, they are by necessity interdependent. In these societies, there is greater freedom from some external controls, but such freedom occurs in concert with the interdependence of individuals, not in conflict with it. Durkheim realized that societies may take many forms and, consequently, that group allegiance can manifest itself in a variety of ways. In both types of societies outlined previously, however, Durkheim stressed that adherence to a common set of assumptions about the world was a necessary prerequisite for maintaining group integrity and avoiding social decay.

Consider each of the following choices separately and select all that apply.

2. Which of the following might be examples of a mechanical solidarity societal formation as explained by the passage?

    ☐ A   A religious order living in a monastery with an evenly distributed division of labor

    ☐ B   A company comprised of a group of architects, carpenters, plumbers, and construction workers who can design and complete all facets of a building project from start to finish

    ☐ C   A xenophobic tribe living in an isolated fishing village amid an uncolonized set of islands

The second form of multiple-choice question offers three choices, but any combination of them could be the correct answer, from a single choice to all three being correct. In order to get the question correct on the test, you must identify all of (and only) the correct choices.

❖ STEP 1   Read the passage strategically.

You've already read the passage strategically, of course. It will come as no surprise that the questions continue to reward you for noting the contrast between Durkheim's two models.

❖ STEP 2   Analyze the question stem.

This question asks you to identify which of three examples meet the criteria supplied by the text to qualify as a society displaying "mechanical solidarity." Notice that the author divides societal formation into "mechanical" and "organic," and the question is only concerned with the former. In a five-choice one-correct-answer question, once you're confident that you have the correct choice, you can move on. You need not give the remaining choices equal consideration. In three-choice questions, on the other hand, don't stop once you spot a correct answer. Evaluate all of the choices. More than one may be correct.

❖ STEP 3   Research the relevant text in the passage.

This question rewards you for identifying which of the three examples meet the criteria supplied by the text to qualify as a mechanical solidarity social formation. The author cites "more traditional and geographically isolated groups" as examples of this sort of group. You also know that the author distinguishes mechanical from organic solidarity on the basis of labor specialization.

❯❯ STEP 4 Make a prediction.

Now, apply your research. You noted the author's illustration of mechanical solidarity groups: "such as more traditional and geographically isolated groups." Make this your prediction.

❯❯ STEP 5 Evaluate the answer choices.

Your prediction makes choice **(C)** easy to select; it uses much of the same terminology. Knowing that *xenophobic* means "fearful of outsiders" helps, but is not necessary for answering that portion of the question. Keep choice **(C)** as an answer, but check the others as well. Choice **(A)** also meets the criteria. A monastic religious order (such as monks) in which the members do all the same tasks without specialization meets the non-specialized distribution of labor portion of the author's definition as well. Only choice **(B)** fails to meet the definition; even though the workers listed may share a singular goal (of creating a house or building), each worker has very specific specialties and abilities—a feature associated with organic solidarity groups.

Apply the Kaplan Method for Reading Comprehension

Now, apply the Kaplan Method to a Reading Comprehension (Select-in-Passage) question:

Question 3 is based on the following passage.

A pioneering figure in modern sociology, French social theorist Emile Durkheim examined the role of societal cohesion on emotional well-being. Believing that scientific methods should be applied to the study of society, Durkheim studied the levels of integration in various social formations and the impact that such cohesion had on individuals within the group. He postulated that social groups with high levels of integration serve to buffer their members from frustrations and tragedies that could otherwise lead to desperation and self-destruction. Integration, in Durkheim's view, generally arises through shared activities and values. Durkheim distinguished between mechanical solidarity and organic solidarity in classifying integrated groups. *Mechanical solidarity* dominates in groups in which individual differences are minimized and group devotion to a common goal is high. Durkheim identified mechanical solidarity among groups with little division of labor and high degrees of cultural similarity, such as among more traditional and geographically isolated groups. *Organic solidarity*, in contrast, prevails in groups with high levels of individual differences, such as those with a highly specialized division of labor. In such groups, individual differences are a powerful source of connection rather than of division. Because people engage in highly differentiated ways of life, they are by necessity interdependent. In these societies, there is greater freedom from some external controls, but such freedom occurs in concert with the interdependence of individuals, not in conflict with it. Durkheim realized that societies may take many forms and, consequently, that group allegiance can manifest itself in a variety of ways. In both types of societies outlined previously, however, Durkheim stressed that adherence to a common set of assumptions about the world was a necessary prerequisite for maintaining group integrity and avoiding social decay.

3. Select the sentence in the passage that explains why a society displaying organic solidarity tends more toward social codependence than does a mechanical societal formation.

This question type asks you to click on the sentence that meets the criteria or provides the information solicited by the question stem.

» STEP 1 Read the passage strategically.

You know from having analyzed the text already that the correct answer will be found somewhere after the introduction of the two forms of societal formations. Keep that in mind.

» STEP 2 Analyze the question stem.

This question rewards you for distinguishing the ways in which societies displaying the two forms of solidarity manifest codependence.

» STEP 3 Research the relevant text in the passage.

Since the question centers on the organic solidarity model, the best place to start looking is in the part of the passage where the author defines and illustrates organic solidarity. There, you find this cause-and-effect statement: "Because people engage in highly differentiated ways of life, they are by necessity interdependent."

» STEP 4 Make a prediction.

Make that sentence your prediction.

» STEP 5 Evaluate the answer choices.

The sentence is the right answer; it explains that because the members of an organic society do not have the same skill sets, they are forced to rely on others for those things they are unable to do or do not have the skill for. Click it and confirm your answer.

KAPLAN'S ADDITIONAL TIPS FOR READING COMPREHENSION QUESTIONS

Express the Main Idea in Your Own Words

Summarizing the main idea of the passage not only forms the foundation of your comprehension of the passage, it's also the starting point for your evaluation of the questions. While not every passage has a specific main idea, each passage does have a topic and scope, both of which you should discern by the end of the first paragraph. If you are halfway through a passage and still have not identified these elements, you may be reading too fast and not outlining or identifying key words and phrases in the text.

Focus on Retaining Ideas, Not Facts

Unlike university coursework, you do not have to memorize or retain any of the dates, details, or minutiae of a GRE passage. If you are asked a question about a specific term or detail within the text, such as a date or place, the question will likely ask "why" or "how" the author used the detail rather than what's true about it. You have the text there to refer back to. In that sense, the GRE is an open-book test. Concern yourself with the ideas, arguments, and conclusions the author presents in order to assess the questions accurately and examine them within the context of the passage.

Concentrate on Using Only What the Passage Gives You

As a smart test taker, you can benefit from a passage about a topic completely foreign to you. Whatever the passage is about, it is still presented using familiar patterns of expository and persuasive writing.

A danger occurs when you encounter topics about which you have pre-existing knowledge. Such knowledge can confuse or muddle your ability to answer a question by clouding or expanding the scope of the piece beyond what's written. To best handle the questions, you must be concerned only with the text itself and not be influenced by outside knowledge that may be at odds with the answer as defined by the passage and the question stem. When it comes to answering GRE Reading Comprehension questions, the passage is your "universe.

While you've no doubt honed an ability to question and critique text, on the GRE you should accept the information given in informative passages as true. The questions reward you for determining correct answers "based on the passage" or "according to the passage," not for answers true in the world at large. Even with persuasive passages, and regardless of your own opinions on the author's subject or point of view, correct answers follow from the evidence and arguments given as the groundwork for the passage.

Do Not Approach Bolded Statement Questions Differently

From time to time, the GRE will highlight words, phrases, clauses, or sentences in the passage in order to ask you about the logic, function, or meaning of the bolded portion. In the most complex of these—which Kaplan designates as Bolded Statement questions—the test highlights two portions of text (clauses or sentences) in the passage. It then asks you to determine the functions of both statements or their relationship to one another. Some of the functions a sentence might serve are these:

- Development of an argument
- Conclusion of an argument
- Evidence supporting a conclusion
- Evidence supporting part of a conclusion
- Evidence supporting an objection to the conclusion
- A secondary argument or support for a secondary argument
- Illustration or example of a point
- A principle underlying an argument

While it's natural to focus primarily or exclusively on the bolded sentences, you may need the entire passage in order to determine the roles played by the highlighted portions. As you read the passage, read strategically to determine the position taken by the author. Identify his argument and its conclusion and note how he supports them or refutes opposing views. While the bolded lines are central to the correct answer, the surrounding material provides key context.

Predict the correct answer. Then, move on to evaluating the choices and eliminating obviously incorrect answers. In Bolded Statement questions, each answer has two parts, one for each highlighted sentence; both must be correct in order for the answer to be correct. If you are unable to predict an answer, or if your prediction is not among the answer choices, eliminate wrong answer choices by looking carefully at the two parts. Get rid of choices in which you find a mischaracterization of the role of a sentence, a reversal of the sentences' roles,

a reference to a sentence not highlighted, or a description of something that does not appear in the passage. Once you've eliminated the obviously incorrect answers, you'll more easily be able to identify the answer that best describes the roles of the sentences.

Do Not Get Misled by Variations on Standard Question Stems

While most questions concern themselves with what is stated in or follows from the passage, some questions will ask you to find an answer that is *not* supported by the passage. Don't confuse "true" with correct. Characterize the choices before you evaluate them. Consider a question stem like this one, for example:

According to the passage, each of the following is commonly associated with inflation EXCEPT:

This question has four answers that are "true" according to the passage, but wrong (because of the call of the question stem). The one correct choice is the "false" answer, the one that does not follow from the text. While you should assume passages to be true, veracity is irrelevant to evaluating the answers. Choices are correct because they follow from the passage and answer the question. They're incorrect when they do not. From time to time, the test makers will ask "Which of the following, if TRUE, most strengthens the argument?" In such cases, treat the five answer choices as facts, but distinguish the correct answer from the incorrect ones based on the effect they have on the reasoning.

Now try the following section of practice passages and questions to drill and strengthen your Reading Comprehension skills. The following passages are representative in terms of length and number of questions associated with passages on the GRE. Complete the thirty questions and use the explanations that follow to gauge your thinking and refine your test-taking skills.

READING COMPREHENSION PRACTICE SET

Basic

Questions 1–3 are based on the following passage.

Could any comic book superheroes exist in real life? According to a physics professor who studies the way science concepts are applied in comics, Superman is a surprising nominee as one who might actually have a chance. Not the flying, heat-vision-using version we know today, says Dr. James Kakalios of the University of Minnesota, but rather the Superman who first appeared in 1938. Jerry Siegel and Joe Shuster imagined a rocket-borne infant refugee whose alien physiology gave him bullet-resistant skin, the strength of 15 strong men, and the ability to leap (not fly) "tall buildings in a single bound." Whereas today's Superman gets his strength from our "yellow sun," the original Superman's power derived from his planet of origin. According to Kakalios, a compact planet with extreme gravity could produce a being who, as a result of adaptation to environmental factors, would have superhuman strength in Earth's lesser gravity. But that planet's ability to bring forth such a being would ultimately result in the planet's own destruction. Its gravitational collapse would be very similar to the planetary death that resulted, fictionally of course, in Superman being sent to our world in the first place.

1. Which of the following is TRUE according to the passage?

   (A) The author believes that a superhuman being might really exist somewhere on Earth.

   (B) The character of Superman is more likely to exist in reality than the character of Batman.

   (C) Superman as he is portrayed today is more powerful than the Superman of 1938.

   (D) Dr. James Kakalios has a large comic book collection.

   (E) Looking for a planet with beings of superhuman strength is pointless because any such planets would have been destroyed.

2. Select the sentence in the passage that identifies the scientific rationale for the possibility of a superhuman being.

Consider each of the following choices separately and select all that apply.

3. According to Dr. Kakalios, which of the following abilities would be possible in a superhuman being?

   [A] The ability to travel unaided through outer space

   [B] The ability to bench-press many times more weight than a normal man

   [C] The ability to jump over a house

Question 4 is based on the following passage.

Richard Wagner's *The Ring of the Nibelung* is perhaps the epitome of a *magnum opus*. If the entire work were to be performed beginning at seven o'clock in the morning, it might not conclude until close to midnight! Despite its immensity, Wagner's epic cycle of four music dramas, filled with familiar melodies such as "Ride of the Valkyries," is still performed and celebrated today. This daunting work is usually divided into a cycle of its four component pieces, which are often performed on successive nights because of the long and arduous level of singing over the course of a full cycle. The performance requirements of *The Ring of the Nibelung* also occasioned a specially constructed opera house in which the orchestra was placed in a covered pit under the stage. This ensured that the size and volume of the orchestra did not drown out the voices of the chorus. This innovation is still in use today. That opera companies are still willing to perform and enthusiasts are still willing to pay for what amounts to multiple consecutive shows is a testament to what some have called the greatest piece of operatic theater ever written.

Consider each of the following choices separately and select all that apply.

4. With which of the following statements would the author be likely to agree?

☐ A Wagner's *Ring of the Nibelung* cycle is too demanding and logistically difficult to be performed.

☐ B An enduring effect of Wagner's *Ring of the Nibelung* cycle is the innovations made to the opera house to accommodate the large orchestra.

☐ C Mammoth works such as *Ring of the Nibelung* are better performed on one day to preserve their full effect.

Questions 5 and 6 are based on the following passage.

Discovered in 2001, the mimic octopus is a creature whose survival abilities are as unique as they are versatile. This talented cephalopod is capable of imitating several different species of creatures found in its environment, and it does so for different purposes. It imitates a crab to get close enough to catch and eat one, it imitates toxic fish to avoid being eaten itself, and it can imitate a predatory sea snake to scare off trespassers. The shape-shifting creature's conscious selection from among multiple forms is an exceptionally rare trait among animals, and one that adds a wrinkle to the more commonly expressed forms of singularly limited camouflage seen in nature. Many species exist that survive in part by resembling sticks, leaves, or other animals. Scientists have suggested that, within these species, members showing adaptive coloring or designs were overlooked by predators while the differently marked members were consumed. The survivors were then left to mate and to pass on their beneficial forms as a natural defense. The mimic octopus's intelligent use of selective disguise suggests a creative and adaptive survival mechanism, more versatile and intriguing than that arising from appearance alone.

5. Select the sentence in the passage that distinguishes how the mimic octopus's camouflage exceeds that of most forms found in nature.

6. The author would most likely agree with which of the following sentences?

   (A) The mimic octopus was probably discovered only recently because of its incredible ability to camouflage itself.

   (B) The mimic octopus's method of conscious and situational disguise discredits current evolutionary theory.

   (C) Mimic octopuses can only imitate the forms of creatures they can see.

   (D) Octopuses must be nearly as intelligent as humans.

   (E) Animal mimicry throughout nature is primarily a defensive mechanism as opposed to a means of attracting food.

Questions 7 and 8 are based on the following passage.

Few today would argue that including women in modern productions of Shakespeare's plays, a practice almost universally forbidden in Shakespeare's time, detracts from the presentation as a whole. However, in realizing gender equality through the assignment of women to female roles, a layer of both added humor and dramatic challenge is removed from several of the bard's works, including a light comedy (*Twelfth Night*), a dark comedy (*The Merchant of Venice*), and a romance (*As You Like It*). In each, a female character, whom Shakespeare would have imagined played by a man, disguises herself as a man. A male actor of Shakespeare's age would have had to move beyond instilling feminine qualities in his character and into sustaining a feminine undercurrent beneath a superficial masculine pretension within an obviously masculine form. To the historic audience of *As You Like It*, the spectacle of a young man pretending to be young Rosalind pretending to be an old man brought additional "fourth wall" humor to the event. That humorous presentation may be lost on today's audiences, for whom assigning one gender to play another within a gender-mixed cast might come across more as a surprising distraction than as an added laugh.

Consider each of the following choices separately and select all that apply.

7. Which of the following options would reflect a modern return to the same gender humor the author describes in the passage?

   A   Changing a male character to a female character and having the role played by a woman

   B   Casting a male actor to play the part of Rosalind in *As You Like It*

   C   Casting a female actor in the role of a male servant in *The Taming of the Shrew*, who disguises himself as a woman

8. Select in the passage the sentence that expresses the author's overall thesis.

Questions 9 and 10 are based on the following passage.

In some key ways, a zoologist's orderly method for identifying and classifying a subject species is at odds with the multi-millennial chaos of adaptive development that led to the species as it is embodied today. If the laws of nature were as rigid as we want our classification system to be, famous taxonomic rebels such as the platypus would be forced, as mammals, to gestate and give birth to live young even if the risk to both parent and child were increased to the point of bringing about the end of the species. We are thus fortunate that the rigid biological nomenclature of science makes concessions for such an unusual marvel, one that not only scorns the basic tenets of its class, but brings new and mystifying qualities to the whole branch of its kingdom. It is hard enough to believe in the existence of a furry, duck-billed, egg-laying, venomous mammal that senses its prey through disturbances in a surrounding electromagnetic field without an unassailable checklist stating that the creature cannot by definition exist.

9. Select the sentence that explicitly states one of the traditional zoological characteristics of a species of mammal.

Consider each of the following choices separately and select all that apply.

10. Which of the following accurately describes the author's intent in writing the passage?

   A   To indicate the shortcomings of using a highly structured classification system to define radically adaptive animals

   B   To express admiration for the unusual abilities of the platypus

   C   To make an argument in favor of changing how scientists classify animals with atypical traits

Intermediate

Question 11 is based on the following passage.

A healthy national economy is normally in oscillation between a period of freely flowing dollars driving the economy to expansion and a more tightly controlled release of money stabilizing it. All of these actions are initiated by the Federal Reserve (the Fed). When the Fed unleashes money into the system with low interest rates, consumer confidence rises, spending increases, business expands, and the economy itself grows. As wealth accumulates, the pricing of goods and services rises rapidly, creating inflation. The Fed neutralizes inflation by clamping down on the flow of money by setting higher interest rates. With less money available, spending and demand diminishes, usually curtailing or lowering prices. **Unfortunately, this balance of control can only operate perfectly in a closed system.** In the world economy, external, universal demands for food and oil fuel create an internal inflationary resonance. Increased flow of money is offset by unchecked inflation, and the economy remains flat. When that happens, the Fed is faced with the no-win condition of *stagflation*: it must attempt to increase the flow of dollars into the economy and see inflation skyrocket disproportionately against economic growth, or restrain spending to control inflation, forcing Americans to see their cumulative wealth dissipate.

11.   What roles do the boldfaced sentences play in the passage?

  (A) The first sentence establishes the author's primary argument, and the second sentence is a detail supporting the argument.

  (B) The first sentence identifies the two subjects of the passage, and the second sentence describes a point of comparison.

  (C) The first sentence states a premise, and the second sentence supplies a criticism of that premise.

  (D) The first sentence defines the primary idea of the passage, and the second sentence states the secondary idea.

  (E) The first sentence provides a definition for the subject of the passage, and the second sentence is an example of the subject.

Questions 12–13 are based on the following passage.

After a successful digital grass roots movement resulted in a hosting appearance by accomplished actress Betty White on the sketch comedy show *Saturday Night Live* (or *SNL*), a second movement appeared to get the revered stateswoman of comedy Carol Burnett to host an episode as well. If successful, it would mark an ironic full circle for the show that imagined itself in the 1970s as a counteragent to the supposedly hackneyed antics of Burnett's own successful sketch comedy show. As *SNL* embarked on a path toward the irreverent humor that continues today, the accessible and sentimental *Carol Burnett Show*, which ended every evening with Burnett giving a gentle tug on her ear in symbolic reverence to her grandmother, had already cultivated an audience with an intimate familiarity and genuine appreciation for the unassuming comedienne. Should such a convergence of these shows finally come to pass, will the current show's stars, whose fan bases combined are probably eclipsed by Burnett's own, encourage the show business legend to engage completely in their particular populist stylings? Or will the show that once denounced Burnett's style be willing at last to give a wink, nod, and ear tug to Burnett's highly regarded comedic sensibilities?

12. Select the sentence that demonstrates that *The Carol Burnett Show* must have been on television prior to *Saturday Night Live*.

13. Which of the following would be the most appropriate title for the passage?

   (A) "The Demise and Return of Classic Comedy"

   (B) "Saturday Night Success"

   (C) "Burnett and *SNL*—Together at Last?"

   (D) "The Internet Brings Back a Laughing Legend"

   (E) "Carol Burnett: The Mother of Sketch Comedy"

Question 14 is based on the following passage.

For the past year, a network television talk-show host has been making fun of the name of a particular brand of chainsaw, the Tree Toppler. The ridicule is obviously taking its toll: in the past 12 months, sales of the Tree Toppler have declined by 15 percent, while the sales of other chainsaws have increased.

14. Which of the following, if true, casts the most serious doubt on the conclusion drawn above?

   (A) The talk-show host who is ridiculing the Tree Toppler name actually owns a Tree Toppler.

   (B) The number of product complaints from owners of the Tree Toppler has not increased in the past year.

   (C) The average price of all chainsaws has increased by 10 percent in the past year.

   (D) The number of stores that sell the Tree Toppler has remained steady for the past year.

   (E) A year ago, a leading consumer magazine rated the Tree Toppler as "intolerably unsafe."

Question 15 is based on the following passage.

With the rise of community file-sharing programs that facilitated the easy distribution of data, which initially were used almost exclusively to disseminate music, artists and recording companies faced the possibility of a massive decrease in album sales. While record labels were unified in calling for swift legal crackdowns against file sharing, artists themselves were divided. No one was excited about the prospect of losing royalties, yet a few musicians imagined that the circumstances might lead to a return of the "bardic tradition," in which a musician's living was made through live performances. With large increases in the number of people with access to an artist's music, it was hoped that a potentially larger fan base would translate into better attended shows and concerts. Talented musicians or acts with entertaining showmanship would thrive while contrived or manufactured music groups would disappear, improving the overall quality of music. To date, that imagined future has failed to appear, in part due to rising ticket costs.

Consider each of the following choices separately and select all that apply.

15. Which of the following statements is suggested by the passage?

    [A] Regardless of the ultimate impact of file sharing on the music industry, two certainties will be a decrease in album sales for musicians and an increase in concert tours.

    [B] A subset of musicians would prefer to make their living as touring performers.

    [C] A musician's profits from concert tours are usually greater than that from record sales.

Question 16 is based on the following passage.

Between 1997 and 2002, the incidence of peanut allergies in young children doubled, according to studies by medical allergists. The sharp rise in peanut and other food allergies in adolescents led scientists and doctors to look for possible causes and contributing factors. **One idea gaining support is the "hygiene hypothesis," which suggests that the human immune system requires contact with a wide range of environmental pathogens in order to strengthen itself.** In a home environment that is kept largely sterile, particularly through the use of antibacterial soaps and sprays, the body does not learn to recognize and later combat some harmful viruses and bacteria. The absence of germs to fight, some theorize, leads the immune system to begin focusing on other, more innocuous substances such as peanuts, milk, and eggs. As a result of the overly clean environment, the developing autoimmune reaction becomes too sensitive to other organisms. Unfortunately, even if there is sufficient evidence to support the hygiene hypothesis, the benefits of that knowledge are mixed. **Few people would want to resort to introducing germs, avoiding vaccines, or purposely living less sanitary lives in hopes of preventing a mere possibility of food allergies.**

16. In the passage, what purpose do the boldfaced sentences serve?

    (A) The first sentence states the main idea of the paragraph, and the second sentence states the secondary idea.

    (B) The first sentence states a counterargument to the author's argument, and the second sentence provides a supporting detail.

    (C) The first sentence identifies a problem, and the second sentence argues a solution.

    (D) The first sentence introduces the main idea of the paragraph, and the second sentence is a supporting statement for the conclusion.

    (E) The first sentence is the primary argument, and the second sentence is a secondary argument.

Questions 17–18 are based on the following passage.

It is possible for a product to become a victim of its own success. When a product is so new, so innovative, or so well marketed that it dominates the marketplace and the mindset of the consumer, it can be easy to associate the product's brand name with the product itself. When a type of product is nearly universally known or referred to by the brand name of one version of the product, the brand name becomes a victim of "genericism." Aspirin (acetylsalicylic acid), the escalator (moving stair), and the pogo stick (hopping toy) are all former brand names whose success and popularity led to such general and widespread use of the name that the inventors or parent companies were unable to maintain their trademark protections and even lost their competitive advantage against similar products described with the term that had once been a definitive brand name. All it takes is one court ruling for a term that has shifted away from its identity as a trusted brand name to become forever identified as a generic product. When this happens, a company is likely to lose a profitable beachhead within the consumer consciousness. Therefore, companies are highly motivated to use lawsuits and advertisements to dissuade others from making product identifications, such as a permutation of the original brand name, that even passingly resemble their trademarks.

The loss of revenue due to a shift to genericism is compounded by the large amounts of money companies may spend in an attempt to keep it from happening. Despite spending millions of dollars in legal and public relations campaigns, the company Kimberly-Clark has been fighting an uphill battle to keep people from referring to all forms of tissues as *Kleenex*. Google has laid heavy pressure on dictionary publishers that include the term *googled* to define the word as a Web search using the Google search engine instead of any Web search. The risk for a company facing a genericized trademark is not only the loss of a profitable brand's trademark but also the sense of superiority that comes with that brand name. Once, people seeking to keep their coffee hot or milk cold for hours would only depend on a Thermos brand vacuum flask. Unfortunately, the product was so successful and in such high demand that the other companies' vacuum flasks became colloquially known as Thermoses as well. The term became so general that any such product is usually identified as a *thermos*, and the Thermos company lost U.S. protections for the trademark. Now, instead of spending to protect its brand name, the company that first created the product, Thermos, LLC, spends its marketing dollars to make sure that, when people "Google" the term *thermos*, pages for their company's stores and products are the first to appear.

17. According to the above passage, which of these statements is NOT true:

    Ⓐ Only one company can refer to its product as "aspirin."

    Ⓑ Kimberly-Clark would prefer that people refer to its product as "Kleenex brand tissues."

    Ⓒ Companies that lose U.S. protection of their trademarks also stand to lose money on the brands associated with those trademarks.

    Ⓓ Genericism is a by-product of a company's successful positioning of a product so that it assumes a place of dominance with the general public.

    Ⓔ Americans' awareness of the distinction between a product and its brand name is key to preventing a trademark from becoming genericized.

18. Select the sentence in the passage that identifies what ultimately is required for a trademark to become fully "genericized."

Question 19 is based on the following passage.

Thousands who suffer heart attacks each year die before reaching a hospital or clinic where they can benefit from the drugs that dissolve clots found in coronary arteries. The Food and Drug Administration recently approved a new blood clot dissolving agent, which a spokesman claimed could save the lives of many people who would otherwise join this group of heart attack victims.

19. Which of the following statements, if true, would most weaken the argument above?

    Ⓐ The new agent must be administered by a team of doctors in a hospital or clinic setting.

    Ⓑ Many heart attack victims die unnecessarily even though they reach a hospital or clinic in time.

    Ⓒ The new agent can be effectively administered prior to the victim's arrival at a hospital or clinic.

    Ⓓ The Food and Drug Administration has already approved agents that are at least as effective as the new drug in dissolving blood clots.

    Ⓔ The new blood clot dissolving agent causes kidney damage and irregular heart rates in some patients.

Advanced

Questions 20 and 21 are based on the following passage.

With computer access for work, education, and personal use reaching near universal saturation, and with many people logging time on more than one networked machine, a vast array of online computers are operated by largely untrained users. These operators' lack of network security awareness presents a large opportunity for hackers and cybercriminals to gain access to sensitive business and personal data. Ironically, it is not these users' computing inexperience that represents the vulnerability. A very small percentage of malicious computer attacks are caused by a "traditional" external attack. Instead of kicking in the door, so to speak, the perpetrators usually convince computer users to open it for them. Through targeted links and ads from dubious websites or fake emails to anonymous contacts made through instant messaging services or social networking sites, cybercriminals rely on people's trusting nature to provide them with the means to infect or gain access to the victims' computers. In some cases, creative criminals will even initiate their attack in the real world, placing advertisements or fake parking tickets on cars that ask the owners to visit a website for more information. The website usually contains invasive software that users then download to their computers.

Consider each of the following choices separately and select all that apply.

20. According to the passage, which of the following are means that the passage suggests cybercriminals can use to illegitimately access another's computer?

   [A] Engage in an external attack over a network.

   [B] Get users to click on a link contained in a deceitful email.

   [C] Use a seemingly innocuous object to get a person to voluntarily visit a specifically created attack site.

21. With which of the following sentences would the author most likely agree?

   (A) Since nearly everyone uses computers, the sheer number of computers in use makes the odds of any one computer being hacked too low to merit concern about security.

   (B) One way to combat cybercrime is to become more suspicious of anonymous requests or messages sent over social networks.

   (C) In order to prevent illegal access to data, only trained personnel should be allowed to use computers.

   (D) If a cybercriminal is unable to trick users into giving access to their machines, the criminal will likely attack the users' machines directly.

   (E) In order to protect their computers, people should refrain from using instant messaging services and social networks.

Questions 22 and 23 are based on the following passage.

One of the strategic principles for success in the stock market is to refrain from having knee-jerk reactions to possibly deceptive fluctuations in the market's or a particular stock's performance. Before reinvesting in a rapidly falling stock, analysts and investors will often wait for the passing of one or more small upward bumps, referred to as "dead cat bounces." The term reflects the somewhat crude idea that even a dead cat will bounce if it falls from a great height. Upticks in a plummeting stock can be caused by short selling, triggered sell-offs, or overly optimistic reactions to changes made by the company, such as replacing an unpopular CEO. Such a small, unimpressive rise is usually followed by another drop-off that surpasses the previous low. While almost exclusively related to the stock market, the term has found occasional use in describing other areas of misleading improvement. Poll numbers for a candidate losing ground near an election sometimes make a brief, illusory surge. In sports, losing teams that make midseason coaching changes sometimes experience a mild surge of energy that translates to one or more wins before the team reverts to form.

22. According to the passage, each of the following is TRUE of a "dead cat bounce" EXCEPT:

  (A) It occurs when a stock shows a small improvement followed by a much greater decline in performance.

  (B) It only occurs in instances where performance is already showing a rapid decline.

  (C) It provides a good opportunity to sell stock at the peak of the "dead cat bounce" before the stock plummets even further.

  (D) It is a term that primarily exists to explain a regularly occurring feature of the stock market.

  (E) It is capable of occurring multiple times within the same stock's downward collapse before the stock's improvement becomes sustainable.

23. Select the sentence in the passage that demonstrates the traditional investment strategy in regard to a stock experiencing or expected to experience a "dead cat bounce."

Questions 24–26 are based on the following passage.

The barely edible rarity known as *casu marzu* is a cheese so dangerous that it has been illegal to sell, serve, or in some cases even possess in its native Italy. And yet, it is one of the most sought-after dishes for weddings there. What starts out as a firm hunk of cheese made from sheep's milk is soaked in brine, smoked, and left in a cellar to age. The step that infringes European food and hygiene laws comes next, when holes are drilled into the cheese so that cheese flies and fly larvae can be inserted into the center of the cheese. The flies are then free to spawn thousands upon thousands of maggots that consume, digest, and expel a fermented cheese by-product. The result is an extremely runny and flowing substance that, live maggots and all, is spread over dry bread or crackers and consumed. In fact, the Italians who produce and eat the cheese today, and do so with the same delight and confidence that their ancestors did hundreds of years ago, insist that the maggots must be alive within the cheese. If they are not, they warn, the cheese has clearly ripened too much and become too toxic for consumption.

This makes the maggots a considerable factor in preparing the cheese. The agile and nimble creatures are said to jump as high as six inches from the cheese with considerable precision, often targeting a potential new host's eyes. They are also quite hardy and, if not thoroughly masticated during eating, might survive passage through the stomach and live on as an internal parasite. As if the danger of fly larvae taking up residence in one's intestines isn't troublesome enough, the liquid excretions from the cheese are capable of burning the skin, eyes, and tongue. Even the cheese itself, properly formed, can cause a burning, itching skin irritation that can last for a week after eating.

All of these gastronomic hazards, some of which can be lethal, belie the fact that the cheese is still a considerable black market item, consumed in sizable amounts in the Sardinia region of Italy, but very little by even the most curious outsiders who must ask why people, particularly people in celebration, would subject themselves to such a concoction. The answer for this, as with many other seemingly unpalatable foods such as raw fish eggs and ground cockroach eaten in other parts of the world, is that the dish has traditionally been seen as an aphrodisiac, thus making it sought after not just for the aforementioned weddings, but also for the bachelor parties that precede them.

24. Based on the preceding passage, with which of the following statements would the author most likely agree?

    Ⓐ Despite the process *casu marzu* goes through in order to be formed, the end product must taste delicious, or else people would not make it.

    Ⓑ Some people are willing to eat foods with potential health risks based on traditional claims about those foods.

    Ⓒ The popularity of *casu marzu* in Sardinia suggests that the laws regarding food and hygiene making the food illegal are not enforced there.

    Ⓓ Long-standing traditions, such as *casu marzu*, should, based on their cultural importance, be given some degree of exemption from legal regulation.

    Ⓔ *Casu marzu*'s continued popularity as a wedding food probably means that claims regarding its effects have a basis in fact.

25. Select the sentence that best explains the violations that have resulted in *casu marzu* being unavailable through traditional outlets.

Consider each of the following choices separately and select all that apply.

26. According to the passage, which of the following are potential health effects of eating *casu marzu*?

    - ☐ A   Larval parasitic infection caused by live maggots passing through the stomach into the intestines
    - ☐ B   Mild intoxication caused by the fermentation process of the cheese
    - ☐ C   Caustic burns to the surface of the tongue caused by the liquid issued by the cheese

Question 27 is based on the following passage.

Archaeologists found the ruins of a Mayan city they named X near the site of another Mayan city that is known to have been destroyed by a major earthquake in 950 A.D. The archaeologists hypothesized that the same earthquake destroyed both cities.

27. All of the following, if true, would strengthen the archaeologists' hypothesis EXCEPT:

    - Ⓐ   The Mayans built all of their cities primarily of masonry, which provides little stability in case of earth tremors.
    - Ⓑ   Records of another society that came to control the region in approximately 1000 A.D. contain no records of either city.
    - Ⓒ   City X does not lie on a fault line, as the neighboring city does.
    - Ⓓ   Archaeologists found no inscriptions written after 950 A.D. in city X, but many written before that date.
    - Ⓔ   The pattern of collapsed buildings in city X is consistent with earthquake damage in other cities destroyed by earthquake.

Question 28 is based on the following passage.

A study of children's television-watching habits by the federal Department of Education found that children aged 7–10 who watched more than 25 hours of television per week performed worse in school than children of the same age who watched fewer than 25 hours of television per week. Therefore, parents of children aged 7–10 should prohibit their children from watching more than 25 hours of television per week.

28. Which of the following, if true, would best strengthen the argument above?

Ⓐ A separate study, by a renowned graduate school of education, found that when parents prohibited their children from watching any television, the children's reading scores increased rapidly and significantly, and stayed high indefinitely.

Ⓑ Children who watched more than 25 hours of television per week also performed worse on measures of physical fitness than children who watched fewer than 25 hours per week.

Ⓒ The television shows that children aged 7–10 are most likely to watch are saturated with advertisements for products, such as toys and candy, of little educational value.

Ⓓ The Department of Education study gave appropriate weight to children of backgrounds representative of children nationwide.

Ⓔ Children who develop a habit of extensive television watching are more likely than others to maintain that habit as an adult.

Questions 29 and 30 are based on the following passage.
Decompression sickness, colloquially known as "the bends," occurs when inert gas bubbles are formed and expelled from organic tissue during rapid ascent following an extended period of prolonged intensive atmospheric pressure. This is most commonly experienced during deepwater dives. Surface divers capable of descending to sufficient depth, or scuba divers using air tanks, supersaturate their lungs with air, which diffuses throughout the body. When a diver remains at high pressure for a sufficiently long time, nitrogen, a gas present in the air and breathed into the body, is driven into the muscle tissue in elevated amounts and subsequently released again as pressure subsides. When pressure on the body decreases as the diver nears the surface, the diver must take care to rise gradually and expel excess gas through the mouth, nose, and ears. Without these pressure balances, the gas bubbles that form in the tissue can disrupt the joints and organs. In mild cases, the diver suffers from painful sensations in the knees, elbows, hips, and shoulders. In extreme cases, the bubbles can impede or rupture blood vessels in the brain or spine, which can lead to paralysis or even death.

29. Select the sentence that identifies the preventative process for circumventing decompression sickness during the conclusion of a deepwater dive.

Consider each of the following choices separately and select all that apply.

30. Which of the following must have occurred in order to initiate a case of decompression sickness in a diver according to the passage?

   A   The person suffering decompression sickness must have experienced a decrease in atmospheric pressure.

   B   A supply of nitrogen sufficient to form high levels of gas bubbles must be present in the muscle tissue of the person suffering decompression sickness.

   C   The person suffering decompression sickness must have used a breathing apparatus, such as a scuba tank that supplies air to a diver.

READING COMPREHENSION PRACTICE SET ANSWER KEY

1. C

2. *"According to Kakalios, a compact planet with extreme gravity could produce a being who, as a result of adaptation to environmental factors, would have superhuman strength in Earth's lesser gravity."*

3. B, C

4. B

5. *"The shape-shifting creature's conscious selection from among multiple forms is an exceptionally rare trait among animals, and one that adds a wrinkle to the more commonly expressed forms of singularly limited camouflage seen in nature."*

6. E

7. B, C

8. *"However, in realizing gender equality through the assignment of women to female roles, a layer of both added humor and dramatic challenge is removed from several of the bard's works, including a light comedy (Twelfth Night), a dark comedy (The Merchant of Venice), and a romance (As You Like It)."*

9. *"If the laws of nature were as rigid as we want our classification system to be, famous taxonomic rebels such as the platypus would be forced, as mammals, to gestate and give birth to live young even if the risk to both parent and child were increased to the point of bringing about the end of the species."*

10. A, B

11. D

12. *"As SNL embarked on a path toward the irreverent humor that continues today, the accessible and sentimental Carol Burnett Show, which ended every evening with Burnett give a gentle tug on her ear in symbolic reverence to her grandmother, had already cultivated an audience with an intimate familiarity and genuine appreciation for the unassuming comedienne."*

13. C

14. E

15. B

16. D

17. A

18. *"All it takes is one court ruling for a term that has shifted away from its identity as a trusted brand name to become forever identified as a generic product."*

19. A

20. A, B, C

21. B

22. C

23. *"Before reinvesting in a rapidly falling stock, analysts and investors will often wait for the passing of one or more small upward bumps, referred to as 'dead cat bounces'."*

24. B

25. *"The step that infringes European food and hygiene laws comes next, when holes are drilled into the cheese so that cheese flies and fly larvae can be inserted into the center of the cheese."*

26. A, C

27. C

28. D

29. *"When pressure on the body decreases as the diver nears the surface, the diver must take care to rise gradually and expel excess gas through the mouth, nose, and ears."*

30. A, B

READING COMPREHENSION PRACTICE SET ANSWERS AND EXPLANATIONS

1. C

You can quickly eliminate choices **(B)** and **(D)** because neither one of these is addressed in the text. Choice **(A)** requires slightly more attentive reading; though the passage explains why Dr. Kakalios believes a superhuman being is plausible, nothing in the passage suggests that he believes one exists on Earth. Similarly, in eliminating choice **(E)**, note that the passage states that a planet capable of producing a superman would eventually be destroyed; it does not state that such planets could not exist now, in a precollapse state. Choice **(C)** is easy to defend, because it makes specific comparisons between the original Superman, who could only leap and had super strength, to the modern version that has developed greater additional powers.

2. *"According to Kakalios, a compact planet with extreme gravity could produce a being who, as a result of adaptation to environmental factors, would have superhuman strength in Earth's lesser gravity."*

Only a few sentences discuss scientific principles. Of those, the correct answer is the one that defines how a superhuman's powers could result from his home environment. The sentence immediately prior attributes Superman's powers to his "planet of origin," but is devoid of any *rationale* explaining "how" or "why" the exceptional physiology came about. The sentence following the correct one describes a scientific analysis of how the high-gravity planet would end but doesn't discuss the possibility of a superhuman being.

3. B, C

Choice **(C)** is a portion of the right answer, because the text reinforces the supposed ability of Superman to leap over a tall building, which would certainly enable him to clear a house. Choice **(A)** can comfortably be ruled out because the passage discusses a "rocket-borne infant" and distinguishes the plausible "Superman" from the character who is able to fly. There is nothing in the text to suggest that Dr. Kakalios imagines a being that could survive unaided in space. Choice **(B)**, on the other hand, is a viable option. The text states that the being Dr. Kakalios considers possible had the strength of 15 strong men. It is therefore reasonable that Superman's strength would allow him to lift much more weight than a normal man, making **(B)** a correct choice as well.

4. B

The correct answer to this question can be discerned from one key detail in the text, in which the passage explains that the performance requirements for the *Ring of the Nibelung* necessitated the construction of a newly designed opera house, and that this innovation is still in use today. With that knowledge, you know that **(B)** applies, because that is the only effect mentioned that is still in use today. You can reject **(A)** because the author explains the technical innovations that have allowed such a work to be performed on a regular basis. Choice **(C)** is incorrect because the author nowhere implies that he disapproves of the multi-night performances, and notes the logistical difficulties of a single-day performance.

5. *"The shape-shifting creature's conscious selection from among multiple forms is an exceptionally rare trait among animals, and one that adds a wrinkle to the more commonly expressed forms of singularly limited camouflage seen in nature."*

This sentence best meets the criterion of describing how the camouflage of the mimic octopus exceeds that of other creatures. The sentence asserts that the creature's ability is rare and elaborates that the mimic octopus's ability to take multiple forms is a step above that of most other camouflaging creatures, which possess only a single form of disguise.

6. E
With five-choice questions that are not specific enough for you to make a prediction, it is better to eliminate than attempt to recognize the correct answer initially. Walking down the list of choices, **(A)** doesn't stand up because no details are given concerning the nature of the mimic octopus's discovery, only its year. The most that the passage asserts regarding the mimic octopus's abilities within the scheme of evolutionary theory is that it "adds a wrinkle." The wording of choice **(B)** is too extreme to follow from the passage. As with **(A)**, choice **(C)** makes an inference without any supporting details in the passage. The passage lists three creatures that the octopus mimics and explains how it uses each of those disguises. Nothing suggests that these are the only creatures it imitates or that sight is required for the mimicking process. Choice **(D)**, which acknowledges the mimic octopus's intelligence, falls outside the scope of the passage, which gives no grounds for comparing it to that of humans. Choice **(E)** is the correct answer, not just because it is left standing after the process of elimination, but also because the passage gives us ample discussion of animal camouflage, describing it primarily as defensive. Only the mimic octopus is described as using camouflage to catch prey.

7. B, C
The aspect of gender humor specified in the text by the author involves an actor of one gender playing the role of the other gender who is then disguised in the form of the actor's original gender. Modern versions of this can be accomplished by a man playing a woman's role disguised as a man, or a woman playing a man's role disguised as a woman. These versions are the ones contained in choices **(B)** and **(C)**. Simply changing the part from its original gender, as in **(A)**, is insufficient.

8. *However, in realizing gender equality through the assignment of women to female roles, a layer of both added humor and dramatic challenge are removed from several of the bard's works, including a light comedy* (**Twelfth Night**), *a dark comedy* (**The Merchant of Venice**), *and a romance* (**As You Like It**).

The task here is the most fundamental in all of Reading Comprehension: find the topic sentence. That sentence, initially identified by the transition "however," clearly outlines the premise of the paragraph: modern productions, which tend to assign roles to actors who are the same gender as their characters, have removed an aspect of humor that was intended in Shakespeare's time. Keep in mind that the author does not argue that such a loss is negative or positive, only that it exists. This is why the passage's initial, evaluative sentence is not correct.

9. *"If the laws of nature were as rigid as we want our classification system to be, famous taxonomic rebels such as the platypus would be forced, as mammals, to gestate and give* *birth to live young even if the risk to both parent and child were increased to the point of bringing about the end of the species."*

With a four-sentence passage, your odds of getting this question right are one-in-four, just on a blind guess. Those odds are better than on a "one right, four wrong" multiple-choice question, but you can do better. Only two sentences—the second and the fourth—discuss mammals. The fourth describes the traits that make the platypus unlike most mammals. From that, you can infer the standard mammalian traits. But, the question asks for a sentence in which qualities are "explicitly" listed. The second sentence, however, states that, to fit properly within the definition of a "mammal," a creature must produce live young.

10. A, B

Reading strategically, you likely discerned the author's dual purposes. They're indicated by key words indicating her opinion and emphases. The passage centers on the limitations of the standard method of zoological classification, which the author chides for being too rigid to accommodate species that don't fall precisely within certain families. That fits choice (A); the author, indeed, "indicate(s) the shortcomings" of the biological taxonomy. Choice (C), on the other hand, goes too far; the author does not suggest an alternative classification system. The author illustrates her point through a discussion of the platypus. In addition to describing its category-defying traits, the author considers it a "marvel," one we're "fortunate" to experience because it's difficult to define. Attending to the author's tone enables you to discern her admiration for the platypus. That tells you to include choice (B) as part of the correct answer.

11. D

In Bolded Statement questions, in which the sentences to be analyzed are pointed out, you are best served by forming a prediction for the correct answer before you consider the choices. You should look for the main idea or argument and then determine how the highlighted sentences (those in boldface on the paper and pencil GRE) apply. By predicting the correct answer, you're less likely to let the choices influence you into thinking a sentence does something it does not. Here, for instance, the passage is informative, not persuasive. This means that choices (A) and (C)—which is only a slight variation on choice (A)—are incorrect. Even without reading the second boldfaced sentence, you can dismiss choice (B) because the description of the first sentence, which introduces a single subject, is inaccurate. You might be able to make an argument for the first part of (E), if you see the explanation of the state of a healthy U.S. economy as a definition. But the second part of choice (E) is derailed by the word "unfortunately" at the onset of the second boldfaced sentence, which suggests not a supporting example but a separate and contrasting idea. Indeed, the second highlighted sentence contains a secondary idea that further refines the main idea. That matches the correct answer, choice (D).

12. *"As SNL embarked on a path toward the irreverent humor that continues today, the accessible and sentimental* Carol Burnett Show, *which ended every evening with Burnett giving a gentle tug on her ear in symbolic reverence to her grandmother, had already cultivated an audience with an intimate familiarity and genuine appreciation for the unassuming comedienne."*

It's easy to presume that the second sentence in the passage, which outlines how *SNL* planned to position itself against the *Carol Burnett Show*, would suffice for this question, but it does not assure that the two shows did not arise simultaneously or even that Burnett's show wasn't following in the footsteps but competing for an audience. Only in the third sentence (the correct answer to this question) do the combined statements of "As *SNL* embarked" and "had already cultivated an audience" guarantee us that Burnett had preceded *SNL* into the sketch comedy arena.

13. C

Titles can be difficult to judge. We've all experienced articles and stories with titles at odds with their content. For the purposes of defining a passage such as this, there are qualifiers you should keep in mind. First, the possible title cannot introduce or fixate on some element of discussion that does not appear in the text. Choice **(E)** fails on that standard; nowhere does the passage posit that Burnett invented sketch comedy. Choice **(A)** stumbles on this point as well; you're never told of a "demise" or death of any form of comedy or of any show. You can tell that Burnett's show no longer runs today, but you get no explanation of the conditions under which that occurred. A title must also be an accurate summary of the main subject or idea. Choice **(B)** is not only too bland, but too general, missing the comparison central to the passage. Choice **(D)** misses the boat by targeting an introductory detail rather than the main idea. Choice **(C)**, which most correctly identifies both the longevity and disparate comedy careers of Burnett and *Saturday Night Live* elaborated on in the passage, is the clear choice.

14. E

This question asks you to cast doubt on the author's conclusion that the talk-show host's ridicule of the Tree Toppler is damaging the chainsaw's sales. To weaken this conclusion, you want an answer choice that presents new information that goes against the stimulus—something that suggests the talk-show host *has not* had undue influence on the sales figures stated by the author.

Choice **(A)** suggests that the host might be engaging in some hypocrisy, but fails to address the Tree Toppler's sales directly, so it is incorrect. Choice **(B)**, if anything, actually *strengthens* the connection between the host's criticism and chainsaw sales, by suggesting that consumers are not otherwise dissatisfied with the Tree Toppler. Choice **(C)** may seem tempting at first, but an increase in the price of *all* chainsaws would not account for the last piece of evidence in the stimulus: Tree Toppler sales have gone down while *sales of other chainsaws have increased*. Choice **(D)** is incorrect on the same grounds as (B): a "steady" level of market penetration, if anything, strengthens the argument. But choice **(E)** does what you want. If the Tree Toppler is "intolerably unsafe," then it is reasonable to assume that sales might decrease, talk-show host or no. Since choice **(E)** introduces a non-talk-show host explanation for the drop in Tree Toppler sales, it weakens the connection and is thus correct.

15. B

As always, each statement needs to be considered on its own merits, using only evidence stated in the passage. Remember that you only have to discredit one aspect of a choice to show that it's invalid. Option **(A)** has multiple parts, and none is supported by the text. Whether or not you agree that the end result of music file sharing can't be determined, the passage does not establish that either the decrease in album sales (which the music industry fears) or an increase in the number of concerts (which some musicians anticipate) has or will come to pass. Option **(B)** has merit, and is a correct answer. Indeed, the passage's main idea is that, with the onset of music file sharing, some musicians were optimistic that they could engage in and support themselves through live performance. Option **(C)**, similarly to **(A)**, has multiple undemonstrated aspects. The passage does not compare the profitability of albums and concerts, either before or after the influence of file sharing. There is no basis in the text for this claim.

16.   D

The topic of this passage, introduced in the first sentence, is food allergies and the search for a possible cause. The next sentence presents the main idea; it defines the "hygiene hypothesis" and asserts that it might explain the rise in adolescent food allergies. Once you have recognized that, you can pass over all choices that do not acknowledge that role for the first bolded sentence, meaning **(B)**, **(C)**, and **(E)** are out. Your understanding of the passage's structure is important, because the conclusion, "Unfortunately, even if there is sufficient evidence to support the hygiene hypothesis, the benefits of that knowledge are mixed," is not one of the bolded sentences. The final, bolded sentence supports that conclusion. This puts choice **(A)** by the wayside and indicates **(D)** as the correct choice.

17.   A

You should immediately identify choice **(A)** as correct, not because general knowledge suggests that more than one brand sells aspirin (don't bring in outside knowledge), but because the text specifically identifies aspirin as a product that lost its brand name protections in the United States. However, this choice is clear-cut only if you read the question stem properly to see that the question asks you to find the choice that is *not* true. The other four choices are defended by the text. The section detailing Kimberly-Clark's battle to retain its control over Kleenex brand tissues supports choice **(B)**, and choice **(C)** is identified in the section that states, "When [genericization] happens, a company is likely to lose a profitable beachhead within the consumer consciousness." The opening sentences state the crux of the premise of choice **(D)**. The hardest to demonstrate to be true is choice **(E)**, but the supporting details for the main idea of the passage illustrate that the key to whether or not a product reaches a state of genericization hinges on the public perception as interpreted by a court of law. Keeping the brand name separate from the product seems to be the overall key to protecting a brand.

18.   *"All it takes is one court ruling for a term that has shifted away from its identity as a trusted brand name to become forever identified as a generic product."*

This can be a tricky question to answer, because an early introduction to the term "genericization" provides a cursory explanation of its cause: "When a type of product is nearly universally known or referred to by the brand name of one version of the product, the brand name becomes a victim of 'genericism.'" However, keeping in mind the Kaplan strategy of analyzing the question stem, you need to take into account that the question demands that you identify what *ultimately* is required. The shift in public consciousness regarding a brand name must, as the passage indicates, be ruled into fact by a court. That ruling, which negates U.S. trademark protections, completes the process of genericization. That makes the statement indicated at the beginning of this answer explanation the correct one.

19.   A

This question asks you to weaken the argument in the stimulus. In the last sentence of the stimulus, a spokesperson says that this dissolving agent will save the lives of many people who would otherwise join "this group of heart attack victims." Which group of heart attack victims? Those who die before reaching a hospital or clinic, who are mentioned earlier in the stimulus.

To weaken the spokesperson's conclusion, you need to find an answer choice that goes against this specific argument. In other words, you want a choice that says people who would die before reaching a hospital *will not be saved* by this drug. Answer Choice **(A)** does this, and it is correct; if the new agent can't be administered outside a hospital or clinic setting, it's not going to make a shred of difference for those who die before they get there.

Choice **(B)** is outside the scope of this argument, as this argument only cares about those who die before they hit the hospital. Choice **(C)** actually *strengthens* the argument, attesting to the agent's ability to save pre-hospital patients. And choices **(D)** and **(E)** both begin suggesting reasons why this new drug might not make a difference, but there is too much uncertainty in each of them: for **(D)**, perhaps the more-effective drugs are not yet in wide usage or have some other caveat; for **(E)**, maybe the lives saved would outweigh those endangered by the side effects.

20.   A, B, C

This is a tough Select One or More question. For the untrained test taker, the difficulty is compounded by the fact that, here, all three choices are correct. Remember not to assume that one of the answers must be wrong. The test makers may write one, two, or all three of the choices to be applicable to the question

stem. In this question, select any answer that lists a way in which the passage tells you a cybercriminal might attack a personal computer. The passage states that direct attack over the network, choice **(A)**, is unlikely, but still a possibility. Likewise, the passage explicitly cites "dubious websites or fake emails," choice **(B)**. The use of "advertisements or fake parking tickets" cited near the end of the passage matches choice **(C)**'s "seemingly innocuous object" reference.

21.   B

This question asks for a choice with which the author would agree. Rule out the choices that are not supported in the text. Choice **(A)** contradicts the author; she states that near-universal computer use increases the security risk. You can infer that the author would agree with choice **(B)**; she cites fraudulent requests and messages from unknown sources on social networks and instant messaging systems as a significant source of cyber-vulnerability. This makes **(B)** the correct answer. In this predominantly informative paragraph, the author makes no claims that come close to either of the controversial suggestions in choices **(C)** and **(E)**. The passage describes the source of the problem, but doesn't recommend policies to fix it. Choice **(D)** receives no support from the passage. The author says indirect attack is more common than direct attack, but doesn't state or suggest that criminals turn to direct attack when their indirect schemes fail.

22.   C

This is a question that asks for the answer choice that is *not* supported by the passage. That means that the four wrong answers will contain statements you can infer from the text. A solid reading of the text gives you all you need to know about the definition and characteristics of a "dead cat bounce" in order to eliminate choices **(A)** "usually followed by another drop-off that surpasses the previous low", **(B)** "before reinvesting in a rapidly falling stock", **(D)** "occasional use in describing other areas", and **(E)** "one or more small upward bumps". Choice **(C)**, on the other hand, is contradicted by the passage. Most investors wait out the "dead cat bounce," meaning it's not likely to be a good time to sell.

23. ***"Before reinvesting in a rapidly falling stock, analysts and investors will often wait for the passing of one or more small upward bumps, referred to as 'dead cat bounces.'"***

Here, the sentence that provides the definition for a "dead cat bounce" also gives you the conventional wisdom investors use in response: Wait out the deceptive event before finding a more opportune time to reinvest.

24.   B
This is an open-ended Inference question. The stem doesn't direct you to a particular detail or piece of text. You know the author's high-level evaluation of *casu marzu* from your roadmap and topic, scope, and purpose summaries. The author describes the food as "barely edible," cites its health risks, and tells you that the claims about its aphrodisiacal qualities are the reason for its continued popularity. Use those broad summaries to eliminate any clearly wrong answer choices. If more than one answer choice remains, use the choices to research the passage. Confirm the correct answer or eliminate the remaining incorrect choices. The author directly contradicts choice **(A)**. Eliminate it. Choice **(B)** may sound overly generic, but read it carefully. Combining the author's list of potential health hazards from eating *casu marzu* with his conclusion

about the reasons for its popularity, you can conclude beyond any doubt that the author would agree with choice **(B)**. Eliminate the remaining choices. The author tells you that those seeking *casu marzu* buy it on the black market, suggesting that he would not agree with choice **(C)**. The author offers no recommendations about policies or regulations on traditional or culturally significant foods. So, choice **(D)** is out. The author tells you that *casu marzu* shares its claim as an aphrodisiac with other traditional foods, but makes no assessment of the claim's validity. Choice **(E)** can be eliminated, too.

25.   *"The step that infringes European food and hygiene laws comes next, when holes are drilled into the cheese so that cheese flies and fly larvae can be inserted into the center of the cheese."*

In the passage's first sentence, you learn that *casu marzu* is illegal to make, sell, and possess. That explains why the cheese is available only on the black market. But this question asks for the sentence that best explains the violations that lead to its illegality. Only in this sentence, highlighting a step in the cheese's creation that violates regulatory standards, does the author explicitly address the reasons that the cheese runs afoul of the regulatory process.

26.   A, C
The author lists many potential health risks to *casu marzu*, so you must be diligent in locating and filing them away as you research the passage. The danger of parasitic infection in the intestines is stated explicitly in the second paragraph, confirming choice **(A)** as a correct answer. The passage also points out that the liquid that comes from the cheese is capable of burning the skin, eyes, and tongue, which confirms **(C)**. Drunkenness, however, is

not mentioned as an effect of the cheese. *Casu marzu* is fermented, but the author makes no mention of an intoxicant byproduct to that process. Choice **(B)**, therefore, is not a part of the answer.

27. C

In this question, we are asked to identify statements that would strengthen the archaeologists' hypothesis, which is outlined above: the same earthquake destroyed both cities in question—City X and its neighbor. However, since this is an EXCEPT question, all the answer choices that match up with the question stem and strengthen the argument will be INCORRECT. The one choice that either weakens the argument or stays neutral on the issue will be our correct answer.

It's a good idea to have a predictive framework before we go to the answer choices here. The best way to support the assertion that both cities were destroyed by the same earthquake is to outline key similarities between them, especially similarities that would predispose them to being destroyed by earthquakes, or evidence that they disappeared at the same time. So anything that makes them look more similar will be *incorrect*.

Choices **(A)**, **(B)**, **(D)**, and **(E)** all fall in line with the fact that the two cities are analogous and were both destroyed around 950 A.D. Answer Choice **(C)**, however, shares a key difference: City X is not on a fault line. Since City X's not being on a fault line would make it undoubtedly *less* likely to be destroyed by an earthquake, Answer Choice **(C)** actually *weakens* the argument, making it the correct answer to this EXCEPT question.

28. D

We need to strengthen the argument in the stimulus here by finding an answer choice that goes along with the last sentence in the stimulus: children aged 7-10 shouldn't watch more than 25 hours of TV per week. Since the author uses a study as his evidence, the most likely way this argument will be strengthened is by bolstering the legitimacy of this evidence. We also want to quickly eliminate answers that are outside the scope of the issue; this will be a particularly large trap because the conclusion here is so specific.

Choice **(A)** might sound very official, but it errs on two crucial details: first, the cited study in **(A)** is about children who are *prohibited* from watching television, not just kept down to 25 hours. It also only mentions "children" as its subjects rather than the age range given by the stimulus. While this choice does toe the line of "less TV equals better grades," it does not strengthen the argument's specific conclusion and doesn't consider the original argument's evidence at all. It is incorrect. Choice **(B)** is out of scope because it ventures into measures of physical fitness rather than performance in school. Incorrect as well. Choice **(C)** is out of scope and incorrect; it offers a possible *explanation* for why TV doesn't educate children, but avoids strengthening this author's specific argument.

Choice **(D)** is correct. If the Department of Education study—the one cited in the stimulus—was appropriately weighted and the sample was representative, then it legitimizes the author's evidence and strengthens his argument.

Choice **(E)**, while perhaps interesting in its own right, joins, **(B)**, and **(C)** in venturing outside the scope of scholastic achievement.

29. *"When pressure on the body decreases as the diver nears the surface, the diver must take care to rise gradually and expel excess gas through the mouth, nose, and ears."*

The phrase "the diver must . . ." indicates that this sentence gives instructions for how to avoid a case of decompression sickness.

30. A, B
The passage outlines the two things necessary for a diver to get a case of the bends: the external cause found in the rapid change in atmospheric pressure caused by a quick ascent from a deep location—that covers choice **(A)**—and the effect in the form of the nitrogen gas bubbles forming too large and too quickly, which must therefore have to be present, as choice **(B)** states, to begin with. The main detail to catch regarding **(C)** is that the author provides an exception for "surface divers capable of descending to sufficient depth," which means that a scuba tank is not a prerequisite for a diver to get the bends.

CHAPTER 5

Verbal Reasoning Practice Set

VERBAL REASONING PRACTICE SET 1

Directions: For each sentence, choose one word for each set of blanks. Select the word or words that best fit(s) the meaning of the sentence as a whole.

1. Despite much informed (i)_____ and a great deal of scientific interest and money invested in research on the subject, the precise nature of the relationship between sunspot cycles and the weather on Earth remains (ii)_____.

Blank (i)	Blank (ii)
(A) confusion	(D) decisive
(B) conjecture	(E) elusive
(C) evidence	(F) clear

2. (i)_____ in crimes committed by juveniles has been noted in recent years. This trend has occurred despite the fact that, over the same period of time, increased attention has been (ii)_____ juvenile delinquency by law enforcement.

Blank (i)	Blank (ii)
(A) A decrease	(D) given to
(B) An escalation	(E) withdrawn from
(C) A decline	(F) requested for

3. The Strait of Bab-el-Mandeb has earned itself the _____ "Gates of Tears" for the large number of fatal disasters that have befallen those attempting its navigation.

   (A) sobriquet

   (B) veneration

   (C) machination

   (D) syncopation

   (E) condemnation

4. Although intended as only a white lie to avoid conflict, the _____, when discovered, stirred the same resentment the original falsehood sought to avoid.

   (A) euphemism

   (B) guile

   (C) candor

   (D) sophism

   (E) mendacity

5. When the vitamin and supplement company issued the report, even the company's most (i)_____ customers questioned it, calling it (ii)_____ used to lure buyers. Within three months, the company (iii)_____ as much in a public announcement, confirming the suspicion.

Blank (i)	Blank (ii)	Blank (iii)
(A) devout	(D) a sanction	(G) conceded
(B) incredulous	(E) an artifice	(H) retaliated
(C) obtuse	(F) an enigma	(I) recuperated

6. While (i) _____ the public outcry for a new approach, the panel encouraged consumers to (ii) _____ current measures to stabilize the problem. These measures, the panel emphasized, had (iii) _____ unemployment in the past.

Blank (i)	Blank (ii)	Blank (iii)
(A) dismissing	(D) steadfastly support	(G) curtailed
(B) acknowledging	(E) vehemently oppose	(H) confirmed
(C) explicating	(F) carefully question	(I) imparted

Questions 7 and 8 are based on the following passage.

The psychoactive herb *Salvia* has garnered a great deal of attention for its use among adolescents. Thousands of online videos have sprung up of teenagers filming their hallucinogenic experiences. Most of this footage is uninspired: it shows the subjects losing focus for approximately seven to ten minutes, followed by enthusiastic claims regarding the transformative experience they underwent. These videos serve to compound parents' fear of neurological damage with the more real horrors of compromised personal privacy, documentation of potentially illegal activities, and a seemingly open invitation to online predators.

7. The author would most likely agree with which of the following sentences?

    (A) *Salvia* is a highly dangerous and addictive substance that causes neurological damage.

    (B) An important protection for our young people is to regulate herbal substances such as *Salvia*.

    (C) Online video sites should require people posting videos of themselves using *Salvia* to prove they are 18 or older.

    (D) People who post *Salvia* videos should be more explicit about the hallucinations they experienced when they come out of the high.

    (E) The videos of teenagers using *Salvia* exemplify multiple concerns faced by today's parents.

Consider each of the following choices separately and select all that apply.

8. Which of the following statements is suggested by the passage?

    [A] The effects of smoking *Salvia* are short-lived, but intense.

    [B] Posting a public video of oneself engaging in the use of mind-altering substances is a cry for help.

    [C] Young people who expose their private drug use could open themselves to being targeted by pushers of more dangerous drugs.

Questions 9 is based on the following passage.

According to recent research, during the final days of planet formation but before planets had fully formed, planetesimals, which were itinerant objects as large as Pluto, may have collided with Earth, Mars, and the moon. It is hypothesized that they deposited siderophiles (elements such as gold, platinum, and palladium) into Earth's crust. Siderophiles are typically drawn to iron, which forms much of the inner core of Earth. Logically, during planet formation, most of these elements would have been drawn into the center of Earth; however, their abundance in Earth's crust has long perplexed scientists. These collisions may also have caused Earth's axis to tilt by 10 degrees and deposited water on the moon.

9. Based on the information in the passage, which of the following best describes planetesimals?

- (A) Free-roaming proto-planets
- (B) Planets that collided with Earth and bounced out of the galaxy
- (C) Objects embedded in Earth's crust
- (D) Highly magnetic bodies that helped form planets
- (E) Large rocks composed of siderophiles

Question 10 is based on the following passage.

Attempts to blame the mayor's policies for the growing inequality of wages are misguided. The sharp growth in the gap in earnings between college and high school graduates in this city during the past decade resulted from overall technological trends that favored the skills of more educated workers. The mayor's response to this problem cannot be criticized, as it would hardly be reasonable to expect him to attempt to slow the forces of technology.

10. Which of the following, if true, casts the most serious doubt on the conclusion drawn in the last sentence in the passage?

- (A) The mayor could have initiated policies that would have made it easier for less-educated workers to receive the education necessary for better-paying jobs.
- (B) Rather than cutting the education budget, the mayor could have increased the amount of staff and funding devoted to locating employment for graduating high school seniors.
- (C) The mayor could have attempted to generate more demand for products from industries that paid high blue-collar wages.
- (D) Instead of reducing the tax rate on the wealthiest earners, the mayor could have ensured that they shouldered a greater share of the total tax burden.
- (E) The mayor could have attempted to protect the earnings of city workers by instituting policies designed to reduce competition from foreign industries.

Directions: For each of the following questions, choose two of the answer choices that, when used to complete the sentence, produce two completed sentences that are similar in meaning.

11. He was _____ spender, as evidenced by his life of luxury, which included a collection of fine wines and jewelry from around the world.

   [A] an exorbitant

   [B] an expedient

   [C] an erratic

   [D] a lavish

   [E] a penitent

   [F] a desultory

12. The campaign party warned the presidential hopeful that he had a centrist public image to uphold. However, he continued to release _____ campaign ads.

   [A] polemical

   [B] hackneyed

   [C] genial

   [D] riveting

   [E] pugnacious

   [F] contentious

13. American consumers responded to a surge in the economy with an increase in spending, countering last year's trend toward _____.

   [A] ambiguity

   [B] parsimony

   [C] benevolence

   [D] opulence

   [E] abundance

   [F] frugality

14. The defendant, charged with conspiring to defraud investors, steered clear of the public eye; nonetheless, the press _____ each day outside the courthouse, hoping to stop him for an interview.

   ☐ A skulked
   ☐ B disseminated
   ☐ C amassed
   ☐ D languished
   ☐ E convened
   ☐ F dispersed

Question 15 is based on the following passage.

The Stone of Scone, originally a Scottish coronation stone, had been held in Westminster Abbey in London from 1296 until Christmas Day 1950, when a quartet of Scottish university students and nationalists liberated the stone. After first hiding it in England, they smuggled it past English roadblocks and brought the stone back to Scotland. The British government initiated a hunt but was unable to locate the stone until its presence at a Scottish Abbey was made known over a year later. The stone was promptly taken back to London, but Scottish protests eventually triumphed, and in 1996 the stone was moved to Scotland. However, despite its position as a national treasure of Scotland, the English consider it to be on loan and expect the Scots to return it when needed for English coronations.

15. Based on the passage's content, what is the author's opinion of the ownership of the Stone of Scone?

   Ⓐ It is the rightful property of England.
   Ⓑ It is the rightful property of Scotland.
   Ⓒ Both countries are part of the British Empire, and therefore it belongs to both.
   Ⓓ Both countries have used it for coronations, and therefore it belongs to both.
   Ⓔ Both countries have legitimate claims, and therefore it is unclear.

Question 16 is based on the following passage.

The word *atom* is derived from the Greek *atomos*, meaning "uncuttable," and was popularized by Democritus as a fundamental, indivisible building block of natural matter around the turn of the fourth century BCE. Although other philosophers across the world developed similar theories, it was not until the turn of the 19th century that the existence of atoms was definitively proved by science. However, at the turn of the 20th century, J.J. Thompson demonstrated the existence of subatomic particles, and these were in turn found to be reducible into elementary (or fundamental) particles. These discoveries, dividing what was previously considered indivisible, have revolutionized physics and spawned a number of subfields. In 2010, the Large Hadron Collider (hadron being a type of subatomic particle) gained international attention for creating the highest-energy man-made particle collisions. It is the hope of particle physicists that experiments using the collider will be able to shed light on a number of fundamental questions about the laws of nature.

16. Which of the following statements is NOT supported by the passage?

    Ⓐ The theory of atoms was proposed long before it was proved.

    Ⓑ The hadron is not the smallest type of particle.

    Ⓒ Students of particle physics hope to answer questions about the laws of nature.

    Ⓓ The atom was first discovered by Democritus.

    Ⓔ The theory of atoms was proposed by multiple philosophers.

Questions 17–20 are based on the following passage.

Cinematic renditions of historic pieces of literature provide an informative glimpse into the cultural and social context in which the films were made. Shakespeare's *Henry V* is a prime example, as it has been in circulation within the English-speaking world for over 400 years and has been reinterpreted in a number of different milieus. Since the source material has not changed, the way in which different artists and directors treat the play indicates not only the predispositions of the interpreter, but also the prevailing social and political views of the audience. This is acutely noticeable in a play like *Henry V,* which is highly charged with nationalistic concerns.

The play was written during the reign of Elizabeth I, when English national identity (and the modern English language) had begun to crystallize and the language and culture we know today approached their present form. It is a historical biography of King Henry V of England, who waged a bloody campaign during The Hundred Years War with the aim of conquering France. The introduction of the play features an adviser to the King explaining, in a confusing and nearly incomprehensible fashion, the justification for Henry's claim to the French throne. The text of the play itself has been interpreted as being ambiguous in its treatment of Henry's character. Henry has a number of rousing, heroic speeches, but he is also shown to be coldly unmerciful, as in the case of his refusal to pardon petty thieves.

Shakespeare's play has been adapted in two famous film versions. The first, directed by Laurence Olivier, was made during the Second World War, immediately before the invasion of Normandy was launched in 1944. Critics of the film have emphasized the pageantry, bravado, and nationalistic undertones of this version. The battle scenes in the film are understated and tame, with little of the carnage that would be expected of a medieval melee. They are shot in beautiful weather, and the actors are clad in radiant colors. The scene with Henry's harsh justice is omitted. *The film was funded, in part, by the British government and is widely understood to have been intended as a propaganda film, made in anticipation of D-day.* The second version, directed by Kenneth Branagh, was made in 1989, only a few years after the Falklands War, and was much harsher in tone. The battle scenes are gory and are shot in gray, dismal weather. The actors wear muddy, blood-smeared costumes reflective of the period. The scene with Henry's harsh justice is included.

17. The primary purpose of this passage is to

   (A) describe Shakespeare's *Henry V*.

   (B) denounce the intrusion of government involvement with the arts.

   (C) describe cinematic interpretation of literature.

   (D) teach the reader about cinematic versions of theater.

   (E) explain the effect of contemporary situations upon interpretation of literature.

Consider each of the following choices separately and select all that apply.

18. The author would most likely agree with which of the following?

   [A] Original works of art are more reflective of their societal contexts than are cinematic adaptations of such works.

   [B] Contemporary events influence the adaptation of historical source material.

   [C] War is likely to produce good cinema.

19. Which of the following most accurately describes the relationship between the highlighted sentences?

    (A) The first is an example of an argument; the second is a counterexample.

    (B) The first is a synthesis of disparate ideas; the second is one of the components of that synthesis.

    (C) The first is the topic of the passage; the second is an argument in support of it.

    (D) The first presents an assertion; the second provides an example to support that assertion.

    (E) The first is a thesis; the second is the antithesis.

20. It can be inferred that the author:

    (A) Regards texts as being open to interpretation.

    (B) Prefers the Olivier version.

    (C) Dislikes Henry.

    (D) Prefers Branagh's version.

    (E) Believes directors should remain as faithful to the original as possible.

PRACTICE SET 1 ANSWER KEY

1. B, E
2. B, D
3. A
4. E
5. A, E, G
6. B, D, G
7. E
8. A
9. A
10. A
11. A, D
12. A, F
13. B, F
14. C, E
15. B
16. D
17. E
18. B
19. D
20. A

PRACTICE SET 1 ANSWERS AND EXPLANATIONS

1. B, E

"Despite" is a road sign that tells you there will be a contrast between the first blank, which is described as "informed," and the description of the state of our knowledge of the sunspot cycle. You can predict that, even if the topic had "much informed *discussion*," the relationship might still "remain *unclear*." Now move on to the answer choices. Choice **(B)** *conjecture* is a good match for *discussion*, but if you didn't see that right away, you could have eliminated the wrong answers. It doesn't make sense to talk about "informed *confusion*," choice **(A)** or "informed *evidence*," choice **(C)**, so **(B)** is the best choice here. For the second blank, the best match for your prediction is choice **(E)** *elusive*. Both choices **(D)** *decisive* and **(F)** *clear* are the opposite of your prediction. Now, plug your choices back into the sentence: "Despite much informed *conjecture*, . . . the relationship between sunspot cycles and the weather on Earth remains *elusive*." That makes sense and is the correct answer.

2. B, D

The detour road sign "despite" in the middle of the sentence helps you to figure this one out. You know that something has happened "despite" increased attention to the issue. Start with the second blank. Predict *shown to* or *paid to*. Since you would expect that, with increased attention, there would be fewer crimes committed by juveniles, predict *an increase* for the first blank. For the second blank, choice **(D)** *given to*, matches your prediction. Choice **(E)** *withdrawn from* is the opposite of your prediction, and you wouldn't expect any results from attention that was just *requested for*, choice **(F)**, a problem. For the first blank, choice **(B)**, *escalation*, matches your prediction. Choices

(A) *decrease* and **(C)** *decline* are the opposite of your prediction. The resulting sentence is logical: "*An escalation* in crimes committed by juveniles has been noted in recent years. This trend has occurred despite the fact that, over the same period of time, increased attention has been *withdrawn* from juvenile delinquency by law enforcement."

3. A

Reading through the sentence, you can see that "Gates of Tears" is a *nickname* or *title* given to the strait; that's sufficient to predict the right answer. Choice **(A)** *sobriquet* means just that—a given name or title. Choice **(B)** *veneration*, meaning "reverence," **(C)** *machination*, meaning "scheme," and **(D)** *syncopation*, meaning "metronomic irregularity" are all words unrelated to the sentence. Choice **(E)** *condemnation* might be tempting because of the negative sense of the name "Gates of Tears"; however, the name itself is not a condemnation, so you should also reject **(E)**.

4. E

This sentence contains two synonyms for the correct answer: *lie* and *falsehood*. Based on them, you can eliminate wrong answers. Choice **(A)** *euphemism* is a word or phrase used to replace a more offensive word or phrase of the same meaning. While euphemisms are intended to avoid offensive expression, they aren't lies or falsehoods. Reject **(A)**. Choice **(B)** *guile* means "cleverness" or "wit," which contrasts with the description of a "white lie." Choice **(C)** *candor* means "frank truth." This is the opposite of what the correct answer must mean. Choice **(D)** *sophism* is a deceptively incorrect argument, one that appears true or appealing, masking a falsehood. Again, there may be some similarities, but you are looking for a word that simply means "falsehood," which choice **(E)** *mendacity* does; that is the correct answer.

5.   A, E, G

The signal word "even" suggests a contrast. What type of customers would you NOT expect to question a company's actions? Choice **(A)** *devout* is often used in a religious context. It means "dedicated," and it is the strongest choice. Choice **(B)** *incredulous* means "skeptical," the opposite of what you want, though *obtuse*, **(C)**, meaning "dim-witted," seems plausible. If you can't choose between *devout* and *obtuse*, fill in the second blank first. Customers would likely question a company's motives if they suspect dishonesty. Choice **(E)** *artifice*, or "ploy," is the only word that works here. If you weren't sure of *artifice*, think of the word *artificial*, which brings to mind something fake. Neither **(D)** *sanction*, which means "authorization," nor **(F)** *enigma*, which means "puzzle" or "mystery," makes sense. You can now see that *devout* is the only choice that fits the first blank. An obtuse customer is not likely to detect an artifice. The sentence ends with a key phrase: "confirming the suspicion." The correct answer for the third blank describes an action taken by the company that would produce that result. Choice **(G)** *conceded* does just that. Choice **(H)** *retaliated* means "got revenge," and **(I)** *recuperated* means "recovered." Neither makes sense in context.

6.   B, D, G

The detour road sign "While" at the beginning of the sentence tells you that the first two blanks will produce opposing phrases. The best combination of choices is **(B)** *acknowledging* ("a desire for change") and **(D)** *steadfastly support* ("current measures"). Choice **(C)**

explicating, meaning "explaining," doesn't make sense; the panel reacts to public outcry rather than explaining it. Choice **(A)** *dismissing* may seem plausible, but it doesn't logically follow a contrast signal in a sentence in which the panel encourages continued support for the current measure. Likewise, in the second blank, neither choice **(E)** *vehemently oppose* nor **(F)** *carefully question* fits the logic of the sentence's construction. Follow the logic of the sentence to fill the last blank. The panel must believe that the current measures have had a positive effect. Only choice **(G)** *curtailed* fits, and it is correct. Choices **(H)** *confirmed* and **(I)** *imparted* suggest—awkwardly—that the measures have caused unemployment.

7.   E

In this Inference question, you are asked to identify the statement that follows from the author's point of view as it's expressed in the passage. The author offers two opinionated statements. He finds the video footage "uninspired" and states that it "serve(s) to compound" parental fears. One of those two statements will be paraphrased in the correct answer. The claim in **(A)** is not actually made in the passage. The author suggests that parents may fear possible neurological damage from *Salvia* but suggests that the other "horrors" are "more real," undermining this statement. Choices **(B)** and **(C)** both go beyond the scope of the passage; the author stops short of recommending solutions for the *Salvia* problem. You can also dismiss choice **(D)** because, although the author does intimate that the videos are rather dull, there is no evidence that the author wants more detail about the experience. Choice **(E)** matches your prediction. It is strongly suggested in the passage's final sentence and therefore is the correct answer.

8. A

Here is another Inference question, this time with the potential for multiple correct answers. You can infer choice **(A)** because the text states that the "spaced out" part only lasts a few minutes but that the experience is intense enough that young people describe it in great detail. There is no evidence for choice **(B)**; the author doesn't opine on the psychological state of *Salvia* users. Choice **(C)** is not suggested by the passage; "online predators," not "drug pushers," are cited as the threat, and *Salvia* is not compared to other drugs.

9. A

Though it is not explicitly stated in the passage, you can, from a few clues, determine that a planetesimal is (1) an object that moved— a sort of wandering body—since they are described as "itinerant," and (2) an object that existed during "planet formation." Choice **(A)** follows from those two inferences and is correct. There is no support for choice **(B)**; the passage makes no mention of objects leaving or bouncing out of the galaxy. You can eliminate choice **(C)** because the passage tells you that components of the planetesimals (the siderophiles) remained in Earth's crust after impact but doesn't say that whole planetesimals did so. Choice **(D)** is beyond the scope of the passage, which doesn't contain information about planetesimals' magnetic characteristics. You can also cross off **(E)** because the passage doesn't describe planetesimals as "rocks," nor does it claim that they are always made up of (or necessarily even contain) siderophiles.

10. A

When asked to cast doubt on a conclusion, as you are here, first locate the author's conclusion. Then, find an answer choice that contradicts it in some way. This question stem explicitly directs you to the last sentence of the passage, where the author is defending the mayor from criticism, asserting that the growing inequality of wages is beyond his control. Since the passage is saying, "This isn't the mayor's fault," predict a correct answer that says, "No, this *is* the mayor's fault."

Answer Choice **(A)** should stand out immediately as going against the passage. If the mayor *could* have initiated policies that would have educated those who are now earning less, then his policies—to be precise, his policy of inaction—*is* at least partially to blame for the problem of wage inequality. This is exactly the sort of additional evidence you want, and choice **(A)** is correct.

The wrong choices largely focus on misleading shifts in terminology from the passage. Choice **(B)** sidesteps the wage issue, as more employment of high school graduates would not necessarily raise their wages. Choice **(C)**'s logic requires that we assume "blue-collar" equals "less-educated," which is too large a shift in terminology. Choice **(D)** only discusses taxes and avoids wages altogether. Choice **(E)** only mentions protection of "city workers," again avoiding the education issue from the passage.

11. A, D

Focus on the straight-ahead road sign "as," which alerts you that the sentence will continue in the same direction. How would you describe a person who spends money on a collection of fine wines? Choice **(A)** *exorbitant* means "excessive" and fits the context. See if you can find a similar word. Choice **(B)** *expedient* looks similar to *expedite*, a word you have likely seen. It means "practical" or "efficient." That might or might not describe the wine connoisseur, and it certainly doesn't match *exorbitant*. Eliminate it. Choice **(C)** *erratic* and choice **(F)** *desultory* are synonyms meaning "inconsistent or unfocused." That doesn't describe a person who collects fine wines. Rule out both of these choices. Choice **(D)** *lavish* means "done in excess"; that matches *exorbitant*, and is the second correct answer. The sentence describes the wine and jewelry collection in a way that suggests excessive spending. Choice **(E)** *penitent* may remind you of the word *repent*. Both words describe regret or remorse, which doesn't make sense in context. That leaves you with choices **(A)** and **(D)**, the only choices that create equivalent sentences.

12. A, F

"However" serves as a detour road sign, indicating that the second sentence differs in tone from the first. Here, the presidential hopeful continued to issue a certain type of ad, despite warnings to maintain a "centrist" image. The correct answers will mean "extreme" or "far right/left." Choice **(A)** *polemical* means "argumentative." This word fits your prediction and the context of the sentence. Look for the other answer to be a synonym for *polemical*. Something that is *hackneyed*, choice **(B)**, lacks in originality. The ads might be unoriginal, but that wouldn't contrast with "centrist." Choice **(C)** *genial* and choice **(D)** *riveting* are too positive to fit the context. Although choice **(E)** *pugnacious* has a negative connotation, it is an adjective used to describe an aggressively stubborn or determined person. Choice **(F)** *contentious* is a perfect match for *polemical* and completes the correct answer.

13. B, F

The word "countering" is a clue that the increase in spending is different from "last year's trend." Predict the correct answers to mean "saving" or "being economical." Choice **(A)** *ambiguity* means "uncertainty." This word does not logically fit the

context of the sentence. Choice **(B)** *parsimony* means "thrift" or "frugality." This makes sense in context and is a correct answer. Choice **(C)** *benevolence* means "kindness" or "generosity." This doesn't describe people who are spending little money. Choice **(D)** *opulence* and **(E)** *abundance* describe an excess, the opposite of what you are looking for. Choice **(F)** *frugality* means economical. This forms the correct synonym pair along with choice **(B)**.

14. C, E

Rearrange and simplify this sentence to make it easier to see the contrast. Try this paraphrase: "The defendant avoided the public, yet the press _____ daily, hoping to interview him." Look for words that suggest what a group of people trying to get somebody's attention would do. Choice **(A)** *skulked* means "moved secretly." The press is not likely to do this when it wants somebody's attention. Choices **(B)** *disseminated* and **(F)** *dispersed* are similar, containing the same prefix *dis-*. Since this prefix means "apart," you can deduce that these two choices are incorrect. In fact, you need two words that mean the opposite of "came apart." Choice **(C)** *amassed* means "gathered." Note that it contains the word *mass*; knowing the root, you can guess the meaning closely enough to pick this as a correct answer. Choice **(D)** *languished* means "weaken," which doesn't make sense in context. Choice **(E)** *convened* means "came together or assembled. This is synonymous with *amassed* and is the other correct answer. This question really brings home the power of word roots. *Con-* means "together," and *-vene* comes from the root VEN meaning "to come or move toward."

15. B

The author uses several terms that indicate his point of view in the passage. Although this is not an argumentative passage, the tone clearly supports choice **(B)**. Words such as "liberated" (indicating the stone was being held unfairly) and phrases such as "national treasure of Scotland" clearly indicate that the author believes the stone to be rightfully Scottish. Choice **(A)** is opposite of the author's opinion, while choices **(C)**, **(D)**, and **(E)** are simply unsupported in the text.

16. D

The correct answer to this question is *not* supported in the passage, meaning it either contradicts the passage or falls outside the scope. The four wrong answers *are* supported. The first two sentences of the passage describe the origin of the theory of atoms prior to their scientific discovery, which allows you to eliminate choice **(A)**; furthermore, the author mentions that "philosophers across the world developed similar theories," which supports—and thus eliminates—choice **(E)**. However, the author describes Democritus as having "popularized" the theory of atoms, which is not the same as first discovering the atom; based on this, choice **(D)** is correct. Choices **(B)** and **(C)** both relate to the discussion of subatomic particles, but because elementary particles are smaller than subatomic particles (an example of the latter being the hadron), you may eliminate **(B)**. The conclusion of the passage supports choice **(C)** in the description of the importance of experiments using the Large Hadron Collider.

17. E

The correct answer to a primary purpose question summarizes what the author is trying to do in the passage. Here, the author uses cinematic depictions of *Henry V* to illustrate how contemporary culture influences the interpretation of art. Choice **(A)** makes an irrelevant comparison. The author discusses the influence of historical and societal context on both Shakespeare's play and the later film adaptations of it but never implies that one is more reflective of its societal context than the other. **(B)** distorts the author's purpose, which is to illustrate the cultural influence, not to judge which influences are positive or negative. **(C)** is too broad; the passage isn't about cinematic interpretations of literature writ large. **(D)** is too general in the same way as choice **(C)**. So, choice **(E)** is the correct answer. It cites the effect of contemporary situations on the interpretation of literature, striking at the heart of what the author explores in the passage.

18. B

Questions of this type have three options, but any or all of them could be correct. You can't stop when you come across one correct answer. Evaluate the choices in light of this author's scope and purpose. Choice **(A)** gets the passage backwards. The author uses *Henry V* to show how social and cultural concerns influence the cinematic readings of the play, not how the films reveal the culture. Choice **(B)** is correct; this paraphrases the author's primary purpose, so he's certain to agree with it. Choice **(C)** is incorrect. The author makes no effort to argue about what makes *good* cinema, only what influences it when it's involved in interpreting classic literary works.

19. D

Questions of this type reward you for understanding the logic of a passage. In this case, the first highlighted sentence is an assertion that lays out the topic and scope of the passage. The second highlighted sentence is a specific example that the author offers to illustrate his main point. Choice **(D)**, the correct answer, hits this prediction squarely. Choice **(A)** is incorrect because the second sentence does not contradict the first. You can reject **(B)** as is mischaracterizes the first sentence;

there is nothing disparate about its components. You can reject **(C)** because it gets the second sentence wrong; the second sentence is an example, not an argument (which would need a conclusion supported by evidence. Choice **(E)** distorts the relationship between the two sentences; the second doesn't contradict the first.

20. A

This is another question that asks you to put yourself in the author's shoes and try to reason from his perspective. The tone of the passage is neutral; even when describing Henry's darker moments, the author passes no judgment. You can therefore reject choice **(C)**, as the author is not doing a character study. Though choices **(B)** and **(D)** are mutually exclusive, they are both incorrect. The author states no preference for either of the film versions he describes. Choice **(E)** is incorrect because the author states no preference for cinematic versions that maintain greater fidelity to the source material. Choice **(A)** is correct; it matches the author's purpose for the passage. In order for cultural events to influence the interpretation of classic literature, such literature must be interpretable.

DIAGNOSTIC TOOL

Tally up your score and write your results in the space provided.

Total

Total Correct: _____ out of 20 correct

Percentage Correct: # you got right × 100 ÷ 20: _____

By Question Type

Text Completion _____ out of 6 correct

Sentence Equivalence _____ out of 4 correct

Reading Comprehension _____ out of 10 correct

Diagnose Your Results

Look back at the questions you got wrong and think about your experience answering them.

VERBAL REASONING PRACTICE SET 2

Directions: For each sentence, choose one word for each set of blanks. Select the word or words that best fit(s) the meaning of the sentence as a whole.

1. Many felt the rules for the scholarship competition had been unfairly administered to the applicant pool and that, furthermore, the judges were _____.

    (A) biased

    (B) adequate

    (C) inept

    (D) impartial

    (E) objective

2. We will face the idea of old age with _____ as long as we believe that it invariably brings poverty, isolation, and illness.

    (A) regret

    (B) apprehension

    (C) enlightenment

    (D) veneration

    (E) reverence

3. Usually an articulate speaker, as he had given many public addresses over the years, the doctor (i) _____ the keynote speech at the oncology convention. It was clear from their expressions that the audience members were overcome with (ii) _____ by the end.

Blank (i)	Blank (ii)
(A) flubbed	(D) rapture
(B) perfected	(E) repulsion
(C) rescinded	(F) bewilderment

4. The author's agent approached the contract signing with (i)_____ as he knew full well the reputation of the publishing industry. The author, finally recognized after years of rejection, was more (ii)_____ by the event.

Blank (i)	Blank (ii)
Ⓐ incertitude	Ⓓ enraptured
Ⓑ hubris	Ⓔ humiliated
Ⓒ cordiality	Ⓕ mortified

5. The hikers were eager to summit Mount Everest and (i)_____ warnings about the dangerous storm approaching the camp. It was only when disaster struck that the (ii) _____ of the situation took hold. By this time, however, the descent was (iii) _____, and the survivors fought for their lives.

Blank (i)	Blank (ii)	Blank (iii)
Ⓐ recollected	Ⓓ gravity	Ⓖ galvanizing
Ⓑ scrutinized	Ⓔ hypocrisy	Ⓗ fortuitous
Ⓒ flouted	Ⓕ prestige	Ⓘ baleful

6. The fact that Mark Twain gave orders for his memoir to remain unpublished for 100 years reflects the author's (i) _____ about its contents. Indeed, releasing his more (ii) _____ observations about the world during his own time would have spurred a public response, one that Twain must have foreseen as (iii) _____.

Blank (i)	Blank (ii)	Blank (iii)
Ⓐ trepidation	Ⓓ quixotic	Ⓖ enigmatic
Ⓑ buoyancy	Ⓔ utopian	Ⓗ detrimental
Ⓒ insouciance	Ⓕ vitriolic	Ⓘ salubrious

Questions 7 and 8 are based on the following passage.

Pancreatic beta cells are responsible within a body for monitoring homeostatic cues from a wide variety of hormonal inputs and in turn regulate the insulin needed to maintain balance in the blood sugar. Researchers studying this signaling system have located three key proteins that relay signals. Understanding how these proteins function within the context of the signaling system can help scientists gain more insight into how diabetes compromises the healthy functioning of the system and how to counteract the impact of diabetes once it is identified.

7. The passage implies which of the following about diabetes research?

(A) When scientists fully understand how these key proteins work, rates of Type II diabetes will be greatly reduced.

(B) Researchers hope to understand the signaling system of pancreatic beta cells in order to replicate an artificial system.

(C) Without a complete understanding of these key proteins, diabetes research is at a standstill.

(D) Future medications for diabetes may include or simulate some of the hormonal cues that pancreatic beta cells monitor.

(E) One way researchers hope to fight diabetes is by stopping the relay signal system in the pancreas by cutting off the proteins.

8. According to the passage, each of the following is true EXCEPT:

(A) The pancreas helps a body to maintain homeostasis.

(B) Diabetes controls the functioning of pancreatic beta cells.

(C) When the pancreas is stimulated, it releases varying amounts of insulin that help to balance blood sugar.

(D) Pancreatic beta cells must interpret a wide array of hormonal information.

(E) Blood sugar can be controlled by insulin.

Question 9 is based on the following passage.

Named after the notorious confidence trickster Charles Ponzi (though not originated by him), the term "Ponzi scheme" describes a particular type of fraud in which individual investors are promised extremely high returns, which are then paid either out of their own money or the money of other investors, creating the appearance of an extremely profitable investment. The entire scheme relies on encouraging investors to donate large amounts of money long-term by offering them the enticement of impossibly high short-term returns. As time progresses, investors who have been paid returns contribute even more money, and new investors are drawn in to the scheme. New payments are used to pay off new investors. Excess money is then kept as profit for the creator of the fraud, rather than to create any tangible profits for the investment itself.

9. According to the passage, which is necessary for a Ponzi scheme to be successful?

   Ⓐ Investors should be tempted into long-term investment by large initial returns.

   Ⓑ The investment plan should demonstrate sustainability over the long term.

   Ⓒ The percentage of the investment's profits going to the creator of the scam should be concealed.

   Ⓓ There should be no paper trails of the fraud.

   Ⓔ The culpability for the fraud should be shared among the confidence trickster and investors.

Question 10 is based on the following passage.

Hay-on-Wye is a small town in Wales, just over the border from England. While once a relatively unknown town, the town rose to fame in the second half of the 20th century as a literary hot spot. Influenced by Richard Booth's opening of a secondhand bookshop in a converted fire station, a number of other entrepreneurs followed suit, until the tiny town held over 30 used bookshops; by the 1970s, it became known around the world as the "Town of Books." Aided by Booth's publicity efforts, Hay-on-Wye was turned from a sleepy market town with fewer than 2,000 inhabitants to a thriving tourist destination. The town now boasts half a million tourists per year and hosts a popular annual literary festival. Booth himself was inducted into the Order of the British Empire for his efforts to encourage tourism.

10. Which of the following is the primary purpose of the passage?

    Ⓐ To argue for the importance of secondhand bookshops

    Ⓑ To describe the life of Richard Booth

    Ⓒ To explain the development of Hay-on-Wye as a literary center

    Ⓓ To highlight Richard Booth's publicity efforts to encourage tourism

    Ⓔ To depict the town of Hay-on-Wye

Directions: For each of the following questions, choose two of the answer choices that, when used to complete the sentence, produce two completed sentences that are similar in meaning.

11. The fashion designer's silk scarf wasn't popular initially; the public found it gaudy until a model discovered the accessory and _____ it.

   [A] vilipended

   [B] disavowed

   [C] engendered

   [D] indulged

   [E] championed

   [F] espoused

12. One of the most commonly perpetuated myths about Einstein is that he failed math; on the contrary, he excelled at the subject, developing _____ it at a young age.

   [A] a predilection for

   [B] an enmity toward

   [C] an acquiescence to

   [D] an antipathy toward

   [E] a penchant for

   [F] a reminiscence about

13. The pundits agreed that the speech was both deeply profound and _____ in its delivery, and it was well received by audiences.

   [A] pellucid

   [B] affable

   [C] militant

   [D] asinine

   [E] perspicuous

   [F] magisterial

14. The two boxers battled toe-to-toe until the final round, when the longtime champion of the ring was finally _____ by his young opponent's stamina.

> [A] exiled
>
> [B] thwarted
>
> [C] decimated
>
> [D] galvanized
>
> [E] annihilated
>
> [F] stymied

Questions 15–17 are based on the following passage.

Characterized as half zebra and half horse, the quagga sounds like a mythical creature, but at one time, it was a very real animal. Only 150 years ago, a great number of quaggas were found in South Africa. Unlike the common zebra, which has black and white stripes that cover its entire body, the quagga has yellow-brown stripes only on its head, neck, and forebody, which gave it its half-horse facade. Its unique appearance caused early explorers to think the quagga was a separate species from the common zebra when it was discovered around 1760, but DNA analysis later revealed that the animal is a subspecies of the zebra. In the 100 years following its discovery, the quagga population diminished. It was frequently hunted for its meat and hide, and settlers who considered the animal a competitor for the grazing of their livestock also callously killed the quagga in great numbers. By 1870, the quagga was no longer found in the wild. The last captive quagga died in 1880 in an Amsterdam zoo. Today, the quagga is categorized as an extinct animal, but researchers in Africa hope to resurrect the native subspecies through genetic modification and selective breeding.

Select only one answer choice.

15. What does the author designate as the primary reason for the quagga going extinct?

> (A) DNA analysis revealed that the quagga was susceptible to diseases brought by domesticated animals.
>
> (B) The quagga did not have enough grazing land.
>
> (C) The quagga was unable to survive in captivity.
>
> (D) Settlers eliminated the species through hunting and extermination.
>
> (E) The quagga did not breed as successfully as the common zebra.

16. With which of the following statements would the author of the passage most likely agree?

- (A) The zebra is a type of quagga.
- (B) Researchers hope to restore the quagga using scientific technology.
- (C) Settlers humanely killed quaggas in an effort to protect their livestock.
- (D) Shortly after the quagga was discovered, its population grew.
- (E) Settlers saw the quagga as a competitor for the prey of their livestock.

Consider each of the following choices separately and select all that apply.

17. Based on the information in the passage, which conclusion can be drawn?

- [A] If it were not for the human influence, the quagga would be a surviving species.
- [B] DNA analysis can help humans better understand the origins of certain species.
- [C] The extinction of species should not be a concern as scientists are able to bring back extinct species through genetic modification.

Questions 18–20 are based on the following passage.

According to a recent survey from the National Institute for Drug Abuse, more U.S. adolescents smoke marijuana than cigarettes. The organization's annual survey revealed an increase in marijuana use among all teen groups and a slight decrease in tobacco use among high school seniors compared to past years. Federal officials speculate that teens are starting to listen to the warnings about the risks of tobacco use but are receiving mixed messages about the safety of marijuana use. While antidrug organizations such as Drug-Free America maintain their message that marijuana impairs judgment and hampers brain development, clinical studies support the medicinal benefits of marijuana, particularly for those suffering from certain cancers and Crohn's disease. These studies have sparked a national debate about the legalization of marijuana. More than a dozen states and the District of Columbia have legalized the use of medical marijuana, and there is a push for the nationwide legalization of the drug. The White House Office of National Drug Control Policy asserts that the message that marijuana use is okay for some is dangerous. The office insists that both policy makers and the general public should be aware of the effect the debate over the legalization of marijuana has on teens' perception of the drug's risk.

Select only one answer choice.

18. The passage implies which of the following about teen drug use?

    Ⓐ The Office of National Drug Control is concerned about teen tobacco use.

    Ⓑ Marijuana has many health benefits for teens.

    Ⓒ Teens are aware of health risks associated with smoking.

    Ⓓ Drug-Free America suspects that teen marijuana use will continue to rise.

    Ⓔ Teens support legislation to legalize marijuana.

19. The passage predicts which of the following would follow the legalization of marijuana?

    Ⓐ It may increase the use of illegal street drugs.

    Ⓑ It may decrease the frequency of teen tobacco use.

    Ⓒ It may cause teens to believe that marijuana use is harmless.

    Ⓓ It may change antidrug organizations' stance on the drug's use.

    Ⓔ It may increase the safety of the drug's use.

20. According to the passage, what is the "mixed message" that teens are receiving about marijuana?

    Ⓐ Its use is acceptable for individuals older than age 18, but not for individuals younger than age 18.

    Ⓑ It has legitimate health benefits for the ill, but it has serious health risks.

    Ⓒ Its use is acceptable in some states, but not acceptable in other states.

    Ⓓ It is safer to use than tobacco, but it is still an unsafe drug.

    Ⓔ Its use is approved by the government, but not by teens' parents.

PRACTICE SET 2 ANSWER KEY

1. A
2. B
3. A, F
4. A, D
5. C, D, I
6. A, F, H
7. D
8. B
9. A
10. C

11. E, F
12. A, E
13. A, E
14. B, F
15. D
16. B
17. B
18. C
19. C
20. B

PRACTICE SET 2 ANSWERS AND EXPLANATIONS

1. A

Here, "furthermore" indicates that the charge of the word in the blank will be consistent with "unfair." Choice **(A)** *biased* is a good synonym for "unfair," and is the correct answer. Choices **(B)**, **(D)**, and **(E)** all list traits one would want in judges. Choice **(C)** *inept* provides a negative trait, but one that challenges the judge's competence, not his fairness.

2. B

First, read the sentence through, noting any structural road signs and/or key words. Here, "as long as" is a structural clue: we view old age in the same way we do poverty, isolation, and illness. Predict that the correct answer matches a word like *fear* or *despair*. Choice **(B)** *apprehension* is a good match. Check the other answers, to confirm that each is incorrect. Choice **(A)** *regret* is tempting, but it applies to something that has already happened, not what you will face in the future. Choice **(C)** *enlightenment* doesn't match the sentence's list of negative conditions. Choices **(D)** *veneration* and **(E)** *reverence* both mean "great respect"; that's a positive way to face old age, but not one that matches the way one would face something likely to bring "poverty, isolation, and illness." That confirms that **(B)** is the right answer. Now, plug the answer into the sentence: "We will face the idea of old age with *apprehension* as long as we believe that it invariably brings poverty, isolation, and illness." This certainly makes sense.

3. A, F

Consider the logic of the sentences before approaching the first blank. It might be tempting to choose a positive word, but the structure and tone suggest a contrast from the "usual."

It might help to put the word *while* in front of *usually*. The only word that suggests the opposite of "articulate speaker" is choice **(A)** *flubbed*, which means "to make a mess of." Choice **(B)** *perfected* means "made no errors" and choice **(C)** *rescind* means "took back." These words don't fit the context of the clause. How might an audience subjected to a flubbed speech feel? You can rule out choice **(D)** *rapture* since it means "extreme joy." That leaves choice **(E)** *repulsion* or "disgust" and choice **(F)** *bewilderment* or "deep confusion." Consider the shades of meaning here: the audience is not likely to respond with an emotion as strong as disgust, especially if the doctor is normally a great speaker. *Bewilderment* is correct.

4. A, D

Since these two sentences include contrasting ideas, try paraphrasing them using a detour sign. For instance, "The agent approached the signing with _____, *but* the author was _____." The second half of the first sentence suggests skepticism about the industry. A skeptical agent would be suspicious of the contract signing. Only choice **(A)** *incertitude*, which means "uncertainty," fits the context. Choices **(B)** *hubris* and **(C)** *cordiality*, meaning "pride" and "friendliness," respectively, are too positive to work. It wouldn't make sense for the author to be **(E)** *humiliated* or **(F)** *mortified*; he's finally received some recognition, after all. You need a word that contrasts with *uncertainty*, and the best fit is choice **(D)** *enraptured*, which means "full of delight."

5. C, D, I

The words "and," "only," and "however" are road signs that help you determine the direction of each sentence and choose the appropriate missing words. Overly eager hikers are unlikely to heed warnings, and choice **(C)** *flouted,* which means "defied" or "ignored," captures this relationship best. Neither choice **(A)** *recollected* nor **(B)** *scrutinized,* both of which suggest examining an issue, fits the context. The second blank will contain a word consistent with one's attitude after a disaster. Choice **(E)** *hypocrisy* refers to insincerity; that might describe the hikers (who'd just flouted the warnings), but not the situation they now find themselves in. Choice **(F)** *prestige,* meaning "status" or "consideration," is inappropriate to the context as well. Only choice **(D)** *gravity,* or "seriousness," makes sense here. While the descent may have been **(G)** *galvanizing,* or "exciting," on some level, it was in the context of a dire situation, so keep looking for a better choice. Choice **(H)** *fortuitous* means "lucky." (If you didn't know its definition, notice that it shares the root of "fortune.") You can infer that it doesn't fit logically in the paragraph. Something **(I)** *baleful* appears threatening, or even deadly; this is the correct answer.

6.   A, F, H

To complete this sentence, look for key words or phrases that give hints about the context. For instance, "gave orders" in the first sentence indicates a strong feeling, perhaps a concern, so try to find a term that plays off this sentiment. Only choice **(A)** *trepidation,* which means "unease," supports the first sentence. Choice **(B)** *buoyancy* means "quick to recover" (think of the buoy floating in the ocean) and **(C)** *insouciance* means "lightheartedness." Both words suggest unconcern, the opposite of how Twain must have felt when ordering his memoirs to remain sealed for a century. The word in the second blank must describe writing that the author wants to keep private for a long time after his death. Choices **(D)** *quixotic* and **(E)** *utopian* have a similar meaning—"idealistic"—and

neither fits the context. Choice **(F)** *vitriolic,* meaning "acidic" or "corrosive," is the best fit. For the third blank, you need a negative word. Choice **(G)** *enigmatic,* or "mysterious," doesn't make sense. If you didn't know **(H)** *detrimental,* or **(I)** *salubrious,* ask what each reminds you of. For instance, think of the word *salve,* which is related to medicine. Indeed, *salubrious* comes from the Latin *salvus,* meaning "promoting health." You need a negative word here, and **(H)** *detrimental* means "damaging." That is the right answer.

7.   D

The correct answer follows from the passage, though it may not be stated explicitly. Choice **(A)** is not implied. Although researchers probably hope to stem the occurrence of diabetes, the passage speaks only of combating the disease's impact. There is also no suggestion in the passage of the hope, expressed in choice **(B)**, of creating an artificial system. Choice **(C)** is too extreme. The passage doesn't imply a "standstill" absent "complete" understanding of the proteins. The wording in choice **(D)** is dense, but it's also broad enough to follow from the passage. Researchers may well use their understanding of the hormonal cues monitored by the proteins to develop the treatments mentioned in the final sentence of the passage. Indeed, **(D)** is the correct response. Finally, **(E)** runs counter to the passage. The researchers hope to understand how to help the relay system work, not how to cut it off. You can eliminate **(E)** confidently.

8.   B

The four wrong answers to this Detail question are found in the passage. The correct answer will either contradict or distort the passage, or fall outside its scope altogether. Choice **(A)** is true; it is stated in the first sentence of the passage. Choice **(B)** seems like it might be true, but reading carefully, it overstates the role of diabetes as described in the passage: diabetes compromises or impairs the ability of the pancreatic beta cells to function, but you're not told that it *controls* those functions. Choice **(C)** is true and is also stated in the passage's first sentence. Choice **(D)** paraphrases the first main claim of the passage. Choice **(E)** comes from the end of the first sentence.

9. A

The correct answer to this Detail question must paraphrase something stated explicitly in the passage. Choice **(A)** restates the author's definition of Ponzi schemes: the use of short-term payoffs to attract long-term investments. That's the correct answer. Choice **(D)** is incorrect because the passage mentions nothing about paper trails; likewise for who should share the culpability described in choice **(E)**. Choice **(C)** is initially tempting, but be careful; the final sentence of the passage explicitly states that the investment does not create any real profits, so **(C)**'s recommendations for how to divvy them up must be incorrect. Choice **(B)** is tempting because the schemes attempt to sucker investors into long-term commitments. But, the schemes needn't be "sustainable" in any case.

10. C

By the time you begin to look at questions accompanying a passage, you should have already determined the scope and purpose of the passage. In this case, the author is purely expository; he just wants to relate or explain how Hay-on-Wye became known for books and literature. Choices **(A)**, **(B)**, and **(D)** are related to the passage's subject matter but don't describe the overall purpose of the passage. Choices **(C)** and **(E)** look relatively similar, and the fact that the passage is about Hay-on-Wye makes **(E)** tempting. But the pas-

sage focuses on a specific aspect of the town, rather than the town as a whole. This aspect is its rise to fame as the "Town of Books," and thus choice **(C)** is your answer.

11. E, F

In this sentence, the words "initially" and "until" function as detour signs, informing you that the idea changes. Since there is a positive change of events, search for a term with a more hopeful meaning. Even if you've never seen choice **(A)** *vilipended*, you've probably seen similar looking words like *vile, revile,* and *vilify.* Given the negative connotation of these words, you can rule out *vilipend,* which means "to dismiss or treat with contempt." Choice **(B)** *disavowed* means "refused to acknowledge or accept." You can tell by the prefix *dis-* ("apart") that the word does not fit the meaning you are looking for. Choice **(C)** *engendered* means "created." Although this word has a positive slant, it doesn't make sense in context. Choices **(D)**, **(E)**, and **(F)** are all possible answers. Consider the shades of meaning and then decide which two words make the most sense. To *champion* or *espouse* means "to support," like a cause. If you *indulge* something, you don't support it as much as yield to it. Choices **(E)** and **(F)** are correct.

12. A, E

The phrase "on the contrary" is a clear turning point in this sentence. Look for a word to fill the blank that suggests a fondness or strong attraction to something. Ask yourself if you know any words that look like choice **(A)** *predilection.* It comes from the same Latin root as *diligent,* which means "attentive" or "careful." Indeed, *predilection* suggests a strong attraction to something, and this fits the meaning you're looking for. You can use a similar strategy to test choices **(B)** *enmity* and **(D)** *antipathy,* two synonyms that have a negative meaning. *Enmity* looks like its related to the word *enemy*, and *antipathy* contains the word parts *anti-*, meaning "against," and *pathos*, meaning "feeling." Both answer choices mean "hatred," and can be ruled out. Choice **(C)** *acquiescence* means "passive acceptance." This is too soft to work in the sentence or in conjunction with *predilection*. Keep searching for a synonym for choice **(A)**. Choice **(E)** *penchant* means "a strong liking" and is the other correct answer. If you didn't know the word *penchant*, you could deduce that choice **(F)** *reminiscence*, or "fond remembrance," doesn't make sense in context. That leaves **(A)** and **(E)** as the best choices.

13.   A, E

The words "both" and "and" alert you that the missing word will have a positive meaning, consonant with "deeply profound" but not necessarily a synonym. Think about what other qualities you would look for in an insightful speech. You may not have seen choice **(A)** *pellucid* before, but it is related to *lucid* and *luminous*. The shared roots, *luc* and *lum*, mean "light." *Pellucid* means "clear in expression," which bears the correct relationship to the word *profound*; you'd want an insightful speech to be clear and understandable. This seems like a strong choice. Choice **(B)** *affable* means "pleasant." This word has a positive connotation but doesn't match *pellucid* at all. Keep this word for now, but only with reservations. Choices **(C)** *militant* and **(F)** *magisterial* could describe a speech that is also profound, but they don't describe how that speech would be delivered. Further, these words have negative connotations and don't fit the tone of the sentence. Choice **(D)** *asinine*, which means "silly" or "stupid," is completely wrong for this sentence. Choice **(E)** *perspicuous* may be unknown to you, but it may look familiar because it comes from the same root as *perspective*. Much like

pellucid, it means "clear," especially in expression or understanding. Since choices **(A)** and **(E)** create truly equivalent sentences, you can rule out **(B)** *affable* with certainty.

14.   B, F

This sentence has no obvious road signs, so look for key descriptive words that might help you. The sentence describes a long, closely fought match in which the young challenger finally prevails. The correct answer is a verb that tells you what happened to the champion at the end. Choice **(A)** *exiled* means "forced out," as from one's country. This doesn't make sense in context. Choice **(B)** *thwarted* means "successfully opposed." This word accurately reflects the outcome of the match. Choices **(C)** *decimated* and **(E)** *annihilated* both mean "destroyed." Given that the two boxers fought "toe-to-toe" until the final round, it doesn't make sense to say that either one destroyed the other. Choice **(D)** *galvanized* means "stimulated." This is a tempting option (the champ could have been inspired by the challenger), but no other answer choice creates a sentence of similar meaning. You need a better fit. Choice **(F)** *stymied* is a synonym for *thwarted* and is the other correct answer.

15.   D

This question asks you to identify a major point in the passage, the *primary* reason for the quagga's extinction. Research leads you to the sentence between those asserting the quagga's decline and its extinction. The quagga was hunted and "callously" exterminated by ranchers who considered it a competitor for their livestock. Choice **(A)** distorts the passage. Settlers considered the quagga a competitor with their herds, but there's nothing to suggest that the domestic species infected the wild animals. Choice **(C)** distorts the passage, which states that the last quagga died in captivity but not that the species' extinction was a result of captivity. Similarly, choice **(E)** distorts that portion of the passage stating that researchers want to revive the quagga using selective breeding of existing, related species. It does not link the quagga's extinction to its breeding habits. Choices **(B)** and **(D)** are both, in a way, related to grazing. Choice **(B)** is incorrect because it ascribes the problem to the quagga's loss of grazing habitat. You never learn that the quagga was left with an insufficient range. The quagga competed with livestock for grazing, which caused settlers to hunt the species to extinction. Choice **(D)** best reflects what the passage states as the primary reason for the quagga's extinction.

16. B

The correct answer may not be stated explicitly in the passage, but it must follow directly from something that is stated there. The passage states that the quagga is a subspecies of the zebra, not the other way around. That makes choice **(A)** incorrect. The passage also contradicts choice **(D)**; its population "diminished" after discovery. Choice **(C)**, which states that settlers "humanely" killed quaggas, contradicts the passage more subtly but just as fatally. In fact, according to the passage, settlers "callously" killed quaggas. Choice **(E)** distorts the passage. The quagga was a competitor for the pasture of settlers' livestock, not their prey. Indeed, grazing animals have no prey. Choice **(B)** is the correct answer, as the last sentence of the passage states that scientists are hoping to spark the species' return.

17. B

This question asks you to evaluate the statement and identify what conclusions you can draw using the information from the passage. Choice **(A)** overstates the passage. Humans were historically responsible for the quagga's extinction. There's no way to deduce what would have happened absent human contact. Choice **(B)** follows from the portion of the passage in which you learn that DNA analysis helped determine that the quagga is a subspecies of the zebra and not a unique species. That's enough to make the broadly worded choice **(B)** a viable conclusion. Choice **(C)** does not provide a viable answer; it assumes too much information. The passage states that researchers are trying to bring back the extinct quagga, but it doesn't say how likely these efforts are to be successful, nor does it opine on how much concern extinctions should provoke.

18. C

Examine the answer choices one at a time and choose the one that follows from the passage. Choice **(A)** states that the Office of National Drug Control is concerned about teen tobacco use. While you may assume this to be a true statement, the passage doesn't state this directly, commenting only on the Office's concern about teen marijuana use. Similarly, it is reasonable to think that choice **(D)** is true, but the passage only addresses Drug-Free America's stance on the risks of marijuana, not the organization's predictions of future use. The passage mentions claimed health benefits of marijuana, but it does not imply choice **(B)**, that marijuana has health benefits for teens. Choice **(C)** is the correct answer. The passage states that officials believe teens to be acting, in part, in response to anti-tobacco warnings. Choice **(E)** may seem reasonable because the passage makes implications about teen perception of the risks of marijuana, but it contains no statements about teens' feelings on the issue of legalization.

19. C

This question asks you to evaluate the possible connections and compare them to the information in the passage. Choice **(A)** seems possible, but the passage contains no information about drug use beyond marijuana and tobacco. Choice **(B)** makes a reference to information about tobacco use, but it distorts the passage, which states that teen tobacco use is down because teens seem to understand the risk of smoking, not because marijuana has been legalized in some states. Choice **(C)** is the most viable choice. The passage states that research on the medical uses of marijuana and the decision to legalize medical marijuana in some states contribute to the message that marijuana is not harmful. Choice **(D)** addresses antidrug organizations' message on marijuana use. This is not a viable choice because the passage states that antidrug organizations maintain their message that marijuana is harmful and gives you no reason to think they would change their views upon legalization. Choice **(E)** is out of scope; the passage does not give any information on how legalizing marijuana will affect the risks of the drug's use.

20. B

This question asks you to identify a detail in the passage. The "mixed message" referred to in the stem is found in the passage's fourth sentence, introduced with the contrast key word "While." That sentence outlines the contrast between antidrug messages (marijuana impairs judgment and hampers brain development) and research about possible health benefits. That matches choice **(B)** to a T. Choice **(E)** misses the scope of the passage by including a statement about the opinions of teens' parents, who aren't mentioned. Choice **(A)** brings in information about the age-appropriateness of marijuana use, another topic that isn't considered in this passage. Choice **(D)** states that marijuana use is safer than tobacco use, but the passage never makes that comparison. Choice **(C)** accurately states the inconsistent legal status of marijuana, but it doesn't answer the question. The mixed message teens receive is about the health effects—not the legality—of marijuana use.

DIAGNOSTIC TOOL

Tally up your score and write your results in the space provided.

Total

Total Correct: _____ out of 20 correct

Percentage Correct: # you got right × 100 ÷ 20: _____

By Question Type

Text Completion _____ out of 6 correct

Sentence Equivalence _____ out of 4 correct

Reading Comprehension _____ out of 10 correct

Diagnose Your Results

Look back at the questions you got wrong and think about your experience answering them.

VERBAL REASONING PRACTICE SET 3

Directions: For each sentence, choose one word for each set of blanks. Select the word or words that best fit(s) the meaning of the sentence as a whole.

1. While most of the crowd was elated at the _____ promises that the politicians made, more cynical observers remained skeptical.

   (A) stolid

   (B) verbose

   (C) whimsical

   (D) extravagant

   (E) diffident

2. In mythology, rarely is a hero completely (i) _____ to any harm; even the greatest heroes have some (ii) _____ part of their body, such as Samson's hair or Achilles's heel.

Blank (i)	Blank (ii)
(A) obdurate	(D) gullible
(B) impervious	(E) impotent
(C) oblivious	(F) susceptible

3. Though pedagogical studies tend to focus on motivation only for struggling students, a teacher's ability to (i) _____ students' passion for the subject is paramount to students' learning. The well-intentioned studies by (ii) _____ educators who design intricate strategies intended to (iii) _____ students' specific struggles entirely miss the point.

Blank (i)	Blank (ii)	Blank (iii)
(A) aggrandize	(D) pedantic	(G) mitigate
(B) foment	(E) naïve	(H) obviate
(C) enervate	(F) ardent	(I) aggravate

4. The ongoing salmon crisis is the result of (i) _____ of problems, among them pollution, introduction of nonnative species, and pesticide use. Such issues speak to decades of (ii) _____ management at the political level. At this point, (iii) _____ solution will require both an understanding of history and foresight of future challenges.

Blank (i)	Blank (ii)	Blank (iii)
Ⓐ a reclamation	Ⓓ methodical	Ⓖ a sustainable
Ⓑ a multitude	Ⓔ rudimentary	Ⓗ an exigent
Ⓒ an exhibition	Ⓕ paltry	Ⓘ a conspicuous

5. Such a (i) _____ manuscript must be approached with (ii) _____. Only the most seasoned editor should be considered for the job.

Blank (i)	Blank (ii)
Ⓐ poignant	Ⓓ circumspection
Ⓑ frivolous	Ⓔ creativity
Ⓒ labyrinthine	Ⓕ fecundity

6. The Perito Moreno Glacier, located inside Glaciers National Park in Patagonia, houses the so-called Curve of the Sighs. This (i) _____ is earned due to the (ii) _____ view of snow-tipped mountains above and icy, slate-hued waters and the foot of the glacier below.

Blank (i)	Blank (ii)
Ⓐ appellation	Ⓓ bucolic
Ⓑ aphorism	Ⓔ calorific
Ⓒ benediction	Ⓕ panoramic

Question 7 is based on the following passage.

Parents of high school students argue that poor attendance is the result of poor motivation. If students' attitudes improve, regular attendance will result. The administration, they believe, should concentrate less on making stricter attendance policies and more on increasing students' learning.

7. Which of the following, if true, would most effectively weaken the parents' argument?

    (A) Motivation to learn can be improved at home, during time spent with parents.

    (B) The degree of interest in learning that a student develops is a direct result of the amount of time he or she spends in the classroom.

    (C) Making attendance policies stricter will merely increase students' motivation to attend classes, not their interest in learning.

    (D) Showing a student how to be motivated is insufficient; the student must also accept responsibility for his or her decisions.

    (E) Unmotivated students do not perform as well in school as other students.

Questions 8–10 are based on the following passage.

The National Aeronautics and Space Administration (NASA) recently discovered a new species of bacteria that has changed our understanding of how living things survive. Deep in the waters of Mono Lake in California, NASA scientists discovered a form of bacteria that uses arsenic to make DNA and proteins. Most life forms are made from six main building blocks: carbon, hydrogen, nitrogen, oxygen, sulfur, and phosphorus. The newfound bacteria, called the *GFAJ-1 strain*, can substitute arsenic for phosphorus. This discovery is remarkable because arsenic is toxic to most known organisms. What's more, the *GFAJ-1 strain* can tolerate high concentrations of arsenic, and it can incorporate the chemical into its cells. Scientists suggest that this discovery has cracked open a new door to what is possible for life elsewhere in the universe, as the new *GFAJ-1 species* has shown that organisms can exist in chemical environments that scientists may not have considered.

Select only one answer choice.

8. Which of the following statements best summarizes the passage?

   (A) The presence of arsenic-based bacteria proves that there is life on other planets.

   (B) Scientists have discovered that arsenic is not toxic to most known organisms.

   (C) The *GFAJ-1 strain* is a unique type of bacteria that has changed scientists' perception of how living organisms survive.

   (D) Scientists need to add a seventh element, arsenic, to the six main building blocks of life.

   (E) Mono Lake is a scientific phenomenon that scientists will be studying for years.

9. According to the information in the passage, the *GFAJ-1 strain* is which of the following?

   (A) A water-based bacteria that has a high tolerance for toxins

   (B) One of the six building blocks of life

   (C) A form of arsenic that is toxic to most living organisms

   (D) A strain of bacteria that incorporates arsenic into its cells

   (E) A form of DNA that does not need phosphorus to grow

Consider each of the following choices separately and select all that apply.

10. Based on the information in the passage, what reasonable conclusion can be drawn?

   ☐ A If a species of bacteria can use arsenic in cell development, it is possible that planets that have high levels of arsenic might be able to support living organisms.

   ☐ B If the *GFAJ-1 strain*'s chemical processes do not follow the same patterns as those of other organisms, the strain must have originated on another planet.

   ☐ C If scientists have discovered a living organism that uses arsenic in place of one of the six building blocks of life, it is possible that there may be other chemicals in addition to arsenic that can support life.

Directions: For each of the following questions, choose two of the answer choices that, when used to complete the sentence, produce two completed sentences that are similar in meaning.

11. After repeated attempts to resolve grievances, 500 sanitation workers went on strike; consequently, city leaders _____ measures to address the issue.

    A flouted

    B concerted

    C contrived

    D consecrated

    E spurned

    F levied

12. By the fifth sequel, the director had become _____ in his delivery; even the most die-hard fans of the series lost interest.

    A convoluted

    B cautious

    C remedial

    D perfunctory

    E unpleasant

    F mundane

13. Within a few short years, the young city council member was able to rise in the political ranks due to her _____ supporters, savvy and skillful team, and incandescent wit.

    A intelligent

    B ardent

    C lenient

    D intrepid

    E zealous

    F recalcitrant

14. In any economy, the success of a business is dependent on two things: the degree to which it can _____ borrowed money and its ability to withstand fluctuations in the market.

   - [A] invert
   - [B] capitalize
   - [C] expound
   - [D] conjure
   - [E] repudiate
   - [F] leverage

Questions 15 and 16 are based on the following passage.

All artists are reputed to suffer to some degree for their art, but some may physically suffer more than others. As part of *The 3rd I* project, a performance artist agreed to have a camera surgically implanted into the back of his head and the footage gathered from the experiment to be uploaded hourly into a website. The surgery involves slicing and lifting folds of skin and implanting the camera into the back of the skull and is excruciating for the artist. Some critics claim that the visceral reaction of hearing about the camera or its insertion may be orchestrated to shock viewers into learning more about the art or the project. Although the camera can be fitted with a lens cap to protect the privacy of those who request it, every single detail of the artist's life is recorded and open for all to view. One might conclude that this project is an extreme example of the Modernists' tendency to take the creation of art as its subject.

15. This passage implies which of the following about performance art?

   - (A) At least some performance art is Modernist in origin.
   - (B) Modern technology affords performance artists a wider audience for conveying political messages.
   - (C) Critics prefer static visual art to performance art because it typically relies less on shock value.
   - (D) By becoming part of the art, a performance artist can convey a powerful message within the art.
   - (E) Performance artists suffer more greatly than other types of artists.

Consider each of the following choices separately and select all that apply.

16. The passage implies that the power of the message of the artwork described in the passage would be substantially weakened if which of the following were to happen?

    A   The content of the video is difficult to make out on-screen.

    B   Most people who see the video on the website don't know how it was made.

    C   Certain shots of the video "go viral" and become something that people across the world discuss in real time.

Questions 17 and 18 are based on the following passage.

To poets of the Modern era, 1910–1940, the Romantic verses of previous generations failed to express the chaos of industrialism and devastation of World War I. Modern poets found new influences when "The International Exhibition of Modern Art" opened at New York's Armory building in February 1913. The Armory Show, as it came to be known, exposed Americans to Modern European artists like Kandinsky, Picasso, and Munch. The show also shattered traditional notions of art and introduced techniques such as abstract cubism, in which objects are fragmented and reassembled. The public was shocked, and the press criticized the show, ridiculing one abstract painting in particular, "Nude Descending a Staircase," by Marcel Duchamp, in which a single figure is captured taking successive steps. Most Modern poets, however, loved the show. William Carlos Williams reportedly burst into laughter when he viewed Duchamp's controversial painting. Williams observed motion in an art form previously limited to still-life. He understood that words no longer had to be static. He began infusing movement into his imagery. New poetic styles sprang to life as other poets applied the techniques of visual art to poetry.

17. The main point of the passage is best stated in which of the following sentences?

    Ⓐ Marcel Duchamp gave Modern American poets a way to express the effects of industrialism and war.

    Ⓑ The general public and the press hated the Armory Show because the pieces did not follow conventional, traditional artistic techniques.

    Ⓒ Using words instead of paint, Modern American poets applied the abstract and cubist techniques of Modern European visual art to poetry.

    Ⓓ One form of art can easily influence and shape another.

    Ⓔ William Carlos Williams was influenced by Marcel Duchamp to apply cubist techniques to his poetry.

Consider each of the following choices separately and select all that apply.

18. Which of the following conclusions is supported by the passage?

    [A] Cubism was too abstract for anyone except other artists to understand.

    [B] Traditional forms of artistic expression were rejected by artists in 1913.

    [C] Artistic forms of expression are shaped by world events, social and political.

Questions 19 and 20 are based on the following passage.

Willa Cather (1873–1947) lived in Nebraska and set her novels *O Pioneers!* and *My Ántonia* in the state, describing the land as intricately as she would a main character. However, Nebraska might not have featured so heavily in Cather's work if she had not grown up in the Shenandoah Valley of Virginia. Until she was nine, she lived in the quaint charm of Willow Shade, her grandfather's 300-acre farm. Amid the lush, wooded vegetation, a rustic bridge covered a creek. Box hedges surrounded the house. Willow trees grew large. In 1883, following the lure of fertile farmland in the West, Cather's family left Willow Shade and crossed six states to reach a new farm in Webster County, Nebraska. The new landscape shocked Cather to the core. She felt erased by flat prairies stretching to the horizon, swallowed by the enormous sky. The stark contrast to the mountains of Virginia etched its influence onto her soul. She grew to love the new land, but never forgot the old. Perhaps that is why she identified with immigrants homesick for Czechoslovakia, Norway, and Sweden, the people she wrote about in *O Pioneers!* and *My Ántonia*. She knew how transplanted they felt.

19. Based on the information in the passage, which assumption MOST likely underlies the passage?

    Ⓐ Cather's novels would have been much different if her family had not moved to Nebraska.

    Ⓑ Cather would not have become an author if her family had not moved to Nebraska.

    Ⓒ Cather did not truly remember or value Virginia because she did not use the state as the setting of her most famous novels.

    Ⓓ It was Cather's compassion for immigrant people, rather than her passion for landscape, that inspired her novels.

    Ⓔ The shock Cather felt in Nebraska and her grief for Virginia deepened her soul and made her an artist.

20. Which best states the author's use of rhetorical structure in the passage?

    (A) The passage is a comparison between the different landscapes of Virginia and Nebraska.

    (B) The passage compares Willa Cather's response to the different landscapes of Virginia and Nebraska.

    (C) The author compares the different landscapes of Virginia and Nebraska as a way to emphasize Willa Cather's experience when she first set eyes on Nebraska.

    (D) The author describes how Willa Cather compared the different landscapes of Virginia and Nebraska when she first set eyes on Nebraska.

    (E) The author compares Willa Cather's use of landscapes in her two most famous novels.

PRACTICE SET 3 ANSWER KEY

1. D
2. B, F
3. B, F, G
4. B, F, G
5. C, D
6. A, F
7. B
8. C
9. D
10. A, C
11. B, C
12. D, F
13. B, E
14. B, F
15. A
16. B
17. C
18. C
19. A
20. C

PRACTICE SET 3 ANSWERS AND EXPLANATIONS

1. D

The key to this question is the contrast between the "elated," or excited, crowd, and the "skeptical," or doubting, cynics. We are looking for a word that would cause the crowd to be excited, but would cast doubt among skeptics. We can immediately eliminate choice **(A)** *stolid* "unemotional," choice **(B)** *verbose* "talkative," and choice **(E)** *diffident* "lacking self-confidence," as these are all negative adjectives for a political speech and would not invoke the excitement of the crowd. Choice **(C)** *whimsical* "fanciful" seems plausible: the crowd may like a fanciful, idealistic promise, while cynics would remain doubtful of its veracity. However, choice **(D)** *extravagant* is a better choice, as it implies an attractive promise that may not be realistic.

2. B, F

Based on the context, you can assume that the blank will describe a hero's ability to be harmed, so you can predict *resistant*, or *unable*, to describe the hero's relationship to harm. Therefore, you can immediately eliminate choice **(A)** *obdurate*, which means the opposite of the predicted meaning. Choice **(C)** *oblivious* may be tempting, but the second part of the sentence is clearly discussing actual bodily harm, not awareness of harm. Choice **(B)** *impervious* means "unable to be pierced" and is the best choice.

For the second blank, you could use the examples of Achilles's heel and Samson's hair to help you along. But whether or not you are familiar with these stories, you can use the straight-ahead road sign of the semicolon: the second part of the sentence carries the same ideas as the first. Since the first part of the sentence suggests that heroes all have some sort of flaw or problem, predict a word that means

"open to harm." Choice **(D)** *gullible* refers to someone who is easily tricked. This is rarely a hero's downfall and is certainly not in the cases of the heroes listed. Choice **(E)** *impotent* describes what might happen to the hero if he or she were open to harm, but it does not work as the predicted meaning itself. Only choice **(F)** *susceptible* carries the correct meaning, "open to harm," and is your answer.

3. B, F, G

There are several good clues to work with in this sentence. The first blank contains a detour road sign. The author begins the sentence saying that "studies tend to focus on motivation only for struggling students," and the detour demonstrates that she would prefer there to be more studies related to motivating all students. Therefore, predict a term that means "increase motivation." For the second blank, use the term "well-intentioned" as a straight-ahead road sign to predict a word that could describe the educators who publish the studies. For the third blank, predict a word that means "improve" or "alleviate" because the intentions of the "well-intentioned studies" should be a positive outcome.

The words after the first blank, "students' passion," take care of the second half of your prediction, "increase motivation," so look for a word that means "increase" or "generate." Choice **(A)** *aggrandize* means to make more important, so that does not work in this context. Choice **(B)** *foment* means "generate" or "encourage," which does work in this context. Choice **(C)** *enervate* means "annoy" and is clearly not the right answer.

For the second blank, a solid prediction would be *thoughtful* or *caring* because those educators would produce well-intentioned studies that may miss the point. Choice **(D)** *pedantic* implies someone who is overly educated and makes a show of his learning; although we can assume a teacher is well educated, this is not apparent or relevant to the paragraph. Similarly, choice **(E)** *naïve* might be inferred, but it is not directly relevant to the context. Choice **(F)** *ardent*, which means "passionate," fits best.

For the third blank, your prediction was *improve* or *alleviate*, and all choices are similar to this meaning. Choice **(H)** *obviate*, which means "to prevent," may seem reasonable, but its meaning is too extreme for this context. The strategies do not prevent struggles, just ease them. Choice **(I)** *aggravate* means "to make worse," which clearly does not work. Choice **(G)** *mitigate* is our best choice as it means to "lessen" or "soften."

4.   B, F, G
Try reading the passage and filling in the blanks with words you already know. Then see which answer choices make the most sense in context. The first blank in this sentence is easiest to fill because of the examples given at the end of the sentence. Choice **(B)** *multitude* means "many" or "a great number," which makes sense given that the list that follows includes only some of the problems, as signaled by the phrase "among them." Even though this makes sense, remember to check the other choices for plausibility. Choice **(A)** *reclamation* means "reformation" and choice **(C)** *exhibition* is a public showing. Neither choice works.

Given the information in the first sentence, you need to locate a word for the second blank that implies a problem. Choice **(F)** *paltry* is the only option with a clearly negative tone, meaning "worthless." Choice **(D)** *methodical* means "done by routine," which doesn't fit. Choice **(E)** *rudimentary* means "basic" and suggests imperfection. However, it's not a strong enough word to meet the tone of the sentence.

A *sustainable* solution is one that will last a long time, so choice **(G)** makes the most sense in the third sentence. Choice **(H)** *exigent,* which means "requiring immediate help," suggests a meaning opposite of what you want, and choice **(I)** *conspicuous,* meaning "obvious," makes sense but is not the best fit for the context.

5.   C, D
Before filling in the two blanks, you need to understand how the second sentence elaborates on the first. Think of what type of manuscript should be approached by a "seasoned editor" and how that editor should conduct her work. **(A)** *poignant* means "emotional." While this makes sense, it doesn't explain why a seasoned editor would be needed. **(B)** *frivolous* means "playful." Choice **(C)** *labyrinthine* means "intricate, complex," like a labyrinth. This is the best fit.

Think about how a complex manuscript should be approached. Skip choice **(D)** *circumspection* for now, if you're unfamiliar with it. Choice **(E)** *creativity* is not quite right—look for an option suggesting attention to detail. Choice **(F)** *fecundity* means "fruitfulness," which doesn't make sense. Going back to *circumspect*, break it down to *circum-*, "around," and *spect*, "to look." *Circumspection* is thoughtfulness around a subject, a metaphorical "looking" around a problem. This is the correct answer.

6.   A, F
The first blank refers to the name "Curve of the Sighs." Each of the answer choices listed could refer to the name, so you must take each singly. Choice **(A)** *appellation* means "nickname," and this is a strong choice. Choice **(B)** *aphorism* refers to a pithy phrase that gives a general truth. It is tempting but doesn't quite fit this meaning. Choice **(C)** *benediction* is a blessing, which does not makes sense here. So **(A)** is the correct choice here.

It is easier to predict the second blank because the view seen at the Curve of the Sighs is described in images just after the blank: the answer must have something to do with viewing a wide, dramatic space. Choice **(F)** *panoramic* makes sense in this blank because it means "wide in scope." This is the right answer. Choice **(D)** *bucolic* may be tempting, but it refers to an area that is fertile or where sheepherding is done—not a glacier. Choice **(E)** *calorific* has the opposite meaning: it means "producing heat."

7. B

You are asked here to weaken the parents' argument, which is outlined in the first sentence of the stimulus: parents believe that poor attendance results from poor motivation. This sets up a cause-and-effect relationship between "poor attendance" and "poor motivation," with poor motivation as the cause and poor attendance as the effect. The parents go on to elaborate on their theory and suggest a plan of action, but this cause-and-effect argument is the central issue.

Since you need to *weaken* this argument, you need to find an answer choice that contradicts or otherwise introduces doubt into this assertion. Choice **(B)** does just this by stating that "the degree of interest in learning that a student develops" (i.e., a student's motivation) is a result of "the amount of time he or she spends in the classroom" (his or her attendance). Choice **(B)** establishes a new cause-and-effect relationship with *attendance* as the cause and *motivation* as the effect. Since this reverses the causality from the initial argument, it weakens the stimulus and is the correct answer.

Wrong choices **(A)**, **(D)**, and **(E)** fail to mention both attendance and motivation and therefore sidestep the issue. Choice **(C)** does mention both concepts, but its stance of decrying strict attendance policies is right in line with the last sentence of the stimulus and would thus *strengthen* rather than weaken the argument.

8. C

This question asks you to identify the most accurate summary of the passage. Use your summary of the topic, scope, and purpose of the passage as a prediction of the correct answer. This author is writing to inform her reader about an exciting discovery: Scientists have discovered a new bacterium whose remarkable ability to use arsenic challenges assumptions about the building blocks of life. That matches the correct answer, choice **(C)**. Choice **(A)** is too extreme; the passage states that the new discovery introduces new possibilities for life in other parts of our universe, but it does not state that this discovery *proves* that there is life in other parts of our universe. Choice **(B)** contradicts the passage; the *GFAJ-1 strain* is "remarkable because arsenic is toxic to most known organisms." Choice **(D)** goes too far; the new bacteria substitute arsenic for phosphorous, but that doesn't mean arsenic should be considered a new "building block." This is, at any rate, far from the passage's main point. Choice **(E)** misses the boat by focusing on the wrong subject and making a prediction that is not supported by information in the passage.

9. D

The correct answer to this question is directly stated in the passage. The *GFAJ-1* is a "new-found bacteria" that can tolerate arsenic and even "incorporate the chemical into its cells." Eliminate choice **(B)** because it states that the *GFAJ-1 strain* is a building block of life, not a bacteria strain that uses some of the building blocks of life as the passage suggests. Eliminate **(C)** because it states that the *GFAJ-1 strain* is a form of arsenic, not a bacteria strain that is arsenic based as the passage suggests. Similarly, eliminate **(E)** because it states that the *GFAJ-1 strain* is a form of DNA, whereas the passage suggests that it develops DNA from arsenic. Choices **(A)** and **(D)** both state that the *GFAJ-1 strain* is a form of bacteria. However, choice **(A)** states that it is a water-based bacteria, which is not supported by information in the passage. Choice **(D)** states that the *GFAJ-1 strain* is a type of bacteria that incorporates arsenic into its cells, which (as you noted above) is directly stated in the passage.

10. A, C

This question asks you to evaluate the statement and identify the conclusions you can validly draw using the information from the passage. Choice **(A)** is a reasonable conclusion because it is based on the statement in the passage that suggests that the discovery of an arsenic-based bacteria has "cracked open a new door to what is possible for life elsewhere in the universe." Choice **(B)** is not based on any information stated in the passage. The passage suggests that the discovery of this new bacteria will lead to the examination of life on other planets, but it does not suggest that the bacteria came from another planet. Choice **(C)** is a reasonable conclusion because the passage states that *GFAJ-1* has shown that "organisms can exist in chemical environments that scientists may not have considered."

11. B, C

The word *"consequently"* means "as a result." Considering the tone of the sentence, think about how city leaders might have responded. Choice **(A)** *flouted* means "disregarded." It's unlikely that city leaders disregarded the issues after such extreme measures by the workers. Look for a word that suggests a more proactive response. Choice **(B)** *concerted* and choice **(C)** *contrived* mean "devised or planned" and fit the

context of the sentence. Although these are likely the correct answers, check the remaining choices just to be sure. Choice **(D)** *consecrated* means "declared sacred," which doesn't make sense and can be eliminated. Choice **(E)** *spurned* has a meaning similar to *flouted*. Like *flouted*, this is opposite to the response that is likely to have occurred. You may be familiar with choice **(F)** *levied* from historical contexts, as in "a tax was levied." The word *levied* means "collected" and doesn't make sense in context. Stick with options **(B)** and **(C)**; they are synonyms and create sentences with similar meanings.

12. D, F

Use the key phrase "lost interest" to determine the tone of the word in the blank. The semicolon separating the two clauses acts as a straight-ahead road sign. You need a negative word to describe the director's work, which has become rote or boring. Choice **(A)** *convoluted* means "intricate." Depending on the type of story, an "intricate" film might be boring or very interesting. There's not enough context to make this choice a logical certainty. **(B)** *cautious* is another choice that could go either way. A "cautious" delivery might make for a better or worse fifth film. Choice **(C)** *remedial* contains the word *remedy*, which means "cure." This does not fit the context of the sentence. Choices **(D)** *perfunctory* and **(F)** *mundane* are synonyms meaning "in a routine manner." They fit the tone of the sentence. You can also rule out choice **(E)** *unpleasant*. Even though the film may be unpleasant, the phrase "by the fifth sequel" suggests fatigue or boredom on the part of the director. Choices **(D)** and **(F)** are correct.

13. B, E

Ask yourself what kind of supporters a young politician would need in order to move up quickly in local government. Choice **(A)** *intelligent* fits in the sentence, so hold on to it for now. Choice **(B)** *ardent* means "eager, full of passion." This word is more precise in context than choice **(A)**, so see if you can find a synonym for it. Choice **(C)** *lenient* is not the best fit for the context. *Lenient* is similar to "tolerant," but it has a negative connotation, implying that a lenient person may allow people to do things they are not supposed to. *Intrepid*, choice **(D)**, means "fearless." This choice is possible but would not fit with *ardent* or *intelligent*, so you can discard it. Somebody who is **(F)** *recalcitrant* is stubborn and resists authority, which doesn't apply here. Choice **(E)** *zealous* is a synonym for *ardent*. Since both *ardent* and *zealous* fit the sentence and are synonyms, you can get rid of *intelligent*. Even though the word fits, no other word matches to create a sentence with the same meaning.

14.   B, F

The straightforward road sign "and" means that the verb for the blank matches "ability" in the accompanying phrase. You're looking for a word that means "use" and that fits with "borrowed money." Choice **(A)** *invert* means "to put upside down or inside out," which doesn't make sense, so eliminate it. Choice **(B)** *capitalize* means "to take advantage of." This describes a business strategy and fits in context. Choice **(C)** *expound* is "to explain." A business will most likely not have to explain its borrowed money as a business strategy—unless it gets into trouble! Choice **(D)** *conjure* means "to imagine or make up." This doesn't work in context. Choice **(E)** *repudiate* means "to reject." Move on to the last choice, **(F)** *leverage*, which is the synonym you needed; like *capitalize*, it means "to take advantage of." Choices **(B)** and **(F)** are the correct answers. This is a good example of a situation where the answers are not quite synonyms, but the words affect the meaning of the sentence similarly.

15.   A

The correct answer to this question will be true based on the passage. With this in mind, **(A)** is the correct answer. If this performance art project is an "example of" Modernist art, it must be the case that at least some performance art is Modernist in origin. Although choice **(B)** may be true in the real world, it is not an implication of the passage. The author says nothing about the political dimensions of the performance. Consider choice **(C)** carefully: critics do comment on this aspect of this project's shock value, but nowhere is it suggested that critics prefer visual art to performance art. This passage doesn't make any assessment of how "powerful" the piece is, so choice **(D)** is incorrect. Choice **(E)** is too vague; the artist described here may suffer more *physically*, but that doesn't translate to a generalized statement that performance artists suffer more that artists of other genres.

16.   B

This Inference question asks you for any and all answers that follow from the passage. According to the critics mentioned in the passage, knowing how the art was created is potentially related to the audience's interest in it. Choice **(A)** doesn't follow from the passage. Nothing suggests that the beauty or clarity of the images produced affects the success of the project. The message is mainly reliant on the concept, not the product, of the art. Thus, choice **(B)** is correct. If the audience doesn't appreciate how the art was made, they may be less interested in it. If choice **(C)** were true, it would likely increase the popularity of the performance and get people thinking about it. This has the opposite effect called for by the question stem.

17.   C

In this question, you are asked to identify the statement that expresses the main point of the passage. The author begins with large concepts and narrows the information to a single specific event and the influence it had on one person. The claim in choice **(A)** is lopsided. The author suggests that poets found new influences in art, not only that of Marcel Duchamp and not only on the subjects of war and industry. The statement in choice **(B)** is supported by the passage, but the reason why the general public reacted negatively to the show is an aside intended to provide context for Williams's response. Choice **(C)** best states the connection made in the paragraph and is the correct response. You can disregard choice **(D)** as too vague and too broad; nothing implies that influence across genres of art is "easy." Choice **(E)** merely states the specific example given to support the main point.

18.   C

This question asks you to evaluate the veracity of the general statements by making inferences using evidence from the passage. The claim in choice **(A)** cannot be supported as there is no proof that all viewers other than artists disliked cubism or that cubism was disliked because it was misunderstood. There is also no evidence to suggest that choice **(B)** is correct. Because artists invented new styles that "shattered traditional notions" does not necessarily mean the artist rejected old styles. Choice **(C)** is supported, as the author of the paragraph directly correlates world events with new forms of artistic expression.

19.   A

This question asks you to make inferences based on the information in the passage. You will need to evaluate each response one by one and weigh its merits. Choices **(A)** and

(B) are similar in that they refer to Cather's motives in becoming an author. The passage does not prove, however, that she wouldn't have become an author at all if she had stayed in Virginia. Choice **(B)** is not the correct answer. You can also rule out choice **(C)**; the author tells you explicitly that Cather remembered Virginia. The fact that she was influenced by Nebraska doesn't mean that she devalued her former home. To support the claim in choice **(D)**, the passage would have to offer summaries of each novel and more information about Cather's relationship to communities of people. You can't draw this inference from the passage. In a literary analysis, an author could possibly support a claim such as the one stated in choice **(E)**. However, based on this passage, **(E)** is emotional hyperbole. Choice **(A)** is the most feasible assumption. According to the passage, Cather certainly would not have written the specific novels she did write if she hadn't moved to Nebraska as a child.

20.   C

The correct answer to this Global question summarizes the passage's structure. The passage certainly compares two landscapes, but to correctly answer this question, you must determine *why* the comparison is made. You can eliminate choice **(A)** because it does not provide a reason for the comparison. Rule out choice **(B)** because prior to seeing Nebraska, Cather had nothing to compare to Virginia. We do not know how she "responded" to her home state. Choice **(C)** includes the main point of the passage—Cather's shock upon first seeing Nebraska and its influence on her writing. Choice **(D)** is not reasonable as you don't know Cather's thought process when she first saw Nebraska. You can also cross off choice **(E)** as there is little to no information about the novels in the passage. Therefore, **(C)** is the correct answer.

DIAGNOSTIC TOOL

Tally up your score and write your results in the space provided.

Total

Total Correct: _____ out of 20 correct

Percentage Correct: # you got right × 100 ÷ 20: _____

By Question Type

Text Completion _____ out of 6 correct

Sentence Equivalence _____ out of 4 correct

Reading Comprehension _____ out of 10 correct

Diagnose Your Results

Look back at the questions you got wrong and think about your experience answering them.

VERBAL REASONING PRACTICE SET 4

Directions: For each sentence, choose one word for each set of blanks. Select the word or words that best fit(s) the meaning of the sentence as a whole.

1. It was apparent that the recordings were _____ remastered, as the vocals were barely audible through the wave of noise.

   (A) maladroitly

   (B) copiously

   (C) ingeniously

   (D) shrewdly

   (E) maliciously

2. He cited financial difficulty as his primary motive in the lucrative robbery; nonetheless, even his own family _____ him.

   (A) deluded

   (B) chastised

   (C) absolved

   (D) venerated

   (E) engulfed

3. The (i)_____ young children were a top priority for their mother and commanded most of her attention. They had such (ii) _____ level of volatile energy that ordinary activities were not enough to keep them occupied for an extended period of time. She devoted herself to channeling their energy into (iii)_____ pursuits.

Blank (i)	Blank (ii)	Blank (iii)
(A) earthy	(D) an eclectic	(G) salutary
(B) froward	(E) a pedestrian	(H) provocative
(C) limpid	(F) a robust	(I) dour

4. The punctilious wine aficionado was a consummate purist when it came to his tastes. He immediately rejected the (i) _____ of two wines. As an alternative, and as a general rule, he preferred a simple, (ii) _____ wine.

Blank (i)	Blank (ii)
Ⓐ amalgamation	Ⓓ pragmatic
Ⓑ dissonance	Ⓔ unadulterated
Ⓒ enigma	Ⓕ opaque

5. The belligerent student did everything in his power to (i)_____ the other students with his behavior and classroom conduct. However, the teacher's calm yet stern discipline, acquired through years of dealing with similar situations, quickly (ii)_____ their reactions.

Blank (i)	Blank (ii)
Ⓐ satiate	Ⓓ exacerbated
Ⓑ antagonize	Ⓔ vacillated
Ⓒ repudiate	Ⓕ assuaged

6. The _____ alumni donors for the university's English department is well-documented and acknowledged. It creates _____ in the allocation of university funds when the time comes to decide the annual budget. As things stand now, the available money goes to other university departments, which are not always the most underfunded or _____.

Blank (i)	Blank (ii)	Blank (iii)
Ⓐ paucity of	Ⓓ an irritation	Ⓖ widespread
Ⓑ preponderance of	Ⓔ a paradox	Ⓗ needy
Ⓒ utility of	Ⓕ a disparity	Ⓘ newsworthy

Questions 7 and 8 are based on the following passage.

British Naval Officer Robert Scott (1868–1912) made his intent to discover the South Pole public, but that did not stop Norwegian explorer Roald Amundsen (1872–1928) from trying to beat him to it. In 1910, Amundsen raced to Antarctica and headed for the pole with 4 crewmen and 52 sled dogs. Scott's party left base camp ten days later with 17 men, 2 motorized sleds, 10 ponies, and 34 dogs. Scott's motor sleds broke down, the ponies had to be shot, and Scott sent all but four men back to base camp. The remaining crewmen hauled the sleds the rest of the way. Amundsen planted the Norwegian flag on the South Pole on December 14, 1911. A demoralized Scott raised the British flag on January 17, 1912. Amundsen and crew skied back to camp in good health. Scott's team, however, walked in temperatures that reached –30°F, losing two men along the way. A blizzard trapped the remaining three in a tent, which became their grave on March 29, 1912. A search party, discovering the tent, built a cairn, or monument of stones, marking the spot with a cross made of skis. When news of Scott's death reached civilization, England fell into mourning. The cross and cairn honoring Robert Scott still stand today.

7. **Which conclusion about the competition between the two explorers does the passage steer the reader toward?**

   (A) Scott would not have died if Amundsen had not forced him to compete.

   (B) Scott never should have tried for the South Pole because he was not a good explorer.

   (C) Amundsen was destined to win the historic conquest of the South Pole.

   (D) The English public followed the race to the South Pole with more interest than the Norwegian public did.

   (E) Despite losing the race to the South Pole, Scott's efforts were heroic.

8. **With which of the following statements is the author most likely to agree?**

   (A) Amundsen's conquest seems anticlimactic compared to Scott's disastrous defeat.

   (B) Scott wanted to conquer the South Pole more than Amundsen did.

   (C) Amundsen was better prepared to discover the South Pole by using commonsense skills suited to Antarctica.

   (D) Amundsen exploited Scott's preparations and ruined his expedition; Scott's defeat was Amundsen's fault.

   (E) Amundsen and Scott both viewed the discovery of the South Pole in part as a competitive race.

Question 9 is based on the following passage.

In the results of a long-term medical study, babies exposed to Mozart's music from the age of four weeks developed into young adults who were, on average, not only better performing scholastically, but also physically more adept than young adults who had not been exposed to Mozart's music from an early age. Therefore, parents who wish to improve the strength and scholastic performance of their children should expose their infants to classical music from the age of four weeks.

Select only one answer choice.

9. Which of the following, if true, best supports the argument above?

   (A) Children who were exposed to Mozart starting at the age of eight weeks also exhibited better scholastic performance as young adults.

   (B) High school students who study music tend to be better at math than those students who do not.

   (C) Long-term medical studies are difficult to undertake and require large amounts of outside funding.

   (D) When infants listen to Mozart's music, it stimulates their brains and increases the rate of brain cell growth.

   (E) Babies who listen to classical music from composers other than Mozart also tend to develop into young adults with greater strength and better scholastic performance than other young adults.

Question 10 is based on the following passage.

A social worker surveyed 200 women, each of whom had recently given birth to her first child. Half of the women surveyed had chosen to give birth in a hospital or obstetrics clinic; the other half had chosen to give birth at home under the care of certified midwives. Of the 100 births that occurred at home, only 5 presented substantial complications, whereas 17 of the hospital births presented substantial complications. The social worker concluded from the survey that the home is actually a safer environment in which to give birth than a hospital or clinic.

Select only one answer choice.

10. Which of the following, if true, most seriously calls the social worker's conclusion into question?

    (A) Women who give birth in hospitals and clinics often have shorter periods of labor than do women who give birth at home.

    (B) Many obstetricians discourage patients from giving birth at home.

    (C) All of the women in the study who had been diagnosed as having a high possibility of delivery complications elected to give birth in a hospital.

    (D) Women who give birth at home tend to experience less stress during labor than women who deliver in hospitals.

    (E) Pregnant doctors prefer giving birth in a hospital.

Directions: For each of the following questions, choose two of the answer choices that, when used to complete the sentence, produce two completed sentences that are similar in meaning.

11. Caligula, one of the great _____ of history, is best remembered for his lavish, bacchanalian feasts, in which participants indulged in every form of excess.

   A   gadflies

   B   sybarites

   C   philanthropists

   D   puritans

   E   wantons

   F   ascetics

12. Arthur looked positively _____; as he hadn't seen his wife, Deirdre, in weeks, the mere sight of her filled him with elation.

   A   ebullient

   B   esurient

   C   peevish

   D   pensive

   E   ecstatic

   F   execrable

13. For all his _____ in chatting with his friends and coworkers, when Cedric actually had a good reason to speak up in a serious conversation, he became taciturn.

   A   oratories

   B   declamations

   C   palaver

   D   blather

   E   epigrams

   F   opining

14. Despite the falling temperature and the inclement weather that lasted for most of the expedition, the hunting party was in a _____ mood.

A disconcerted

B jocund

C garrulous

D genial

E histrionic

F sententious

Questions 15–17 are based on the following passage.

The reversal of the Chicago River in 1900 is considered one of the greatest engineering feats of all time. The project involved building a deep channel through miles of solid bedrock in an effort to make the waters of the Chicago River—and its associated untreated sewage—flow out of Chicago and away from Lake Michigan, which was the source of the city's water supply. The project seemed impossible at the time, but it was deemed necessary after a flood in 1885 caused the Chicago River to foul the city's water supply and subsequently killed almost 12 percent of the population as a result of exposure to cholera and other water-borne diseases. In 1889, engineers started construction on the 28-mile channel that would connect Lake Michigan at Chicago with the Des Plaines River at Lockport, Illinois. This complex task gave workers the ability to isolate and reverse the flow of the Chicago River. At the end of the yearlong project, the city's water supply became safer and the river's new mouth at Lake Michigan became a major port that served thousands of ships each year.

Select only one answer choice.

15. Which one of the following statements reflects a major point of the passage?

Ⓐ Sewage disposal was a serious problem in Chicago during the late 1800s.

Ⓑ Water-borne diseases can spread easily and kill large populations.

Ⓒ The reversal of the Chicago River is a tremendous accomplishment in the field of engineering.

Ⓓ The reversal of the Chicago River opened the river's mouth to Lake Michigan.

Ⓔ Connecting Lake Michigan to the Des Plaines River was a key component of plans to reverse the flow of the Chicago River.

Consider each of the following choices separately and select all that apply.

16. Using the details from the passage, what can one infer about why the reversal of the Chicago River is considered one of the greatest engineering feats of all time?

   - [A] The logistics of drilling through 28 miles of bedrock and connecting rivers was extremely difficult.
   - [B] The river-reversal project in Chicago was successful, whereas similar projects were unsuccessful in several other cities.
   - [C] The project proved that strong engineering can make things that seem impossible possible.

Select only one answer choice.

17. Which one of the following was NOT a benefit of reversing the Chicago River?

   - (A) Engineers created a cure for water-borne illnesses.
   - (B) The city's engineers gained recognition for completing an impressive project.
   - (C) Citizens received safer drinking water.
   - (D) The city became a major port for industry.
   - (E) Lake Michigan became a cleaner body of water.

Question 18 is based on the following passage.

The Hague Convention for the Protection of Cultural Property in the Event of Armed Conflict (1954) was an international response to the destruction of cultural artifacts during World War II. Overseen by the United Nations Educational, Scientific, and Cultural Organization (UNESCO), the parties that participated in the convention (numbering over 100) pledged to safeguard locations and items of cultural significance during armed conflict, as well as preempt possible threats to the preservation of culture during times of peace. The Hague Convention is significant in that it formally established in its preamble that "damage to cultural property belonging to any people whatsoever means damage to the cultural heritage of all mankind, since each people makes its contribution to the culture of the world." However, it is difficult to enforce, particularly in the case of pieces of cultural heritage that are claimed by multiple States. An example of this is the possession of some of the Dead Sea Scrolls in the aftermath of the Six Day War (1967), a hotly debated topic between Jordan and Israel today. Both countries are signatories to the convention, but both claim their efforts to hold the scrolls amount to rightful possession, rather than theft as forbidden in the convention.

18. Which of the following statements about the Hague Convention of 1954 is
    NOT supported by the passage?

    Ⓐ It was a reaction to despoliation and destruction of cultural heritage
       during World War II.

    Ⓑ It asserted the international significance of all cultural heritage.

    Ⓒ It is the focus of controversy in some cases even to this day.

    Ⓓ It is overseen by a division of the United Nations.

    Ⓔ It included strong and effective measures for enforcement.

Questions 19 and 20 are based on the following passage.

An idea that has gained renewed currency in recent years is that the proliferation of
information technology has a deleterious effect on interpersonal relationships. Neil
Postman, in his book *Amusing Ourselves to Death*, asserted that television, as a medium,
was incapable of fostering intelligent, meaningful discourse around a given subject.
Postman wrote his book in the 1980s, when cable television was first becoming widely
available. In it, he discusses the way that putatively "serious" news programs are inherently trite. Terse reports on serious, weighty issues such as the war in Iraq are juxtaposed with trivial information, such as celebrity gossip. Often the two are linked, one
after another, by the phrase "and now…." This leaves the viewer unable to emotionally
respond to something traumatic, as he is bombarded with disparate pieces of information in rapid succession. Instant access to a glut of information impoverishes genuine
experiences, as it deprives the information of a meaningful context for interpretation.

19. Select the sentence in the passage in which the author cites a concrete example
    of how mass media has a desensitizing effect.

Consider each of the following choices separately and select all that apply.

20. Based on his views as they're expressed in the passage, Postman would likely
    agree with which of the following statements?

    ☐ A Information technologies, such as smartphones, are unlikely to provide
          meaningful contexts in which to interpret information.

    ☐ B Television programs inherently lack intelligent, meaningful discourse.

    ☐ C The medium in which factual content is delivered can be an important
          factor in how that content is interpreted.

PRACTICE SET 4 ANSWER KEY

1. A
2. B
3. B, F, G
4. A, E
5. B, F
6. A, F, H
7. E
8. E
9. E
10. C
11. B, E
12. A, E

13. C, D
14. B, D
15. C
16. A, C
17. A
18. E
19. *"Terse reports on serious, weighty issues such as the war in Iraq are juxtaposed with trivial information, such as celebrity gossip."*
20. A, C

PRACTICE SET 4 ANSWERS AND EXPLANATIONS

1. A

The word *as* signals a continuation of ideas—the vocals were hard to hear because of the way the recordings were mastered. The answer is **(A)** *maladroitly*, which means "unskillfully" or "bunglingly." Choices **(B)** *copiously*, **(C)** *ingeniously*, and **(D)** *shrewdly* are not in line with what you're looking for—these words suggest more time and care than was spent. Choice **(E)** *maliciously* is too harsh. It's doubtful the recordings were mastered with intent to harm.

2. B

Even with the road sign *nonetheless*, a contrast is not immediately clear. Consider the tone of the phrase "even his own family," which suggests an element of surprise at the family's response. Choice **(A)** *deluded* means "misled," which doesn't fit the context. Choice **(B)** *chastised* means "scolded," which makes sense, since the robber would expect his family's support, not scolding. Choices **(C)** *absolved* and **(D)** *venerated* imply support—rule these out. The last choice, **(E)** *engulfed*, doesn't make sense in context.

3. B, F, G

It's difficult to predict for the first blank, as all you're told is that the children were time-consuming for their mother. You need more contextual clues, so move on to the second blank. Here, you're looking for something to describe the children's energy level. Their energy is characterized as "volatile" ("explosive"), so they must have an *intense* level of energy. Make that your prediction. Choice **(F)** *robust* ("vigorous") fits perfectly. Choices **(D)** *eclectic* ("varied") and **(E)** *pedestrian* ("ordinary") don't make sense. Now that you know the children are high-energy, you can predict

something like "unruly" for the first blank, since that blank describes the children. Looking at the answer choices, choice **(B)** *froward*, meaning "not easily controlled," works perfectly. Choice **(A)** *earthy* means "crude," so that is wrong, and **(C)** *limpid*, which means "calm or untroubled," is the opposite of what you need. For the final blank, remember that the mother is trying to direct the children's energy towards something "constructive" so that they will make productive use of their time. This is close to choice **(G)** *salutary*, which means "beneficial" or "useful," and that's your answer. Choice **(H)** *provocative* ("provoking to anger or desire") and **(I)** *dour* ("gloomy") do not make sense in this context, as they do not describe pursuits that parents would encourage for their children.

4. A, E

The key to this sentence is the description of the wine aficionado (or expert) as a "purist," or someone who insists on the purity of things. Since he rejects the first blank, you can assume it will be an antonym of *pure*. You can predict *mixture*, which fits in the context. However, he prefers the second blank, so this should be a synonym of *pure* and the contextual word, "simple."

For the first blank, the best match for your prediction is choice **(A)** *amalgamation*. This is an exact synonym of your prediction, *mixture*. Choice **(B)** *dissonance*, which means "a disagreeable combination," seems plausible. A purist would definitely find a mixture of two wines to be dissonant. However, we need a word that states this mixture has occurred for the sentence to make sense. Similarly, choice **(C)** *enigma* means "puzzle," which may also be applicable to such a mixture but, again, lacks the necessary meaning of "mixture." For the second blank, choice **(E)** *unadulterated* matches your prediction best. Choice **(D)** *pragmatic* means "practical" and does not fit as well as *unadulterated* in context. The wine aficionado does not prefer something for its practicality but for the taste; therefore, this choice would be misleading in the sentence. Choice **(F)** *opaque*, which means "impossible to see through," may similarly be applicable to the wine; however, nowhere in the sentence is the color implied or relevant.

5. B, F

Since the student is described as "belligerent," meaning "aggressive," you can assume he will be attempting to provoke the other students. Later in the sentence, the road sign word "however" appears, which indicates a turn of events when the teacher takes over. You can predict *aggravate* for the first blank and *calmed* or *lessened* for the second blank. For the first blank, the best match for your prediction is **(B)** *antagonize*, which means "provoke." Choice **(A)** *satiate* means "to satisfy," which is inconsistent with the idea of belligerence. Choice **(C)** *repudiate* means "to reject the validity of," which, although it may antagonize the students, lacks the direct connotation of *aggravate*. For the second blank, choice **(F)** *assuaged* is the best match to your prediction. Choice **(D)** *exacerbated*, which means "worsened," is the exact opposite of what you are looking for. Choice **(E)** *vacillated* means "to be indecisive," which sounds plausible but does not match the prediction as well as *assuaged,* or "calmed."

6. A, F, H

Start tackling this question by looking at the last sentence. You know that the money is going to other departments, which are not necessarily the most underfunded. Therefore, you know there aren't enough donors to the English department, or they aren't generous enough. You can predict something that means "lack of" for the first blank. Choice **(A)** *paucity of*, which means "shortage," works perfectly. Hang on to that one. For the second blank, you need something that contrasts what the English department gets with what the other ones get. *Discrepancy* works nicely. That eliminates choice **(E)** *paradox*—this is not contrary to what might be expected. Choice **(D)** *irritation* is very tempting but wrong. Although this situation is certainly irritating, choice **(F)** *disparity* better matches your prediction of "discrepancy." The final blank will describe the department in a manner similar to "underfunded," with which it is paired. You can therefore reject choices **(G)** *widespread* and **(I)** *newsworthy* as being incorrect. That leaves **(H)** *needy*, which matches well with "underfunded."

7. E

This is an Inference question. The correct answer, though not directly stated in the passage, must follow from the text. Take the choices one by one and ask what the author is trying to persuade you to believe. Choice **(A)** is not implied. Historians may speculate, but no one can know whether Scott's expedition would have gone any differently without Amundsen in the race. The passage does not support choice **(B)**; it doesn't evaluate Scott's abilities as an explorer. You can cross **(C)** off the list: there is no evidence that the author subscribes to fate or destiny. Cross off **(D)**, too. Though the race was of national significance, the author does not describe Norway's response to victory. Choice **(E)** matches the tone of the passage, which portrays Scott's struggles in a heroic light despite his failure to reach the South Pole first. Choice **(E)** is the correct answer.

8. E

The correct answer to this question will follow from the passage. While the reader may or may not come to the conclusion expressed in choice **(A)**, the author makes no evaluation of which expedition was more "climactic." Choice **(B)** is an irrelevant comparison; the author says nothing to imply which explorer had greater desire or motivation. Choice **(C)** seems reasonable but misses the scope of the passage. The author doesn't attribute Amundsen's success or Scott's failure to "preparation" or "common sense." Choice **(D)** is too harsh to find support in this passage. The author doesn't attribute any sinister motives to either explorer. That leaves choice **(E)**, which you know is the correct answer. While the author never makes this statement directly, he tells you that Amundsen was "trying to beat" Scott and that Scott was "demoralized" to have arrived at the pole after Amundsen.

9. E

A question stem that asks us to "support" an argument is asking you to *strengthen* the argument, which means you want an answer choice that makes the author's conclusion *more likely* to come about, either by introducing additional evidence or shoring up potential flaws in the author's argument.

So what potential flaws does this author have? Well, the author employs a subtle shift in terminology. His main piece of evidence is a study about babies that listened to Mozart from a very young age; however, his conclusion in the last sentence recommends the broader category of "classical music." Someone looking to criticize this argument could easily say, "Perhaps Mozart's music has some special educational qualities, and other classical music would not produce the same effects." Therefore, since you are asked to strengthen the argument, the best way to do so would be to shore up this flaw and find an answer choice that says other classical music will produce the same proven results as Mozart.

Choice **(E)** matches that prediction perfectly, citing similar results from other classical composers. It is correct.

The wrong answer choices all step outside the scope in various ways: choices **(A)** and **(D)** continue to sing the praises of Mozart, but don't bring in those other classical composers we were looking for; choice **(B)** discusses development of high school students rather than young children; and choice **(C)** is completely off base, as the viability of these studies is not a point at issue here.

10. C

To call the social worker's conclusion into question, the first step is to find it, which is easily located here by using the key word "concluded" in the last sentence of the stimulus. Since the social worker concludes that the home is safer than the hospital (for giving birth, at least), you'll want to find an answer choice that gives some reason why the home might *not* be as safe as it seems.

The extensive information in this question stem is fertile ground in which to make a solid prediction: The social worker's study showed that substantial complications arose in a larger proportion of hospital births than home births. But what if the women who gave birth in hospitals were otherwise predisposed to complications in some way? If there were such a factor, the extra complications in the hospital births could be explained by non-location-related reasons, and the social worker's argument would be weakened.

Choice **(C)** matches the prediction well: in stating that women in the study who knew they might have complications *chose* to give birth in hospitals, the hospital is not necessarily more dangerous than the home.

Although choices **(A)**, **(B)**, **(D)**, and **(E)** all place speculations on home and/or hospital births one way or the other, none of them so directly attacks the social worker's evidence—none even mentions the study—and so all are incorrect.

11. B, E

You don't need to know who Caligula was to be able to answer this question: you simply need to recognize how he is being described, and be able to follow the direction the sentence is taking. Caligula is characterized as being remembered for "bacchanalian feasts," which are basically drunken revelries. This is reinforced by the fact that the participants indulged in "every form of excess." Therefore, you can predict that the blank, which describes Caligula, will mean something like "glutton." Choices **(D)** *puritans* (morally strict persons) and **(F)** *ascetics* (those who renounce worldly indulgences) can both be rejected. Choice **(A)** *gadflies* are "irritating people," so that doesn't fit in this context. Choice **(B)** *sybarites* are people devoted to luxury and pleasure, so that one certainly works. That leaves choices **(C)** *philanthropists* ("humanitarians") and **(E)** *wantons* ("those who live luxuriantly"). Humanitarians aren't necessarily people who indulge in excess, and *wantons* creates a sentence with a meaning similar to the one created by *sybarites*. They're your answers.

12. A, E

The word "as," after the semicolon, is a straight-ahead road sign, indicating that the sentence will continue its original direction. You have to figure out how Arthur looked upon seeing his wife, based on the fact that seeing her filled him with "elation." "Elation" means "exultant gladness," so a good prediction for the blank would be *happy*. That allows you to get rid of choice **(B)** *esurient*, which means "hungry," and **(D)** *pensive*, which means "thoughtful," as those don't work in this context. Choices **(C)** *peevish* ("annoyed") and **(F)** *execrable* ("detestable") have strongly negative meanings, so they're the opposite of what you need. Choices **(A)** *ebullient* ("high-spirited") and **(E)** *ecstatic* ("delighted") both create sentences that say Arthur was happy when he saw his wife.

13. C, D

The phrase "for all his" that begins the sentence is a detour road sign that sets up a contrast. When Cedric has a good reason to talk, he becomes taciturn ("quiet"). Therefore, when he has no particular reason to talk, he probably "babbles on" or "chatters idly." You can therefore reject choices that describe meaningful, articulate, or pithy speech. Choices **(A)** *oratories* and **(B)** *declamations* are both "eloquent public speeches," so they are the opposite of what you need. Choice **(E)** *epigrams* are witty sayings, so you can reject that as well. Choice **(F)** *opining* has a neutral charge, so that is wrong. Choices **(C)** *palaver* and **(D)** *blather* are both words that describe meaningless chatter. They're the correct answers.

14. B, D

"Despite" is a classic detour road sign indicating that the sentence will change direction. You're told that the weather is bad, which normally puts people in a "foul" mood, so the blank must have a meaning opposite of that because of the detour road sign. "Happy" works well. Based on that prediction, you can reject **(A)** *disconcerted*, as that means "upset," and **(E)** *histrionic*, as that means "melodramatic." Choice **(C)** *garrulous* means "chatty," so that does work in this context, but no other answer choice creates a similar sentence. Choice **(F)** *sententious* means "given to excessive moralizing," so that doesn't work in this context. Choice **(B)** *jocund*, meaning "jolly," works and creates a sentence similar to the one created by **(D)** *genial* (warm and friendly.) They're your answers.

15.   C

This Global question asks you to identify the main point of the passage. To determine the correct answer, you will need to examine each choice one by one. While **(A)** refers to one of the major reasons for the reversal of the Chicago River, it is not a major point of the passage because it does not address the main subject of the passage, which is the Chicago River itself. Similarly, **(B)** does not reference the main subject. It refers to one of the issues that helped launch the project to reverse the river, but not the actual river. Choices **(C)**, **(D)**, and **(E)** each reference the Chicago River, but only **(C)** mentions it as a major engineering feat, making **(C)** the best choice. **(D)** and **(E)** reference only minor components of the passage (specific details of the project).

16.   A, C

This Function question asks you to evaluate the statements and identify the one(s) that states *why* the river-reversal project was considered a great engineering feat. Choice **(A)** can be inferred because the passage uses words such as "solid" to describe the bedrock and "complex" to describe the process of connecting the rivers. These words suggest that the job was difficult. Choice **(B)** cannot be inferred because the passage does not compare the Chicago River project to any others. Choice **(C)** can be inferred because the statement references a section of the passage that states that

the project seemed impossible but in the end it was successful.

17.   A

This is an Evaluation question that rewards you for identifying the statement that does *not* follow from the passage. That means that each of the four wrong answers is stated or implied in the text. Choice **(E)** is a benefit of the project implied by the section of the passage that states that untreated sewage no longer flowed into Lake Michigan after the river was reversed. Choice **(D)** is a result of the project stated directly in the passage. Choice **(C)** also paraphrases the passage, which stated directly that the city's water became "safer." Choice **(B)** follows from the passage's first sentence: the Chicago project "is considered one of the greatest engineering feats." Choice **(A)** distorts the passage. Engineers didn't "cure" the diseases mentioned in the passage; they made it possible to prevent them in Chicago's drinking water.

18.   E

To answer this question, you must reexamine the passage and determine which of the choices is *not* supported by the passage—often these questions require very careful thinking. Choice **(A)** is the first one you can eliminate because it directly paraphrases the statement in the first sentence of the paragraph about the reason the Hague Convention was adopted. Likewise for choice **(B)**, which is confirmed by the quote taken from the convention's preamble, stating that "each people makes its contribution to the culture of the world." Choice **(C)** refers to the example of the dispute over ownership of the Dead Sea Scrolls following the Six Day War. Choice **(D)** follows from the second sentence of the passage. The Hague Convention is overseen by UNESCO, which, as the name implies, is a division of the

United Nations. Choice **(E)**, however, directly contradicts the latter portion of the passage, which states that the Hague Convention is difficult to enforce. Therefore, this is the correct answer.

19. "Terse reports on serious, weighty issues such as the war in Iraq are juxtaposed with trivial information, such as celebrity gossip."

This sentence is the only one in the passage that offers a concrete example. The other likely candidate, "This leaves the viewer unable to emotionally respond to something traumatic, as he is bombarded with disparate pieces of information in rapid succession," describes the result. That doesn't answer the question, which calls for a sentence that illustrates *how* mass media has such an effect.

20. A, C

This question is asking you to infer Postman's position from what the brief selection tells you about his views. Choice **(A)** is correct because the author noted that Postman thought "instant access to a glut of information" reduced meaningful context for that information. Thus, he would likely apply this reasoning to newer information technology that has the same effect. Choice **(B)** is subtly wrong. Postman, you're told, thought television, *as a medium*, incapable of fostering intelligent discourse; you cannot conclude that he, therefore, thinks that no intelligent discourse appears in any television program. In fact, part of Postman's problem with the medium is that serious topics are juxtaposed with frivolous items. Postman would definitely agree with the statement in choice **(C)**. Given his views on television, as a medium, and those in the final sentence of the passage, you can infer that he believes that media influence how information is interpreted.

DIAGNOSTIC TOOL

Tally up your score and write your results in the space provided.

Total

Total Correct: _____ out of 20 correct

Percentage Correct: # you got right × 100 ÷ 20: _____

By Question Type

Text Completion _____ out of 6 correct

Sentence Equivalence _____ out of 4 correct

Reading Comprehension _____ out of 10 correct

Diagnose Your Results

Look back at the questions you got wrong and think about your experience answering them.

VERBAL REASONING PRACTICE SET 5

Directions: For each sentence, choose one word for each set of blanks. Select the word or words that best fit(s) the meaning of the sentence as a whole.

1. A responsible business owner may easily feel _____ between her concern for the well-being of her employees and the challenges of financial shortfalls.

   - (A) affinity
   - (B) tension
   - (C) uneasiness
   - (D) trepidation
   - (E) dejection

2. The controversy surrounding the election dragged on for months, and the lack of a definite victor _____ governance and left people anxious about the future of their leadership.

   - (A) facilitated
   - (B) augmented
   - (C) forestalled
   - (D) lowed
   - (E) abetted

3. The busboy was known for his diligence rather than his celerity. During his shifts, he worked (i)_____ when cleaning up after customers. Though the chef initially found it annoying, he came to appreciate having things done thoroughly rather than (ii)_____.

Blank (i)	Blank (ii)
(A) perfunctorily	(D) haphazardly
(B) sedulously	(E) expediently
(C) desperately	(F) disingenuously

4. The colonel believed that even a minor (i)_____ the rules demanded his attention. It could not go (ii)_____ if he were to maintain discipline. In his eyes, obedience and order were of the utmost importance.

Blank (i)	Blank (ii)
Ⓐ adherence to	Ⓓ unappreciated
Ⓑ respect for	Ⓔ unobserved
Ⓒ infraction of	Ⓕ unpunished

5. Jurisprudence requires a dispassionate approach on the part of the judge or arbiter. Law and custom require that a definite (i) _____ be made in every case, regardless of how strong the winning argument seems. Therefore, a judge is forced to behave as if a verdict is (ii)_____. This is true even when, in fact, the evidence may not be (iii)_____.

Blank (i)	Blank (ii)	Blank (iii)
Ⓐ deadlock	Ⓓ negotiable	Ⓖ conclusive
Ⓑ dispute	Ⓔ irrelevant	Ⓗ accessible
Ⓒ determination	Ⓕ self-evident	Ⓘ substantiated

6. As a result of poor planning and disorganization, the young team (i)_____ attacking the root of the problem. This went on until there was no other recourse left to them. They were obliged to (ii)_____ a (iii)_____, last-minute solution to the problem.

Blank (i)	Blank (ii)	Blank (iii)
Ⓐ expedited	Ⓓ implement	Ⓖ measured
Ⓑ postponed	Ⓔ envision	Ⓗ premeditated
Ⓒ accelerated	Ⓕ reject	Ⓘ desperate

Questions 7–9 are based on the following passage.

Painting is a process that is ordinarily associated with a brush and a palette, but as an artist who was far from ordinary, Jackson Pollock used neither when creating some of his most famous works. Pollock (born in 1912) is one of the most influential figures in American painting. His unique style of painting and artistic point of view made him stand out from his contemporaries. Pollack painted in an entirely abstract manner. Instead of using an easel, he placed his canvases on the floor or against a wall. Employing a "drip and splash" method, Pollack poured and dripped his paint from the can onto the canvas. Instead of brushes, he manipulated the paint with sticks and knives. Pollack's works created a new, "all-over" style of painting in which there is no focal point and no differentiation is made between areas of the painted surface. His scattered painting style may be a reflection of his unstable mental state, as he was known to battle depression and alcoholism. While his volatile personality may have contributed to his legacy, Pollock will primarily be remembered for his tremendous contributions to the art world.

Select only one answer choice.

7. The primary purpose of this passage is to address which of the following issues related to Pollock as an artist?

   Ⓐ How he developed his unique style

   Ⓑ How his methods influenced future artists

   Ⓒ Whether his personal life affected his work

   Ⓓ How his methods affected the art world's concept of art

   Ⓔ Whether he should be revered for his work

8. The passage states each of the following EXCEPT:

   Ⓐ Pollock's work was similar to that of his peers.

   Ⓑ The all-over painting method placed no importance on any particular piece of the painting.

   Ⓒ Pollock suffered from mental health issues.

   Ⓓ Pollock's "drip and splash" method created art without the use of conventional painting tools.

   Ⓔ Pollock's legacy will reflect his artistic ability.

9. Based on the information in the passage, which word best describes Pollock as an artist?

   Ⓐ Plain

   Ⓑ Gloomy

   Ⓒ Inventive

   Ⓓ Literal

   Ⓔ Traditional

Question 10 is based on the following passage.

In the field of Kafka studies and its various related subfields, perhaps the most controversial figure is Max Brod, Franz Kafka's publisher, biographer, and closest friend. Although it is thanks to Brod that we possess any of Kafka's writing—Kafka only allowed his writing to be published at Brod's insistence and had asked Brod to burn all his writing upon his death, which Brod did not do—Brod is considered by many Kafka specialists and enthusiasts to have possessed a meager understanding of his friend's writing and importance. A prolific writer, Brod's writing has in time been greatly overshadowed by Kafka's, and many find his compositions to be blunt and crude when compared to Kafka's abstruse elegance; this contrast was further emphasized by their personalities, with Brod being gregarious and a notorious womanizer, whereas Kafka was withdrawn and shy. Based on this contrast, many in the field of Kafka studies feel that Brod—being the only channel through which we know Kafka—in some ways tainted the "pure" Kafka in the editorial process, and the search for unpublished manuscripts of Kafka (free of Brod's influence) has become for many an obsession.

10. According to the passage, why is Max Brod described as a "controversial figure"?

   Ⓐ Although Brod was Kafka's closest friend, many wonder if Kafka objected to Brod's editorial alterations of his writing.

   Ⓑ Because of the divergence of their upbringings, Brod and Kafka had difficulty seeing eye to eye with one another.

   Ⓒ Although he is the only source of Kafka's writings, Brod is thought to have poorly understood Kafka's writing.

   Ⓓ Brod's lascivious behavior repulsed Kafka, who wished for someone more refined to edit his work.

   Ⓔ Upon Kafka's death, Brod burned all of Kafka's remaining writings, suggesting that he did not properly recognize his friend's incredible talent.

Directions: For each of the following questions, choose two of the answer choices that, when used to complete the sentence, produce two completed sentences that are similar in meaning.

11. Terrance was _____ student, always eager to participate and try his best; unfortunately, his low test scores did not reflect his efforts.

   ☐ A ☐ a pedantic

   ☐ B ☐ an animated

   ☐ C ☐ an apathetic

   ☐ D ☐ a pragmatic

   ☐ E ☐ an assiduous

   ☐ F ☐ a prudent

12. In addition to having sharp teeth and claws, the maned wolf emits _____ musk, which acts as a defense mechanism in the wild.

    A   a malodorous

    B   a pristine

    C   a soporific

    D   a pungent

    E   an estimable

    F   a charming

13. The first baseman and shortstop were both talented players with Hall of Fame credentials, but their _____ relationship exacerbated the chaos in the locker room.

    A   venerable

    B   prudent

    C   volatile

    D   stolid

    E   inimical

    F   stoic

14. Although the old woman had lived through the Great Depression, she _____ spent her money on her grandchildren, giving them everything she didn't have growing up.

    A   liberally

    B   scrupulously

    C   capriciously

    D   meticulously

    E   lavishly

    F   flintily

Questions 15 and 16 are based on the following passage.

Few babies born to HIV-infected mothers carry the disease *in utero*, even though HIV is a blood-borne virus and there is a constant flow of blood through the umbilical cord that could infect the growing fetus. As genetic testing has demonstrated, this is because the human fetal immune system may develop separately from the adult immune system, and it may provide a measure of protection. When exposed to foreign cells, immune cells "activate" to become T-cells, which defend the organism. Fetal T-cells seem to be more tolerant of HIV and do not cause the reactions typically seen in HIV infection; these cells recognize the foreign cells but do not fight them, and the virus is not stimulated to destroy the T-cells, as happens when an individual has full-blown AIDS.

15. Which sentence provides the best summary of the passage?

    (A) Foreign cells cannot enter fetuses' bloodstreams as easily as they can enter the bloodstreams of adults.

    (B) The reason few fetuses contract HIV from infected mothers is that their mothers' T-cells protect them.

    (C) The fetal immune system may not be similar to the adult immune system.

    (D) T-cells affected by HIV are not activated in the fetal immune response and therefore remain more tolerant of foreign cells.

    (E) Fetuses do not contract HIV *in utero* because the fetal immune system operates differently than the adult system.

Consider each of the following choices separately and select all that apply.

16. Which of the following statements are suggested by the passage?

    [A] Fetuses are better protected from HIV than their mothers because of their respective immune systems.

    [B] If researchers could find a way to stop T-cells in adults from activating, adults would have the same health benefit as fetuses.

    [C] Fetal immune systems are more complicated than those of adults.

Questions 17 and 18 are based on the following passage.

While days of the chain gang are long gone, the effects of meaningful labor during imprisonment demonstrate marked benefits to both the prisoner and society. Some of these benefits take the forms of reduced recidivism, increased job skills and employability, and improved quality of life. In fact, corporations have hired jails to have their inmates perform work from manufacturing to telemarketing. However, some critics argue that prisoners who work are little more than bonded slaves, earning nothing for their labor and forced to do work that may be beyond their physical or mental capacity.

Others are more concerned about the economic factors of cheap, noncompetitive labor or issues involved in giving inmates responsibility for critical components of products or providing them with lists of addresses and telephone numbers.

17. The author would most likely agree with which of the following sentences?

    (A) Working may offset deleterious psychological conditions to which prisoners are exposed.

    (B) Too many lawsuits filed against jails involve prisoners being forced to perform work they are not physically equipped to handle.

    (C) Telemarketing corporations are the main entities that stand to profit from inmates working for free or at low cost.

    (D) People in jail lack the mental skill needed to perform more challenging work.

    (E) Adjusting the current model of inmate labor to have prisoners work for money or reduced sentences would improve the penal system.

18. Choose the sentence in the passage that provides support for the main argument.

Questions 19 and 20 are based on the following passage.

The current worldwide economic recession has forced state governments to reevaluate how tax dollars should be spent. A recent statement from the Iowa State legislature indicated that they were considering cutting state-funded sabbaticals for professors working within the publicly funded Iowa University system. The justification has been that this is an inefficient use of funds, which could be better allocated elsewhere or cut out of the tax code. Critics cited the high cost of paying a professor's salary for the entire year in which they do not work. They also suggested that taxpayers should not pay for professors to take time off from teaching to write a book on a subject such as ancient mythology. There is a strong counterargument, however, which points out that not all faculty sabbaticals are, by necessity, unprofitable. Aside from the benefit of the increase of knowledge, it is not entirely clear how a sabbatical may, ultimately, return on its investment. A genetics professor who, during her sabbatical, discovers a new drug treatment methodology, for example, could potentially generate millions of dollars in grant money for the university's research department.

19. Which of the following is likely to be an opinion of the author of this passage?

    (A) Public funding for sabbaticals should be cut.

    (B) The value produced by a faculty sabbatical cannot be determined prior to the sabbatical.

    (C) Professors should only teach, not engage in outside research.

    (D) The goal of a university should be to conduct abstract research that leads to practical applications.

    (E) The study of genetics is a more worthwhile pursuit than that of mythology.

Consider each of the following choices separately and select all that apply.

20. Which of the following statements is suggested by the passage?

    A   As a result of the sabbatical system, universities are doing less meaningful research than they once did.

    B   As a state, Iowa has a lower percentage of professors whose primary responsibility is teaching.

    C   Some state legislators feel that taxpayers should not have to indirectly pay for research that will not benefit them.

PRACTICE SET 5 ANSWER KEY

1. B
2. C
3. B, E
4. C, F
5. C, F, G
6. B, D, I
7. D
8. A
9. C
10. C
11. B, E
12. A, D

13. C, E
14. A, E
15. E
16. A
17. A
18. *"Some of these benefits take the forms of reduced recidivism, increased job skills and employability, and improved quality of life."*
19. B
20. C

PRACTICE SET 5 ANSWERS AND EXPLANATIONS

1. B

The sentence tells you that a relationship exists between concerns for the well-being of employees and the challenges of financial shortfalls. The two are being contrasted, so a reasonable prediction would be *stress*. Scanning the answers, you'll notice choice **(B)** *tension*, which is a synonym for stress, fits perfectly. Choice **(A)** *affinity* is the opposite of the prediction. Choice **(C)** *uneasiness* is close but does not address the conflict between the two concern as well as *tension*. Choices **(D)** *trepidation* and **(E)** *dejection* are too negatively charged for this context; nothing in the sentence indicates that the business owner is frightened or sad, respectively.

2. C

The people are anxious because they do not know who will be leading them, which will *limit* or *hinder* leadership or governance; your answer will reflect this. Choices **(A)** *facilitated*, **(B)** *augmented*, and **(E)** *abetted* all have meanings of "strengthened" or "increased." Choice **(D)** *lowed* might be tempting because it resembles "lowered," but the verb "low" means to make the sound of a cow. Choice **(C)** *forestalled* is the only option that means "restricted" or "slowed down."

3. B, E

The detour road sign "rather than" indicates that the busboy has one of two contrasting qualities: "diligence" ("thoroughness") rather than "celerity" ("speed"). He is not quick, yet he is thorough. The chef initially disliked the busboy's work habits, but the detour road sign "though" indicates that he has come to like them, since thoroughness can be more important that rapidity. For the first blank, you need a word that means something like thoroughly. Choice **(B)** *sedulously*, which means "perseveringly," works well. Choice **(A)** *perfunc-*

torily "superficial" is the opposite of what you need, and **(C)** *desperately* doesn't make any sense in this context. There is more information available on the second blank. The word "rather" appears again as a detour road sign. The sentence mirrors the earlier contrast in the question. The chef has come to appreciate the busboy's thoroughness even though the busboy isn't *fast*. Choice **(E)** *expediently* means "quickly," and matches the prediction perfectly. Choice **(D)** *haphazardly* means "sloppily." While someone who works too fast might be sloppy, nothing in these sentences implies that the busboy's work has this characteristic.

4. C, F

You read that the colonel wants to "maintain discipline" and that order is of paramount importance to him. From that context, you can determine that a *breaking of* the rules will not be tolerated. Make this your prediction for the first blank. For the second, predict that this could not go *unpunished*. For the first blank, the best match is choice **(C)** *infraction of*. Both choices **(A)** *adherence to* and **(B)** *respect for* are the opposite of your prediction. The best fit for the second blank is choice **(F)** *unpunished*. Choice **(D)** *unappreciated* doesn't make sense in context, and if the infraction was *unobserved*, choice **(E)**, the colonel wouldn't know about it: "The colonel believed that even a minor *infraction of* the rules . . . could not go *unpunished* if he were to maintain discipline."

5. C, F, G

Here, "law and custom" require that something definite be made in a courtroom—predict *verdict* for the first blank. If a verdict must be reached, predict that the judge may have to assume that a verdict is *always possible* when, in fact, the evidence might not be *compelling*. For the first blank, choice **(A)** *deadlock* might have sounded tempting, since you often hear about "deadlocked juries," but this is the opposite of what you need. A *dispute*, choice **(B)**, is what is settled in a courtroom, not what is reached there. The best choice here is choice **(C)** *determination*. For the second blank, you can rule out choice **(E)** *irrelevant* immediately, since the verdict is the most relevant thing in a courtroom. You might have initially liked choice **(D)** *negotiable* because sometimes the outcomes of trials are negotiated, but once a verdict is reached, it might be appealed but it cannot be negotiated. Choice **(F)** *self-evident* is the best choice for the second blank. For the third blank, while it's not an exact match to your prediction, the most logical choice is **(G)** *conclusive*. It's illogical to say that the evidence may not be *accessible*, choice **(H)**, or *substantiated*, choice **(I)**; without at least some evidence, there generally wouldn't even be a trial. "[Because] law and custom require that a definite *determination* be made, . . . a judge is forced to behave as if a verdict is *self-evident*, . . . when in fact, the evidence may not be *conclusive*."

6.   B, D, I

The sentences provide context clues to the missing words. You learn that they did something until only one option remained open to them, something consistent with "a . . . last-minute solution." You're also told that the team was disorganized and that they planned poorly. Since the solution was last-minute, predict that they must have *put off their work* until they had no other recourse than to *attempt* a *frantic* last-minute solution. For the first blank, the best match for your prediction is choice **(B)** *procrastinated*. Choices **(A)** *expedited* and **(C)** *accelerated* are both inconsistent with needing "a . . . last-minute solution." For the second blank, the closest match to your prediction is choice **(D)** *implement*. Choice **(E)** *envision* might have been

tempting, but if all they had to do was *envision* a solution, it doesn't seem that time would have been an issue. And since they waited until the last minute, it isn't likely they'd *reject* a solution, choice **(F)**. For the third blank, the best match for your prediction is choice **(I)** *desperate*. Choice **(G)** *measured* is inconsistent with waiting until the last minute to find a solution, and *premeditated*, choice **(H)**, is the opposite of last minute. "[They] procrastinated . . . until there was no . . . recourse [but to] implement a desperate, last-minute solution to the problem."

7.   D

The correct answer states the passage's primary purpose. The wrong answers will, therefore, miss the main point, either by distorting the scope of the passage or by concentrating on a specific detail from the text. Choice **(A)** is not directly addressed in this passage. While the passage speculates that Pollock's scattered style could be the result of his personality, how the style was originally developed is not addressed. There is also no mention of choice **(B)**; the author doesn't describe *how* Pollack's methods influenced future artists, just *that* they did. Choice **(C)** is mentioned in the passage but is not the primary purpose of the passage; it is only a secondary issue. The primary purpose of this passage is to address choice **(D)**, how Pollack's methods affected the art world. Pollock changed the art world by creating an all-over style of painting. The author gives a lot of credit to Pollock and states that Pollock has made "tremendous contributions to the art world." The author does not address the proper critical response to Pollack, and certainly not whether he should be revered for his work. Therefore, choice **(E)** is not a viable choice.

8.   A

The correct answer to this Detail EXCEPT question is the one with a statement *not* listed in the passage. When describing Pollock's painting methods, the author mentions that Pollock did not use paintbrushes or an easel when employing his "drip and splash" method. As paintbrushes and easels are conventional painting tools, you can determine that **(D)** is true based on the passage and therefore not the correct choice. The author also mentions that the "all-over" style of painting makes no differentiation between areas of the painted surface; therefore, choice **(B)** follows from the passage and is incorrect. Near the end of the passage, the author mentions Pollock's problems with depression and an "unstable mental state" and that he is remembered for these problems. That makes **(C)** and **(E)** incorrect choices. Choice **(A)** actually contradicts the passage. The author states that Pollock's unique style of painting and artistic point of view made him stand out from his contemporaries, implying that Pollock did not mirror his peers or contemporaries. Thus, **(A)** is the correct choice.

9. C

None of these words is in the passage, so you will have to base your choice on context clues. In the beginning of the passage, the author states that Pollock was "far from ordinary," had a "unique style," and created a "new" way of painting. That makes choices **(A)** and **(E)** clearly incorrect. When describing Pollock's artistic point of view, the author states that he paints in an abstract manner. Because "abstract" is an antonym for "literal," **(D)** is not the correct choice. The passage indicates that inventing a new style and new techniques of painting is what Pollock is best known for, making **(C)** the best choice. Choice **(B)** is probably the trickiest wrong answer. The passage mentions that Pollock was depressed, but the question asked how the passage described Pollock *as an artist*, not as a person. The passage doesn't suggest that Pollack's art is "gloomy." Therefore, **(B)** is not a viable choice.

10. C

The reasons Brod is described as a controversial figure are a major focus of this passage, so researching this question should give you little trouble. The correct answer comes from the sentence in which the author tells you what "many in the field" feel about Brod: He was incapable of appreciating Kafka's work despite being its sole caretaker. Choice **(A)**, while saying nothing that directly contradicts the passage, is not supported by the passage, either. No mention is made of Kafka's feelings towards Brod's editing. That's the first choice you can eliminate. Choices **(B)** and **(D)** both possess language not contained in the passage. The passage does not discuss Kafka's and Brod's upbringings or Kafka being "repulsed" by Brod's lifestyle. Choice **(E)** sounds reminiscent of the passage, but the passage describes Kafka's wish to have his writing burned, a wish Brod denies. Choice **(E)** misstates this situation and is, thus, also incorrect. Choice **(C)**, however, paraphrases the concern of those in the field who believe that Brod did not really comprehend Kafka's writing (although he saw its importance). That is the correct answer.

11. B, E

The key to this question is the detour road sign "unfortunately." Terrance's low test scores are the exact opposite of what you would expect from a student such as him. You know he is an eager student who always tries his best and participates in class; any of these positive associations could fit in the blank. This allows you to immediately eliminate choice **(A)** *pedantic* "stodgy" and **(F)** *prudent* "restrained," which are direct opposites of our predictions. Choice **(C)** *apathetic* can be rejected for the same reason. Contrasting Terrance's ability with his idealistic actions eliminates choice **(D)** *pragmatic*, which means "realistic as opposed to idealistic." The remaining two answer choices, **(B)** *animated,* "lively" and **(E)** *assiduous,* "persistent," both create sentences that describe the type of student who would continue to participate in class when he is not experiencing success.

12.   A, D

If the maned wolf's musk acts as a "defense mechanism," it probably smells pretty bad. So you can predict *foul-smelling* for the blank. For this reason, you can eliminate choice **(B)** *pristine* "fresh," "uncorrupted," which suggests the exact opposite of a foul musk, and choice **(E)** *estimable* "admirable," which suggests only a positive attitude toward the smell. Choice **(F)** *charming* can be rejected for similar reasons. Choice **(C)** *soporific* is completely irrelevant to the sentence, as sleep is not indicated anywhere in the context. Choices **(A)** malodorous, "bad-smelling," and **(D)** *pungent* "sharp-smelling" best fit your original prediction of *foul-smelling*.

13.   C, E

Reading this sentence all the way through reveals that the missing word describes a relationship that "exacerbates," or "worsens," a chaotic situation. For this reason, you can immediately eliminate choices **(A)** *venerable* and **(B)** *prudent*, as they characterize a relationship as respectful and restrained, the opposite of the relationship described here. Choice **(D)** *stolid* "unemotional, lacking sensitivity" seems plausible at first glance, as it suggests a negative relationship. Likewise for choice **(F)** *stoic*, "indifferent to pleasure or pain." However, the context key word "chaos" sentence suggests an emotional (albeit negative) relationship. Therefore, choice **(C)** *volatile* "easily aroused" and **(E)** *inimical* "hostile" are the best choices. They indicate the hostile, chaotic relationship that the sentence suggests.

14.   A, E

"Although" is a detour road sign, indicating that the sentence will change direction. So, although

the woman lived through the Great Depression, she can now give her grandchildren the things she couldn't afford growing up. Choice **(F)** *flintily* is wrong, as this implies she was not kindly disposed to spending money. This reasoning also eliminates choices **(B)** *scrupulously* and **(D)** *meticulously* as these imply a restraint with money. Choice **(C)** *capriciously* is plausible, but implies a carelessness that is not evidenced in the passage. Therefore, choice **(A)** *liberally* and choice **(E)** *lavishly* are the best choices, as they indicate exuberant spending, opposite of the frugality typical of the Depression.

15.   E

In this question, you are asked to select the best summary of the passage. The main idea of the passage is that fetal immune systems do not operate in the same way as adult immune systems, and that provides protection from HIV to the developing fetus. Choice **(E)** paraphrases that summary and is indeed the answer. Choice **(A)** is not true according to the passage; HIV can enter the bloodstream, but the T-cells are tolerant and don't activate, which allows the HIV to pass through without attacking the T-cells. Choice **(B)** is outside the scope; nothing is said in the passage about the mothers' T-cells. Choice **(C)** is true according to the passage, but it is not a complete summary. The critical component of HIV resistance is not included in this choice. Choice **(D)** gets the facts from the passage wrong. According to the passage, T-cells activate in the fetal immune system but do not fight HIV in the typical way.

16.   A

This question asks you to evaluate the statements and select those that can be validly inferred from the passage. Choice **(A)** summarizes the passage's main point. It's one correct answer. Choice **(B)** seems reasonable, but the passage doesn't go this far. Differences between the adult and fetal immune systems beyond their respective responses to HIV may make this statement untrue. There is nothing in the passage to suggest that choice **(C)** is a valid inference. The passage does not compare the complexity of the adult and fetal immune systems.

17. A

This question asks you to evaluate possible explanations and compare them to your understanding of the information in the passage. Choice **(A)** follows from that portion of the passage in which the author tells you that prisoners see "quality of life" improvements as the result of working. Choice **(B)** falls completely outside the scope of the passage. The author says nothing about lawsuits challenging prison work programs. Choice **(C)** distorts the passage. Telemarketing is one of the jobs prisoners perform, but so is manufacturing (and maybe others). Nothing suggests that telemarketing firms have the most to gain from using prison labor. Choice **(D)** is cited as a concern of some critics, but nothing suggests that the author agrees with them. Nor can you determine whether the author would agree with choice **(E)**. The suggestion in **(E)** might address the concerns of some critics, but again, you don't know that the author shares those concerns.

18. "Some of these benefits take the forms of reduced recidivism, increased job skills and employability, and improved quality of life."

This sentence supports the main claim that is set up in the first sentence: "While days of the chain gang are long gone, the effects of meaningful labor during imprisonment demonstrate marked benefits to both the prisoner and society." The remainder of the passage contains counterarguments and their supporting evidence.

19. B

This question rewards you for paying attention to the author's attitude and opinions. For the most part, this author takes a neutral tone. He states facts and reports the debate over sabbaticals, but doesn't appear to take a side in that debate. Choice **(A)** is one of the sides in the debate. Nothing in the passage suggests that the author agrees with the anti-sabbatical crowd. Choice **(B)** is the correct answer. The author points out that it is not clear, prior to a sabbatical, whether the result will be profitable. He offers the biotechnology example to illustrate this point. Choice **(C)** is wrong because the author doesn't opine on this issue; he suggests a defense of research through his inclusion of the biotechnology example. Choice **(D)** is the flip side of **(C)**; while the author is positively disposed to research, nothing suggests that he considers it the sole (or even primary) mission of universities. You can reject choice **(E)** as a comparison irrelevant to the scope of this passage.

20. C

This question asks you to evaluate the statements and identify which you can infer from the passage. Choice **(A)** is incorrect because it goes beyond the scope of what the passage implies; nowhere does the author say that there is insufficient research being done within the university system or ascribe blame to the sabbatical system. Choice **(B)** may be tempting, but it is wrong. The passage employs the Iowa debate to illustrate the point, but it doesn't provide any information that compares Iowa to other states. Choice **(C)** is the only correct answer. The author mentions the example of a professor writing a book on ancient mythology during sabbatical to imply that some legislators may not consider that an adequately beneficial work product.

DIAGNOSTIC TOOL

Tally up your score and write your results in the space provided.

Total

Total Correct: _____ out of 20 correct

Percentage Correct: # you got right × 100 ÷ 20: _____

By Question Type

Text Completion _____ out of 6 correct

Sentence Equivalence _____ out of 4 correct

Reading Comprehension _____ out of 10 correct

Diagnose Your Results

Look back at the questions you got wrong and think about your experience answering them.

VERBAL REASONING PRACTICE SET 6

Directions: For each sentence, choose one word for each set of blanks. Select the word or words that best fit(s) the meaning of the sentence as a whole.

1. After getting expelled from school, Patricia refused to attend any future family functions, petrified that her stern family would _____ her.

   (A) venerate

   (B) stigmatize

   (C) vex

   (D) emulate

   (E) deride

2. The filmmaker's highly controversial work was a _____ in bringing the style of Dogme 95 to the forefront of the film industry.

   (A) lament

   (B) anachronism

   (C) catalyst

   (D) anomaly

   (E) paradox

3. Male sperm whales, recognizable by their astonishing size, are normally (i)_____ creatures; however, when they are jealously guarding their territory, they have been known to (ii)_____ ships that they feel have encroached too far.

Blank (i)	Blank (ii)
(A) docile	(D) ignore
(B) aggressive	(E) follow
(C) powerful	(F) attack

4. Opponents of affirmative action by quota, the practice of hiring on the basis of race or sex as well as (i)_____, maintain that both the hired and the rejected suffer (ii)_____ when not judged on their abilities alone.

Blank (i)	Blank (ii)
Ⓐ status	Ⓓ nepotism
Ⓑ creed	Ⓔ parity
Ⓒ competence	Ⓕ injustice

5. Ancient Greek philosophers tried to (i)_____ contemporary notions of change and stability in the physical composition of the world around them. They did so by (ii)_____ the existence of the atom. For them, the atom was (iii)_____ particle from which all varieties of matter are formed.

Blank (i)	Blank (ii)	Blank (iii)
Ⓐ reconcile	Ⓓ denying	Ⓖ a mythical
Ⓑ eliminate	Ⓔ ignoring	Ⓗ an indivisible
Ⓒ confirm	Ⓕ postulating	Ⓘ a munificent

6. As a general rule, feuds between individuals or groups tend to arise in societies that (i)_____ centralized government because public justice, such as the kind meted out by a strong, centralized authority or sophisticated judicial system, is difficult to (ii)_____. In such societies, it is therefore not surprising that private recourse is more (iii)_____.

Blank (i)	Blank (ii)	Blank (iii)
Ⓐ espouse	Ⓓ identify	Ⓖ objectionable
Ⓑ lack	Ⓔ enforce	Ⓗ effective
Ⓒ affirm	Ⓕ recognize	Ⓘ brutal

Questions 7 through 8 are based on the following passage.

Ludwig Wittgenstein asserted that with the publication of his *Tractatus Logico-Philosophicus* he had solved all philosophical problems and retired to teach mathematics at the secondary level. He believed he had achieved this through his exploration of the logic of language, which he referred to as his "picture theory" of language. Wittgenstein's contention was that the world consisted of a collection of interconnected "facts" that created "pictures" of the world through propositions. These propositions are meaningful if they picture matters of empirical fact, such as "Meri is six feet tall."

In order for these linguistic pictures to accurately represent facts, they must have the same logical structure as matters of empirical fact.

The problem is that philosophical propositions, such as "Truth is beauty," are not matters of empirical fact. Since language itself is based on this relationship, philosophers cannot extricate themselves from the realm of language in order to actually *say* anything about whether or not the "pictures" have the same logical structure as the facts. One important consequence of this argument is that it is nonsensical to discuss philosophical problems. The propositions that philosophers commonly make are not technically wrong but nonsensical. For Wittgenstein, the ultimate goal of philosophy itself is not the actual study or pursuit of "truth." Philosophy has more to do with clarifying the relationship between language and truth than truth itself. The *Tractatus* ends up subverting its own claims by concluding that the kind of propositions of which it is composed are senseless. The most commonly quoted excerpt from the book is the proposition, "What we cannot speak about we must pass over in silence."

7. The author believes Wittgenstein would likely agree with which of the following statements?

   (A) The truth is not beautiful.

   (B) Beauty is not truthful.

   (C) Something cannot be both truthful and beautiful.

   (D) The proposition "Truth is beauty," is nonsensical.

   (E) Beauty is the same as truth.

8. Based on the context of the passage, the author's use of the word "empirical" most nearly means which of the following?

   (A) Verifiable by experimentation

   (B) True

   (C) Subjective

   (D) Nonsensical

   (E) Typical

Question 9 is based on the following passage.

According to a recent study, advertisements in medical journals often contain misleading information about the effectiveness and safety of new prescription drugs. The medical researchers who wrote the study concluded that the advertisements could result in doctors' prescribing inappropriate drugs to their patients.

9. The researchers' conclusion would be most strengthened if which of the following were true?

- (A) Advertisements for new prescription drugs are an important source of revenue for medical journals.

- (B) Editors of medical journals are often unable to evaluate the claims made in advertisements for new prescription drugs.

- (C) Doctors rely on the advertisements as a source of information about new prescription drugs.

- (D) Advertisements for new prescription drugs are typically less accurate than medical journal articles evaluating those same drugs.

- (E) The Food and Drug Administration, the government agency responsible for drug regulation, reviews advertisements for new drugs only after the ads have already been printed.

Question 10 is based on the following passage.

Marcus Tullius Cicero was a Roman statesman and philosopher in the final years of the Republic and remains one of the greatest and most influential orators in Western history. Among his many famous tracts and speeches, one of the most remarkable remains the first Catilinarian Oration, a condemnation of the senator Lucius Sergius Catiline for his role in a conspiracy against the Republic. Enraged at having lost the election for consulship the previous year to Cicero, his political rival, Cataline wove a plot to assassinate Cicero and several other senators to ensure his victory in the election of 63 BCE. When the plot was uncovered and foiled, the election was postponed, and the Senate meeting moved to a more secure location the following day to discuss the conspiracy. Cataline arrived at the Senate, shocking the entire Senate, but Cicero quickly recovered and delivered the first Catilinarian Oration, a masterpiece of oratory skill, which prompted the rest of the Senate to denounce Cataline as a traitor. Cataline fled the city with his conspirators and was killed a year later in battle with Republican soldiers.

10. What is the topic of this passage?

- (A) The works of Marcus Tullius Cicero
- (B) The effects of the first Catilinarian Oration
- (C) The Catilinarian conspiracy
- (D) The first Catilinarian Oration
- (E) Famous orations

Directions: For each of the following questions, choose two of the answer choices that, when used to complete the sentence, produce two completed sentences that are similar in meaning.

11. Many Americans in the 1950s may have found the idea of a black president _____, but society has changed in many ways since then.

    - [A] farcical
    - [B] puerile
    - [C] superannuated
    - [D] implausible
    - [E] perfidious
    - [F] fastidious

12. Located in what is perhaps the most geographically remote state in the Union, Hawaii's isolated Molokai Island is known for its hidden, untouched, and _____ beaches.

    - [A] morose
    - [B] immaculate
    - [C] dilapidated
    - [D] placid
    - [E] pristine
    - [F] imperturbable

13. Hot yoga, a practice that takes place in a 95-degree-plus room, clears toxins out of the body through perspiration, leaving a practitioner with a sense of _____.

    - [A] disarray
    - [B] turbulence
    - [C] purgation
    - [D] quintessence
    - [E] ablution
    - [F] exhilaration

14. The doctor told Joe he needed to lose weight, so he began to make more _____ choices when going out to dinner.

     A   abstemious

     B   detrimental

     C   gluttonous

     D   acerbic

     E   loquacious

     F   austere

Question 15 is based on the following passage.

One of the most famous and influential music theorists of the latter half of the 20th century, John Cage is remembered for being to music what Marcel Duchamp was to art—someone who constantly questioned what defined music. One of his best-known interests was in removing the creator, the personal influence, from music and instead creating music based on natural patterns and chance (aleatory music). One of his famous works involved music created by laying musical bars over astrological maps and assigning notes based on the location of the stars and planets. Another famous work (perhaps his most famous), 4'33", consisted of three movements all entirely of rests: the music, rather, was created by the ambient sounds of and around the performance hall. His stated goal was to remove personal agency and purpose from music and let music act as a reflection of the natural chaos of the world, rather than as an effort to organize and improve nature.

15. According to the passage, which of the following best paraphrases John Cage's philosophy of music?

     Ⓐ   Music must be radically changed from our current notions.

     Ⓑ   Music should be based in nature rather than on individual purpose.

     Ⓒ   Music is not really anything, but rather whatever we wish it to be.

     Ⓓ   Music is a reflection of the personal agency of the composer.

     Ⓔ   Music is inherently without meaning.

Questions 16–18 are based on the following passage.

Coffee has long been the subject of research due to its popularity as an early-morning pick-me-up and its distinct taste and aroma. Although it has often been laden with a reputation for being potentially unhealthy, many studies have shown that the opposite is true; in fact, coffee has been tied to a wide range of benefits. The acid in coffee can contribute to heartburn, and the caffeine can raise blood pressure, but when consumed in moderation (a few regular cups a day), these disadvantages are minimized.

Although coffee was once linked to cancer, that association has long been dispelled. Instead, coffee may contribute to the prevention of certain types of cancers due to its high volume of antioxidants. Minerals found in coffee, like magnesium and chromium, help the body control blood sugar by influencing insulin, and this may contribute to preventing diabetes. Similarly, although researchers aren't sure why, coffee drinkers seem to have a better chance than do non–coffee drinkers of fighting off Parkinson's disease and dementia as they age. In the short term, coffee is low in calories, stimulates alertness and concentration, and, for some people, lengthens their attention spans.

16. Which statement best summarizes the reading passage?

- Ⓐ The more coffee a person consumes, the healthier he or she will be.
- Ⓑ The benefits of drinking coffee appear to outweigh the disadvantages.
- Ⓒ Drinking coffee can prevent Parkinson's disease and dementia.
- Ⓓ Coffee consumption is unrelated to the incidence of cancer.
- Ⓔ Caffeine is the cause of high blood pressure.

Consider each of the following choices separately and select all that apply.

17. What can you infer from the passage?

- ☐ A Decaffeinated coffee offers the same benefits as caffeinated coffee.
- ☐ B If they are high in antioxidants, berries can help prevent cancer.
- ☐ C Insulin has an effect on diabetes.

18. The author would most likely disagree with which of the following statements?

- ☐ A Stimulants are inherently bad for the human body.
- ☐ B It is possible for coffee to be a part of a healthy diet.
- ☐ C Decaffeinated coffee does not have the same benefits as caffeinated coffee.

Questions 19 and 20 are based on the following passage.

In December 2010, the Federation Internationale de Football Association (FIFA), the global governing body of soccer, announced that the 2022 World Cup would be held in Qatar. Immediately, a swirl of controversy surrounded the decision, which followed previous allegations that certain FIFA members had accepted monetary bribes in exchange for their bid votes. Soccer fans questioned how Qatar was able to win the bidding process over other bidders, such as the United States, Australia, South Korea, and Japan. In addition to the logistical problem of oppressive heat during the summer months in which the World Cup is traditionally held, Qatar is a controversial choice because of allegedly discriminatory legislation and its restrictive alcohol policy, which some claim is at odds with the activities typical of a sporting event. Additionally, Qatar would have to build venues for the event from scratch. Nonetheless, FIFA officials insist that this furthers the goal of spreading soccer to new places.

19. Which of the following is likely to be an opinion of the author of this passage?

    (A) FIFA is a corrupt and unethical organization.

    (B) It is improbable that Qatar will be adequately prepared for the 2022 World Cup.

    (C) Japan was most deserving of winning the 2022 World Cup bid.

    (D) Qatar is a controversial choice to host the 2022 World Cup.

    (E) Soccer fans will be unlikely to travel to Qatar for the 2022 World Cup.

Consider each of the following choices separately and select all that apply.

20. Which of the following statements is suggested by the passage?

    [A] FIFA is likely to face criticism and come under scrutiny in the following months.

    [B] The country of Qatar is likely to change in some ways as a result of hosting the 2022 World Cup.

    [C] The choice of Qatar to host the 2022 World Cup is enough evidence to abolish FIFA and replace it.

PRACTICE SET 6 ANSWER KEY

1.	B	11.	A, D
2.	C	12.	B, E
3.	A, F	13.	C, E
4.	C, F	14.	A, F
5.	A, F, H	15.	B
6.	B, E, H	16.	B
7.	D	17.	B, C
8.	A	18.	A
9.	C	19.	D
10.	D	20.	A, B

PRACTICE SET 6 ANSWERS AND EXPLANATIONS

1. B

Using what you know about the "stern family" and their feelings toward failure, you can assume the blank will be a word with some negative connotation. You can also deduce this negative aspect by Patricia's fear ("petrified") of seeing her family. This eliminates choices **(A)** *venerate* and **(D)** *emulate*, as they both indicate positive feelings. Choice **(C)** *vex* "annoy" can also be eliminated, as it indicates Patricia's irritation towards her family, which is not evidenced by the context. Choice **(E)** *deride* "to speak ill of" seems plausible; she may fear being teased. However, the reference to her "stern family" indicates a severity of feeling. Therefore, choice **(B)** *stigmatize* "disgrace or shame" captures the attitude of the family toward her expulsion.

2. C

The key to this sentence is the relationship of the film to the film style of Dogme 95. We can predict the word *start* for the blank. For that reason, you can eliminate choice **(A)** *lament* "expresses grief," as it directs attention to the past, not the future as is the case in this sentence. Similarly, you can eliminate choice **(E)** *paradox* "a contradiction," which is irrelevant to the beginning of a new fad. Choices **(B)** *anachronism* and **(D)** *anomaly* are both plausible, as a controversial work is likely to be out of place. However, choice **(C)** *catalyst* "something that brings about a change in something else" is the correct answer; it best fits your predicted word *start*, and it directly describes the relationship between the film and the change in the film industry.

3. A, F

The first word here will describe what type of creatures male sperm whales normally are. The detour road sign "however" between the clauses indicates that a contrasting point will be made. In the second clause, we learn that something happens when the whales "are jealously guarding their territory." Predict that the whales *attack* ships when they're guarding their territory and are *gentle* when they're not. For the first blank, choice **(A)** *docile* is the best match for your prediction; choices **(B)** *aggressive* and **(C)** *powerful* are more descriptive of the whales when they're guarding their territory. For the second blank, choice **(F)** *attack* is a perfect match for our prediction: "Male sperm whales . . . are normally *docile* creatures; however, when they are jealously guarding their territory, they have been known to *attack* ships."

4. C, F

For the first blank, there are a few clues to pay attention to. The phrase set off with commas will define "affirmative action by quota." The road sign "as well as" directly before the blank tells us that there is a basis upon which people are being hired other than race or sex. Because the rest of the sentence states that people suffer when they are not judged on their abilities alone, the missing word in the first blank must mean *abilities*. The second blank will have a negative connotation, since the opponents believe that people "suffer" from it. For the first blank, the best match is choice **(C)** *competence*. Choice **(A)** *status* and choice **(B)** *creed* have no necessary connection to the idea of ability. For the second blank, choice **(D)** *nepotism* means "favoritism for family members," which, while it might have a negative connotation, is not related to affirmative action by quota. Choice **(E)** *parity* means "equality," which has a positive connotation. The best choice for the second blank is choice **(F)** *injustice*: "Opponents of affirmative action by quota, the practice of hiring on the basis of race or sex as well as *competence*, maintain that both the hired and the rejected suffer *injustice* when not judged on their abilities alone."

5.   A, F, H

These philosophers were trying to do something with the notions of "change and stability." The first thing you should notice is that change and stability are starkly opposing ideas, so predict that they were trying to *harmonize* the two ideas. The way they tried to do this was to do something concerning the existence of a particle that could explain both change and stability—predict *hypothesizing*. You're told that this particle is the atom from which all varieties of matter are formed, which would include both changing and stable things. The third blank will describe the atom in some way. This blank is difficult to predict, so you'll need to evaluate the answer choices in context. For the first blank, choice **(A)** *reconcile* is a good match for your prediction. Neither choice **(B)** *eliminate*, nor choice **(C)** *confirm*, takes into account the opposing forces of change and stability. In the second blank, choice **(F)** *postulating* matches your prediction. Neither choice **(D)** *denying* the existence of the atom, nor choice **(E)** *ignoring* it, would have helped the philosophers reconcile the concepts of change and stability. Moving on to the third blank, choice **(G)** *mythical* doesn't work—these philosophers didn't see atoms as the stuff of myth, but rather as a plausible hypothesis. Choice **(H)** *indivisible* seems promising—although you now know that atoms can be split, this was not known at the time of the Greek philosophers—but check choice **(I)** just in case. *Munificent* means

"generous" or "bountiful"; this wouldn't be a logical way to describe a particle.

6.   B, E, H

The word "because" is a straight-ahead road sign that indicates a close connection between the first two clauses. The first clause tells you that feuds tend to arise in societies that have a certain relationship with centralized government. In the second clause, you learn more about these societies—there is something difficult about public justice in them. The second sentence, in turn, tells you that this difficulty has an effect on the concept of "private recourse." These must be societies that *don't have* strong, centralized governments—because "public justice is difficult to *obtain*," private recourse becomes "more *common*." For the first blank, choice **(B)** *lack* matches your prediction. Societies that *espouse*, choice **(A)**, or *affirm*, choice **(C)**, central governments are the opposite of what you're looking for. For the second blank, the best fit is choice **(E)** *enforce*. It doesn't make sense to say that "public justice is difficult to *identify*," choice **(D)**, or *recognize*, choice **(F)**. For the third blank, *effective*, choice **(H)**, while not an exact match for your prediction, works best in context. Choice **(G)** *objectionable* is the opposite of what you need here: you may find the concept of "private recourse" objectionable, but those in the societies referred to in the sentence would not. Choice **(I)** *brutal* is not supported by the information in the sentence: "Feuds tend to arise in societies that *lack* centralized government; when public justice is difficult to *enforce*, private recourse is more *effective*."

7.   D

The passage itself is largely concerned with the philosophical relationship between logical reasoning and language. The author notes that Wittgenstein distinguishes between propositions that are "pictures" of empirical fact, and those that are not. The statement "Truth is beauty," falls into the latter category. Since it is a matter of nonempirical fact, you cannot determine if the linguistic picture (the proposition "Truth is beauty.") has the same logical structure as the fact itself. Therefore it is nonsensical. Choice (D) is your answer.

8. A

The word "empirical" has the meaning of "measurable." That's close to choice (A) *verifiable by experimentation*, which makes sense in the context of the passage. You can't measure truth or beauty, but you can measure how tall someone is, which is cited as an example of an empirical fact.

9. C

This question stem asks you to find an answer choice that would strengthen the researchers' conclusion outlined in the second sentence of the stimulus: the researchers believe that misleading drug advertisements in medical journals might lead doctors to prescribe the wrong drugs. Any answer choice that makes this *more* likely will be correct; therefore, look for a choice that further suggests doctors will end up prescribing inappropriate drugs based on misleading ads.

Choice (C) does this perfectly. By asserting that doctors actually depend on the advertisements for information, it strengthens the bond between the researchers' evidence and their conclusion and therefore strengthens their argument. Choice (A) is outside the scope of this issue—the journals' revenues have no direct connection to the prescribing of drugs. Choice (B) critiques the wrong party—even if *editors of medical journals* can't discern true claims from false, maybe doctors still can. Neither choice (D) nor (E) tells you anything

new. Both support the notion that advertisements are inaccurate or misleading, but the falsehood of the ads is already established in the passage, so neither (D) nor (E) will further strengthen the researchers' argument regarding actual prescriptions.

10. D

Remember: the topic is the general area of the passage, while the scope is the specific purpose or focus of the passage—you should have already determined these before you began attacking the question or questions following the passage. In the case of this passage, some of the choices are *too* broad to be the topic—choice (A) is too broad because only one of Cicero's works is discussed, and likewise for (E) because only one oration is discussed. Choice (C) relates to the passage, but it is the setting of the passage, not the topic. Choices (B) and (D) may look similar, but you should be able to choose between them—(B) is too narrow to be the topic and is more akin to a possible scope. Choice (D) is the correct answer because it describes the general topic of the passage (the first Catilinarian Oration) rather than specific aspects of it.

11. A, D

You can use the word "but" in the sentence to deduce that the environment in the 1950s was not the same as it is now. In other words, Barack Obama became the first African-American to be elected president of the United States in 2008, and the phrase "but society has changed" in the sentence implies that Americans in the 1950s would not have expected such an occurrence. Choice (E) *perfidious* "faithless," "disloyal," "untrustworthy" and (F) *fastidious* "careful with details" can both be ruled out. These are words more likely to be used to describe people than events and ideas and would thus not make sense in this context.

While **(B)** *puerile*, which means "childish, imma- ture, or silly," could be used to describe an occurrence or event, it wouldn't make sense to describe an election of a president. Choice **(C)** *superannuated* describes something that is out-of-date or obsolete, which would be in conflict with the idea of social progress. That leaves choice **(A)** *farcical* "absurd," "ludicrous" and **(D)** *implausible* "improbable," "inconceiv- able". Both these words render a sentence that means about the same thing. At the beginning of the Civil Rights Movement, people would have found the idea of a black president far- fetched, rendering it both absurd and incon- ceivable during that era.

12. B, E

You can infer from the words "isolated," "hid- den," and "untouched" that the blank must be in line with these adjectives. It wouldn't make sense for a beach to be hidden, untouched, and **(A)** *morose* "gloomy and sullen" or **(C)** *dilapidated* "in disrepair or run-down," so you can eliminate these choices. Choices **(D)** *placid* "calm" and **(F)** *imperturbable* "incapable of being disturbed" are both tempting options because it is possible that an isolated beach would be both of these things. But the sen- tence doesn't rule out the possibility that the beaches could be less than placid, and just because a beach hasn't been touched yet doesn't mean it is immune from being dis- turbed in the future. You are left with choice **(B)** *immaculate*, "without stain or flaw," and **(E)** *pristine* "untouched," "uncorrupted," which are both synonyms of the adjectives used else- where in the sentence and therefore the cor- rect answers.

13. C, E

If your body has been cleared of toxins through sweating from exercise, there is no reason to believe that you would feel a sense of **(A)** *disar- ray* or **(B)** *turbulence*, which are both terms for disorder. Additionally, choice **(D)** *quintessence*, doesn't make sense in this context, since it is a word for a most typical example or concen- trated essence. **(F)** *exhilaration* may seem like a plausible choice if you or a friend has ever described yoga as leaving you in a state of being energetic or filled with happiness. But nothing from this particular sentence implies that a person would feel especially happy after finishing a hot yoga session. Rather, this sen- tence highlights the fact that sweating plays a role in cleansing a person's body. Therefore, the correct choices are **(C)** *purgation* "the pro- cess of cleansing or purification" and **(E)** *ablu- tion* "the act of cleansing".

14. A, F

If Joe is making an effort to lose weight, it would be in his best interest to make healthy choices when going out to dine. Therefore, making a **(C)** *gluttonous* "tending to eat and drink excessively" or a **(B)** *detrimental* "caus- ing harm or injury" choice for dinner would be the opposite of what he should be doing. He may choose an **(D)** *acerbic* "bitter," "sharp in taste" dish for dinner, but there's no telling if that would be a healthy or unhealthy choice. Because the adjective in question applies to food, choice **(E)** *loquacious* makes no sense since it means "talkative." This leaves choices **(A)** *abstemious* "moderate in appetite" and **(F)** *austere* "stern," "strict", which make sense when describing a selection that someone on a diet would make.

15. B

The key to understanding this question is to determine how the author of the passage describes John Cage's approach to music. In the passage, the author describes Cage as being concerned with "removing the creator, the personal influence, from music and instead creating music based on natural patterns." This points immediately to choice **(B)**, a paraphrase of this statement. That answer is correct, but you should take care to eliminate the other options to ensure your correct response. Choice **(A)** may seem to describe Cage's radical departure from traditional music, but the departure itself is not described as his motivation. Choices **(C)** and **(E)** are, in essence, paraphrases of one another, claiming that music has no real definition. While this relates to Cage's question of what defined music, neither choice correctly describes his philosophy of music. Choice **(D)** is clearly incorrect because it directly contradicts the paraphrase of the passage seen in **(B)**. Choice **(B)** is the correct answer.

16. B

While the general sentiment of this passage appears to be in support of coffee, it does not state that the benefits are proportionate to consumption as outlined in choice **(A)**. In fact, it recognizes that there are downsides to drinking coffee and implies that drinking it to excess could exacerbate these problems by saying that the disadvantages are minimized when coffee is consumed in moderation. Instead, choice **(B)** is the statement that most closely aligns with the message of the passage. The use of the word "appear" acknowledges the fact that there are still unknowns about coffee that researchers are studying. Although the passage states that coffee may help a person fight off Parkinson's disease and dementia, you can infer from the passage that the link is merely a correlation and not necessarily a cause-and-effect relationship, rendering **(C)** inaccurate. The passage states that coffee does not *cause* cancer, as was once believed,

but that it's now known to have some properties that help fight cancer, which means choice **(D)** is false. Choice **(E)** isn't correct because, although caffeine can be a cause of high blood pressure, it is certainly possible that someone with a low caffeine intake can have high blood pressure as well.

17. B, C

This question asks you to evaluate the statements and identify what you can infer, using material from the passage. Taking each individually, choice **(A)** may be true, but this particular passage does not address research done on both varieties of coffee. Because the antioxidants in coffee help contribute to fighting cancer, it can be inferred that choice **(B)** is correct because any other food or drink that contains antioxidants would carry the same properties. Similarly, you may deduce that if blood sugar impacts diabetes, and the magnesium and chromium in coffee interact with a person's insulin, thereby changing a person's blood sugar, choice **(C)** *insulin has an effect on diabetes* is correct.

18. A

While the passage does recognize one downside of caffeine as a stimulant (high blood pressure), it also points out a handful of benefits (higher levels of alertness and concentration as well as longer attention spans.) Therefore, the author is likely to disagree with choice **(A)**. It is likely that the author would agree with choice **(B)**, since coffee has been "tied to a wide range of benefits." Although there is no evidence to say that the author would disagree with choice **(C)**, because the author doesn't address research on different types of coffee, you can't infer anything about whether or not the author would disagree with that statement.

19. D

This question rewards you for correctly summarizing the author's scope and purpose in writing the passage. For the most part, this author remains objective despite reporting a controversial decision. Choice **(A)** is the attitude of some critics of the decision to have Qatar as host, but the author doesn't express agreement with the critics. The passage claims that Qatar will need to build facilities, but the author doesn't assess the likelihood that the country will or will not be ready for the World Cup by 2022; thus, choice **(B)** is incorrect. The author cites other countries that some felt were deserving, but doesn't himself state a preference for who should host the Cup; that knocks out choice **(C)**. Choice **(D)** is the correct answer. Without acknowledging whether the criticism is warranted, the author states that Qatar is a controversial choice. Choice **(E)** is out of scope; the likelihood that fans will attend the World Cup in Qatar simply isn't addressed in the passage.

20. A, B

This question asks you to evaluate the statements and identify any and all that you can infer, using material from the passage. Choice **(A)** follows from the passage, which reports that FIFA has already been criticized for its decision. Choice **(B)**, too, follows from the passage. Whether there are cultural or political changes as a result of hosting this global event, Qatar will at least have new stadiums and infrastructure, which the passage says must be built in anticipation of 2022. Choice **(C)** is far too extreme to qualify as a correct answer. The most rabid critics may feel this way, but nothing in the passages offers such a strong opinion.

DIAGNOSTIC TOOL

Tally up your score and write your results in the space provided.

Total

Total Correct: _____ out of 20 correct

Percentage Correct: # you got right × 100 ÷ 20: _____

By Question Type

Text Completion _____ out of 6 correct

Sentence Equivalence _____ out of 4 correct

Reading Comprehension _____ out of 10 correct

Diagnose Your Results

Look back at the questions you got wrong and think about your experience answering them.

PART THREE

Verbal Content Review

CHAPTER 6

Vocabulary

UNDERSTANDING VOCABULARY

Overview

A strong vocabulary is the greatest asset you can bring to the GRE Verbal Reasoning sections. Text Completion and Sentence Equivalence questions reward you for knowing the meanings of a large number of words. Similarly, the passages in the Reading Comprehension section contain dense, complex passages and are accompanied by questions that require you to determine the meaning of words and sentences from context.

Building a good vocabulary takes time—a lifetime for most people. However, you can increase your GRE vocabulary quickly. There are a few reasons for this:

1. The GRE tests the same words repeatedly.

Knowing the words that the GRE Test Makers love to use gives you a big head start in increasing your GRE vocabulary. We have included the words that appear most often on the GRE in this chapter in the "Words in Context" section. Start learning the meanings of these words as soon as you can.

2. The GRE does not test the exact definitions of words. If you have some idea of what the word means, you can usually determine the correct answer.

You don't need to know the exact definitions of words to achieve a good verbal score on the GRE. It's better to know something about ten words than everything about one word. This is why learning words in groups is a powerful technique. We have included common word groups found on the GRE in this chapter.

Knowing the meanings of common word roots can be helpful in two ways. First, knowing the meaning of word roots can help you guess at the meanings of unfamiliar words you encounter on the GRE. Second, when you're learning new vocabulary, it's more effective to study words in groups rather than individually. Learning several words that are related by a common root will help you to learn more words faster. We have included a list of common GRE word roots in this chapter.

Once you've looked over the top GRE words and the sections on word groups, roots, and words in context, you can hone your skills using the exercises that follow each section.

Basics of Vocabulary Building

The way most people build their vocabularies is by reading words in context. Reading is ultimately the best way to increase your vocabulary, although it also takes the most time. Of course, some types of reading material contain more GRE vocabulary words than others. You should get into the habit of reading high-level publications, such as the *Wall Street Journal*, the *Economist*, and the *New York Times*. (Because you'll have to read from the computer screen on test day, we recommend you read these publications online, if possible. And if you read lengthy articles that require scrolling, so much the better.)

WORD GROUPS

Learning words in groups is an efficient way of increasing your GRE vocabulary, since the GRE often tests only the general sense of a word. Assume you saw the following Sentence Equivalence question on the test:

The prime minister _____ the actions of the cabinet member; her sanctimonious tone indicated that she wanted to put distance between herself and the lurid implications of the scandal.

- denounced
- rephrased
- extirpated
- maligned
- impugned
- exculpated

If you looked up *denounce* in a dictionary, you'd see something like this:

de•nounce (dî-nouns′) transitive verb, de•nounced, de•nounc•ing, de•nounc•es [Middle English: denouncen, denounsen, fr. Latin denoncier, fr. de + nuntiare to report, announce, fr. nuntius messenger]

1. To declare (a person, an idea, behavior, a philosophy) to be censurable or evil; stigmatize or accuse, especially publicly and indignantly; inveigh against openly
2. *archaic* to announce in a public, formal, and solemn manner: to declare or publish something disastrous
3. to inform against: declare or expose a lawbreaker to the authorities
4a. *obsolete* to indicate or portend
4b. *archaic* to announce in a warning or threatening manner
5. to proclaim formally and publicly the ending of a treaty or pact
6. *Mexican Law* to offer for record legal notice of a claim for a mining concession on land held by the government

Synonym see CRITICIZE

Do you need to know all this to answer the question? No—all you need to know is that *denounce* means something like "criticize." And in the time it took you to learn the meaning of *denounce* from the dictionary, you could have memorized a whole list of other words that also mean something like "criticize": *aspersion, berate, calumny, castigate, decry, defame/defamation, denounce, deride/derisive, diatribe,* **impugn**, *rebuke,* and others. Note that *impugn* is in this list: this Sentence Equivalence question is made dramatically easier! This is why learning words in groups is a better general strategy for beefing up your GRE vocabulary than working slowly through the dictionary.

Just remember, the categories in which these words are listed are *general* and not to be taken for the exact definitions of the words.

BOLD

| audacious | courageous | dauntless |

CHANGING QUICKLY

| capricious | mercurial | volatile |

HESITATE

| dither | oscillate | teeter |
| vacillate | waver | |

ACT QUICKLY

| abrupt | apace | headlong |
| impetuous | precipitate | |

INNOCENT/INEXPERIENCED

| credulous | gullible | ingenuous |
| naive | novitiate | tyro |

DIFFICULT TO UNDERSTAND

abstruse	ambiguous	arcane
bemusing	cryptic	enigmatic
esoteric	inscrutable	obscure
opaque	paradoxical	perplexing
recondite	turbid	

EASY TO UNDERSTAND

articulate	cogent	eloquent
evident	limpid	lucid
pellucid		

SMART/LEARNED

astute	canny	erudite
perspicacious		

CRITICIZE/CRITICISM

asperity　*censure*　*ignominy / ignominious*

fulmination
fulminate
vehement speech

aspersion	belittle	berate
calumny	castigate	decry
defame/defamation	denounce	deride/derisive
diatribe	disparage	excoriate
gainsay	harangue	impugn
inveigh	lambaste	obloquy
objurgate	opprobrium	pillory
rebuke	remonstrate	reprehend
reprove	revile	tirade
vituperate		

CAROUSAL

indulging in pleasure / corrupt

bacchanalian	depraved *adj*	dissipated *adj*
iniquity	libertine	libidinous
licentious	reprobate	ribald
salacious	sordid	turpitude

TRUTH

candor/candid	fealty	frankness
indisputable	indubitable	legitimate
probity	sincere	veracious
verity		

FALSEHOOD

meretricious

apocryphal	canard	chicanery
dissemble	duplicity	equivocate
erroneous	ersatz	fallacious
feigned	guile	mendacious
mendacity	perfidy	prevaricate
specious	spurious	

slander

BITING (as in wit or temperament)

acerbic	acidulous	acrimonious
asperity	caustic	mordant
mordacious	trenchant	

PRAISE

acclaim	accolade	aggrandize
encomium	eulogize	extol
fawn	laud/laudatory	venerate

homage

panegyric

HARMFUL

redoubtable = to be feared

baleful	baneful	deleterious
inimical	injurious	insidious
minatory	perfidious	pernicious

malign

TIMID/TIMIDITY

lacking self confidence

craven	diffident	pusillanimous
recreant	timorous	trepidation

BORING

soporific = cause sleep

banal	fatuous	hackneyed
insipid	mundane	pedestrian
platitude	prosaic	quotidian *ordinary*
trite		

WEAKEN

adulterate	enervate	exacerbate
inhibit	obviate	stultify
undermine	vitiate	

ASSIST

abet	advocate	ancillary
bolster	corroborate	countenance
espouse	mainstay	munificent
proponent	stalwart	sustenance

HOSTILE / Unfriendly

antithetic	churlish	curmudgeon
irascible	malevolent	misanthropic
truculent	vindictive	

STUBBORN

implacable	inexorable	intractable
intransigent	obdurate	obstinate
recalcitrant	refractory	renitent
untoward	vexing	

BEGINNING/YOUNG

| burgeoning | callow | engender |
| inchoate | incipient | nascent |

GENEROUS/KIND

altruistic	beneficent	clement
largess	magnanimous	munificent
philanthropic	unstinting	

GREEDY

avaricious	covetous	mercenary
miserly	penurious	rapacious
venal		

TERSE
concise

| compendious | curt | laconic |
| pithy | succinct | taciturn |

OVERBLOWN/WORDY

bombastic	circumlocution	garrulous
grandiloquent	loquacious	periphrastic
prolix	rhetoric	turgid
verbose		

DICTATORIAL

authoritarian	despotic	dogmatic
hegemonic	hegemony	imperious
peremptory	tyrannical	

HATRED

abhorrence	anathema	antagonism
antipathy	detestation	enmity
loathing	malice	odium
rancor		

BEGINNER/AMATEUR

dilettante	fledgling	neophyte
novitiate	proselyte	tyro

LAZY/SLUGGISH

indolent	inert	lackadaisical
languid	lassitude	lethargic
phlegmatic	quiescent	slothful
torpid		

PACIFY/SATISFY

ameliorate	appease	assuage
defer	mitigate	mollify
placate	propitiate	satiate
slake		

FORGIVE

absolve	acquit	exculpate
exonerate	expiate	palliate
redress	vindicate	

POOR

destitute	esurient	impecunious
indigent		

FAVORING/NOT IMPARTIAL

ardent/ardor	doctrinaire	fervid
partisan	tendentious	zealot

DENYING OF SELF

abnegate	abstain	ascetic
spartan	stoic	temperate

WALKING ABOUT

ambulatory	itinerant	meander
peripatetic		

INSINCERE

disingenuous	dissemble	fulsome
ostensible	unctuous	

PREVENT/OBSTRUCT

discomfit	encumber	fetter
forfend	hinder	impede
inhibit	occlude	

ECCENTRIC/DISSIMILAR

aberrant	anachronism	anomalous
eclectic	esoteric	discrete
iconoclast		

FUNNY

chortle	droll	facetious
flippant	gibe	jocular
levity	ludicrous	raillery
riposte	simper	

SORROW

disconsolate	doleful	dolor
elegiac	forlorn	lament
lugubrious	melancholy	morose
plaintive	threnody	

DISGUSTING/OFFENSIVE

defile	fetid	invidious
noisome	odious	putrid
rebarbative		

WITHDRAWAL/RETREAT

abeyance	abjure	abnegation
abortive	abrogate	decamp
demur	recant	recidivism
remission	renege	rescind
retrograde		

DEATH/MOURNING

bereave	cadaver	defunct
demise	dolorous	elegy

knell	lament	macabre
moribund	obsequies	sepulchral
wraith		

COPY

counterpart	emulate	facsimile
factitious	paradigm	precursor
quintessence	simulated	vicarious

EQUAL

equitable	equity	tantamount

UNUSUAL

aberration	anomaly	iconoclast
idiosyncrasy		

WANDERING

discursive	expatiate	forage
itinerant	peregrination	peripatetic
sojourn		

GAPS/OPENINGS

abatement	aperture	fissure
hiatus	interregnum	interstice
lull	orifice	rent
respite	rift	

HEALTHY

beneficial	salubrious	salutary

ABBREVIATED COMMUNICATION

abridge	compendium	cursory
curtail	syllabus	synopsis
terse		

WISDOM

adage	aphorism	apothegm
axiom	bromide	dictum
epigram	platitude	sententious
truism		

FAMILY

conjugal	consanguine	distaff
endogamous	filial	fratricide
progenitor	scion	

NOT A STRAIGHT LINE

askance	awry	careen
carom	circuitous	circumvent
gyrate	labyrinth	meander
oblique	serrated	sidle
sinuous	undulating	vortex

INVESTIGATE

appraise	ascertain	assay
descry	peruse	

TIME/ORDER/DURATION

anachronism	antecede	antedate
anterior	archaic	diurnal
eon	ephemeral	epoch
fortnight	millennium	penultimate
synchronous	temporal	

BAD MOOD

bilious	dudgeon	irascible
pettish	petulant	pique
querulous	umbrage	waspish

EMBARRASS

abash	chagrin	compunction
contrition	diffidence	expiate
foible	gaucherie	rue

HARDHEARTED

asperity	baleful	dour
fell	malevolent	mordant
sardonic	scathing	truculent
vitriolic	vituperation	

NAG

admonish	cavil	belabor
enjoin	exhort	harangue
hector	martinet	remonstrate
reproof		

PREDICT

augur	auspice	fey
harbinger	portentous	precursor
presage	prescient	prognosticate

LUCK

adventitious	amulet	auspicious
fortuitous	kismet	optimum
portentous	propitiate	propitious
providential	serendipity	talisman

NASTY

fetid	noisome	noxious

HARSH-SOUNDING

cacophony	din	dissonant
raucous	strident	

PLEASANT-SOUNDING

euphonious	harmonious	melodious
sonorous		

laud = panegyric = praise
homage, tribute, encomium

WORD GROUPS EXERCISE

Directions: Choose the TWO synonyms that can correctly complete the sentence.

[NOTE: While the questions in this exercise are not in GRE format, the task of choosing synonyms is good practice for the kind of thinking rewarded by Sentence Equivalence questions.]

1. The incoming freshman found the 300-level Intermediate Macroeconomic Analysis course _____; he simply did not possess the necessary background knowledge.

   (A) recondite

   (B) ardent

   (C) enigmatic

   (D) noxious

   (E) salubrious

2. The man encountered a series of _____ events on his way to work, from finding $20 on the ground to winning concert tickets off the radio.

   (A) lugubrious

   (B) fortuitous

   (C) gibe

   (D) din

   (E) propitious

3. The accountant became more _____ after she failed to save the company from bankruptcy.

   (A) volatile

   (B) torpid

   (C) lackadaisical

   (D) munificent

   (E) acrimonious

4. Generally, parents punish bad behavior and _____ good behavior in order to teach their children.

   (A) ameliorate

   (B) exculpate

   (C) ribald

   (D) laud

   (E) extol

5. A child may find jokes about bodily functions humorous while an adult finds them _____.

   (A) caustic

   (B) noisome

   (C) pernicious

   (D) odious

   (E) credulous

6. After spending 15 years teaching in the inner city and volunteering at homeless shelters on the weekends, it was clear the teacher was _____.

   (A) clement

   (B) disingenuous

   (C) penurious

   (D) rapacious

   (E) altruistic

7. A _____ melody filled the band room the first time the fourth graders played their chosen instruments.

   (A) sonorous

   (B) strident

   (C) jocular

   (D) diffident

   (E) raucous

8. My sister often found her friend's conversations about celebrities and fashion _____; she was more interested in politics and science.

   (A) hackneyed

   (B) banal

   (C) limpid

   (D) trenchant

   (E) perspicacious

9. The student was able to reduce wordiness and rewrite the paper in such a _____ manner that the page count fell from 20 to 12.

   (A) garrulous

   (B) succinct

   (C) mordacious

   (D) compendious

   (E) arcane

10. After feeding the stray cat every day for a week, I watched the once _____ animal develop the audacity to walk up to my door and wait for food.

    (A) craven

    (B) churlish

    (C) iconoclastic

    (D) truculent

    (E) timorous

11. While the author swore her novel was not intended to _____ a classic novel, the syntax, diction, and plot were identical to a classic work of fiction.

    (A) abridge

    (B) bereave

    (C) emulate

    (D) facsimile

    (E) rescind

12. The professor answered the question in such a _____ way that the student was left confused and without a straightforward explanation.

    (A) respite
    (B) circuitous
    (C) sententious
    (D) oblique
    (E) presage

13. Instead of taking one piece of candy from the bowl, the _____ child took five.

    (A) avaricious
    (B) ingenuous
    (C) salubrious
    (D) dour
    (E) rapacious

14. In order to _____ her crying baby, the mother gently rocked the infant and sang a lullaby.

    (A) abet
    (B) dither
    (C) mollify
    (D) obviate
    (E) placate

15. The biologist was _____ when he spoke about the characteristics of the red-eyed tree frog, because he spent nine years studying the animal in its natural habitat.

    (A) perspicacious
    (B) libidinous
    (C) ersatz
    (D) erudite
    (E) acidulous

16. The executive regretted her _____ action, when it later became clear that she had approved the proposal without having access to complete information.

    (A) precipitate

    (B) impecunious

    (C) discursive

    (D) impetuous

    (E) mordacious

17. The _____ side effects of chocolate ingestion can be extremely detrimental for dogs.

    (A) insipid

    (B) deleterious

    (C) injurious

    (D) irascible

    (E) vexing

18. Adam's bout of bronchitis _____ his ability to get into peak shape for the outdoor track season.

    (A) admonished

    (B) inhibited

    (C) ameliorated

    (D) stultified

    (E) exhorted

19. Being denied a partial scholarship from her dream school proved _____ for Katie because she received a full scholarship to a different school where she met her future husband.

    (A) providential

    (B) serendipitous

    (C) raucous

    (D) scathing

    (E) temporal

20. Her constantly _____ demeanor eventually discouraged Kara's friends from inviting her to social functions.

    (A) irascible

    (B) propitious

    (C) euphonious

    (D) salutary

    (E) querulous

21. The failing economy led the company into an extended _____, resulting in substantial financial losses.

    (A) demise

    (B) precursor

    (C) hiatus

    (D) lull

    (E) recant

22. The teacher's _____ response to the girl's question deterred the student from raising her hand for the rest of the semester.

    (A) caustic

    (B) indigent

    (C) fulsome

    (D) droll

    (E) acerbic

23. Although I've been to her house several times, I've never seen her _____ little cat because he is constantly hiding.

    (A) venal

    (B) insipid

    (C) torpid

    (D) timorous

    (E) diffident

24. It wasn't a surprise that with Kristen's creativity and _____ tastes, her new restaurant was praised as "truly original."

    (A) eclectic

    (B) noxious

    (C) iconoclastic

    (D) morose

    (E) vitriolic

25. Sick of being continually _____ by her mother, Erica decided it was finally time to move out of the house and into her own apartment.

    (A) ascertained

    (B) harangued

    (C) abashed

    (D) admonished

    (E) lulled

26. One of the most simple but _____ things we can do is drink lots of water and stay hydrated.

    (A) lugubrious

    (B) beneficial

    (C) salubrious

    (D) sinuous

    (E) ludicrous

27. Once he realized the inconvenience entailed by holding up his end of the deal, Aaron tried to _____ his promise to help his friend move.

    (A) recant

    (B) lament

    (C) renege on

    (D) curtail

    (E) descry

28. Although many _____ can seem trite and jaded, most of them do have a lot of truth to them.

    Ⓐ aphorisms

    Ⓑ scions

    Ⓒ labyrinths

    Ⓓ advocates

    Ⓔ adages

29. Despite her dreams of exploring South America after graduating college, Caroline settled into a less-than-satisfying office job to _____ her parents.

    Ⓐ abet

    Ⓑ appease

    Ⓒ placate

    Ⓓ stultify

    Ⓔ inhibit

30. Because of the capabilities resulting from scientific advancements, identical twin births are far less of an _____ than they were 50 years ago.

    Ⓐ aberration

    Ⓑ abatement

    Ⓒ ancillary

    Ⓓ anomaly

    Ⓔ accolade

ANSWER KEY FOR WORD GROUPS EXERCISE

1. recondite, enigmatic
2. fortuitous, propitious
3. torpid, lackadaisical
4. laud, extol
5. noisome, odious
6. beneficent, altruistic
7. strident, raucous
8. hackneyed, banal
9. succinct, compendious
10 craven, timorous
11. emulate, facsimile
12. circuitous, oblique
13. avaricious, rapacious
14. mollify, placate
15. perspicacious, erudite
16. precipitate, impetuous
17. deleterious, injurious
18. inhibited, stultified
19. providential, serendipitous
20. irascible, querulous
21. hiatus, lull
22. caustic, acerbic
23. timorous, diffident
24. eclectic, iconoclastic
25. harangued, admonished
26. beneficial, salubrious
27. recant, renege on
28. aphorisms, adages
29. appease, placate
30. aberration, anomaly

ANSWERS AND EXPLANATIONS FOR WORD GROUPS EXERCISE

1. A, C

Recondite and *enigmatic* both mean "confusing." *Ardent* means "strong" or "passionate." *Noxious* means "bad smelling" and *salubrious* means "healthful."

2. B, E

Fortuitous and *propitious* both mean "luck." *Lugubrious* means "sorrow." *Gibe* means "funny" and *din* means "harsh-sounding."

3. B, C

Torpid and *lackadaisical* both mean "lazy" or "sluggish." *Volatile* means "changing quickly." *Munificent* means "assist" and *acrimonious* means "biting" (as in wit or temperament).

4. D, E

Laud and *extol* both mean "praise." *Ameliorate* means "pacify" or "satisfy." *Exculpate* means "forgive" and *ribald* means "carousal."

5. B, D

Noisome and *odious* both mean "disgusting" or "offensive." *Caustic* means "biting" (as in wit or temperament). *Pernicious* means "harmful" and *credulous* means "innocent" or "inexperienced."

6. A, E

Beneficent and *altruistic* both mean "generous" or "kind." *Disingenuous* means "insincere." *Penurious* and *rapacious* both mean "greedy."

7. B, E

Strident and *raucous* both mean "harsh-sounding." *Sonorous* means "pleasant-sounding."

Jocular means "funny" and *diffident* means "timid."

8. A, B

Hackneyed and *banal* both mean "boring." *Limpid* means "easy to understand." *Trenchant* means "biting" (as in wit or temperament) and *perspicacious* means "smart" or "learned."

9. B, D

Succinct and *compendious* both mean "terse." *Garrulous* means "overblown" or "wordy." *Mordacious* means "biting" (as in wit or temperament) and *arcane* means "difficult to understand."

10. A, E

Craven and *timorous* both mean "timid." *Churlish* means "rude" or "hostile." *Iconoclastic* means "destructive" or "unorthodox" and *truculent* means "defiant."

11. C, D

Emulate and *facsimile* both mean "copy." *Abridge* means "to shorten or abbreviate." *Bereave* means "sadden" (especially by a death) and *rescind* means "revoke" or "cancel."

12. B, D

Circuitous and *oblique* both mean "not a straight line." *Respite* means a "gap" or "opening." *Sententious* means "wise" and *presage* means a "prediction."

13. A, E

Avaricious and *rapacious* both mean "greedy." *Ingenuous* means "innocent" or "inexperienced." *Salubrious* means "healthy" and *dour* means "hardhearted."

14. C, E

Mollify and *placate* both mean to "pacify" or "satisfy." *Abet* means "assist." *Dither* means "hesitate" and *obviate* means "weaken."

15. A, D

Perspicacious and *erudite* both mean "smart" or "learned." *Libidinous* means "carousal." *Ersatz* means a "falsehood" and *acidulous* means "biting" (as in wit or temperament).

16. A, D

Precipitate and *impetuous* both mean "acting quickly"; in this case, the context is negative, implying that the executive acted *too* quickly, given the information that was not yet available to her. *Impecunious* means "poor," and *discursive* means "wandering." *Mordacious* means "biting," as in wit or temperament.

17. B, C

Deleterious and *injurious* both mean "harmful." *Insipid* means "boring." *Irascible* means "hostile" and *vexing* means "stubborn."

18. B, D

Inhibited and *stultified* both mean "prevented" or "hindered." *Admonished* means "nagged" or "reprimanded." *Ameliorated* means "made better" and *exhorted* means "strongly urged."

19. A, B

Providential and *serendipitous* both refer to "luck." *Raucous* means "harsh-sounding."

Scathing means "critical" or "harmful." *Temporal* means "of, related to, or limited by time."

20. A, E

Irascible and *querulous* both mean "argumentative" or "irritable." *Propitious* means "favorable." *Euphonious* means "pleasant-sounding" and *salutary* means "beneficial."

21. C, D

Hiatus and *lull* both mean a "pause" or "break." *Demise* means an "end" or "termination." *Precursor* means a "predecessor" and *recant* means to "take back."

22. A, E

Caustic and *acerbic* both mean "biting" or "sharp" (as in sharp-tongued). *Indigent* means "poor." *Fulsome* means "insincere" and *droll* means "funny."

23. D, E

Timorous and *diffident* both mean "timid." *Venal* means "greedy" or "bribable." *Insipid* means "boring" and *torpid* means "lazy" or "sluggish."

24. A, C

Eclectic, meaning "diverse," and *iconoclastic*, meaning "non-conforming" or "challenging the established way," both come from the ECCENTRIC/DISSIMILAR word group. *Noxious* means "toxic" or "nasty." *Morose* means "sad" or "glum" and *vitriolic* means "hurtful."

25. B, D

Harangued and *admonished* both mean "scolded." *Ascertained* means "determined." *Abashed* means "ashamed" or "embarrassed." *Lulled* means "paused" or "calmed."

26. B, C

Beneficial and *salubrious* both mean "healthy" or "beneficial." *Lugubrious* means "somber" or "sorrowful." *Sinuous* means "winding" or "twisting" and *ludicrous* means "absurd."

27. A, C

Recant and *renege* both mean "to take back." *Lament* means "to grieve." *Curtail* means to "limit" or "shorten" and *descry* means to "investigate."

28. A, E

Aphorisms and *adages* are both "sayings." *Scions* are "descendants." *Labyrinths* are "mazes" and *advocates* are "supporters or defenders of a cause."

29. B, C

Recant and *renege on* both mean "to take back." *Abet* means "assist." *Stultify* means "weaken" or "hinder" and *inhibit* means to "slow down" or "restrain."

30. A, D

Aberration and *anomaly* both mean an "abnormality" or "irregularity." *Abatement* means "suppression" or "termination." *Ancillary* means "subsidiary" or "auxiliary." An *accolade* is a "tribute" or "reward."

WORD ROOTS

Introduction to the Word Root List

The following list presents some of the most common word roots—mostly Greek and Latin—that appear in English. Learning to recognize these word roots is a great help in expanding your vocabulary. Many seemingly difficult words yield their meanings easily when you recognize the word roots that make them up. *Excrescence*, for example, contains the roots *ex-*, meaning "out or out of," and *cresc-*, meaning "to grow"; once you know this, the meaning of *excrescence*, an outgrowth (whether normal, such as hair, or abnormal, such as a wart) is easily deduced.

The list concentrates on Latin and Greek roots because these are the most frequently used to form compound words in English, and because they tend not to be self-explanatory to the average reader. Each entry gives the root in the most common form or forms in which it appears in English, with a brief definition. (The definition does not cover all the shades of meaning of the given root, only the most important or the most broadly applicable.) The rest of the entry is a list of some of the common English words derived from this root; this list is only intended to provide a few examples of such words, and not be exhaustive. Some words are naturally found under more than one entry. The words themselves are not defined. We hope the Word Root List will encourage you to turn to the GRE Minidictionary or, better yet, to a complete dictionary.

A, AN   **NOT, WITHOUT**
amoral, anarchy, anomalous, anonymous, aseptic, asexual, atheism, atrophy

AB   **FROM, AWAY, APART**
abdicate, abduct, abhor, abject, abnormal, abrupt, absent, abuse, averse

ABLE, IBLE   **CAPABLE OF, WORTHY OF**
changeable, durable, indubitable, inevitable, infallible, irreducible, laudable, tolerable, variable

AC, ACR   **SHARP, SOUR**
acerbic, acetate, acid, acrid, acrimony, acumen, acute

ACOU   **HEARING**
acoustic

AD, A   **TO**
(Often *d* is dropped and the first letter to which *a* is prefixed is doubled.) adapt, adequate, adumbrate, advocate, accede, adduce,

affiliate, aggregate, allocate, annunciation, appall, arrest, assiduous, attract

AMBI, AMPHI **BOTH, ON BOTH SIDES, AROUND**
ambidextrous, ambient, ambiguous, ambition, ambivalent, amphibian, amphitheater

AMBL, AMBUL **WALK**
amble, ambulance, ambulatory, perambulator, preamble

ANIM **MIND, SPIRIT, BREATH**
animadversion, animal, animate, animosity, equanimity, magnanimity, pusillanimous, unanimity

ANT, ANTE **BEFORE**
ancient, antecedent, antechamber, antediluvian, anterior, anticipate, antiquity

ANTI, ANT **AGAINST, OPPOSITE**
antagonism, anticlimax, antidote, antipathy, antiphony, antipodes, antithesis

AQUA, AQUE **WATER**
aquamarine, aquarium, aquatic, aquatint, aqueduct, subaqueous

ARD **BURN**
ardent, ardor, arson

AUTO, AUT **SELF**
autism, autobiography, autocracy, autograph, automaton, autonomous, autopsy

BEL, BELL **BEAUTIFUL**
belle, embellish

BELL, BELLI **WAR**
antebellum, bellicose, belligerent, rebellion

BEN, BENE **WELL, GOOD**
benediction, benefactor, benevolent, benign

BI, BIN **TWO**
bicameral, bicycle, bifocals, bifurcate, bilateral, binoculars, binomial, biped, combination

BON, BOUN	**GOOD, GENEROUS**	
	bonus, bountiful, bounty, debonair	
BREV, BRID	**SHORT, SMALL**	
	abbreviate, abridge, brevet, breviary, breviloquent, brevity, brief	
BURS	**PURSE, MONEY**	
	bursar, bursary, disburse, reimburse	
CARN	**FLESH**	
	carnage, carnal, carnival, carnivorous, charnel, incarnate	
CAUS, CAUT	**BURN**	
	caustic, cauterize, cautery, encaustic, holocaust	
CED, CESS	**YIELD, GO**	
	abscess, accede, access, accessory, ancestor, antecedent, cession, concede, exceed, excess, intercede, precede, proceed, recede, recess, recession, secede, succeed	
CELER	**SPEED**	
	accelerate, celerity, decelerate	
CENT	**HUNDRED, HUNDREDTH**	
	bicentennial, cent, centennial, centigrade, centigram, centiliter, centimeter, centipede, century, percent	
CHROM	**COLOR**	
	chromatic, chrome, chromosome, monochromatic	
CHRON	**TIME**	
	anachronism, chronic, chronicle, chronological, chronometer, synchronize	
CIRCUM	**AROUND**	
	circumference, circumlocution, circumnavigate, circumspect, circumstance	
CO, COM, CON	**WITH, TOGETHER**	
	coeducation, coefficient, coincide, communicate, communist, compare, concert, concubine, conflict, cooperate, correspond	
CONTRA, CONTRO, COUNTER	**AGAINST**	
	contradict, contrary, controversy, counter, counteract, counterattack, counterfeit, countermand, counterpart, counterpoint, encounter	

CORD, CARD	**HEART**
	accord, cardiac, cardiograph, cardiology, concord, cordial, discord, record
CORP, CORS	**BODY**
	corporate, corps, corpse, corpulent, corpus, corpuscle, corset, incorporation
COSM	**ORDER, UNIVERSE, WORLD**
	cosmetic, cosmic, cosmology, cosmonaut, cosmopolitan, cosmos, microcosm
CRED	**TRUST, BELIEVE**
	accredit, credentials, credible, credit, creditable, credo, credulity, creed, incredible, incredulous
CRYPT	**HIDE**
	apocryphal, crypt, cryptic, cryptography
CULP	**FAULT, BLAME**
	culpable, culprit, exculpate, inculpate
CUMB, CUB	**LIE DOWN**
	concubine, cubicle, incubate, incubus, incumbent, recumbent, succubus, succumb
CYN, CAN	**DOG**
	canine, cynic
DE	**DOWN, OUT, AWAY FROM, APART**
	dehydrate, deject, depend, deport, depress, descend, describe, devalue
DELE	**ERASE**
	dele, delete, indelible
DEXT	**RIGHT HAND, RIGHT SIDE**
	ambidextrous, dexterity, dexterous
DI	**DAY**
	dial, diary, dismal, diurnal, meridian, quotidian

DIA   **THROUGH, ACROSS**
diadem, diagnosis, diagonal, diagram, dialect, dialogue, diameter, diaphanous, diaphragm, diarrhea, diatribe

DIC, DICT, DIT   **SPEAK**
abdicate, benediction, condition, contradict, dedicate, dictate, dictator, diction, dictionary, dictum, ditto, edict, indicate, indict, interdict, malediction, predicament, predicate, predict, valedictorian, verdict

DIS, DI   **AWAY, APART**
disagreeable, discard, discern, disdain, dismay, dismiss, distant, diverge

DOL   **GRIEVE**
condole, condolence, doleful, dolor, indolent

DORM   **SLEEP**
dormant, dormitory

DORS   **BACK**
dorsal, endorse

DUC, DUCT   **LEAD**
adduce, conduce, conduit, deduce, duct, duke, educate, induction, misconduct, produce, reduce, seduce, traduce, viaduct

DULC   **SWEET**
dulcet, dulcified, dulcimer

DUR   **HARD, LASTING**
dour, durable, duration, duress, during, endure, obdurate, perdurable

E, EX, EC   **OUT**
eliminate, emanate, eradicate, erase, evade, evict, evince, exact, excavate, except, excerpt, excise, excite, exclusive, excommunicate, excrescence, execute, exhale, exile, exit

EGO   **SELF**
ego, egocentric, egoism, egotist

EQU   **EQUAL**
adequate, equable, equation, equator, equilibrium, equinox, equivocate

ERR	WANDER
	aberration, errant, erratic, erroneous, error

EU	WELL, GOOD
	eugenics, eulogy, euphemism, euphony, euphoria, euthanasia

FAL	LIABLE TO ERR, TO DECEIVE
	default, fail, fallacy, false, faux pas, infallible

FATU	FOOLISH
	fatuity, fatuous, infatuate

FERV	BOIL
	effervescent, fervent, fervid, fervor

FI, FID	FAITH
	affiance, affidavit, confidant, fealty, fidelity, fiducial, fiduciary

FLAGR, FULG, FULM	BURN, SHINE
	conflagration, effulgent, flagrant, fulgent, fulminate, refulgent

FLECT, FLEX	BEND, TURN
	circumflex, deflect, flex, flexible, inflection, reflect

FUG	FLEE
	centrifuge, fugitive, fugue, refuge, refugee, subterfuge

FUM	SMOKE
	fume, fumigate, perfume

GEN	BIRTH, CLASS, KIN
	congenital, degenerate, engender, eugenics, gender, gene, general, generation, generosity, genesis, genetics, genial, genital, genius, gentile, gentility, gentle, gentry, ingenious, ingenuity, ingenuous, progeny, progenitor, regenerate

GNI, GNO, COGN,	KNOW
	agnostic, cognition, cognizance, diagnosis, gnomic, ignore, incognito,
CONN	prognosis, quaint, recognize, reconnaissance, reconnoiter

GRAM, GRAPH	**WRITE, DRAW**
	anagram, diagram, epigram, epigraph, grammar, grammarian, gramophone, graph, graphic, graphite, phonograph, photograph, program, telegram
GREG	**FLOCK**
	aggregate, congregate, egregious, gregarious, segregate
HAP	**BY CHANCE**
	haphazard, hapless, happen, happily, happy, mayhap, mishap
HEMI	**HALF**
	hemiptera, hemisphere, hemistich
HETERO	**OTHER**
	heterodox, heterodyne, heterogeneous, heterosexual
HOL	**WHOLE**
	catholic, holocaust, hologram, holograph, holistic
HOMO	**SAME (from Greek)**
	homogeneous, homogenize, homologue, homonym, homophone, homoptera, homosexual, homotype
HUM	**EARTH**
	exhume, humble, humility, posthumous
ICON	**IMAGE, IDOL**
	icon, iconic, iconoclast, iconography, iconology
IM, IN	**NOT**
	(Often *n* is dropped and the first letter to which *i* is prefixed is doubled.) illogical, immature, immutable, imperfect, improvident, indigestible, inhospitable, innocuous, intolerant, irrelevant
IN, IM, I	**IN, ON**
	(Often *n* is dropped and the first letter to which *i* is prefixed is doubled.) illuminate, imbibe, immigrate, impact, incantation, induct, infer, irrigate
INTER	**BETWEEN, AMONG**
	intercept, interchange, interfere, interject, interpret, interval
INTRA	**INSIDE, WITHIN**
	intramural, intrastate, intravenous

IT, ITER	**WAY, JOURNEY**
	ambition, circuit, initial, itinerant, itinerary, reiterate, transit

JOC	**JOKE**
	jocose, jocular, jocularity, jocund, joke

JOUR	**DAY**
	adjourn, journal, journey

JUD	**JUDGE**
	adjudicate, judiciary, judicious, prejudice

JUG, JUNCT	**JOIN**
	adjunct, conjugal, conjunction, injunction, junction, junta, subjugate, subjunctive

JUR	**LAW**
	abjure, adjure, conjure, injure, juridical, jurisdiction, jurisprudence, jurist, jury, perjury

JUV	**YOUNG**
	juvenile, juvenilia, rejuvenate

LANG, LING	**TONGUE**
	bilingual, language, linguistics

LAUD	**PRAISE**
	cum laude, laud, laudable, laudatory

LAV, LAU, LU	**WASH**
	ablution, laundry, lava, lavatory, lave

LAX, LEAS, LES	**LOOSE**
	lax, laxative, laxity, lease, leash, lessee, lessor, relax, release

LEC, LEG, LEX	**READ, SPEAK**
	dialect, lectern, lecture, legend, legible, lesson, lexicographer, lexicon

LEV	**LIFT, LIGHT (WEIGHT)**
	alleviation, elevate, leaven, lever, levitate, levity, levy, relieve

LI, LIG	**TIE, BIND**
	ally, league, liable, liaison, lien, ligament, ligature, oblige, religion, rely

LIBER   **FREE**
delivery, illiberal, liberal, liberality, liberate, libertine, livery

LITH   **STONE**
acrolith, lithography, lithoid, lithology, lithotomy, megalith, monolith

LOG, LOQU   **SPEECH, THOUGHT**
biology, circumlocution, colloquial, dialogue, ecology, elocution, eloquent, geology, grandiloquent, interlocutor, locution, logic, loquacious, monologue, obloquy, soliloquy, ventriloquism, zoology

LUC, LUX   **LIGHT (BRIGHTNESS)**
elucidate, lucid, lucubrate, luster, pellucid, translucent

MACRO   **GREAT, LONG**
macrobiotics, macrocephalous, macrocosm

MAG, MAX,   **GREAT**
MAJ, MAS   magistrate, magnanimous, magnate, magnificent, magnify, magniloquent, magnitude, majesty, major, majority, master, maxim, maximum, mistress

MAL   **BAD**
maladroit, malady, malediction, malefactor, malevolence, malice, malinger

MAN, MANU   **HAND**
amanuensis, emancipation, manacle, manage, maneuver, manifest, manipulate, manner, manual, manufacture, manuscript

MAND, MEND   **COMMAND, ORDER**
command, countermand, demand, mandate, mandatory, recommend, remand, reprimand

MEDI   **MIDDLE**
immediate, intermediate, mean, media, median, mediate, medieval, mediocre, medium

MEGA   **LARGE, GREAT**
megalithic, megalomania, megalopolis, megaphone, megaton

MICRO	**VERY SMALL**
	microbe, microcosm, micron, microorganism, microphone, microscope
MIS	**BAD, WRONG, HATE**
	misadventure, misanthropist, misapply, miscarry, mischance, mischief, misconstrue, miscount, misfit, misinterpret
MOLL	**SOFT**
	emollient, mild, mollify, mollusk
MOB, MOM, MOT, MOV	**MOVE**
	automobile, demote, immovable, locomotion, mob, mobile, mobility, mobilize, momentous, momentum, motion, motive, motor, move, mutiny, promote, removable
MON, MONO	**ONE**
	monarchy, monastic, monism, monk, monochord, monogram, monograph, monolithic, monologue, monomania, monosyllable, monotonous
MOR, MORT	**DEATH**
	amortize, immortal, morbid, moribund, mortality, mortgage, mortification, mortuary
MULT	**MANY**
	multiplex, multiply, multitudinous
MUT	**CHANGE**
	commute, immutable, mutability, mutation, mutual, permutation, transmute
NASC, NAT, GNA	**BIRTH**
	cognate, innate, nascent, natal, native, natural, nature, pregnant, renaissance
NAU, NAV	**SHIP, SAILOR**
	astronaut, circumnavigate, cosmonaut, nauseous, nautical, naval, nave, navy
NEO	**NEW**
	neolithic, neologism, neophyte, neoplasm
NIHIL	**NOTHING, NONE**
	annihilate, nihilism

NOC, NOX, NEC	**HARM**
	innocent, innocuous, internecine, noxious, nuisance, obnoxious, pernicious
NOCT, NOX	**NIGHT**
	equinox, noctambulant, nocturnal, nocturne
NOM, NYM	**NAME**
	anonymous, antonym, cognomen, denominator, homonym, misnomer, nomenclature, nominal, nominate, noun, pronoun, pseudonym, renowned, synonym
NON	**NOT**
	nonconformist, nonentity, nonpareil, nonpartisan
NOV	**NEW**
	innovate, nova, novel, novelty, novice, novitiate, renovate
NULL	**NOTHING**
	annul, null, nullify, nullity
OB	**AGAINST**
	obdurate, obliterate, oblong, obloquy, object, obstacle, obstreperous, obstruct
OMNI	**ALL**
	omnibus, omnipotent, omnipresent, omniscient, omnivorous
ONER	**BURDEN**
	exonerate, onerous, onus
OSS, OSTE	**BONE**
	osseous, ossicle, ossiferous, ossify, ossuary, ostectomy, osteopathy
PALP	**FEEL**
	palpable, palpate, palpitation
PAN, PANT	**ALL**
	panacea, pandemic, pandemonium, panegyric, panoply, panorama, pantheon, pantomime
PATH	**SUFFER, FEEL**
	antipathy, apathy, empathy, pathetic, pathology, pathos, sympathy

PEC	**MONEY** impecunious, peculation, pecuniary
PED	**CHILD, EDUCATION** encyclopedia, pedagogue, pedant, pediatrician
PED, POD	**FOOT** arthropod, expedient, impede, pedal, pedestal, pedestrian, pedigree, pediment, tripod
PEL	**DRIVE, PUSH** appellate, appellation, compel, dispel, expel, impel, propel
PEN, PENE	**ALMOST** antepenult, peninsula, penult, penultimate, penumbra
PERI	**AROUND** pericardium, perihelion, perimeter, perineum, periphery, periscope
PHIL	**LOVE** bibliophile, necrophilia, philanthropy, philately, philharmonic, philogyny, philology, philosophy
PHOB	**FEAR** claustrophobia, hydrophobia, phobia, phobic, xenophobia
PHON	**SOUND** antiphony, euphony, megaphone, phonetics, phonograph, polyphony, saxophone, symphony, telephone
PLAC	**PLEASE** complacent, implacable, placate, placebo, placid
PLE, PLEN, PLET	**FILL, FULL** accomplishment, complement, complete, deplete, implement, plenary, plenipotentiary, plenitude, plenty, replenish, replete, supplement
POLY	**MANY** polyandry, polygamy, polyglot, polygon, polyhedron, polynomial, polysyllable, polytechnic, polytheism

PORT — **CARRY**
comport, deportment, disport, export, import, important, portable, portage, porter, portfolio, portly, purport, rapport, reporter, supportive, transport

POST — **BEHIND, AFTER**
posterior, posterity, postern, posthumous, postmeridian, postmortem, postpone, postprandial, postscript, postwar, preposterous

POT — **DRINK**
potable, potation, potion

PRE — **BEFORE, IN FRONT**
preamble, precaution, preclude, precocity, precursor, predecessor, predict, preface, prefigure, prelate, premonition, prescribe, president

PRI, PRIM — **FIRST**
primary, primal, prime, primeval, primordial, pristine

PRO — **IN FRONT, BEFORE**
problem, proboscis, procedure, proceed, proclaim, proclivity, procrastinate, procure, propound, prostrate, protest

PROP, PROX — **NEAR**
approximate, propinquity, proximate, proximity

PROT, PROTO — **FIRST**
protagonist, protocol, prototype, protozoan

PSEUD, PSEUDO — **FALSE**
pseudepigrapha, pseudoclassic, pseudomorph, pseudonym, pseudopod, pseudoscientific

PUG, PUN — **HIT, PRICK**
expunge, impugn, poignant, pugilist, pugnacious, punch, punctual, punctuate, pungent, repugnant

PYR — **FIRE**
pyre, pyromania, pyrometer, pyrosis, pyrotechnic

QUAD, QUAR, QUAT — **FOUR**
quadrant, quadrille, quadrinomial, quadruple, quadruplets, quart, quarter, quaternary

QUIE, QUIT	**QUIET, REST**
	acquiesce, acquit, coy, disquiet, quiescent, quiet, quietude, quietus, quit, requiem, requital, tranquil
QUIN, QUINT	**FIVE**
	quincunx, quinquennial, quintessence, quintile, quintillion, quintuple
RACI, RADI, RAMI	**ROOT, BRANCH**
	deracinate, eradicate, radical, radish, ramification, ramiform, ramify
RE	**BACK, AGAIN**
	recline, refer, regain, remain, reorganize, repent, request
RECT	**STRAIGHT, RIGHT**
	correct, direct, erect, rectangle, rectify, rectilinear, rectitude, rector
REG	**KING, RULE**
	interregnum, realm, regal, regent, regicide, regime, regiment, region, regular, regulate
RETRO	**BACKWARD**
	retroactive, retroflex, retrograde, retrospective
RUB, RUD	**RED**
	rouge, rubella, rubicund, rubric, ruby, ruddy, russet
RUD	**CRUDE**
	erudite, rude, rudimentary, rudiments
SACER, SACR, SANCT	**HOLY**
	consecration, desecrate, execrate, sacerdotal, sacrament, sacred, sacrifice, sacrilege, sacristy, sacrosanct, saint, sanctify, sanctimonious, sanction, sanctity, sanctuary, sanctum
SAL	**SALT**
	salary, saline
SAG, SAP, SAV	**TASTE, THINK**
	insipid, sagacious, sagacity, sage, sapient, savant, savor
SALU, SALV	**HEALTH, SAVE**
	safe, salubrious, salutary, salute, salvage, salvation, salve, savior
SAN	**HEALTHY**
	sane, sanitarium, sanitation, sanity

SANG   **BLOOD**
                    consanguinity, sanguinary, sanguine

SAT   **ENOUGH**
                    asset, dissatisfied, insatiable, sate, satiate, satisfy, saturate

SCRIB, SCRIPT, **WRITE**
SCRIV   ascribe, circumscription, conscript, describe, indescribable, inscription, postscript, prescribe, proscribe, scribble, scribe, script, scripture, scrivener, subscribe, transcription

SE   **DOWN, OUT, AWAY, APART**
                    secede, seclude, secret, secrete, secure, sedition, seduce, segregate, select, separate

SED, SID   **SIT**
                    assiduous, dissident, insidious, preside, reside, residue, séance, sedate, sedative, sedentary, sediment, sedulous, session, siege, subside, supersede

SEM   **SEED, SOW**
                    disseminate, semen, seminal, seminar, seminary

SEMI   **HALF**
                    semicircle, semicolon, semiconscious, semifluid

SEN   **OLD**
                    senate, senescent, senile, senior, sire

SEQU, SECU,   **FOLLOW**
SUE, SUI   consecutive, consequent, execute, executive, non sequitur, obsequious, obsequy, persecute, prosecution, pursue, sequel, sequence, subsequent, sue, suitable, suite, suitor

SIN, SINU   **BEND, FOLD**
                    cosine, insinuate, sine, sinuous, sinus

SOL   **ALONE**
                    desolate, isolate, sole, soliloquize, solipsism, solitude, solo

SOL   **SUN**
                    parasol, solar, solarium, solstice

SOMN   **SLEEP**
                    insomnia, somnambulist, somniferous, somniloquist, somnolent

SOPH	**WISDOM**
	philosopher, sophism, sophist, sophisticated, sophistry, sophomore
SOURC, SURG, SURRECT	**RISE**
	insurgent, insurrection, resource, resurge, resurrection, source, surge
SPEC, SPIC	**LOOK, SEE**
	aspect, auspicious, circumspect, conspicuous, despicable, expect, inspect, introspection, perspective, perspicacious, perspicuous, prospectus, respectable, retrospect, specimen, spectacle, spectator, specter, spectrum, suspect, suspicious
SPIR	**BREATH**
	aspire, conspire, expire, inspire, perspire, respirator, spirit, spiritual, sprightly, sprite, suspire, transpire
STRICT, STRING, STRAN	**TIGHT**
	astringency, constrain, constrict, district, restriction, strain, strait, strangle, strict, stringent
SUA	**PLEASE**
	assuage, dissuade, persuade, persuasive, suasion, suave, sweet
SUB	**UNDER**
	subdivide, subdue, subjugate, subjunctive, sublunary, submarine, submerge, subordinate, subpoena, subscribe, subside, substitute, subterfuge, subterranean, suburb
SUMM	**HIGHEST**
	consummate, sum, summary, summit
SUPER, SUR	**ABOVE**
	insuperable, superabound, superannuated, superb, supercharge, supercilious, superficial, superfluous, superior, superlative, supernatural, supernumerary, supervise, surmount, surpass, surrealism, survey
SYM, SYN	**TOGETHER**
	symbiosis, symmetry, sympathy, symposium, synonym, synthesis
TACIT	**SILENT**
	reticent, tacit, taciturn

TACT, TAG, TAM, TANG	**TOUCH** contact, contagious, contamination, contiguous, cotangent, intact, intangible, integral, tact, tactile, tangent, tangential
TEST	**BEAR WITNESS** attest, contest, detest, intestate, protest, testament, testify, testimonial
THERM	**HEAT** diathermy, thermal, thermesthesia, thermometer, thermonuclear, thermophilic, thermos, thermostat
TIM	**FEAR** intimidate, timid, timidity, timorous
TORP	**STIFF, NUMB** torpedo, torpid, torpor
TOR, TORQ, TORT	**TWIST** contort, distort, extort, retort, torch, torment, torque, torsion, tort, tortuous, torture
TOX	**POISON** antitoxin, intoxication, toxemia, toxic, toxicology, toxin
TRANS	**ACROSS, BEYOND** intransigent, transcend, transcontinental, transcribe, transient, transmit, transpire, transport
ULT	**LAST, BEYOND** penultimate, ulterior, ultimate, ultimatum, ultramarine, ultramontane, ultraviolet
UMBR	**SHADOW** adumbrate, penumbra, somber, umber, umbrage, umbrella
UN	**NOT** unaccustomed, unruly, unseen, untold, unusual
UND	**WAVE** abound, abundance, inundate, redundant, undulant, undulate
UNI, UN	**ONE** reunion, unanimous, unicorn, uniform, union, unison, unit, unite, unity, universe

URB   **CITY**

exurbanite, suburban, urban, urbane, urbanity, urbanization

VAIL, VAL   **STRENGTH, USE, WORTH**

ambivalent, avail, convalescent, countervailing, equivalent, evaluate, invalid, prevalent, valediction, valiant, valid, valor, value

VER   **TRUE**

aver, veracious, verdict, verify, verily, verisimilitude, verity, very

VERB   **WORD**

adverb, proverb, verb, verbal, verbalize, verbatim, verbose, verbiage

VERD   **GREEN**

verdant, verdigris, verdure

VIL   **BASE, MEAN**

revile, vile, vilify, vilification

VIRU   **POISON**

virulence, virulent, viruliferous, virus

VIT, VIV   **LIFE**

convivial, revival, revive, survive, vital, vitality, vivacious, vivid, viviparous, vivisection

VOC, VOU   **CALL, WORD**

advocacy, advocate, avow, convocation, convoke, equivocal, evoke, invocation, invoke, provoke, revoke, vocabulary, vocal, vocalist, vocation, vociferous, vouch, vouchsafe

VOL   **WISH**

"benevolent," "malevolent," "volant," "volatile," "volition," "volley," "voluntary"

VOLU, VOLV   **ROLL, TURN**

circumvolve, convolution, devolve, evolve, involution, revolt, revolve, voluble, volume, voluminous, volute

WORD ROOTS EXERCISES

Choose the word that correctly completes the sentence. Make sure to pay attention to structural road signs and key words, and use familiar roots to guide your choice.

1. The play's theme was interesting; however, the (*animated, acerbic*) monologues dampened our appreciation of the author's skills.

2. Although poets are stereotypically considered contemplative and gentle souls, composing dulcet rhymes about the vagaries of life, some of our most famous poets have been (*belligerent, breviloquent*), frequently drunk, or even criminal.

3. The intern was a delight; she completed her tasks with professionalism, (*celerity, cautery*), and good sense.

4. Flemish primitive painters such as Jan Van Eyck used a greenish substance called (*saline, verdigris*) in their portraits.

5. The math professor wrote a formula to calculate every (*neologism, permutation*) of the set of infinite numbers.

6. Some behaviors are learned, while some are (*innocuous, innate*).

7. Because they had been old friends, the general shook the diplomat's hand with a (*somnolent, sanguinary*) air.

8. You can easily recognize (*rubella, toxemia*) because of the raised, red spots on the skin.

9. Some people consider desecration of the American flag to be treasonous or even an act of terrorism, but others refuse to impart such (*sacrosanct, sagacious*) respect to what they consider a mere symbol.

10. In frog anatomy, the major muscles of the shoulder extend from the (*dorsal, quadriceps*) area, across the shoulder joint, and into the arms.

11. At the end of the service, the general's wife gave an impromptu (*convocation, valediction*), which truly venerated his memory and profoundly moved many attendees.

12. Some families organized an effort to bring about the (*restriction, viaduct*) of the sales of illegal fireworks at the neighborhood convenience store.

13. The dog still enjoyed its vigorous morning romps through the park, but its stiff joints and patchy fur betrayed signs of (*dexterity, senescence*).

14. Around dinner time, a delicious smell (*emanated, adjourned*) from the kitchen.

15. The monorail train arrived at the station in 20-minute (*conduits, intervals*).

16. A military (*fealty, junta*) was set up to determine which party ruled, now that the old, corrupt regime had been deposed.

17. The sounds of early jazz on a Victrola are particularly (*redolent, indelible*) of my grandmother, as I always enjoyed those scratchy records in her house.

18. My brother was the intrepid one in the family; though I was by no means (*ambivalent, pusillanimous*), he always managed to outdo me in daredevildom.

19. The teacher was so (*peripatetic, acoustic*) in class that when the maintenance department removed the chair at his desk, he didn't notice for weeks.

20. It was (*indubitable, laudatory*) that Inez would earn the scholarship because she clearly had the best grades and most experience.

21. I felt I had to (*succumb, intercede*) when I saw the child struggling to swim to the side and the lifeguard failed to respond in time.

22. The mad scientist in the movie attached a special (*diathermy, chronometer*) to the time machine with which the passengers could control the year they wanted to travel to.

23. We were afraid that the (*perspicuous, taciturn*) visitor did not like the presentation because she sat quietly and asked no questions.

24. Although we often remember breakthrough artists, such as LL Cool J and Run DMC as the originators of rap, (*seminal, pedantic*) artists such as the Sugarhill Gang and the Fatback Band remind us that rap really started on the street and not in a studio.

25. As much as he practiced and tried to improve, Jack remained (*maladroit, pellucid*) at swimming.

26. While (*jocularity, gentility*) is appreciated in informal conversations with coworkers and colleagues, it is best not to overdo it in formal meetings such as interviews.

27. The appraiser thought she discovered an (*aberrant, indolent*) design in the antique carpet, but after further research, she determined that the pattern was actually consistent with designs in contemporaneous fashions and ornaments.

28. Since many toddlers go through a phase of independence, caregivers should be prepared to deal with frustrated, (*obdurate, dismal*) two-year-olds and provide patient support for this developmental process.

29. The princess arrived not in full regalia but in plain clothes; the young ladies who had hoped to spy a beautiful woman with a flowing gown and bejeweled (*diadem, heterodoxy*) were bewildered.

30. Whenever she is nervous, my sister becomes very (*liberal, loquacious*), so when she chatted away as we were walking through the woods, I suspected she thought we might be lost.

ANSWER KEY FOR WORD ROOTS EXERCISES

1. acerbic
2. belligerent
3. celerity
4. verdigris
5. permutation
6. innate
7. sanguinary
8. rubella
9. sacrosanct
10. dorsal
11. valediction
12. restriction
13. senescence
14. emanated
15. intervals

16. junta
17. redolent
18. pusillanimous
19. peripatetic
20. indubitable
21. intercede
22. chronometer
23. taciturn
24. seminal
25. maladroit
26. jocularity
27. aberrant
28. obdurate
29. diadem
30. loquacious

ANSWERS AND EXPLANATIONS FOR WORD ROOTS EXERCISES

1. ACERBIC

The root ANIM in *animated* should clue you in to the meaning: "active or living." The root of *acerbic,* AC, provides a clue to the meaning: "sharp or sour."

2. BELLIGERENT

The root BELL relates to war and fighting, and *belligerent* refers to someone who is quick to get into a fight. You may recognize the roots BREV ("brief") and LOQ ("speak") in *breviloquent,* which means "terse" or "brief."

3. CELERITY

The root CELER relates to speed, and *celerity* means "alacrity" or "briskness." The word *cautery* contains the root CAUT, which refers to burning. *Cautery* means "burning" or "scarring."

4. VERDIGRIS

The root VERD is the clue to the right answer. VERD refers to green, and *verdigris* is a green pigment used by artists. The root SAL refers to salt, and a *saline* solution is salty, like tears.

5. PERMUTATION

The root MUT is the clue in this word, which refers to a change or transformation. A *permutation* is one of the possible changes or elements in a set. NEO means new and LOG refers to words. A *neologism* is a new word.

6. INNATE

The answer to this one is a little complicated: the prefix IN has a different meaning in each option. NAT refers to birth, and the prefix IN means "internal" or "inside." Something *innate* is born into you. The word *innocuous* contains the root NOX. The prefix IN negates the meaning: an *innocuous* substance is one that will not harm you.

7. SANGUINARY

In this sentence, the friendly handshake is the clue. SANG in the word *sanguinary* refers to blood. In the Middle Ages, blood was considered to be the humor (or fluid) that caused or related to friendliness, and a *sanguinary* handshake is a friendly one. On the other hand, SOMN refers to sleep, so a *somnolent* handshake, if such a thing could exist, would cause the diplomat to get very tired.

8. RUBELLA

Although *toxemia* contains the root TOX, which means "poisonous," the rash's signature red bumps suggest the answer *rubella,* which contains the root RUB meaning "red."

9. SACROSANCT

Sacrosanct means "extremely sacred"; you may have guessed this because it contains both SACR and SANCT, both of which mean "holy." *Sagacious* means "wise" and contains the root SAG, which refers to having acute perception.

10. DORSAL

If you know anatomy or you spend time at the gym, this may have been an easy one. *Dorsal* contains the root DORS, which relates to an organism's back. The *quadriceps* is a group of four (QUAD means "four") muscles in the legs.

11. VALEDICTION

A *valediction* contains the roots VAL ("strength" or "worth") and DICT ("say"). A *valediction* is a speech given to commemorate someone or speak of his or her worth. The root CON means "together" and the root VOC means "call"; a *convocation* is a group of people who have been called together. The gathering was a *convocation*, but the speech was a *valediction*.

12. RESTRICTION

Restriction contains the root STRICT, which means "tight." A *viaduct* contains the roots VIA ("through") and DUCT ("lead"). Since the families wanted to tighten the laws regarding sales of illegal fireworks, *restriction* is your answer.

13. SENESCENCE

Senescence contains the root SEN, which refers to aging or growing old. *Senescence* is the same as maturity or old age. *Dexterity* contains the root DEXT, which refers to the right side of an organism. Because most people in the world are right-handed, and are therefore more agile with their right hands, *dexterity* has come to mean the same as *agility*. (If you're a lefty, remember this point of contention, and the root and word will stick with you on the test!)

14. EMANATED

Emanated contains the root E meaning "out," and indeed, it means "coming out" as a smell. *Adjourned* contains the roots A, which means "without," and JOUR, which means "day." *Adjourned* means "finished for the day."

15. INTERVALS

The root INTER means "between" or "among," and an *interval* is the time that passes between two or more repeating events. The word *conduits* contains the roots CON ("together") and DUC ("lead"). *Conduits* are ways to get from one place to another.

16. JUNTA

The root in *junta*, JUNCT, means "join," and a *junta* is a group of people who come together for a specific purpose. The root in *fealty* is harder to see—FID or FI—and means "faith" or "loyalty."

17. REDOLENT

The roots in these two words look similar, but don't get them confused. *Redolent* actually means "smells of," from the root REDOL of the same meaning. It's used to mean "reminiscent" or "suggestive" and fits well in the sentence. DELE means "erase"; something that is *indelible* cannot be erased.

18. PUSILLANIMOUS

The root in *pusillanimous* is ANIM, which means "life." The other root, not given in the list, is PUSIL, which means "weak." Someone who is *pusillanimous* is "craven" or "cowardly". The word *ambivalent* contains the prefix AMBI ("both") and the root VAL ("strength") and means "pulled with equal force by two choices." NOTE: It is a common error to use ambivalent to mean "unsure." In some cases, *unsure* is synonymous with *ambivalent*, but in many cases, *ambivalent* is the incorrect word.

19. PERIPATETIC

The root PERI ("around") and PED ("walk") provide the strongest clues as to the meaning of *peripatetic*, "given to walking around." *Acoustic* contains the root ACOU meaning "hearing," which does not relate to this sentence.

20. INDUBITABLE

The root DUB (not given in the list) refers to doubt, and something that is *indubitable* cannot be doubted (the root IN means "not"). The root LAUD means "praise" or "honor." A *laudatory* celebration is one that is in honor of the guest.

21. INTERCEDE

The root INTER ("between") and CEDE ("go") give the meaning of *intercede* plainly: "to go between or go into a situation." The root CUMB refers to lying down or giving in, which is the meaning of *succumb*.

22. CHRONOMETER

The roots CHRON ("time") and METER ("measure") should give you the meaning of *chronometer*: "a clock." Similarly DIA ("through") and THERM ("heat"), the roots in *diathermy*, clues you into that meaning: "heating inside a body, usually through electricity."

23. TACITURN

The root TACIT means "silent," and a *taciturn* person does not speak very much. The root SPIC ("look" or "see") is a clue to the meaning of *perspicuous*: "clear or lucid."

24. SEMINAL

The root SEM refers to seeds or sowing. A *seminal* work is one that influences others (think of a seminal work as sowing creative seeds). The word *pedantic* contains the root PED (the same root as in *pediatric*) that means "child" or "teach." A *pedantic* person

is a teacher (and carries the connotation of being too much of a know-it-all!).

25. MALADROIT

The root MAL ("bad") and the word *adroit* should give you a certain meaning to the word *maladroit*: "clumsy." You may recognize the root in *pellucid*, LUC, meaning "light." Follow those instincts: *pellucid* means "translucent" or "perfectly clear."

26. JOCULARITY

You may notice the root JOC ("joke") in the word *jocularity*. *Jocularity* is "joking around" or "having a sense of humor." The word *gentility* contains the root GEN, which refers to birth or class. *Gentility*, or good manners, has been historically expected of the upper classes in society. It does not mean that only the well-off have such manners, but you can remember this connection for the exam.

27. ABERRANT

The root AB ("from") and the root ERR ("wander") provide strong clues to the word *aberrant*, which means "different" or "off." The word *indolent* contains the root IN ("not") and DOL ("grieve"). If you think of someone who does not grieve (and possibly does not care) when something or someone is lost, you can see how the word *indolent* means "lazy" or "irresponsible."

28. OBDURATE

The roots in *obdurate*, OB ("against") and DUR ("strong") give away the meaning: "stubborn." The roots in *dismal* are actually DI ("day") and MAL ("bad"). Indeed, a *dismal* day is usually pretty lousy.

29. DIADEM

Remember that the root DIA means "through" or, as in this case, "across." A *diadem* is a band of jewels worn like a crown (across the head). A *heterodoxy* is a belief or opinion (DOX) different from or at odds with (HETERO) the norm. Its antonym is "orthodoxy."

30. LOQUACIOUS

The root in *loquacious*, LOQU, refers to speech. A *loquacious* person is a talker. The root in *liberal* refers to freedom (LIBER), and those who hold *liberal* or *libertarian* ideas tend to allow more freedom to individuals to make their own choices in life.

WORDS IN CONTEXT

Some words appear on the GRE more than others. The following words all turn up regularly on the test, although some turn up more than others. You should start by learning these words, and the groups of words that have similar meanings to them.

The top 12 words on the GRE are:

ANOMALY	ASSUAGE	ENIGMA
EQUIVOCAL	ERUDITE	FERVID
LUCID	OPAQUE	PLACATE
PRECIPITATE	PRODIGAL	ZEAL

The next 20 most popular words are:

ABSTAIN	ADULTERATE	APATHY
AUDACIOUS	CAPRICIOUS	CORROBORATE
DESICCATE	ENGENDER	EPHEMERAL
GULLIBLE	HOMOGENOUS	LACONIC
LAUDABLE	LOQUACIOUS	MITIGATE
PEDANT	PRAGMATIC	PROPRIETY
VACILLATE	VOLATILE	

The next 20 most popular words after these are:

ADVOCATE	ANTIPATHY	BOLSTER
CACOPHONY	DERIDE	DISSONANCE
ENERVATE	EULOGY	GARRULOUS
INGENUOUS	LETHARGIC	MALLEABLE
MISANTHROPE	OBDURATE	OSTENTATION
PARADOX	PHILANTHROPIC	PREVARICATE
VENERATE	WAVER	

The 180 Top GRE Words In Context

ABATE: to reduce in amount, degree, or severity

As the hurricane's force ABATED, the winds dropped and the sea became calm.

Words with similar meanings:

EBB	LAPSE	LET UP
MODERATE	RELENT	SLACKEN
SUBSIDE	WANE	

ABSCOND: to leave secretly

The patron ABSCONDED from the restaurant without paying his bill by sneaking out the back door.

Words with similar meanings:
FLEE   DECAMP   ESCAPE

ABSTAIN: to choose not to do something

During Lent, practicing Catholics ABSTAIN from eating meat.

Words with similar meanings:
FORBEAR   REFRAIN   WITHHOLD

ABYSS: an extremely deep hole

The submarine dove into the ABYSS to chart the previously unseen depths.

Related words:
ABYSSAL: pertaining to great depth
ABYSMAL: extremely bad

Words with similar meanings:
CHASM   VOID

ADULTERATE: to make impure

The restaurateur made his ketchup last longer by ADULTERATING it with water.

Related words:
UNADULTERATED: pure
ADULTERY: an illicit relationship; an affair

Words with similar meanings:
DOCTOR

ADVOCATE: to speak in favor of

The vegetarian ADVOCATED a diet containing no meat.

Related words:
ADVOCACY: active support for

Words with similar meanings:
BACK   CHAMPION   SUPPORT

AESTHETIC: concerning the appreciation of beauty

Followers of the AESTHETIC Movement regarded the pursuit of beauty as the only true purpose of art.

Related words:
AESTHETE: someone unusually sensitive to beauty
AESTHETICISM: concern with beauty

Words with similar meanings:

ARTISTIC	TASTEFUL

AGGRANDIZE: to increase in power, influence, and reputation

The supervisor sought to AGGRANDIZE himself by claiming that the achievements of his staff were actually his own.

Words with similar meanings:

AMPLIFY	APOTHEOSIZE	AUGMENT
DIGNIFY	ELEVATE	ENLARGE
ENNOBLE	EXALT	GLORIFY
MAGNIFY	SWELL	UPLIFT
WAX		

ALLEVIATE: to make more bearable

Taking aspirin helps to ALLEVIATE a headache.

Words with similar meanings:

ALLAY	ASSUAGE	COMFORT
EASE	LESSEN	LIGHTEN
MITIGATE	PALLIATE	RELIEVE

AMALGAMATE: to combine; to mix together

Giant Industries AMALGAMATED with Mega Products to form Giant-Mega Products Incorporated.

Related words:
AMALGAM: a mixture, especially of two metals

Words with similar meanings:

ADMIX	BLEND	COMBINE
COMMINGLE	COMMIX	COMPOUND
FUSE	INTERMINGLE	INTERMIX
MERGE	MINGLE	MIX

AMBIGUOUS: doubtful or uncertain; able to be interpreted several ways

The directions he gave were so AMBIGUOUS that we disagreed on which way to turn.

Related words:

AMBIGUITY: the quality of being ambiguous

Words with similar meanings:

CLOUDY	DOUBTFUL	DUBIOUS
EQUIVOCAL	INDETERMINATE	NEBULOUS
OBSCURE	UNCLEAR	VAGUE

AMELIORATE: to make better; to improve

The doctor was able to AMELIORATE the patient's suffering using painkillers.

Words with similar meanings:

AMEND	BETTER	IMPROVE
PACIFY	UPGRADE	

ANACHRONISM: something out of place in time

The aged hippie used ANACHRONISTIC phrases like "groovy" and "far out" that had not been popular for years.

Words with similar meanings:

ARCHAISM	INCONGRUITY

ANALOGOUS: similar or alike in some way; equivalent to

In a famous argument for the existence of God, the universe is ANALOGOUS to a mechanical timepiece, the creation of a divinely intelligent "clockmaker."

Related words:

ANALOGY: a similarity between things that are otherwise dissimilar
ANALOGUE: something that is similar in some way to something else

Words with similar meanings:

ALIKE	COMPARABLE	CORRESPONDING
EQUIVALENT	HOMOGENEOUS	PARALLEL
SIMILAR		

ANOMALY: deviation from what is normal

Albino animals may display too great an ANOMALY in their coloring to attract normally colored mates.

Related words:

ANOMALOUS: deviating from what is normal

Words with similar meanings:

ABERRANCE	ABERRATION	ABNORMALITY
DEVIANCE	DEVIATION	IRREGULARITY
PRETERNATURALNESS		

ANTAGONIZE: to annoy or provoke to anger

The child discovered that he could ANTAGONIZE the cat by pulling its tail.

Related words:

ANTAGONISTIC: tending to provoke conflict

ANTAGONIST: someone who fights another

Words with similar meanings

CLASH	CONFLICT	INCITE
IRRITATE	OPPOSE	PESTER
PROVOKE	VEX	

ANTIPATHY: extreme dislike

The ANTIPATHY between the French and the English regularly erupted into open warfare.

Words with similar meanings:

ANIMOSITY	ANIMUS	ANTAGONISM
AVERSION	ENMITY	HOSTILITY
REPELLENCE		

APATHY: lack of interest or emotion

The APATHY of voters is so great that less than half the people who are eligible to vote actually bother to do so.

Words with similar meanings:

COOLNESS	DISINTEREST	DISREGARD
IMPASSIVITY	INDIFFERENCE	INSENSIBILITY
LASSITUDE	LETHARGY	LISTLESSNESS
PHLEGM	STOLIDITY	UNCONCERN
UNRESPONSIVENESS		

ARBITRATE: to judge a dispute between two opposing parties

Since the couple could not come to agreement, a judge was forced to ARBITRATE their divorce proceedings.

Related words:

ARBITRATION: a process by which a conflict is resolved

ARBITRATOR: a judge

Words with similar meanings:

ADJUDGE	ADJUDICATE	DECIDE
DETERMINE	JUDGE	MODERATE
REFEREE	RULE	

ARCHAIC: ancient, old-fashioned

Her ARCHAIC Commodore computer could not run the latest software.

Related words:

ARCHAISM: an outdated word or phrase

Words with similar meanings:

ANCIENT	ANTEDILUVIAN	ANTIQUE
BYGONE	DATED	DOWDY
FUSTY	OBSOLETE	OLD-FASHIONED
OUTDATED	OUTMODED	PASSÉ
PREHISTORIC	STALE	SUPERANNUATED
SUPERSEDED	VINTAGE	

ARDOR: intense and passionate feeling

Bishop's ARDOR for landscape was evident when he passionately described the beauty of the scenic Hudson Valley.

Related words:

ARDENT: expressing ardor; passionate

Words with similar meanings:

DEVOTION	ENTHUSIASM	FERVENCY
FERVIDITY	FERVIDNESS	FERVOR
FIRE	PASSION	ZEAL
ZEALOUSNESS		

ARTICULATE: able to speak clearly and expressively

She is such an ARTICULATE defender of labor that unions are among her strongest supporters.

Words with similar meanings

ELOQUENT	EXPRESSIVE	FLUENT
LUCID	SILVER-TONGUED	SMOOTH-SPOKEN

ASSUAGE: to make something unpleasant less severe

Like many people, Philip Larkin used alcohol to ASSUAGE his sense of meaninglessness and despair.

Words with similar meanings:

ALLAY	ALLEVIATE	APPEASE
COMFORT	CONCILIATE	EASE
LIGHTEN	MITIGATE	MOLLIFY
PACIFY	PALLIATE	PLACATE
PROPITIATE	RELIEVE	SOOTHE
SWEETEN		

ATTENUATE: to reduce in force or degree; to weaken

The Bill of Rights ATTENUATED the traditional power of government to change laws at will.

Words with similar meanings:

DEBILITATE	DEVITALIZE	DILUTE
ENERVATE	ENFEEBLE	RAREFY
SAP	THIN	UNDERMINE
UNDO	UNNERVE	WATER
WEAKEN		

AUDACIOUS: fearless and daring

"And you, your majesty, may kiss my bum!" replied the AUDACIOUS peasant.

Related words:
AUDACITY: the quality of being audacious

Words with similar meanings:

ADVENTURESOME	AGGRESSIVE	ASSERTIVE
BOLD	BRAVE	COURAGEOUS
DARING	DAUNTLESS	DOUGHTY
FEARLESS	GALLANT	GAME
HEROIC	INTREPID	METTLESOME
PLUCKY	STOUT	STOUTHEARTED
UNAFRAID	UNDAUNTED	VALIANT
VALOROUS	VENTURESOME	VENTUROUS

AUSTERE: severe or stern in appearance; undecorated

The lack of decoration makes Zen temples seem AUSTERE to the untrained eye.

Related words:
AUSTERITY: severity, especially poverty

Words with similar meanings:

BLEAK	DOUR	GRIM
HARD	HARSH	SEVERE

BANAL: predictable, clichéd, boring

He used BANAL phrases like "Have a nice day," or "Another day, another dollar."

Related words:
BANALITY: the quality of being banal

Words with similar meanings:

BLAND	BROMIDIC	CLICHÉD
COMMONPLACE	FATUOUS	HACKNEYED
INNOCUOUS	INSIPID	JEJUNE
MUSTY	PLATITUDINOUS	PROSAIC
QUOTIDIAN	SHOPWORN	STALE
STEREOTYPIC	THREADBARE	TIMEWORN
TIRED	TRITE	VAPID
WORN-OUT		

BOLSTER: to support; to prop up

The presence of giant footprints BOLSTERED the argument that Sasquatch was in the area.

Words with similar meanings:

BRACE	BUTTRESS	PROP
SUPPORT	SUSTAIN	UNDERPIN
UPHOLD		

BOMBASTIC: pompous in speech and manner

Mussolini's speeches were mostly BOMBASTIC; his boasting and outrageous claims had no basis in fact.

Related words:
BOMBAST: pompous speech or writing

Words with similar meanings:

BLOATED	DECLAMATORY	FUSTIAN
GRANDILOQUENT	GRANDIOSE	HIGH-FLOWN
MAGNILOQUENT	OROTUND	PRETENTIOUS
RHETORICAL	SELF-IMPORTANT	

CACOPHONY: harsh, jarring noise

The junior high orchestra created an almost unbearable CACOPHONY as they tried to tune their instruments.

Words with similar meanings:

CHAOS	CLAMOR	DIN
DISCORD	DISHARMONY	NOISE

CANDID: impartial and honest in speech

    The observations of a child can be charming since they are CANDID and unpretentious.

Words with similar meanings:

DIRECT	FORTHRIGHT	FRANK
HONEST	OPEN	SINCERE
STRAIGHT	STRAIGHTFORWARD	UNDISGUISED

CAPRICIOUS: changing one's mind quickly and often

    Queen Elizabeth I was quite CAPRICIOUS; her courtiers could never be sure which of their number would catch her fancy.

Related words:
CAPRICE: whim, sudden fancy

Words with similar meanings:

ARBITRARY	CHANCE	CHANGEABLE
ERRATIC	FICKLE	INCONSTANT
MERCURIAL	RANDOM	WHIMSICAL
WILLFUL		

CASTIGATE: to punish or criticize harshly

    Americans are amazed at how harshly the authorities in Singapore CASTIGATE perpetrators of what would be considered minor crimes in the United States.

Words with similar meanings:

ADMONISH	CHASTISE	CHIDE
REBUKE	REPRIMAND	REPROACH
REPROVE	SCOLD	TAX
UPBRAID		

CATALYST: something that brings about a change in something else

    The imposition of harsh taxes was the CATALYST that finally brought on the revolution.

Related words:
CATALYZE: to bring about a change in something else

CAUSTIC: biting in wit

    Dorothy Parker gained her reputation for CAUSTIC wit from her cutting, yet clever, insults.

Words with similar meanings:

ACERBIC	BITING	MORDANT
TRENCHANT		

CHAOS: great disorder or confusion

In most religious traditions, God created an ordered universe from CHAOS.

Related words:

CHAOTIC: jumbled, confused

Words with similar meanings:

CLUTTER	CONFUSION	DISARRANGEMENT
DISARRAY	DISORDER	DISORDERLINESS
DISORGANIZATION	JUMBLE	MESS
MUDDLE	SCRAMBLE	SNARL
TOPSY-TURVINESS	TURMOIL	

CHAUVINIST: someone prejudiced in favor of a group to which he or she belongs

The attitude that men are inherently superior to women and therefore must be obeyed is common among male CHAUVINISTS.

Words with similar meanings:

PARTISAN

CHICANERY: deception by means of craft or guile

Dishonest used car salespeople often use CHICANERY to sell their beat-up old cars.

Words with similar meanings:

ARTIFICE	CONNIVING	CRAFTINESS
DECEPTION	DEVIOUSNESS	MISREPRESENTATION
PETTIFOGGERY	SHADINESS	SNEAKINESS
SOPHISTRY	SUBTERFUGE	UNDERHANDEDNESS

COGENT: convincing and well-reasoned

Swayed by the COGENT argument of the defense, the jury had no choice but to acquit the defendant.

Related words:

COGITATE: to think deeply

Words with similar meanings:

CONVINCING	PERSUASIVE	SOLID
SOUND	TELLING	VALID

CONDONE: to overlook, pardon, or disregard

Some theorists believe that failing to prosecute minor crimes is the same as CONDONING an air of lawlessness.

Words with similar meanings:

EXCULPATE	EXCUSE	PARDON
REMIT		

CONVOLUTED: intricate and complicated

Although many people bought *A Brief History of Time*, few could follow its CONVOLUTED ideas and theories.

Words with similar meanings:

BYZANTINE	COMPLEX	ELABORATE
INTRICATE	KNOTTY	LABYRINTHINE
PERPLEXING	TANGLED	

CORROBORATE: to provide supporting evidence

Fingerprints CORROBORATED the witness's testimony that he saw the defendant in the victim's apartment.

Words with similar meanings:

AUTHENTICATE	BACK	BEAR OUT
BUTTRESS	CONFIRM	SUBSTANTIATE
VALIDATE	VERIFY	

CREDULOUS: too trusting; gullible

Although some 4-year-olds believe in the Easter Bunny, only the most CREDULOUS 9-year-olds also believe in him.

Related words:
CREDULITY: the quality of being credulous

Words with similar meanings:

NAIVE	SUSCEPTIBLE	TRUSTING

CRESCENDO: steadily increasing in volume or force

The CRESCENDO of tension became unbearable as Evel Knievel prepared to jump his motorcycle over the school buses.

DECORUM: appropriateness of behavior or conduct; propriety

The countess complained that the vulgar peasants lacked the DECORUM appropriate for a visit to the palace.

Related words:

DECOROUS: conforming to acceptable standards

Words with similar meanings:

CORRECTNESS	DECENCY	ETIQUETTE
MANNERS	MORES	PROPRIETY
SEEMLINESS		

DEFERENCE: respect, courtesy

The respectful young law clerk treated the Supreme Court justice with the utmost DEFERENCE.

Related words:

DEFER: to delay; to show someone deference
DEFERENTIAL: courteous and respectful

Words with similar meanings:

COURTESY	HOMAGE	HONOR
OBEISANCE	RESPECT	REVERENCE
VENERATION		

DERIDE: to speak of or treat with contempt; to mock

The awkward child was often DERIDED by his "cooler" peers.

Related words:

DERISION: mockery and taunts
DERISIVE: in a mocking manner

Words with similar meanings:

GIBE	JEER	MOCK
RIDICULE	SCOFF	SNEER
TAUNT		

DESICCATE: to dry out thoroughly

After a few weeks of lying on the desert's baking sands, the cow's carcass became completely DESICCATED.

Related words:

DESICCANT: something that removes water from another substance

Words with similar meanings:

DEHYDRATE	DRY	PARCH

DESULTORY: jumping from one thing to another; disconnected

Diane had a DESULTORY academic record; she had changed majors 12 times in three years.

Words with similar meanings:

AIMLESS	DISCONNECTED	ERRATIC
HAPHAZARD	INDISCRIMINATE	OBJECTLESS
PURPOSELESS	RANDOM	STRAY
UNCONSIDERED	UNPLANNED	

DIATRIBE: an abusive, condemnatory speech

The trucker bellowed a DIATRIBE at the driver who had cut him off.

Words with similar meanings:

FULMINATION	HARANGUE	INVECTIVE
JEREMIAD	MALEDICTION	OBLOQUY
TIRADE		

DIFFIDENT: lacking self-confidence

Steve's DIFFIDENT manner during the job interview stemmed from his nervous nature and lack of experience in the field.

Words with similar meanings:

BACKWARD	BASHFUL	COY
DEMURE	MODEST	RETIRING
SELF-EFFACING	SHY	TIMID

DILATE: to make larger; to expand

When you enter a darkened room, the pupils of your eyes DILATE to let in more light.

Words with similar meanings:

AMPLIFY	DEVELOP	ELABORATE
ENLARGE	EXPAND	EXPATIATE

DILATORY: intended to delay

The congressman used DILATORY measures to delay the passage of the bill.

Words with similar meanings:

DRAGGING	FLAGGING	LAGGARD
LAGGING	SLOW	SLOW-FOOTED
SLOW-GOING	SLOW-PACED	TARDY

DILETTANTE: someone with an amateurish and superficial interest in a topic

Jerry's friends were such DILETTANTES that they seemed to have new jobs and hobbies every week.

Words with similar meanings:

AMATEUR	DABBLER	SUPERFICIAL
TYRO		

DIRGE: a funeral hymn or mournful speech

Melville wrote the poem "A DIRGE for James McPherson" for the funeral of a Union general who was killed in 1864.

Words with similar meanings:

ELEGY	LAMENT

DISABUSE: to set right; to free from error

Galileo's observations DISABUSED scholars of the notion that the sun revolved around the Earth.

Words with similar meanings:

CORRECT	UNDECEIVE

DISCERN: to perceive; to recognize

It is easy to DISCERN the difference between butter and butter-flavored topping.

Related words:
DISCERNMENT: taste and cultivation

Words with similar meanings:

CATCH	DESCRY	DETECT
DIFFERENTIATE	DISCRIMINATE	DISTINGUISH
ESPY	GLIMPSE	KNOW
SEPARATE	SPOT	SPY
TELL		

DISPARATE: fundamentally different; entirely unlike

Although the twins appear to be identical physically, their personalities are DISPARATE.

Words with similar meanings:

DIFFERENT	DISSIMILAR	DIVERGENT
DIVERSE	VARIANT	VARIOUS

DISSEMBLE: to present a false appearance; to disguise one's real intentions or character

The villain could DISSEMBLE to the police no longer—he admitted the deed and tore up the floor to reveal the body of the old man.

Words with similar meanings:

ACT	AFFECT	ASSUME
CLOAK	COUNTERFEIT	CAMOUFLAGE
COVER UP	DISGUISE	DISSIMULATE
FAKE	FEIGN	MASK
MASQUERADE	POSE	PRETEND
PUT ON	SHAM	SIMULATE

DISSONANCE: a harsh and disagreeable combination, often of sounds

Cognitive DISSONANCE is the inner conflict produced when long-standing beliefs are contradicted by new evidence.

Words with similar meanings:

CLASH	CONTENTION	DISCORD
DISSENSION	DISSENT	DISSIDENCE
FRICTION	STRIFE	VARIANCE

DOGMA: a firmly held opinion, often a religious belief

Linus's central DOGMA was that children who believed in the Great Pumpkin would be rewarded.

Words with similar meanings:

CREED	DOCTRINE	TEACHING
TENET		

DOGMATIC: dictatorial in one's opinions

The dictator was DOGMATIC—he, and only he, was right.

Words with similar meanings:

AUTHORITARIAN	BOSSY	DICTATORIAL
DOCTRINAIRE	DOMINEERING	IMPERIOUS
MAGISTERIAL	MASTERFUL	OVERBEARING
PEREMPTORY		

DUPE: to deceive; a person who is easily deceived

Bugs Bunny was able to DUPE Elmer Fudd by dressing up as a lady rabbit.

Words with similar meanings:

BEGUILE	BETRAY	BLUFF
COZEN	DECEIVE	DELUDE

FOOL	HOODWINK	HUMBUG
MISLEAD	TAKE IN	TRICK

ECLECTIC: selecting from or made up from a variety of sources

Budapest's architecture is an ECLECTIC mix of eastern and western styles.

Words with similar meanings:

BROAD	CATHOLIC	SELECTIVE

EFFICACY: effectiveness

The EFFICACY of penicillin was unsurpassed when it was first introduced; the drug completely eliminated almost all bacterial infections for which it was administered.

Related words:

EFFICACIOUS: effective; productive

Words with similar meanings:

DYNAMISM	EFFECTIVENESS	EFFICIENCY
FORCE	POWER	PRODUCTIVENESS
PROFICIENCY	STRENGTH	VIGOR

ELEGY: a sorrowful poem or speech

Although Thomas Gray's "ELEGY Written in a Country Churchyard" is about death and loss, it urges its readers to endure this life and to trust in spirituality.

Related words:

ELEGIAC: like an elegy; mournful

Words with similar meanings:

DIRGE	LAMENT

ELOQUENT: persuasive and moving, especially in speech

The Gettysburg Address is moving not only because of its lofty sentiments but also because of its ELOQUENT words.

Words with similar meanings:

ARTICULATE	EXPRESSIVE	FLUENT
MEANINGFUL	SIGNIFICANT	SMOOTH-SPOKEN

EMULATE: to copy; to try to equal or excel

The graduate student sought to EMULATE his professor in every way, copying not only how she taught, but also how she conducted herself outside of class.

Words with similar meanings:

APE	IMITATE	SIMULATE

ENERVATE: to reduce in strength

The guerrillas hoped that a series of surprise attacks would ENERVATE the regular army.

Related words:
UNNERVE: to deprive of strength or courage

Words with similar meanings:

DEBILITATE   ENFEEBLE   SAP
WEAKEN

ENGENDER: to produce, cause, or bring about

His fear and hatred of clowns was ENGENDERED when he witnessed the death of his father at the hands of a clown.

Words with similar meanings:

BEGET   GENERATE   PROCREATE
PROLIFERATE   REPRODUCE   SPAWN

ENIGMA: a puzzle; a mystery

Speaking in riddles and dressed in old robes, the artist gained a reputation as something of an ENIGMA.

Words with similar meanings:

CONUNDRUM   PERPLEXITY

ENUMERATE: to count, list, or itemize

Moses returned from the mountain with tablets on which the commandments were ENUMERATED.

Words with similar meanings:

CATALOG   INDEX   TABULATE

EPHEMERAL: lasting a short time

The lives of mayflies seem EPHEMERAL to us, since the flies' average life span is a matter of hours.

Words with similar meanings:

EVANESCENT   FLEETING   MOMENTARY
TRANSIENT

EQUIVOCATE: to use expressions of double meaning in order to mislead

When faced with criticism of his policies, the politician EQUIVOCATED and left all parties thinking he agreed with them.

Related words:

EQUIVOCAL: undecided; trying to deceive

EQUIVOCATION: the act or state of equivocating

Words with similar meanings:

AMBIGUOUS   EVASIVE   WAFFLING

ERRATIC: wandering and unpredictable

The plot seemed predictable until it suddenly took a series of ERRATIC turns that surprised the audience.

Related words:

ERRANT: straying, mistaken, roving

Words with similar meanings:

CAPRICIOUS   INCONSTANT   IRRESOLUTE
WHIMSICAL

ERUDITE: learned, scholarly, bookish

The annual meeting of philosophy professors was a gathering of the most ERUDITE, well-published individuals in the field.

Related words:

ERUDITION: extensive knowledge or learning

Words with similar meanings:

SCHOLASTIC   LEARNED   WISE

ESOTERIC: known or understood by only a few

Only a handful of experts are knowledgeable about the ESOTERIC world of particle physics.

Words with similar meanings:

ABSTRUSE   ARCANE   OBSCURE

ESTIMABLE: admirable

Most people consider it ESTIMABLE that Mother Teresa spent her life helping the poor of India.

Related words:

ESTEEM: high regard

Words with similar meanings:

ADMIRABLE   COMMENDABLE   CREDITABLE
HONORABLE   LAUDABLE   MERITORIOUS

PRAISEWORTHY   RESPECTABLE   VENERABLE
WORTHY

EULOGY: speech in praise of someone
His best friend gave the EULOGY, outlining his many achievements and talents.

Words with similar meanings:
COMMEND   EXTOL   LAUD

EUPHEMISM: use of an inoffensive word or phrase in place of a more distasteful one
The funeral director preferred to use the EUPHEMISM "sleeping" instead of the word "dead."

Words with similar meanings:
CIRCUMLOCUTION   WHITEWASH

EXACERBATE: to make worse
It is unwise to take aspirin to try to relieve heartburn; instead of providing relief, the drug will only EXACERBATE the problem.

Words with similar meanings:
ANNOY   AGGRAVATE   INTENSIFY
IRRITATE   PROVOKE

EXCULPATE: to clear from blame; prove innocent
The adversarial legal system is intended to convict those who are guilty and to EXCULPATE those who are innocent.

Words with similar meanings:
ABSOLVE   ACQUIT   CLEAR
EXONERATE   VINDICATE

EXIGENT: urgent; requiring immediate action
The patient was losing blood so rapidly that it was EXIGENT to stop the source of the bleeding.

Words with similar meanings:
CRITICAL   IMPERATIVE   NEEDED
URGENT

EXONERATE: to clear of blame
The fugitive was EXONERATED when another criminal confessed to committing the crime.

Words with similar meanings:

ABSOLVE	ACQUIT	CLEAR
EXCULPATE	VINDICATE	

EXPLICIT: clearly stated or shown; forthright in expression

The owners of the house left a list of EXPLICIT instructions detailing their house sitter's duties, including a schedule for watering the house plants.

Related words:
EXPLICABLE: capable of being explained
EXPLICATE: to give a detailed explanation

Words with similar meanings:

CANDID	FRANK	STRAIGHTFORWARD
UNEQUIVOCAL		

FANATICAL: acting excessively enthusiastic; filled with extreme, unquestioned devotion

The stormtroopers were FANATICAL in their devotion to the Emperor, readily sacrificing their lives for him.

Words with similar meanings:

EXTREMIST	FIERY	FRENZIED
ZEALOUS		

FAWN: to grovel

The understudy FAWNED over the director in hopes of being cast in the part on a permanent basis.

Words with similar meanings:

BOOTLICK	GROVEL	PANDER
TOADY		

FERVID: intensely emotional; feverish

The fans of Maria Callas were particularly FERVID, doing anything to catch a glimpse of the great opera singer.

Related words:
FERVENT: enthusiastic
FERVOR: passion

Words with similar meanings:

BURNING	IMPASSIONED	PASSIONATE
VEHEMENT	ZEALOUS	

FLORID: excessively decorated or embellished

The palace had been decorated in a FLORID style; every surface had been carved and gilded.

Words with similar meanings:

BAROQUE	ELABORATE	FLAMBOYANT
ORNATE	OSTENTATIOUS	ROCOCO

FOMENT: to arouse or incite

The protesters tried to FOMENT feeling against the war through their speeches and demonstrations.

Words with similar meanings:

AGITATE	IMPASSION	INFLAME
INSTIGATE	KINDLE	

FRUGALITY: a tendency to be thrifty or cheap

Scrooge McDuck's FRUGALITY was so great that he accumulated enough wealth to fill a giant storehouse with money.

Words with similar meanings:

ECONOMICAL	PARSIMONY	PRUDENCE
SPARING		

GARRULOUS: tending to talk a lot

The GARRULOUS parakeet distracted its owner with its continuous talking.

Words with similar meanings:

EFFUSIVE	LOQUACIOUS

GREGARIOUS: outgoing, sociable

She was so GREGARIOUS that when she found herself alone she felt quite sad.

Words with similar meanings:

AFFABLE	COMMUNICATIVE	CONGENIAL
SOCIABLE		

GUILE: deceit or trickery

Since he was not fast enough to catch the roadrunner on foot, the coyote resorted to GUILE in an effort to trap his enemy.

Related words:

GUILELESS: innocent, without trickery

Words with similar meanings:

ARTIFICE	CHICANERY	CONNIVERY
DUPLICITY		

GULLIBLE: easily deceived

The con man pretended to be a bank officer so as to fool GULLIBLE bank customers into giving him their account information.

Related words:

GULL: a person who is easily tricked

Words with similar meanings:

CREDULOUS	EXPLOITABLE	NAIVE

HOMOGENOUS: of a similar kind

The class was fairly HOMOGENOUS, since almost all of the students were senior journalism majors.

Related words:

HOMOGENIZED: thoroughly mixed together

Words with similar meanings:

CONSISTENT	STANDARDIZED	UNIFORM
UNVARYING		

ICONOCLAST: one who opposes established beliefs, customs, and institutions

His lack of regard for traditional beliefs soon established him as an ICONOCLAST.

Words with similar meanings:

MAVERICK	NONCONFORMIST	REBEL
REVOLUTIONARY		

IMPERTURBABLE: not capable of being disturbed

The counselor had so much experience dealing with distraught children that she seemed IMPERTURBABLE, even when faced with the wildest tantrums.

Related words:

PERTURB: to disturb greatly

Words with similar meanings:

COMPOSED	DISPASSIONATE	IMPASSIVE
SERENE	STOICAL	

IMPERVIOUS: impossible to penetrate; incapable of being affected
A good raincoat is IMPERVIOUS to moisture.

Words with similar meanings:
RESISTANT   IMPREGNABLE

IMPETUOUS: quick to act without thinking
It is not good for an investment broker to be IMPETUOUS, because much thought should be given to all the possible options.

Related words:
IMPETUS: impulse

Words with similar meanings:
IMPULSIVE   PRECIPITATE   RASH
RECKLESS   SPONTANEOUS

IMPLACABLE: unable to be calmed down or made peaceful
His rage at the betrayal was so great that he remained IMPLACABLE for weeks.

Related words:
PLACATE: to make peaceful

Words with similar meanings:
INEXORABLE   INTRANSIGENT   IRRECONCILABLE
RELENTLESS   REMORSELESS   UNFORGIVING
UNRELENTING

INCHOATE: not fully formed; disorganized
The ideas expressed in Nietzsche's mature work also appear in an INCHOATE form in his earliest writing.

Words with similar meanings:
AMORPHOUS   INCOHERENT   INCOMPLETE
UNORGANIZED

INGENUOUS: showing innocence or childlike simplicity
She was so INGENUOUS that her friends feared that her innocence and trustfulness would be exploited when she visited the big city.

Related words:
INGÉNUE: a naive girl or young woman
DISINGENUOUS: giving a false impression of innocence

Words with similar meanings:

ARTLESS	GUILELESS	INNOCENT
NAIVE	SIMPLE	UNAFFECTED

INIMICAL: hostile, unfriendly

Even though a cease-fire had been in place for months, the two sides were still INIMICAL to each other.

Words with similar meanings:

ADVERSE	ANTAGONISTIC	DISSIDENT
RECALCITRANT		

INNOCUOUS: harmless

Some snakes are poisonous, but most species are INNOCUOUS and pose no danger to humans.

Words with similar meanings:

BENIGN	HARMLESS	INOFFENSIVE

INSIPID: lacking interest or flavor

The critic claimed that the painting was INSIPID, containing no interesting qualities at all.

Words with similar meanings:

BANAL	BLAND	DULL
STALE	VAPID	

INTRANSIGENT: uncompromising; refusing to be reconciled

The professor was INTRANSIGENT on the deadline, insisting that everyone turn the assignment in at the same time.

Words with similar meanings:

IMPLACABLE	INEXORABLE	IRRECONCILABLE
OBDURATE	OBSTINATE	REMORSELESS
RIGID	UNBENDING	UNRELENTING
UNYIELDING		

INUNDATE: to overwhelm; to cover with water

The tidal wave INUNDATED Atlantis, which was lost beneath the water.

Words with similar meanings:

DELUGE	DROWN	ENGULF
FLOOD	SUBMERGE	

IRASCIBLE: easily made angry

Attila the Hun's IRASCIBLE and violent nature made all who dealt with him fear for their lives.

Related words:
IRATE: angry

Words with similar meanings:

CANTANKEROUS	IRRITABLE	ORNERY
TESTY		

LACONIC: using few words

She was a LACONIC poet who built her reputation on using words as sparingly as possible.

Words with similar meanings:

CONCISE	CURT	PITHY
TACITURN	TERSE	

LAMENT: to express sorrow; to grieve

The children continued to LAMENT the death of the goldfish weeks after its demise.

Words with similar meanings:

BEWAIL	DEPLORE	GRIEVE
MOURN		

LAUD: to give praise; to glorify

Parades and fireworks were staged to LAUD the success of the rebels.

Related words:
LAUDABLE: worthy of praise
LAUDATORY: expressing praise

Words with similar meanings:

ACCLAIM	APPLAUD	COMMEND
COMPLIMENT	EXALT	EXTOL
HAIL	PRAISE	

LAVISH: to give unsparingly (v.); extremely generous or extravagant (adj.)

She LAVISHED the puppy with so many treats that it soon became overweight and spoiled.

Words with similar meanings:

BESTOW	CONFER	EXTRAVAGANT
EXUBERANT	LUXURIANT	OPULENT
PRODIGAL	PROFUSE	SUPERABUNDANT

LETHARGIC: acting in an indifferent or slow, sluggish manner

The clerk was so LETHARGIC that, even when the store was slow, he always had a long line in front of him.

Words with similar meanings:

APATHETIC	LACKADAISICAL	LANGUID
LISTLESS	TORPID	

LOQUACIOUS: talkative

She was naturally LOQUACIOUS, which was a problem in situations in which listening was more important than talking.

Related words:
ELOQUENCE: powerful, convincing speaking
LOQUACITY: the quality of being loquacious

Words with similar meanings:

EFFUSIVE	GARRULOUS	VERBOSE

LUCID: clear and easily understood

The explanations were written in a simple and LUCID manner so that students were immediately able to apply what they learned.

Related words:
LUCIDITY: clarity
LUCENT: glowing with light

Words with similar meanings:

CLEAR	COHERENT	EXPLICIT
INTELLIGIBLE	LIMPID	

LUMINOUS: bright, brilliant, glowing

The park was bathed in LUMINOUS sunshine, which warmed the bodies and the souls of the visitors.

Related words:
ILLUMINATE: to shine light on
LUMINARY: an inspiring person

Words with similar meanings:

INCANDESCENT   LUCENT   LUSTROUS
RADIANT   RESPLENDENT

MALINGER: to evade responsibility by pretending to be ill

A common way to avoid the draft was by MALINGERING—pretending to be mentally or physically ill so as to avoid being taken by the Army.

Related words:
LINGER: to be slow in leaving

Words with similar meanings:

SHIRK   SLACK

MALLEABLE: capable of being shaped

Gold is the most MALLEABLE of precious metals; it can easily be formed into almost any shape.

Words with similar meanings:

ADAPTABLE   DUCTILE   PLASTIC
PLIABLE   PLIANT

METAPHOR: a figure of speech comparing two different things; a symbol

The METAPHOR "a sea of troubles" suggests a lot of troubles by comparing their number to the vastness of the sea.

Related words:
METAPHORICAL: standing as a symbol for something else

Words with similar meanings:

ANALOGY   COMPARISON

METICULOUS: extremely careful about details

To find all the clues at the crime scene, the investigators METICULOUSLY examined every inch of the area.

Words with similar meanings:

CONSCIENTIOUS   PRECISE   SCRUPULOUS

MISANTHROPE: a person who dislikes others

The character Scrooge in *A Christmas Carol* is such a MISANTHROPE that even the sight of children singing makes him angry.

MITIGATE: to soften; to lessen

A judge may MITIGATE a sentence if she decides that a person committed a crime out of need.

Words with similar meanings:

ALLAY	ALLEVIATE	ASSUAGE
EASE	LIGHTEN	MODERATE
MOLLIFY	PALLIATE	TEMPER

MOLLIFY: to calm or make less severe

Their argument was so intense that it was difficult to believe any compromise would MOLLIFY them.

Words with similar meanings:

APPEASE	ASSUAGE	CONCILIATE
PACIFY		

MONOTONY: lack of variation

The MONOTONY of the sound of the dripping faucet almost drove the research assistant crazy.

Related words:

MONOTONE: a sound that is made at the same tone or pitch

Words with similar meanings:

DRONE	TEDIUM

NAIVE: lacking sophistication or experience

Having never traveled before, the hillbillies were more NAIVE than the people they met in Beverly Hills.

Related words:

NAIVETÉ: the state of being naive

Words with similar meanings:

ARTLESS	CREDULOUS	GUILELESS
INGENUOUS	SIMPLE	UNAFFECTED

OBDURATE: hardened in feeling; resistant to persuasion

The president was completely OBDURATE on the issue, and no amount of persuasion would change his mind.

Words with similar meanings:

INFLEXIBLE	INTRANSIGENT	RECALCITRANT
TENACIOUS	UNYIELDING	

OBSEQUIOUS: overly submissive and eager to please

The OBSEQUIOUS new associate made sure to compliment her supervisor's tie and agree with him on every issue.

Related words:

OBEISANCE: a physical show of respect or submission, such as a bow

Words with similar meanings:

COMPLIANT	DEFERENTIAL	SERVILE
SUBSERVIENT		

OBSTINATE: stubborn, unyielding

The OBSTINATE child could not be made to eat any food that he disliked.

Words with similar meanings:

INTRANSIGENT	MULISH	PERSISTENT
PERTINACIOUS	STUBBORN	TENACIOUS

OBVIATE: to prevent; to make unnecessary

The river was shallow enough to wade across at many points, which OBVIATED the need for a bridge.

Words with similar meanings:

FORESTALL	PRECLUDE	PROHIBIT

OCCLUDE: to stop up; to prevent the passage of

A shadow is thrown across the Earth's surface during a solar eclipse, when the light from the sun is OCCLUDED by the moon.

Words with similar meanings:

BARRICADE	BLOCK	CLOSE
OBSTRUCT		

ONEROUS: troublesome and oppressive; burdensome

The assignment was so extensive and difficult to manage that it proved ONEROUS to the team in charge of it.

Words with similar meanings:

ARDUOUS	BACKBREAKING	BURDENSOME
CUMBERSOME	DIFFICULT	EXACTING
FORMIDABLE	HARD	LABORIOUS
OPPRESSIVE	RIGOROUS	TAXING
TRYING		

OPAQUE: impossible to see through; preventing the passage of light

The heavy buildup of dirt and grime on the windows almost made them OPAQUE.

Related words:
OPACITY: the quality of being obscure and indecipherable

Words with similar meanings:
OBSCURE

OPPROBRIUM: public disgrace
After the scheme to embezzle from the elderly was made public, the treasurer resigned in utter OPPROBRIUM.

Words with similar meanings:

DISCREDIT	DISGRACE	DISHONOR
DISREPUTE	IGNOMINY	INFAMY
OBLOQUY	SHAME	

OSTENTATION: excessive showiness
The OSTENTATION of the Sun King's court is evident in the lavish decoration and luxuriousness of his palace at Versailles.

Related words:
OSTENSIBLE: apparent

Words with similar meanings:

CONSPICUOUSNESS	FLASHINESS	PRETENTIOUSNESS
SHOWINESS		

PARADOX: a contradiction or dilemma
It is a PARADOX that those most in need of medical attention are often those least able to obtain it.

Words with similar meanings:

ANOMALY	IRONY

PARAGON: model of excellence or perfection
She is the PARAGON of what a judge should be: honest, intelligent, hardworking, and just.

Words with similar meanings:

APOTHEOSIS	IDEAL	QUINTESSENCE
STANDARD		

PEDANT: someone who shows off learning
The graduate instructor's tedious and excessive commentary on the subject soon gained her a reputation as a PEDANT.

Related words:
PEDANTIC: making an excessive display of learning

PERFIDIOUS: willing to betray one's trust
    The actress's PERFIDIOUS companion revealed all of her intimate secrets to the gossip columnist.

Related words:
PERFIDY: deceit, treachery

Words with similar meanings:
    DISLOYAL   FAITHLESS   TRAITOROUS
    TREACHEROUS

PERFUNCTORY: done in a routine way; indifferent
    The machinelike bank teller processed the transaction and gave the waiting customer a PERFUNCTORY smile.

Words with similar meanings:
    APATHETIC   AUTOMATIC   MECHANICAL

PERMEATE: to penetrate
    This miraculous new cleaning fluid is able to PERMEATE stains and dissolve them in minutes!

Related words:
IMPERMEABLE: unable to be permeated

Words with similar meanings:
    IMBUE   INFUSE   SUFFUSE

PHILANTHROPY: charity; a desire or effort to promote goodness
    New York's Metropolitan Museum of Art owes much of its collection to the PHILANTHROPY of private collectors who willed their estates to the museum.

Related words:
PHILANTHROPIST: someone who is generous and desires to promote goodness

Words with similar meanings:
    ALTRUISM   HUMANITARIANISM

PLACATE: to soothe or pacify
    The burglar tried to PLACATE the snarling dog by saying, "Nice doggy," and offering it a treat.

Related words:
PLACID: tolerant; calm
IMPLACABLE: unable to be made peaceful

Words with similar meanings:
APPEASE   CONCILIATE   MOLLIFY

PLASTIC: able to be molded, altered, or bent
The new material was very PLASTIC and could be formed into products of vastly different shapes.

Words with similar meanings:
ADAPTABLE   DUCTILE   MALLEABLE
PLIANT

PLETHORA: excess
Assuming that more was better, the defendant offered the judge a PLETHORA of excuses.

Words with similar meanings:
GLUT   OVERABUNDANCE   SUPERFLUITY
SURFEIT

PRAGMATIC: practical as opposed to idealistic
While daydreaming gamblers think they can get rich by frequenting casinos, PRAGMATIC gamblers realize that the odds are heavily stacked against them.

Related words:
PRAGMATISM: a practical approach to problem solving

Words with similar meanings:
RATIONAL   REALISTIC

PRECIPITATE: to throw violently or bring about abruptly; lacking deliberation
Upon learning that the couple married after knowing each other only two months, friends and family members expected such a PRECIPITATE marriage to end in divorce.

Related words:
PRECIPICE: a steep cliff
PRECIPITATION: weather phenomena, like rain or snow, that falls from the sky
PRECIPITOUS: very steep

Words with similar meanings:

ABRUPT	HASTY	HEADLONG
HURRIED	ILL-CONSIDERED	IMPETUOUS
IMPULSIVE	PROMPT	RASH
RECKLESS	SUDDEN	

PREVARICATE: to lie or deviate from the truth

Rather than admit that he had overslept again, the employee PREVARICATED and claimed that heavy traffic had prevented him from arriving at work on time.

Words with similar meanings:

EQUIVOCATE	LIE	PERJURE

PRISTINE: fresh and clean; uncorrupted

Since concerted measures had been taken to prevent looting, the archeological site was still PRISTINE when researchers arrived.

Words with similar meanings:

INNOCENT	UNDAMAGED

PRODIGAL: lavish; wasteful

The PRODIGAL son quickly wasted all of his inheritance on a lavish lifestyle devoted to pleasure.

Related words:
PRODIGALITY: excessive or reckless spending

Words with similar meanings:

EXTRAVAGANT	LAVISH	PROFLIGATE
SPENDTHRIFT	WASTEFUL	

PROLIFERATE: to increase in number quickly

Although he only kept two guinea pigs initially, they PROLIFERATED to such an extent that he soon had dozens.

Related words:
PROLIFIC: very productive or highly able to reproduce rapidly

Words with similar meanings:

BREED	MULTIPLY	PROCREATE
PROPAGATE	REPRODUCE	SPAWN

PROPITIATE: to conciliate; to appease

The management PROPITIATED the irate union by agreeing to raise wages for its members.

Related words:
PROPITIOUS: advantageous, favorable

Words with similar meanings:
| APPEASE | CONCILIATE | MOLLIFY |
| PACIFY | PLACATE | |

PROPRIETY: correct behavior; obedience to rules and customs
The aristocracy maintained a high level of PROPRIETY, adhering to even the most minor social rules.

Related words:
APPROPRIATE: suitable for a particular occasion or place

Words with similar meanings:
| DECENCY | DECORUM | MODESTY |
| SEEMLINESS | | |

PRUDENCE: wisdom, caution, or restraint
The college student exhibited PRUDENCE by obtaining practical experience along with her studies, which greatly strengthened her résumé.

Related words:
PRUDE: someone who is excessively concerned with propriety
PRUDISH: prissy and puritanical

Words with similar meanings:
ASTUTENESS	CIRCUMSPECTION	DISCRETION
FRUGALITY	JUDICIOUSNESS	PROVIDENCE
THRIFT		

PUNGENT: sharp and irritating to the senses
The smoke from the burning tires was extremely PUNGENT.

Words with similar meanings:
| ACRID | CAUSTIC | PIQUANT |
| POIGNANT | STINGING | |

QUIESCENT: motionless
Many animals are QUIESCENT over the winter months, minimizing activity in order to conserve energy.

Related words:
QUIESCENCE: state of rest or inactivity

Words with similar meanings:

DORMANT   LATENT

RAREFY: to make thinner or sparser

Since the atmosphere RAREFIES as altitudes increase, the air at the top of very tall mountains is too thin to breathe.

Related words:

RAREFACTION: the process of making something less dense

Words with similar meanings:

ATTENUATE   THIN

REPUDIATE: to reject the validity of

The old woman's claim that she was Russian royalty was REPUDIATED when DNA tests showed she was of no relation to them.

Words with similar meanings:

DENY   DISAVOW   DISCLAIM
DISOWN   RENOUNCE

RETICENT: silent, reserved

Physically small and RETICENT in her speech, Joan Didion often went unnoticed by those upon whom she was reporting.

Words with similar meanings:

COOL   INTROVERTED   LACONIC
STANDOFFISH   TACITURN   UNDEMONSTRATIVE

RHETORIC: effective writing or speaking

Lincoln's talent for RHETORIC was evident in his beautifully expressed Gettysburg Address.

Words with similar meanings:

ELOQUENCE   ORATORY

SATIATE: to satisfy fully or overindulge

His desire for power was so great that nothing less than complete control of the country could SATIATE it.

Related words:

SATE: to fully satisfy or overindulge
INSATIABLE: incapable of being satisfied

Words with similar meanings:

CLOY	GLUT	GORGE
SURFEIT		

SOPORIFIC: causing sleep or lethargy

The movie proved to be so SOPORIFIC that soon loud snores were heard throughout the theater.

Related words:
SOPOR: deep sleep

Words with similar meanings:

HYPNOTIC	NARCOTIC	SLUMBEROUS
SOMNOLENT		

SPECIOUS: deceptively attractive; seemingly plausible but fallacious

The student's SPECIOUS excuse for being late sounded legitimate, but was proved otherwise when his teacher called his home.

Words with similar meanings:

ILLUSORY	OSTENSIBLE	PLAUSIBLE
SPURIOUS	SOPHISTICAL	

STIGMA: a mark of shame or discredit

In *The Scarlet Letter*, Hester Prynne was required to wear the letter "A" on her clothes as a public STIGMA for her adultery.

Related words:
STIGMATIZE: to disgrace; to label with negative terms or reputation

Words with similar meanings:

BLEMISH	BLOT	OPPROBRIUM
STAIN	TAINT	

STOLID: unemotional; lacking sensitivity

The prisoner appeared STOLID and unaffected by the judge's harsh sentence.

Words with similar meanings:

APATHETIC	IMPASSIVE	INDIFFERENT
PHLEGMATIC	STOICAL	UNCONCERNED

SUBLIME: lofty or grand

The music was so SUBLIME that it transformed the rude surroundings into a special place.

Related words:
SUBLIMATE: to elevate or convert into something of higher worth
SUBLIMINAL: existing outside conscious awareness

Words with similar meanings:

AUGUST	EXALTED	GLORIOUS
GRAND	MAGNIFICENT	MAJESTIC
NOBLE	REGAL	RESPLENDENT
SUPERB		

TACIT: done without using words

Although not a word had been said, everyone in the room knew that a TACIT agreement had been made about which course of action to take.

Related words:
TACITURN: silent, not talkative

Words with similar meanings:

IMPLICIT	IMPLIED	UNDECLARED
UNSAID	UNUTTERED	

TACITURN: silent, not talkative

The clerk's TACITURN nature earned him the nickname "Silent Bob."

Related words:
TACIT: done without using words

Words with similar meanings:

LACONIC	RETICENT

TIRADE: long, harsh speech or verbal attack

Observers were shocked at the manager's TIRADE over such a minor mistake.

Words with similar meanings:

DIATRIBE	FULMINATION	HARANGUE
OBLOQUY	REVILEMENT	VILIFICATION

TORPOR: extreme mental and physical sluggishness

After surgery, the patient experienced TORPOR until the anesthesia wore off.

Related words:
TORPID: sluggish, lacking movement

Words with similar meanings:

APATHY	LANGUOR

TRANSITORY: temporary, lasting a brief time

The reporter lived a TRANSITORY life, staying in one place only long enough to cover the current story.

Related words:

TRANSIT: to pass through; to change or make a transition

TRANSIENT: passing quickly in and out of existence; one who stays a short time

Words with similar meanings:

EPHEMERAL	EVANESCENT	FLEETING
IMPERMANENT	MOMENTARY	

VACILLATE: to sway physically; to be indecisive

The customer held up the line as he VACILLATED between ordering chocolate chip or rocky road ice cream.

Words with similar meanings:

DITHER	FALTER	FLUCTUATE
OSCILLATE	WAVER	

VENERATE: to respect deeply

In a traditional Confucian society, the young VENERATE their elders, deferring to the elders' wisdom and experience.

Related words:

VENERABLE: old, worthy of respect

Words with similar meanings:

ADORE	HONOR	IDOLIZE
REVERE		

VERACITY: truthfulness; accuracy

She had a reputation for VERACITY, so everyone trusted her description of events.

Related words:

VERITY: truth

VERACIOUS: filled with truth and accuracy

Words with similar meanings:

CANDOR	EXACTITUDE	FIDELITY
PROBITY		

VERBOSE: wordy

The professor's answer was so VERBOSE that his student forgot what the original question had been.

Related words:
VERBALIZE: to put into words
VERBATIM: using the exact words; word for word
VERBIAGE: lots of words that are usually superfluous

Words with similar meanings:

LONG-WINDED	LOQUACIOUS	PROLIX
SUPERFLUOUS		

VEX: to annoy

The old man who loved his peace and quiet was VEXED by his neighbor's loud music.

Related words:
VEXATION: a feeling of irritation

Words with similar meanings:

ANNOY	BOTHER	CHAFE
EXASPERATE	IRK	NETTLE
PEEVE	PROVOKE	

VOLATILE: easily aroused or changeable; lively or explosive

His VOLATILE personality made it difficult to predict his reaction to anything.

Words with similar meanings:

CAPRICIOUS	ERRATIC	FICKLE
INCONSISTENT	INCONSTANT	MERCURIAL
TEMPERAMENTAL		

WAVER: to fluctuate between choices

If you WAVER too long before making a decision about which testing site to register for, you may not get your first choice.

Words with similar meanings:

DITHER	FALTER	FLUCTUATE
OSCILLATE	VACILLATE	

WHIMSICAL: acting in a fanciful or capricious manner; unpredictable

The ballet was WHIMSICAL, delighting the children with its imaginative characters and unpredictable sets.

Related words:

WHIM: a fancy or sudden notion

Words with similar meanings:

| CAPRICIOUS | ERRATIC | FLIPPANT |
| FRIVOLOUS | | |

ZEAL: passion, excitement

She brought her typical ZEAL to the project, sparking enthusiasm in the other team members.

Related words:

ZEALOT: a fanatic

Words with similar meanings:

| ARDENCY | FERVOR | FIRE |
| PASSION | | |

WORDS IN CONTEXT EXERCISES

1. Which sentence uses the word **capricious** correctly, in meaning and form?

   (A) When it rained during the picnic, the party shivered under a tree until John's fiancée laughed, lifting the party's *capricious* mood.

   (B) Senators debated several *capricious* economic issues until the budget had been balanced.

   (C) Jane's mother speculated that her daughter's failing grades were due to her carefree, *capricious* nature.

2. Which sentence uses the word **misanthrope** correctly, in meaning and form?

   (A) Intelligent students are usually *misanthropes* because they tend to study hard in school.

   (B) The *misanthrope* liked to go deer hunting with his friends each summer to add to his collection.

   (C) Although he did well in graduate school, Gary is too much of a *misanthrope* to succeed as a professor.

3. Which sentence uses the word **paragon** correctly, in meaning and form?

   Ⓐ Firefighters are often the biggest *paragons* of smoke detectors, fire extinguishers, and other forms of fire safety.

   Ⓑ The decorated army commander was a *paragon* of team leadership, discipline, and professionalism.

   Ⓒ The chief of police did not support his *paragon* views on crime reduction.

4. Which sentence uses the word **venerate** correctly, in meaning and form?

   Ⓐ In ancient times, kings and great warriors were *venerated* by being buried with many riches.

   Ⓑ To regain control of his soccer team, the coach *venerated* players who were not taking the sport seriously.

   Ⓒ When the retailer *venerated* the brass bed frame, the antique piece looked like new.

5. Which sentence uses the word **cacophony** correctly, in meaning and form?

   Ⓐ The discordant music was a dreadful *cacophony* of synthesizer, accordion, and bells.

   Ⓑ Due to hip surgery, her *cacophony* was off-balance and clumsy.

   Ⓒ The novel's premise was so weak that the very *cacophony* of the motivation was questionable.

6. Which sentence uses the word **chicanery** correctly, in meaning and form?

   Ⓐ The cashmere sweater was light as *chicanery*, as if knit of the softest goose feathers.

   Ⓑ The smells of oregano and *chicanery* wafted from the kitchen into the living room.

   Ⓒ Though he is usually good at detecting *chicanery*, that swindler cheated him out of a month's pay.

7. Which sentence uses the word **impetuous(ly)** correctly, in meaning and form?

   A) She maintained a fiercely *impetuous* hold on her job title and never let anyone else perform the office duties.

   B) Because she'd experienced his rage before, she approached her boss *impetuously* with the updated meeting outline.

   C) She answered the questions on the form *impetuously*, filling them in randomly and without consideration.

8. Which sentence uses the word **vacillating** correctly, in meaning and form?

   A) The music stopped suddenly and the *vacillating* silence was deafening.

   B) After vacillating for days over whether to go to the doctor, she finally made an appointment when the swelling worsened dramatically.

   C) The *vacillating* motion of the hammock rocked her to sleep in the sun.

9. Which sentence uses the word **obstinate** correctly, in meaning and form?

   A) Old maps and charts are too imprecise to give *obstinate* locations of geographic landmarks.

   B) The new features added to the cell phone, including Internet access and photography, make it an *obstinate* piece of equipment.

   C) Her *obstinate* political philosophy allowed her to see her own conditioned, inherited beliefs only.

10. Which sentence uses the word **apathy** correctly, in meaning and form?

    A) The abhorrent criminal sneered maliciously, while the uninterested detective looked on with *apathy*.

    B) Even wearing a heavy cape and tight corset, the opera singer carried herself across the stage with great *apathy*.

    C) When the delicate gardenia blossoms opened, a scented *apathy* filtered through the air.

11. Which sentence uses the word **banal** correctly, in meaning and form?

   (A) The protesting crowd quickly formed a *banal* and crossed it to reach the locked offices of the politicians.

   (B) Thoughtful as her overtures were, his sister's insistence on traditions as *banal* as birthday cards and candles on the cake irritated him.

   (C) Her effervescent light-heartedness made a *banal* impression on him.

12. Which sentence uses the word **castigate** correctly, in meaning and form?

   (A) They stayed a long time by the shore, to watch the boats *castigate* in the setting sun.

   (B) She wrote the paper last night so she was fully prepared for her professor to *castigate* her weak efforts.

   (C) She insisted on chewing vigorously to *castigate* her food before swallowing.

13. Which sentence uses the word **cogent** correctly, in meaning and form?

   (A) The doctor presented *cogent* reasons for continuing the treatment.

   (B) The doctor prepared a *cogent* supply of medical resources for the patient.

   (C) Not all forms of cancer have symptoms *cogent* to only one prescribed type.

14. Which sentence uses the word **lavish** correctly, in meaning and form?

   (A) Her efforts to create a *lavish* party to entertain her new in-laws were flawless.

   (B) Her *lavish* disdain for her professor began to draw the attention of the whole class.

   (C) He kept his skin disorder *lavish* by concealing it discreetly beneath long sleeves.

15. Which sentence uses the word **garrulous** correctly, in meaning and form?

   (A) The *garrulous* guest regaled the party with songs and stories all evening.

   (B) The police set out to apprehend the *garrulous* thief who stole the vehicle.

   (C) The student developed a *garrulous* model to illustrate her geography assignment.

16. Which sentence uses the word **pungent** correctly, in meaning and form?

    (A) The scent of mold assaulted her senses with its *pungent* odor.

    (B) The babysitter developed a *pungent* fondness for the children she cared for.

    (C) Nobody associated with the *pungent* student who lost his temper so easily.

17. Which sentence uses the word **onerous** correctly, in meaning and form?

    (A) Her *onerous* view of the world became apparent during the debate when she mistook libertarianism for liberalism.

    (B) In the fall, the responsibility of driving her brother to practice became more *onerous* because he played twice as many fall sports as summer sports.

    (C) Chad grew concerned that chemicals were being used for a more *onerous* purpose than to study medicine.

18. Which sentence uses the word **plethora** correctly, in meaning and form?

    (A) The new student's hilarious stories brought a lot of *plethora* to the straitlaced campus.

    (B) The newlyweds' home was filled with a *plethora* of gifts, flowers, and letters wishing them good fortune.

    (C) Elephants *plethora* before they begin a long journey.

19. Which sentence uses the word **taciturn** correctly, in meaning and form?

    (A) After his wife died, the widower grew isolated and became *taciturn* in public.

    (B) Her *taciturn* fear of public speaking caused her palms to sweat and her heart to flutter.

    (C) *Taciturn* by nature, she spoke to anyone who would listen about any subject on her mind.

20. Which sentence uses the word **efficacy** correctly, in meaning and form?

    (A) The man fought with fierce *efficacy*, but ultimately lost the boxing match.

    (B) The car owner decided that a damaged fender was too negligible to warrant making an *efficacy*.

    (C) Due to the *efficacy* of his business, a store owner was able to open another branch.

21. Which sentence uses the word **repudiate** correctly, in meaning and form?

    (A) The leftover crumbs, dirty plates, and chocolate-smudged faces helped them *repudiate* what they had for dessert.

    (B) The investor *repudiated* the business plan once she demonstrated that it was nothing more than a pyramid scheme.

    (C) Gamblers work hard to conceal ticks and behaviors that might *repudiate* their strategies.

22. Which sentence uses the word **deferential** correctly, in meaning and form?

    (A) The courts make it clear that *deferential* behaviors will not be tolerated during jury selection.

    (B) The miscreant kicked rocks into the yard next door with a *deferential* attitude toward the homeowners.

    (C) The young man guided his grandmother with *deferential* patience to her car.

23. Which sentence uses the word **dupe** correctly, in meaning and form?

    (A) When the boy's cousin revealed a well-known secret, the boy had to *dupe* surprise.

    (B) No one would ever *dupe* to interrupt the patriarch of the family during mealtimes.

    (C) She *duped* her boyfriend into believing she lived in a better neighborhood.

24. Which sentence uses the word **stolid** correctly, in meaning and form?

    (A) She painted the landscape with *stolid* and acrylic paints.

    (B) Mother complained about the *stolid* couple who stayed so much later than all the other guests.

    (C) The *stolid* professor remained unmoved by the students' story of how they had missed the exam because of the blizzard.

25. Which sentence uses the word **zealous** correctly, in meaning and form?

    (A) He had a *zealous* crush on her that he was much too shy to make known.

    (B) The candidate's *zealous* campaign made a big impression on his supporters.

    (C) He had a *zealous* feeling for his boss and always made snide comments right to his face.

26. Which sentence uses the word **implacable** correctly, in meaning and form?

    (A) Observing a young couple, the older woman felt an *implacable* grief for her lost youth.

    (B) She could never convince her *implacable* son to eat anything but his favorite foods.

    (C) The violinist in the subway station played with an *implacable* skill that no one even recognized.

27. Which sentence uses the word **insipid** correctly, in meaning and form?

    (A) Despite its enormous popularity, the book struck Tom as *insipid*, lacking creativity and inspiration.

    (B) With *insipid* legal maneuvering, the lawyer connected the witness to the crime.

    (C) Homeless shelters handle the poverty of those on the streets by providing *insipid* food and comfort.

28. Which sentence uses the word **transient** correctly, in meaning and form?

    (A) The thin girl pulled a shawl over her chilled, *transient* shoulders.

    (B) The sophomore regretted socializing with such *transient* abandon during his freshman year.

    (C) For a sudden, *transient* moment, the actor seemed to forget his lines completely.

29. Which sentence uses the word **naive** correctly, in meaning and form?

    (A) The film critic's *naive* comment about the classic film illustrated his lack of experience.

    (B) The shape of the yew bushes grew more *naive* when she stopped trimming them.

    (C) The pain in her side grew so intensely *naive* that she doubled over.

30. Which sentence uses the word **audacity** correctly, in meaning and form?

    (A) The *audacity* with which she voiced her complaints startled everyone in the room.

    (B) She left her parents' home in *audacity* to their wishes that she stay.

    (C) Finally leaving her parents' home, she was able to embrace her autonomy and make choices of her own *audacity*.

ANSWER KEY FOR WORDS IN CONTEXT EXERCISES

1.	C	16.	A
2.	C	17.	B
3.	B	18.	B
4.	A	19.	A
5.	A	20.	C
6.	C	21.	B
7.	C	22.	C
8.	B	23.	C
9.	C	24.	C
10.	A	25.	B
11.	B	26.	B
12.	B	27.	A
13.	A	28.	C
14.	A	29.	A
15.	A	30.	A

For further explanation, please see the "Words in Context" section of this chapter (pages 256-295), containing definitions and sample sentences for all vocabulary words tested in this exercise.

PART FOUR

Analytical Writing

CHAPTER 7

The Issue Essay

THE ISSUE ESSAY

The first of the Analytical Writing essay tasks is the Issue essay. On the Issue essay, you are given a point of view about which you'll have to form an opinion and then provide a well-supported and justifiable case for that opinion. The Issue essay requires you to construct your own argument by making claims and providing evidence to support your position on a given issue. The directions will ask you to take a position on the issue and instruct you to explain your position convincingly, using reasons and/or examples to back up your assertions.

For the assignment topic, expect a one- to two-sentence prompt that discuss a broad, general issue, sometimes presenting only one point of view, sometimes presenting two conflicting points. Either way, the test will present a statement that can reasonably be either supported or opposed. Your job is to form an opinion on the topic and make a case for that opinion.

The directions for the Issue essay will look like this:

Directions: You will be given a brief quotation that states or implies a topic of general interest, along with explicit instructions on how to respond to that topic. Your response will be evaluated according to how well you:

- Respond to the specific directions the task gives you.
- Reflect on the complexities of the issue.
- Organize and develop your thoughts.
- Support your reasoning with relevant examples.
- Express yourself in standard written English.

The following is a list of the types of possible Issue essay tasks you might encounter on the GRE Analytical Writing section:

Write a response in which you examine your own position on the statement. Explore the extent to which you either agree or disagree with it, and support your reasoning with evidence and/or examples. Be sure to reflect on ways in which the statement might or might not be true, and how this informs your thinking on the subject.

Write your own response to the recommendation in which you discuss why you either agree or disagree with it. Support your response with evidence and/or examples. Use a hypothetical set of circumstances to illustrate the consequences of accepting or rejecting the recommendation, and explain how this informs your thinking.

Develop a response to the claim in which you discuss whether or not you agree with it. Focus specifically on the most powerful or compelling examples that could be used to refute your position.

Write a response in which you determine which view bears the closest resemblance to your own. In justifying your reasoning and supporting your position, be sure to include your reaction to both of the views presented.

Develop a response to the claim in which you discuss whether or not you agree with it. Focus specifically on whether or not you agree with the reason upon which the claim is based.

Write a response discussing your reaction to the stated policy. Justify your reasoning for the position you take. Explain the potential consequences or implications for implementing such a policy and how this informs your position.

The Kaplan Method for Analytical Writing

- **STEP 1 Take the issue/argument apart.**
- **STEP 2 Select the points you will make.**
- **STEP 3 Organize, using Kaplan's essay templates.**
- **STEP 4 Type your essay.**
- **STEP 5 Proofread your work.**

How the Kaplan Method for Analytical Writing Works

Here's how the Kaplan Method for Analytical Writing works for the Issue essay:

◆ **STEP 1 Take the issue apart.**

Read the assignment and consider both sides of the issue. Use your scratch paper throughout Steps 1–3. Restate the issue in your own words. Consider the other side of the issue, and put that into your own words as well.

◆ **STEP 2 Select the points you will make.**

After you consider what both sides of the issue mean, think of reasons and examples for both sides and decide which side you will support or the extent to which you agree with the stated position.

◆ **STEP 3 Organize, using Kaplan's essay templates.**

Organize your thoughts by outlining what you want to say, so that you'll be able to approach the actual writing process confidently and focus on expressing your ideas clearly. In the introduction, restate the prompt in your own words, state whether you agree or disagree, and give a preview of the supporting points you plan to make. In the middle paragraphs, give your points of agreement (or disagreement) and provide support. Determine the evidence you'll use to support each point. Be sure to lead with your best argument. Think about how the essay as a whole will flow. Conclude by summing up your position on the issue.

◆ **STEP 4 Type your essay.**

You shouldn't proceed with this step until you've completed the three preceding ones. Graders have a limited amount of time in which to read your essay, so start out and conclude with strong statements. Be emphatic and concise with your prose, and link related ideas with transitions. This will help your writing flow and make things easier on the grader. Furthermore, you'll save time and energy by preparing your essay before you start typing it.

◆ **STEP 5 Proofread your work.**

Save enough time to read quickly through the entire essay. Look for errors you can address quickly: capitalization, paragraph divisions, double-typed words, general typos, and small grammatical errors.

Apply the Kaplan Method for Analytical Writing to the Issue Essay

Now, apply the Kaplan Method for Analytical Writing to a sample Issue prompt:

Claim: High school students should be graded on a pass/fail basis, rather than a scaled system of letter grades (A–F).

Reason: It is more important to assess whether or not students have a basic command of the subjects they take than how they fare against their peers.

Develop a response to the claim in which you discuss whether or not you agree with it. Focus specifically on whether or not you agree with the reason upon which the claim is based.

▶ STEP 1 Take the issue apart.

Your first step is to dissect the issue. Take notes on your scratch paper. Start by restating the issue, and the claim it is based on, in your own words: "We should grade high school students as either pass or fail because we only need to know if they understand the material, while ranking them against their peers is less important." Now, consider the other side of the issue—in your own words: "We need a scaled grading system to be able to measure students against one another, as this is important for college admissions."

▶ STEP 2 Select the points you will make.

Your job, as stated in the directions, is to decide whether or not you agree with the statement and then to explain your decision. Some would argue that the use of scaled grades is useless, as well as demoralizing for students who test poorly. Others would say that it's imperative that we use them, as their use allows colleges and universities to distinguish between applicants. Which side do you take? Remember, this isn't about showing the essay graders your deep-seated beliefs about education—it's about demonstrating that you can formulate an argument and communicate it clearly. The position you choose for the Issue essay doesn't have to be one you actually believe in. Quickly jot down on your scratch paper the pros and cons of each side, and choose the side for which you have the most relevant support. For this topic, that process might go something like this:

Arguments *for* the use of scaled grades:

- It helps colleges differentiate between applicants.
- It will help schools determine how far behind their peers poorly performing students are.

· Grades are useful as long as they are consistently applied, and steps can be taken to make sure they aren't subjective.

Arguments *against* the use of scaled grades:

· They are subjectively determined and therefore useless as an assessment.
· They are damaging to students' self-esteem.
· Pass/fail allows schools to determine if students understand the material at a high enough level to graduate them.

Again, it doesn't matter which side you take. Strictly speaking, there is no *right* answer, as far as ETS is concerned. Let's say that in this case you decide to argue against the claim. Remember, the prompt asks you to argue for or against the use of a scaled grading system for high school students, and also to focus specifically on the reason upon which the claim is based.

▸ STEP 3 Organize, using Kaplan's essay templates.

You should already have begun to think out your arguments—that's how you picked the side you support in the first place. Now is the time to write your arguments, including those that weaken the opposing side. You're writing these notes for yourself, so feel free to use abbreviations.

Paragraph 1: We should not dispense with a grading scale in favor of a pass/fail rubric.
Paragraph 2: Scaled grades are important in college admissions.
Paragraph 3: Accurate grades can help identify students who are either in need of specialized help or advanced placement.
Paragraph 4: Grades are useful as long as they are applied consistently.
Paragraph 5: The grading scale serves an important function both pedagogically and within society.

▸ STEP 4 Type your essay.

Remember, open up with a general statement indicating that you understand the issue and then assert your position. From there, make your main points.

Sample Issue Essay 1

Proponents of a "pass/fail" grading rubric have made a case over the years that a scaled grading rubric, such as the traditional "A to F" method, should be dispensed with in favor of a system in which students would either pass or fail their classes. However, a close examination of the issue reveals that doing so would be detrimental to student welfare, as well as to society at large. The reason upon which the claim is based, that ensuring students have a basic command of the material is more important than comparing them to their peers, is misplaced as a justification for changing the grading scale that schools use.

First, we must consider the effect that such a change in assessment would have on society. Colleges and universities depend on a grading system that allows them to assess the relative academic skills of their applicant pool. One of the most expedient ways to provide that comparative scaffolding is a scaled grading system in the secondary school system. This allows institutions of higher learning to meaningfully distinguish between applicants, as a homogenous mass of "passes" would be difficult to choose from in a nonarbitrary way. Our higher education system works because it can determine, on the basis of empirical data, what students are most academically gifted at and best suited for. Grading helps to filter the right people into the right vocations (or, at a minimum, vocations to which they are well suited).

Second, the more precise and accurate a grading system is, the more accurately the school system can determine the specific needs of individual children. Different children learn in different ways and at different rates. For example, there are children who are very proficient in mathematics but less so in language arts and reading. Scaled grades allow schools to assess how far along students are compared to their peers, and to then place them in the appropriate class with appropriate instruction, be it advanced or remedial. A student who is precociously gifted in foreign languages will not be as encouraged to pursue it if her evaluation does not go beyond the knowledge that her command of the subject is sufficient to pass the course.

A final consideration is that the reason upon which the claim is based does not necessarily lead to the claim as a conclusion. A scaled grading rubric does allow the system to determine whether or not students have reached the minimum threshold of academic ability to graduate high school. It provides for the additional benefit of being a more precise indicator of a student's grasp of the material. Some have contended that grading from A to F is detrimental to students' self-esteem. Logically, however, this is far outweighed by the disservice done to our youth by allowing them to leave high school without the best possible education.

❖ STEP 5 Proofread your work.

Be sure to allot a few minutes after you have finished writing to review your essay. Although you don't have to write a grammatically flawless essay to score well, you should review it to correct some of the obvious mistakes. You can practice your writing skills in Chapter 9: Writing Foundations.

Assessment of Sample Issue Essay 1: "Outstanding," Score of 6

Now we'll look at how this essay would have been scored on the actual GRE Analytical Writing section:

This essay is carefully constructed throughout, enabling the reader to move effortlessly from point to point as the writer examines the multifaceted implications of the issue. The writer begins by acknowledging arguments for the opposing side, and then uses his thesis statement ("However, a close examination of the issue reveals that doing so would be detrimental to student welfare, as well as to society at large") to explain his own position on the issue. He proceeds to provide compelling reasons and examples to support the premise, and then takes the argument to an effective conclusion. The writing is clean and concise, and the grammar and usage errors minor enough not to lower the score. Sentence structure is varied, and diction and vocabulary are strong and expressive.

PACING STRATEGY

You'll have a limited amount of time to show the graders that you can think logically, analyze critically, and express yourself in clearly written English. Consequently, you'll need to know ahead of time how you're going to approach each essay. The Kaplan Method for Analytical Writing will help you plan and execute a clear, organized essay in the amount of time allotted. Note that the following timing guidelines are suggestions for how you should most effectively divide the 30 minutes you'll have for each of the essays. Different writers go through different steps at their own pace, so don't feel chained to the breakdown of time described here. As you practice, you'll get a better sense of the amount of time you need to spend on each step to produce the best essay possible.

Analyze an Issue

Number of Questions 1

Time per Question 30 minutes

Keep these estimates in mind as you prepare for the test. If you use them as you work the practice items, you will be comfortable keeping to the same amounts of time on test day.

» **STEP 1 Take the issue/argument apart: 2 minutes**

» **STEP 2 Select the points you will make: 4 minutes**

» **STEP 3 Organize, using Kaplan's essay templates: 2 minutes**

» **STEP 4 Type your essay: 20 minutes**

» **STEP 5 Proofread your work: 2 minutes**

Scoring

The essay scoring for the Analytical Writing section is *holistic*, which means that the graders base your score on their overall impression of your essay, rather than deducting specific point values for errors. A holistic score emphasizes the interrelationship of content, organization, and syntax, and denotes the unified effect of these combined elements. The scoring scale is from 0 to 6, with 6 being the highest score. Two graders will read and score each essay. If their scores differ by more than 1 point, a third reader will also score the essay.

Although the Analytical Writing section comprises two separate essays, ETS reports a single score that represents the average of your scores for the two essays, rounded up to the nearest half-point. You will receive your essay score, along with your official score report, within 10–15 days of your test date.

The Scoring Rubric

Each of the two essays requires different reasoning and presentation, so each has slightly different grading criteria. However, the following rubric will give you a general idea of the guidelines graders have in mind when they score Analytical Writing essays.

6: "Outstanding" Essay

- Insightfully presents and convincingly supports an opinion on the issue or a critique of the argument
- Communicates ideas clearly and is generally well organized; connections are logical
- Demonstrates superior control of language: grammar, stylistic variety, and accepted conventions of writing; minor flaws may occur

5: "Strong" Essay

- Presents well-chosen examples and strongly supports an opinion on the issue or a critique of the argument
- Communicates ideas clearly and is generally well organized; connections are logical
- Demonstrates solid control of language: grammar, stylistic variety, and accepted conventions of writing; minor flaws may occur

4: "Adequate" Essay

- Presents and adequately supports an opinion on the issue or a critique of the argument
- Communicates ideas fairly clearly and is adequately organized; logical connections are satisfactory

- Demonstrates satisfactory control of language: grammar, stylistic variety, and accepted conventions of writing; some flaws may occur

3: "Limited" Essay

- Succeeds only partially in presenting and supporting an opinion on the issue or a critique of the argument
- Communicates ideas unclearly and is poorly organized
- Demonstrates less than satisfactory control of language: contains significant mistakes in grammar, usage, and sentence structure

2: "Weak" Essay

- Shows little success in presenting and supporting an opinion on the issue or a critique of the argument
- Struggles to communicate ideas; essay shows a lack of clarity and organization
- Meaning is impeded by many serious mistakes in grammar, usage, and sentence structure

1: "Fundamentally Deficient" Essay

- Fails to present a coherent opinion and/or evidence on the issue or a critique of the argument
- Fails to communicate ideas; essay is seriously unclear and disorganized
- Lacks meaning due to widespread and severe mistakes in grammar, usage, and sentence structure

0: "Unscorable" Essay

- Completely ignores topic
- Attempts to copy the task
- Written in a language other than English or contains indecipherable text

ISSUE ESSAY PRACTICE PROMPTS

The following is a list of sample Issue essay prompts like those you might encounter on the GRE Analytical Writing section. Those preceded by an asterisk (*) have a sample essay response in the subsequent section of the chapter:

Issue 1:

Some people believe that strong relationships can only develop after conflict and resolution have enabled the partners to speak openly and trust deeply. Others believe that each conflict creates rifts in a relationship that can never be repaired, weakening its foundation.

Write a response in which you determine which view bears the closest resemblance to your own. In justifying your reasoning and supporting your position, be sure to include your reaction to both of the views presented.

Issue 2:

Claim: Military training strategies, such as unit cohesion and drilling, are powerful techniques to use in a classroom.

Reason: These strategies allow students to focus on a task and think like a team, supporting one another to reach a goal.

Develop a response to the claim in which you discuss whether or not you agree with it. Focus specifically on whether or not you agree with the reason upon which the claim is based.

Issue 3:

A nation should ultimately be responsible for the health, welfare, and prosperity of its own citizens.

Write a response discussing your reaction to the stated policy. Justify your reasoning for the position you take. Explain the potential consequences or implications of implementing such a policy and how this informs your position.

*Issue 4:

People who work in the arts and humanities should earn less than those who work in the sciences and economics because the benefit of the arts and humanities to the population is less important than that of scientific or economic endeavors.

Write your own response to the recommendation in which you discuss why you either agree or disagree with it. Support your response with evidence and/or examples. Use a hypothetical set of circumstances to illustrate the consequences of accepting or rejecting the recommendation, and explain how this informs your thinking.

*Issue 5:

Some people argue that confidence and optimism are critical to achieving a dream, while others believe that selfless hard work is the only way to reach a goal.

Write a response in which you determine which view bears the closest resemblance to your own. In justifying your reasoning and supporting your position, be sure to include your reaction to both of the views presented.

*Issue 6:

Claim: The study of a nation's prominent historical leaders and figures is a poor way to study its history.

Reason: The clearest lens through which to view a nation's history is the welfare of its entire population.

Develop a response to the claim in which you discuss whether or not you agree with it. Focus specifically on whether or not you agree with the reason upon which the claim is based.

*Issue 7:

Educational institutions have a responsibility to dissuade students from pursuing fields of study in which they are unlikely to succeed.

Develop a response to the claim in which you discuss whether or not you agree with it. Focus specifically on the most powerful or compelling examples that could be used to refute your position.

*Issue 8:

The main reason we should study history is to ensure that we do not repeat the mistakes of the past.

Write a response in which you examine your own position on the statement. Explore the extent to which you either agree or disagree with it, and support your reasoning with evidence and/or examples. Be sure to reflect on ways in which the statement might or might not be true, and how this informs your thinking on the subject.

Issue 9:

Governments in democratic societies should not restrict the public's access to information, even if it is of a sensitive or classified nature.

Write a response in which you examine your own position on the statement. Explore the extent to which you either agree or disagree with it, and support your reasoning with evidence and/or examples. Be sure to reflect on ways in which the statement might or might not be true, and how this informs your thinking on the subject.

Issue 10:

Professors who work at public universities should not automatically be entitled to periodic sabbaticals, because sabbaticals are expensive and do not necessarily yield anything of value in return.

Write your own response to the recommendation in which you discuss why you either agree or disagree with it. Support your response with evidence and/or examples. Use a hypothetical set of circumstances to illustrate the consequences of accepting or rejecting the recommendation, and explain how this informs your thinking.

Issue 11:

The U.S. should dispense with regulated speed limits on interstate highways, since drivers rarely abide by them.

Write a response discussing your reaction to the stated policy. Justify your reasoning for the position you take. Explain the potential consequences or implications for implementing such a policy and how this informs your position.

Issue 12:

Claim: The educational curriculum for young children should emphasize social skills and the arts over math and reading skills.

Reason: Such a curriculum would foster important moral and social development in children and lead to them becoming well-adjusted adults.

Develop a response to the claim in which you discuss whether or not you agree with it. Focus specifically on whether or not you agree with the reason upon which the claim is based.

Issue 13:

Some economists use the measure of the total value of goods and services that a country produces annually, called the "gross domestic product," or GDP, as the measure of a nation's economic health. Others contend that the GDP is an inadequate measure, because it fails to take into account many important factors, such as unequal distribution of wealth and the health of the environment, that affect people's quality of life.

Write a response in which you determine which view bears the closest resemblance to your own. In justifying your reasoning and supporting your position, be sure to include your reaction to both of the views presented.

Issue 14:

Claim: It is in the best interest of the U.S. government to cease funding the National Aeronautics and Space Administration (NASA).

Reason: The cost of a federal agency like NASA is gargantuan, and the returns on the investment are limited. Funding could be better allocated to dealing with pressing social problems, such as homelessness and poverty.

Develop a response to the claim in which you discuss whether or not you agree with it. Focus specifically on the most powerful or compelling examples that could be used to refute your position.

Issue 15:

The only way to have a meaningful interaction with a foreign culture is, not simply to learn the language, but to live within that culture for an extended period of time.

Write a response in which you examine your own position on the statement. Explore the extent to which you either agree or disagree with it, and support your reasoning with evidence and/or examples. Be sure to reflect on ways in which the statement might or might not be true, and how this informs your thinking on the subject.

ISSUE ESSAY SAMPLE ESSAYS AND EXPLANATIONS

Here are sample top-scoring essays to five of the sample Issue prompts found in the previous section. Remember that an essay does not have to be perfect to receive a top score. Review these essays and note the qualities that earned them a score of 6.

Issue 4:

People who work in the arts and humanities should earn less than those who work in the sciences and economics because the benefit of the arts and humanities to the population is less important than that of scientific or economic endeavors.

Write your own response to the recommendation in which you discuss why you either agree or disagree with it. Support your response with evidence and/or examples. Use a hypothetical set of circumstances to illustrate the consequences of accepting or rejecting the recommendation, and explain how this informs your thinking.

Sample Response

The average American, when asked whether people who work in the sciences or economics should be paid more than people who work in the arts or humanities, would probably say yes. Scientific progress benefits society by making life easier and more enjoyable for the population. The study and regulation of economics enables society to develop and interact with people around the world. These two fields surely generate substantial, quantifiable benefit to the population. At first blush it seems logical to infer that people working in these fields should be compensated more generously. However, we do not determine payment for a group purely by measuring the benefit they create for society. It is difficult to quantify, purely in dollars, how much a professional golfer or a middle school math teacher actually contributes to the population. Furthermore, one cannot categorically assert that the fields of science and economics generate more benefit than arts and humanities. Deciding how much one person or field of study is responsible for the generation of a discrete amount of wealth is difficult. For these reasons, among others, such a recommendation should not be followed.

First, a method for measuring financial reimbursement for different types of occupations must be determined. In an ideal world, wages would be based on merit and contribution to the benefit of society. Things are not that simple in the "real" world. Consider the following two professions: a custodian at a hospital, and a researcher working on theoretical physics in an advanced technology laboratory. The two are working concurrently: the custodian disinfects a hospital bed so a new patient can be admitted, and the physicist calculates the results of a test to prove String Theory. Determining which of the two is contributing more to the benefit of society is difficult. The two workers most likely make substantially different wages. The usual justification for the discrepancy in the wages is that many people can do the custodian's job, while very few can do the researcher's job. Thus, the difference in wage is not based on merit or benefit to society at large, but upon basic supply and demand (limited supply of advanced intelligence and high demand for that skill). Justifying earnings in this way does not attend to the fact that the custodian's duties are still quite necessary. An antiseptic environment such as a hospital could not possibly function without the contributions of the custodial staff.

Secondly, in addition to determining fair compensation, determining the benefit to the population as a whole is problematic. Not all people necessarily agree that scientists and economists benefit society more than artists and those who work the humanities. Imagine that the recommendation was actually put into effect. If society were to provide reduced incentives for teachers, the education of the population as a whole would suffer. Future generations of scientists and economists would be less well equipped to make important scientific or economic contributions. Education is holistic, and draws upon a broad range of disciplines, from the Arts and Humanities to Economics and the Sciences. Even though teachers' contributions to such benefits are indirect and less easily quantified, they are still unassailably real. A scientist can never publish a groundbreaking, economically lucrative discovery if she is never taught to write in grammar school.

In the final analysis, it is difficult to assert that science offers a greater benefit to the population than art. Firstly, it is an inherently subjective value judgment and is not empirically determined. Secondly, even if we try to determine quantitatively how much "work" has been put into such profitable endeavors in the sciences and economics.

Analysis

This essay is particularly well constructed; the author begins by acknowledging the argument for compensating at a higher rate people who work in the sciences or economics than people who work in the humanities. While admitting that the argument seems to make sense, he asserts that this is not necessarily the case. He takes the contrary point of view, and his position is nuanced. He cites two basic assumptions upon which the recommendation depends, neither of which are necessarily founded. The first is that we reward people fairly according to the work they do. The second is that it is difficult to determine, quantitatively, how much someone has contributed to a job or endeavor. The author cites the example of teachers. Without teachers, scientists and economists would never be able to develop intellectually to the point where they can make their contributions. There are a few grammatical errors, as would occur under normal test conditions, but they will not detract from the score. Essays with some small errors or imperfections can still earn a score of 6. For these reasons, this essay receives a score of 6.

Issue 5:

Some people argue that confidence and optimism are critical to achieving a dream, while others believe that selfless hard work is the only way to reach a goal.

Write a response in which you determine which view bears the closest resemblance to your own. In justifying your reasoning and supporting your position, be sure to include your reaction to both of the views presented.

Sample Response

Rather than relying solely on self-assurance and a positive outlook, sustained levels of effort and industry must be maintained in order to reach a goal. While some claim that a positive outlook alone can bring about good things, and others say only a nose-to-the-grindstone attitude will get you where you want to be, it seems to me that the former flows from the latter. Most truly successful people are positive and confident hard workers who derive confidence from their work ethic. Goal-seeking people put in so much time and energy because they actually believe that those goals are achievable and probable results of their efforts. This in itself is characteristic of a positive outlook and leads me to believe that these two attitudes can exist independently, but, hard work is the key ingredient to successfully achieving a goal.

Personally, while my constant optimism certainly helps me to maintain my strong work ethic, my ability to achieve a goal is grounded in hard work. When obstacles and set-backs occur, I am able to convince myself that a goal is still attainable and that a particular situation will improve if I put in the necessary work. I can offer, as anecdotal evidence, an instance in which I had three papers due on the same day for three different classes. I felt overwhelmed, as I had gotten a late start on all of them, but what motivated me was the knowledge that working hard would ultimately lead me to success. A positive attitude could not write my papers, but I was positive as a result of my drive to work hard. What pushes me to stay focused and determined is the conviction that hard work will lead directly to accomplishing a goal. While I do believe that they work best in union, there are certainly benefits to each goal-seeking approach mentioned earlier.

Hard work often results in measurable progress, a gain of experience, and skill development, to name a few. This, in and of itself, will inculcate a positive attitude that will reinforce that strong work ethic. Maintaining a positive outlook and remaining self-confident can help goal-seekers stay persistent and focused despite the inevitable setbacks that occur on the road to reaching any goal. Although these goal-seeking approaches both do have positive outcomes and can individually result in the achievement of goals, goals can only be successfully attained if the goal-seeker is driven by an indefatigable work ethic.

Analysis

This essay is a solid 6. The author adopts a personal, first-person tone, which is acceptable in this case, as that is what the prompt calls for. She tackles the issue head-on, offering her position that hard work is the key factor in achieving a dream. She goes one step further and points out that optimism can be a byproduct of such a work ethic. The personal anecdote cited in the second paragraph is perfectly suited to reinforcing the author's point. The structure of the essay is taut, and the writing is without superfluous fluff. Although the essay is in the first person, the author avoids needless self-reference. There are a few grammatical errors, as would occur under normal test conditions, and they will not detract from the score. Essays with some small errors or imperfections can still earn a score of 6. For these reasons, this essay receives a score of 6

Issue 6:

Claim: The study of a nation's prominent historical leaders and figures is a poor way to study its history.

Reason: The clearest lens through which to view a nation's history is actually the welfare of all its people.

Develop a response to the claim in which you discuss whether or not you agree with it. Focus specifically on whether or not you agree with the reason upon which the claim is based.

Sample Response

This claim is poorly supported because if a nation has had poor leaders, the people will, in turn, suffer. On a much smaller scale, how a child is raised is a reflection of how their parents raised them. If parents are attentive and loving, the children will, most likely, display similar attributes. Similarly, with regards to leaders and nations, if a leader actually cares about his country and its people, the standard of living in that country will reflect that care. People will be happier and have fewer worries. Studying historical figures, therefore, provides as much of a bellwether as studying the welfare of the people they lead.

If one were to examine the situation of a crumbling country, such as 1980s Zimbabwe, for example, one would see a prime example that backs up the above statement. The leader was corrupt and did not know how to properly run a country and, as a result, people fled the country and many who stayed starved and had very little money. In fact, the currency itself was practically worthless. With a leader who knows what he's doing, and actually cares about his citizens, Zimbabwe has the potential to thrive, and its people would have full pockets and full bellies.

Ancient Egypt can be cited as a counterexample to the claim. We know a great deal about Egypt's culture and achievements, and our knowledge comes from studying Egypt's leaders and rulers, not the welfare of its common people. The fact that Egypt's leaders were autocratic despots is beside the point; we know a great deal about Egypt's achievements and what life was like there through the study of the Pharaohs (even if the conditions for the average person were morally indefensible).

As John Donne once said, "no man is an island." This theme reflects throughout our history, for if a leader feels as though he or she is all that matters, the people under such a leader are going to suffer the consequences of his or her self-serving leadership decisions. No leader will ever be perfect, but if he or she has the right focus—that is, his people's welfare—then the decisions will be a reflection of his caring heart. A country's history will have its up and downs, but if it is able to learn from its mistakes, that can make all the difference.

A nation's history is certainly not solely about the leaders of countries and what each of them as individuals are able to accomplish, but how a leader conducts him or herself will reflect on how his or her citizens are living. If a leader becomes too power-hungry, the citizens are going to struggle as a result. Consider the situation with Hitler and Nazi Germany. He wanted ultimate control, and at whose cost? That's right, the people's. History is never one-sided, of course, and a bad leader does not necessarily mean that the country's citizens are also bad. However, a leader should be aware that how he or she behaves will affect other countries' views of his or her country. After all, if citizens are happy and content, then there will be less trouble to be recorded in the history books.

Analysis

This essay is emphatically and passionately argued. The author begins by immediately providing a justification for arguing the contrary of the claim. He insists that without great leaders, the people will suffer. He supports his position with compelling evidence, drawing on notable periods of history, such as ancient Egypt, which he uses as a counterexample to refute the claim. He uses this example to support a second counterargument, which is that the study of the pharaohs and their achievements has taught us a great deal about ancient Egypt. There are a few grammatical errors, as would occur under normal test conditions, and they will not detract from the score. Essays with some small errors or imperfections can still earn a score of 6. The diction is straightforward, but effective, which is what counts when it comes to grading. For these reasons, this essay receives a score of 6.

Issue 7:

Educational institutions have a responsibility to dissuade students from pursuing fields of study in which they are unlikely to succeed.

Develop a response to the claim in which you discuss whether or not you agree with it. Focus specifically on the most powerful or compelling examples that could be used to refute your position.

Sample Response

Educational institutions have a great many responsibilities on their shoulders; apart from giving future generations an idea of what the real world is like and how it functions, they also allows students to build on and develop their own personal beliefs and abilities. Any skills that you possess today are partially the result of your own hard work, but also of the institutions and people who taught you the meaning of hard work. There can be no question that all students need some form of guidance when learning who they are, how the world works, and their role in it. There are limits as to what educational institutions should do. If another person takes it upon themselves to dissuade a student against a certain career (solely for the reason that they might not succeed), what does that say about belief in the student's ability? There can be no hope for the world or for future generations if students are told by the very people teaching them that there are fields of study in which they will never succeed.

There is little question that educators should be honest about certain fields; there are inescapable realities about each of them. Politics is complex; medical professions require a strong stomach. What must be addressed, however, is that if a particular student feels a heightened interest towards the practice of any profession, should somebody else be the one to speak negatively about it? Imagine somebody telling Martin Luther King, Jr. all those years ago that his dreams would never succeed. What kind of society would we be living in if somebody had tried to dissuade him from the advancement of civil liberties? Consider Thomas Edison. He tried to produce the light bulb (or incandescent lamp) hundreds of times before it actually worked. Suppose somebody told him to give up after the first three or four attempts —how would that have worked out?

Eleanor Roosevelt is quoted as saying that "the future belongs to those who believe in the beauty of their dreams." It is a direct contradiction to everything the educational institutions stand for if they take upon themselves a responsibility to dissuade students from going into a particular field. If it is unlikely they will succeed, why is the field being taught? Why bother teaching it if there is no future for it?

All of the arguments aside, the responsibilities of educational institutions should not be second-guessed. The incredible knowledge and fortitude of all who take part in student education ought to be applauded (especially if you can read this). However, it is overstepping the boundaries of teaching to say that all educators have a responsibility to dissuade students from going into an unsuccessful career. Based on the education each student has been given, they have each earned the right to make that decision on their own, not because the institution told them so.

Analysis

This essay tackles a socially sensitive issue in a respectful and candid way. The author begins by acknowledging a powerful argument in support of the position. She does concede that schools should be honest about a student's chances of success in a difficult field (i.e., medicine or politics). While acknowledging this, she constructs an argument that asserts that institutions inculcate not only a specific set of skills, but also a reverence for learning and passion for dreams and ideas. She underscores this by citing examples such as Martin Luther King and Thomas Edison. There are a few grammatical errors, as would occur under normal test conditions, and they will not detract from the score. Essays with some small errors or imperfections can still earn a score of 6. The author uses rhetorical questions only sparingly and for good effect. For these reasons, this essay receives a score of 6.

Issue 8:

The main reason we should study history is to ensure that we do not repeat the mistakes of the past.

Write a response in which you examine your own position on the statement. Explore the extent to which you either agree or disagree with it, and support your reasoning with evidence and/or examples. Be sure to reflect on ways in which the statement might or might not be true, and how this informs your thinking on the subject.

Sample Response

While civilization has made several noted strides, other events throughout time have been denied and swept under the carpet. Although these situations are preferred to be forgotten, they often serve as warning signals that help prevent us from causing the same faults again. This is why the study of our past is crucial to the success of our present and future.

A prime example of a moment in history that is important to study in order to prevent a reoccurrence is the Holocaust. Around the 1930s through the mid 1940s, Hitler and Nazi supporters took the lives of over six million Jews, Gypsies, homosexuals, and other groups of people across Europe that were deemed threats to the Aryan race. While Hitler continued carrying out his plans for the genocide, authoritative figures and religious sects, such as President Roosevelt and the Catholic Church, were accused of neglecting to save victims. Nazi attempts to cover up the horrific events of the Holocaust were generally unsuccessful. However, despite war crime trials, records, and survivor accounts, some still deny the genocide ever occurred. Personal accounts, artifacts, and historical texts have helped open the eyes of several citizens to what really happened. This has helped prevent many populations from becoming clouded by feelings of uncertainty over the differences of others and allowing hatred to escalate to events similar to the Holocaust.

It can be argued that history should be taught in schools for other reasons. It helps students develop critical reading and analytical writing skills that will be useful in most career paths, as well as in college. It also provides a meaningful context in which to interpret contemporary political and social events. For example, it is difficult to understand the nuances and complexities of the precarious situation in the Middle East without a solid understanding of the history of the region. However, while this is certainly true, properly understood it is also part and parcel of the reason cited in the argument. Providing a proper context for interpreting contemporary events will only help in avoiding the mistakes of the past. Therefore, this reason can be subsumed into the overarching one presented by the argument.

In several instances, history has proved to repeat itself. People who ignore events like the Holocaust follow the saying that "Ignorance is bliss." Past warning signs left unaddressed have allowed citizens in some African countries to become genocide victims today. Despite the pain of reality, shedding light on yesterday's mistakes will help us prevent the same ones tomorrow.

Analysis

This essay is well constructed. The author agrees with the statement, and cites a specific set of examples (i.e., atrocities being "swept under the rug") as the best proof of the statement. The author moves on to specifically offer Nazi Germany as a prominent example. She also attends to possible alternative reasons for studying history, but deftly points out that those can all be ultimately "subsumed" into the reason for studying history that is advocated by the Issue statement. The writing is largely clear and direct. The use of diction is skillful and varied, but at the same time not bombastic or excessive. Pretentious word choice can sometimes be used to camouflage weak writing, but in this case diction supports content. For all these reasons, this essay receives a score of 6.

CHAPTER 8

The Argument Essay

THE ARGUMENT ESSAY

The second type of Analytical Writing essay type you have to contend with is the Argument essay. Here, you're given an argument that contains a conclusion and supporting evidence. The writer tries to persuade you of something (her conclusion) by citing facts or premises (her evidence). You should read the "argument" with a critical eye. Be on the lookout for unstated *assumptions* in the way the writer moves from evidence to conclusion. You aren't asked to agree or disagree with the author's *position* or *conclusion*; instead, the directions ask you to express how convincing you find the argument to be. You must analyze the reasoning used in the argument. Every argument presented for this GRE essay is flawed. To make your case, first analyze the argument itself and evaluate its use of evidence; then, explain how a different approach or more information would make the argument better (or possibly worse).

The directions for the Argument essay will look like this:

Directions: You will be presented with a short passage that asserts an argument or position, along with explicit instructions on how to respond to the passage. Your response will be evaluated according to how well you:

· Respond to the specific directions the task gives you.
· Analyze and interpret important elements of the passage.
· Organize and develop your analysis.
· Support your reasoning with relevant examples.
· Express yourself in standard written English.

The following is a list of the types of possible Argument essay tasks you might encounter on the GRE Analytical Writing section:

Write a response in which you describe specific examples or evidence needed to evaluate the argument and how those examples or evidence would weaken or strengthen the argument.

Write a response in which you explain what information would be necessary in order to decide whether the recommendation and the argument on which it is based are reasonable. Be sure to explain how the answers to these questions or pieces of information would help to evaluate the recommendation.

Write a response in which you discuss what questions would need to be answered to decide how likely the stated recommendation is to yield the predicted result. Be sure to explain how the answers to these questions would help to evaluate the recommendation.

Write a response in which you discuss what questions would need to be answered in order to assess the reasonableness of both the prediction and the argument upon which it is based. Be sure to explain how the answers to these questions would help to evaluate the prediction.

Write a response in which you discuss one or more viable alternatives to the proposed explanation. Justify, with support, why your explanation could rival the proposed explanation and explain how your explanation(s) can plausibly account for the facts presented in the argument.

The Kaplan Method for Analytical Writing

- ○ **STEP 1 Take the issue/argument apart.**
- ○ **STEP 2 Select the points you will make.**
- ○ **STEP 3 Organize, using Kaplan's essay templates.**
- ○ **STEP 4 Type your essay.**
- ○ **STEP 5 Proofread your work.**

How the Kaplan Method for Analytical Writing Works

Here's how the Kaplan Method for Analytical Writing works for the Argument essay:

❖ STEP 1 Take the argument apart.

The first step in deconstructing an argument is to identify the conclusion, that is, the main point the author is trying to make. After you've nailed down the conclusion, your next step is to locate the evidence used to support the conclusion. Finally, identify the unstated assumptions (pieces of evidence that are not explicitly stated but that are necessary for the evidence to lead validly to the conclusion). Note any terms that are ambiguous and need definition.

STEP 2 Select the points you will make.

Identify all the important assumptions needed to link the evidence to the conclusion. Think of additional evidence that would strengthen or weaken those assumptions.

STEP 3 Organize, using Kaplan's essay templates.

Organize your thoughts by outlining how the essay, as a whole, will flow. In the introduction, show that you understand the argument by putting it into your own words. Point out the author's conclusion and the evidence she uses to support that conclusion. In each of the middle paragraphs, identify flaws in the author's reasoning. Detail the unstated assumption(s) and explain why the argument is logically invalid if the assumptions prove unfounded. In your second to last paragraph, address ways to strengthen the argument and provide examples of evidence that would confirm the unstated assumption(s). Conclude by saying that, without such evidence, you are not persuaded.

STEP 4 Type your essay.

You shouldn't proceed with this step until you've completed the three preceding ones. Essay graders have a limited amount of time to work with, so start out and conclude with strong statements. Be emphatic and concise with your prose, and use transitions to link related or contrasting ideas. This will help your writing flow and make your essay easier for the grader to follow.

STEP 5 Proofread your work.

Save enough time to read through your response in its entirety. As you do so, have a sense of the errors you are liable to make.

Apply the Kaplan Method for Analytical Writing to the Argument Essay

Now, apply the Kaplan Method for Analytical Writing to a sample Argument prompt:

The following memorandum is from the Edwintown City Council:

"This year, in view of our pledge to be more environmentally conscious, we will be requiring all homeowners within the city limits to recycle their glass, plastic, and paper waste. According to a recent study by Edwintown University, the volume of litter in Edwintown and its surrounding environs has increased by 20 percent over the past 15 years. The only way to combat this blight is for our citizens to actively make an effort to recycle their trash. By enforcing recycling laws for all houses within the city limits, we will improve the aesthetic and public health conditions of our area."

Write a response in which you discuss what questions would need to be answered to decide how likely the stated recommendation is to yield the predicted result. Be sure to explain how the answers to these questions would help to evaluate the recommendation.

❖ STEP 1 Take the argument apart.

Conclusion (the point the author is trying to make): The only way to combat this blight is for our citizens to actively make an effort to recycle their trash. Enforcing recycling laws will improve town conditions.

Evidence (premises or facts offered to support the conclusion): According to a recent study by Edwintown University, the volume of litter in Edwintown and its surrounding environs has increased by 20 percent over the past 15 years.

Assumptions (unspoken conditions or beliefs necessary for the conclusion to make sense in light of the evidence):

- A city-wide required program for glass, paper, and plastic recycling will help citizens become more aware of the environment.
- The recycling program will improve upon the "aesthetic and public health conditions" in the area.

❖ STEP 2 Select the points you will make.

Analyze the use of evidence in the argument. Determine whether there's anything relevant that's not discussed:

- Whether or not there was any form of environmental regulations in the past that succeeded or failed
- Whether or not Edwintown University's study also discovered any particular habits of the citizens in the surrounding area that greatly contributed to the increase in the litter volume
- Whether or not Edwintown residents were recycling voluntarily even without enforcement
- Whether the type of trash produced in Edwintown can be recycled
- Whether Edwintown's trash is disposed of in a way that is aesthetically displeasing or that results in health risks

Also determine what types of evidence would make the argument stronger or more logically sound. In this case, we need more information to support the government's decision to implement recycling regulations and increase citizen awareness:

- Evidence that there will be incentives for citizen cooperation and participation
- Evidence that the government will support the community to help them meet the new requirements

· Evidence that the guidelines will be effective: have they already been applied to another community and produced effective improvements?

STEP 3 Organize, using Kaplan's essay templates.

For an essay on this topic, your opening sentences may look like this:

There has been a recent push for greater environmental awareness. This often includes governmental regulations designed to increase community participation, such as recycling laws. The memorandum from the Edwintown City Council exemplifies a positive strategy for impacting the local environment, but without more concrete evidence, the results predicted by the city council are speculative at best.

Paragraph 1: The argument is that recycling regulations will help improve the overall environment of the surrounding area.
Paragraph 2: The Edwintown University study needs to release additional details and findings.
Paragraph 3: The city council needs to describe more recycling strategies.
Paragraph 4: What incentives will community members have for following the recycling program?
Paragraph 5: For community support, the city council needs to release more evidence and strategies for its environmental improvement plans.

Use your notes as a working outline. In Argument essays, you'll primarily address the ways in which the assumptions are unsupported. You will also recommend new evidence you'd like to see and explain why. Remember to lead with your strongest points.

STEP 4 Type your essay.

Begin writing your essay now. Your essay for this assignment might look like the following sample.

Sample Argument Essay

There has been a recent push for greater environmental awareness. This often includes governmental regulations designed to increase community participation, such as recycling laws. The memorandum from the Edwintown City Council exemplifies a positive strategy for impacting the local environment, but without more concrete evidence, the results predicted by the city council are speculative at best.

To win support for their anticipated recycling program, the Edwintown City Council should release extensive information from Edwintown University's study. According to the city council, the study found that litter increased in the urban area over the past 15 years by 20 percent. We don't, however, know what the makeup of this litter was and whether the items responsible for the increase are recyclable. If the increase has been primarily in discarded electronics, for example, recycling could be difficult or expensive.

A second question that goes unaddressed in the statement is whether there are other factors that may contribute to the success or failure of the initiative. If, for example, there has been a loss in economic resources that decreased the number of recycling bins in public areas, there may have been an increase in trash disposed of in garbage bins. Oftentimes, studies of this nature will also compare other communities with similar environmental situations. To assess Edwintown's program, we should know whether nearby areas decided to implement similar regulations and whether they proved to be beneficial or useless. Knowing the answers to these questions would help the community pinpoint the specific changes that are needed to increase the regulations' enforceability and usefulness.

Along with providing a more intense examination of the university's study, the city council should also outline citizen participation. If Edwintonians have already been recycling, even without a requirement to do so, the new plan is unlikely to have much of an effect. To assess the potential efficacy of the plan, we'd need to know the current levels of recycling in the city. Other specifics of the plan are missing, too. Are there particular products, for example, that the city is or is not prepared to recycle? How can citizens decrease the amount of nonrecyclable waste they produce? Would other household actions, such as developing a compost pile, also help the environment? Giving citizens this kind of information would add to the advantages of the proposal and increase their willingness to embrace new regulations.

Additionally, the city council should detail their methods for enforcing the recycling regulations. At this point, we can only speculate on the effect that various enforcement mechanisms—fines, public service, and so on—would have on citizen participation. Related to this question is the issue of how easy it will be to participate. If citizens can simply put the recycling out for pickup, participation levels should be high. If, on the other hand, they have to travel a distance and deliver recycling to a collection center, enforcement will be much more difficult. Possible disciplinary actions and incentives alike will stimulate citizen awareness and participation.

The city council's desire to improve environmental conditions is admirable. However, citizens need to know more about the program before they can be expected to follow new regulations. A community's lack of support for governmental action generally stems from a desire for facts. Possible future efforts on behalf of the city council to inform citizens how and why their recycling regulations would be beneficial will help ensure cooperation.

> **STEP 5   Proofread your work.**

Be sure to allot some time after you have finished writing to review your essay. While a few grammatical errors here and there won't harm your score, having enough of them will, as will a few so severe that the meaning of the essay is lost. Make sure the graders are as favorably disposed to you as possible; a well-written essay makes their job a bit less tedious.

Assessment of Sample Argument Essay 1: "Outstanding," Score of 6
Now we'll look at how this essay would have been scored on the actual GRE Analytical Writing section:

This outstanding response demonstrates the writer's insightful analytical skills. The introduction notes the prompt's specious reasoning occasioned by unsupported assumptions and a lack of definition and evidence. The writer follows this up with a one-paragraph examination of each of the root flaws in the argument. Specifically, the author exposes these points undermining the argument:

- A city-wide required program for glass, paper, and plastic recycling will help citizens become more aware of the environment.
- The recycling program will improve upon the "aesthetic and public health conditions" in the area.

Each point receives thorough and cogent development (given the time constraints) in a smooth and logically organized discourse. There are a few grammatical flaws, but minor issues or grammar and mechanics will not prevent an outstanding essay from scoring a 6. This essay is succinct, economical, and generally error-free, with sentences that vary in length and complexity, while the diction and vocabulary are precise and expressive.

PACING STRATEGY

You'll have a limited amount of time to show the graders that you can think logically, analyze critically, and express yourself in clearly written English. Consequently, you'll need to know ahead of time how you're going to approach each essay. The Kaplan Method for Analytical Writing will help you plan and execute a clear, organized essay in the allotted time. Note that the following timing guidelines are suggestions for how you should most effectively divide the 30 minutes you'll have for each of the essays. Different writers go through different steps at their own pace, so don't feel chained to the breakdown of time described here. As you practice, you'll get a better sense of the amount of time you need to spend on each step to produce the best essay possible.

Analyze an Argument

Number of Questions 1

Time per Question 30 minutes

Keep these estimates in mind as you prepare for the test. Use them as you work the practice items so you'll be comfortable keeping to the same amounts of time on test day.

- » **STEP 1 Take the issue/argument apart: 2 minutes**
- » **STEP 2 Select the points you will make: 4 minutes**
- » **STEP 3 Organize, using Kaplan's essay templates: 2 minutes**
- » **STEP 4 Type your essay: 20 minutes**
- » **STEP 5 Proofread your work: 2 minutes**

Scoring

The essay scoring for the Analytical Writing sections is *holistic*, which means that the graders base your score on their overall impression of your essay, rather than deducting specific point values for errors. A holistic score emphasizes the interrelationship of content, organization, and syntax, and denotes the unified effect of these combined elements.

The scoring scale is from 0 to 6, with 6 being the highest score. Two graders will read and score each essay. If their scores differ by more than 1 point, a third reader will also score the essay. Although the Analytical Writing section comprises two separate essays, ETS reports a single score that represents the average of your scores for the two essays, rounded up to the nearest half-point. You will receive your essay score, along with your official score report, within 10–15 days of your test date.

The Scoring Rubric

Each of the two essays requires different reasoning and presentation, so each has slightly different grading criteria. However, the following rubric will give you a general idea of the guidelines graders have in mind when they score Analytical Writing essays.

6: "Outstanding" Essay

- · Insightfully presents and convincingly supports an opinion on the issue or a critique of the argument

· Communicates ideas clearly and is generally well organized; connections are logical
· Demonstrates superior control of language: grammar, stylistic variety, and accepted conventions of writing; minor flaws may occur

5: "Strong" Essay

· Presents well-chosen examples and strongly supports an opinion on the issue or a critique of the argument
· Communicates ideas clearly and is generally well organized; connections are logical
· Demonstrates solid control of language: grammar, stylistic variety, and accepted conventions of writing; minor flaws may occur

4: "Adequate" Essay

· Presents and adequately supports an opinion on the issue or a critique of the argument
· Communicates ideas fairly clearly and is adequately organized; logical connections are satisfactory
· Demonstrates satisfactory control of language: grammar, stylistic variety, and accepted conventions of writing; some flaws may occur

3: "Limited" Essay

· Succeeds only partially in presenting and supporting an opinion on the issue or a critique of the argument
· Communicates ideas unclearly and is poorly organized
· Demonstrates less than satisfactory control of language: contains significant mistakes in grammar, usage, and sentence structure

2: "Weak" Essay

· Shows little success in presenting and supporting an opinion on the issue or a critique of the argument
· Struggles to communicate ideas; essay shows a lack of clarity and organization
· Meaning is impeded by many serious mistakes in grammar, usage, and sentence structure

1: "Fundamentally Deficient" Essay

· Fails to present a coherent opinion and/or evidence on the issue or a critique of the argument
· Fails to communicate ideas; essay is seriously unclear and disorganized

- Lacks meaning due to widespread and severe mistakes in grammar, usage, and sentence structure

0: "Unscorable" Essay

- Completely ignores topic
- Attempts to copy the task
- Written in a language other than English or contains undecipherable text

ARGUMENT ESSAY PRACTICE PROMPTS

The following is a list of sample Argument essay prompts like those you might encounter on the GRE Analytical Writing section. Those preceded by an asterisk (*) have a sample essay response in the subsequent section of the chapter:

Argument 1:

The following memorandum is from the production manager of SingSong radio:

"This year, in deference to our many listeners who do not celebrate any of the winter holidays, we will not play holiday music related to any religion on our station. According to an online survey of our listeners, fewer than 20 percent indicated that they enjoy listening to religious songs. Eighty percent noted in the survey that if SingSong began broadcasting religious music (of any faith or denomination), they would "dramatically" reduce their listening hours.

Therefore, to retain our listeners during the holidays, we will respectfully decline any requests for holiday music this year."

Write a response in which you discuss what questions would need to be answered to decide how likely the stated recommendation is to yield the predicted result. Be sure to explain how the answers to these questions would help to evaluate the recommendation.

Argument 2:

Fifty years ago, an entomologist in Ballaland identified a new species of beetle: the scalawag. This beetle is nearly identical to the Andover mop beetle, but is slightly larger. A recent comparison of a colony of Ballaland beetles and Andover mop beetles demonstrates that the two beetles may be more similar than previously thought. The range of size between the largest beetle and the smallest beetle was identical in both colonies, and, as the beetles were physically identical in every other way, it was concluded that the two species were actually the same and that the differences in behavior and diet could be attributed to differences in habitat. Some biologists suggest that before a proposed interbreeding experiment is conducted, more research on behavior and diet of the two beetle species should be conducted.

Write a response in which you discuss what questions would need to be answered in order to assess the reasonableness of both the recommendation and the argument upon which it is based. Be sure to explain how the answers to these questions would help to evaluate the recommendation.

Argument 3:

The following is a letter to the editor of a psychology journal:

"The data collected from a variety of studies now suggest a relationship between the medicine Hypathia and heightened risk of anxiety in patients afflicted with bipolar disorder. In 1950, before Hypathia was widely used to treat bipolar disorder, relatively few patients were diagnosed as anxious or had symptoms that suggested anxiety. However, in five studies published between 2005 and 2010, more than 60 percent of the subjects with bipolar disorder who took Hypathia demonstrated symptoms of anxiety or reported having episodes of heightened anxiety."

Write a response in which you discuss one or more viable alternatives to the proposed explanation. Justify, with support, why your explanation could rival the proposed explanation and explain how your explanation(s) can plausibly account for the facts presented in the argument.

*Argument 4:

A recently issued five-year study on the common cold investigated the possible therapeutic effect of a raw food diet. Raw foods contain antioxidants that boost the immune system. While many foods are naturally rich in antioxidants, food-processing companies also sell isolated antioxidants. The five-year study found a strong correlation between a raw food diet and a steep decline in the average number of colds reported by study participants. A control group that increased their antioxidant intake using supplements did not have a decrease in the number of colds. Based on these study results, some health experts recommend a raw food diet over the use of packaged antioxidants.

Write a response in which you discuss what questions would need to be answered in order to assess the reasonableness of both the recommendation and the argument upon which it is based. Be sure to explain how the answers to these questions would help to evaluate the recommendation.

*Argument 5:

The following was written as part of an application for a permit to congregate by a religious group in the city of Gustav:

"We plan to meet at the Hunter Pavilion on the north side of the park. We expect about 200 attendees. Although we do plan to celebrate our message in words and song, we will be mindful of others who are sharing the park on that day. We have found that in the past, when our group meets in a public space, we run the risk of harassment by those who do not agree with our message. Therefore, we would like to hire five security officers to protect our congregants from religious intolerance. We would like to post one guard at the entrance to the park and others, who will dress in plain clothes, at the perimeter of our gathering. We hope you understand and will endorse this request."

Write a response in which you describe what specific examples or evidence is needed to evaluate the argument and how those examples or evidence would weaken or strengthen the argument.

*Argument 6:

The following memo appeared in the newsletter of the Happy Sun Happy Moon daycare center:

"Since the road construction on I-72 has begun, we've noticed that parents are picking up their children after the center is officially closed. Effective immediately, parents who pick up their children more than five minutes after closing will have to pay a $10 fee. Parents who pick up their children more than one hour after closing will be subject to an additional $30 fee. We predict this will encourage parents to leave earlier from work to pick up their children on time each day."

Write a response in which you discuss what questions would need to be answered to decide how likely the stated recommendation is to yield the predicted result. Be sure to explain how these answers would help to evaluate the recommendation.

*Argument 7:

In 1992, many farmers in Jalikistan began using a hormone designed to produce larger cows that would produce more milk. Since then, childhood obesity in Jalikistan has grown by 200 percent. The amount of milk and dairy consumed by children in this area has not increased or decreased. Children in the same area who are lactose intolerant, and who drink almond milk or soymilk, have not had the same increase in childhood obesity. The only clear explanation is that the introduction of the hormone is responsible for the increase in childhood obesity in that area.

Write a response in which you discuss one or more viable alternatives to the proposed explanation. Justify, with support, why the alternatives could rival the proposed explanation and explain how those explanation(s) plausibly account for the facts presented in the argument.

*Argument 8:

The following appeared in a memo from an advertisement by Pest Protection, Inc.:

"Gardens along the coast are already being infested by the mill bug, a slimy purple pest that can decimate a vegetable garden in seconds flat. If you live within 100 miles of the coast, you need the Pest Protection cure today. Thousands of satisfied customers who have used our chemical-free treatments have never had mill bug problems. One treatment per year will ensure that you never have to lose your valuable crops to this pest."

Write a response in which you examine the underlying assumptions of the argument. Be sure to explain how the argument hinges on these assumptions and what the implications are for the argument if the assumptions prove unfounded.

Argument 9:

The following appeared in a letter to the Director of the Department of Motor Vehicles:

"The use of cell phones while driving is a source of great concern to the community, particularly to parents with young children. Teenage drivers, who are the most likely to text or talk on the phone while driving, are among the most dangerous. In our county alone there were 75 fatalities from traffic collisions. If we raise the legal driving age from 16 to 20, the problem would largely be solved because the most dangerous drivers would no longer be on the road."

Write a response in which you discuss what questions would need to be answered in order to assess the reasonableness of both the prediction and the argument upon which it is based. Be sure to explain how the answers to these questions would help to evaluate the prediction.

Argument 10:

The following memorandum is from the Media Director of the Athletic Department at Burtsdale University:

"We have decided to recommend that the school no longer offer free student access to University athletic events, regardless of level, sport, or gender of the participants.

Our policy in the past has been to sell tickets only to events with significant popularity, such as men's Division I football and basketball games, and other nationally televised events. Although other sports do not typically sell out, or generate the same level of interest outside the student body, we feel it is unfair to Division II sports and the women's teams not to charge admission to their events as well. Charging admission to all events is the only way to treat all athletic teams equitably."

Write a response in which you describe what specific examples or evidence is needed to evaluate the argument and how those examples or evidence would weaken or strengthen the argument.

Argument 11:

The following is from an editorial in a legal journal:

"It is now apparent, based on data that has been collated from several independent studies, that asbestos is the cause of lung cancer, emphysema, and other respiratory illnesses in the miners of Coal Valley. The studies show a high incidence of such ailments among the miners, far higher than that of the general population. In 1920, before the mine opened, relatively few miners were known to have had such conditions. Studies published in 1960, 1980, and 2000 show that the incidence of such ailments has risen dramatically among the miners of Coal Valley."

Write a response in which you discuss one or more viable alternatives to the proposed explanation. Justify, with support, why your explanation could rival the proposed explanation and explain how your explanation(s) can plausibly account for the facts presented in the argument.

Argument 12:

The following is an excerpt from a letter to the editor of the *Billington Bugle*:

"There is no possible downside to the community in bringing the Grand Prix to Billington. Though it has not proved financially successful in other cities that have hosted the race, this will not be the case for Billington. The race's course will run through the economic center of downtown, and the organizers of the event have offered to pay to repave the downtown streets through which the race will run. Those streets are in such disrepair that having them repaired will be a tremendous boon to the city. Furthermore, though most downtown businesses (aside from restaurants and food vendors) will likely be shut down for three days, the influx of tourist dollars will be immense. Finally, the international prestige of hosting such a race will raise the city's profile significantly, generating new interest in doing business here."

Write a response in which you describe what specific examples or evidence is needed to evaluate the argument and how those examples or evidence would weaken or strengthen the argument.

Argument 13:

The following is a recommendation from the Board of Directors of the Cheshire College Preparatory Academy:

"We recommend that Cheshire College Preparatory Academy dispense with the use of standardized tests as an entrance requirement. Cheshire has been an elite school for more than 100 years, but we have recently seen a decline in enrollments. We have had particular difficulty in attracting students from nonlegacy families (those who have never had a member attend Cheshire). We do not require entrance exams for legacy applicants, and those enrollments have not declined. Cutting the standardized entrance requirement will allow us to better compete with Surrey Academy, which recently dropped its exam requirements and concurrently overtook Cheshire in enrollments."

Write a response in which you discuss what questions would need to be answered to decide how likely the stated recommendation is to yield the predicted result. Be sure to explain how the answers to these questions would help to evaluate the recommendation.

Argument 14:

The Supreme Court of the United States must be composed in such a way that it accurately reflects the demographics of the country. As the highest court in the land, it functions as the final arbiter of justice. In a multicultural and multiethnic society, with a variety of races, creeds, and beliefs, it is imperative that the backgrounds of the justices on the court reflect that diversity. Since our society is not homogenous, our judicial system must follow suit. Otherwise, it will be impossible to fairly represent the views, beliefs, and cultural norms of the entire country.

Write a response in which you describe what specific examples or evidence is needed to evaluate the argument and how those examples or evidence would weaken or strengthen the argument.

Argument 15:

The problem of poorly trained teachers that has plagued the state public school system is bound to become a good deal less serious in the future. The state has initiated comprehensive guidelines that oblige state teachers to complete a number of required credits in education and educational psychology at the graduate level before being certified.

Write a response in which you discuss how well reasoned you find the argument. In your response, describe specific examples or evidence needed to evaluate the argument and how those examples or evidence would weaken or strengthen the argument.

ARGUMENT ESSAY SAMPLE ESSAYS AND EXPLANATIONS

Here are sample top-scoring essays to five of the sample Argument prompts found in the previous section. Remember that an essay does not have to be perfect to receive a top score. Review these essays and note the qualities that earned them each a score of 6.

Argument 4:

A recently issued five-year study on the common cold investigated the possible therapeutic effect of a raw food diet. Raw foods contain antioxidants that boost the immune system. While many foods are naturally rich in antioxidants, food-processing companies also sell isolated antioxidants. The five-year study found a strong correlation between a raw food diet and a steep decline in the average number of colds reported by study participants. A control group that increased their antioxidant intake using supplements did not have a decrease in the number of colds. Based on these study results, some health experts recommend a raw food diet over the use of packaged antioxidants.

Write a response in which you discuss what questions would need to be answered in order to assess the reasonableness of both the recommendation and the argument upon which it is based. Be sure to explain how the answers to these questions would help to evaluate the recommendation.

Sample Response

The fields of health and medicine offer constant breakthroughs and varying viewpoints to today's society. Popular nutritional foods and eating habits supported for several years are now up for debate. With that said, new recommendations, such as the inclusion of raw foods in a balanced diet that boosts the immune system, should be proven before they're practiced.

One question that is important to address over claims that a study proved the successful use of raw food to fight against the common cold is which foods were included in the study. If the foods discussed in the study are fruits and vegetables, which are already commonly consumed raw, people would be more apt to accept the study results. However, if the study used raw meats, the population may be hesitant to embrace a diet change due to previous claims of diseases. These elements should be addressed before a public claim is made.

Along with addressing the type of raw food that was used in the study, scientists should also discuss the control group that was used. Oftentimes, the immune system of a younger person will differ from that of an older person. Was the control group composed of healthier, younger citizens, or older ones who are more prone to catching the common cold? The representativeness of the samples would affect the validity of the study results.

In addition to supplying information with regard to the demographics of the control group, the designers of the study should also disclose the environmental factors that may have influenced the control group. Were members of the control group, which used supplements, also parents who were exposed to school children who attend school and are more susceptible to catching colds? Were the parties who consumed raw foods also exercising more frequently than the control group? These factors may dissuade society, or reinforce the importance of other elements of a healthy immune system.

With new studies presented to the population each day, it becomes difficult to distinguish reputable ones from those that may need more evidence. The addition of raw foods in the average healthy diet may bring controversy. Nonetheless, society will continue to adapt to lifestyle suggestions when adequate proof is provided.

Analysis

The author successfully identifies and analyzes this argument's recommendation: raw food diets should take the place of packaged antioxidants. In the opening paragraph, the author states her position: the safety of new diets should be proved before being implemented. The essay then points out an unanswered question on which the argument depends. Namely, is it raw vegetables or meats that are being advocated in this diet? In the subsequent paragraphs, the author identifies flaws, particularly those involving the study's methodology, in the assumptions and perceptively suggests what needs to be known to make the recommendation stronger, and how knowing this information would help in evaluating this recommendation.

The author also cites these points undermining the argument:

1. The assumption that the control group was diverse in terms of age and health
2. Environmental factors that affect populations

Throughout the essay, the author uses well-organized paragraphs—each starts with a broad statement followed by supporting statements—and her ideas logically flow from one sentence to the next. She uses succinct, economical diction and alternates between complex and simple sentences. The essay remains focused and clear throughout, earning a score of 6.

Argument 5:

The following was written as part of an application for a permit to congregate by a religious group in the city of Gustav:

"We plan to meet at the Hunter Pavilion on the north side of the park. We expect about 200 attendees. Although we do plan to celebrate our message in words and song, we will be mindful of others who are sharing the park on that day. We have found that in the past, when our group meets in a public space, we run the risk of harassment by those who do not agree with our message. Therefore, we would like to hire five security officers to protect our congregants from religious intolerance. We would like to post one guard at the entrance to the park and others, who will dress in plain clothes, at the perimeter of our gathering. We hope you understand and will endorse this request."

Write a response in which you describe what specific examples or evidence is needed to evaluate the argument and how those examples or evidence would weaken or strengthen the argument.

Sample Response

The Bill of Rights was designed to protect the rights of the American People in the best way possible without infringing on the rights of others. Assuming that this situation takes place in the United States, this group should have the right to carry out all the requests written in this application. The main issues in question seem to be covered under freedom of religion, freedom of speech, and freedom to congregate, all of which are protected by the U.S. Constitution.

We can assume, by the request for security guards, that this group is not looked upon with favor by the community. Unfortunately for their opponents, if they go through the proper channels (such as applying for permits like this one seems to be), they are within their legal rights to gather and practice their religious ceremony nonviolently. Thus, one important question that needs to be answered in order to evaluate this argument is whether this is the proper permit and whether their request is within the laws and regulations of the city. It is one of the foundational ideals in the creation of this country that practicing an unpopular religion is entirely protected. Some of the founders of the early colonies came here to be safe from religious persecution. It would be hypocritical to cast aside a group because their views are unpopular.

The hiring of private security officers could potentially pose problems for this group. The county police force should be in charge of, and capable of, maintaining the peace in the area. It is the job of the police force to protect citizens from being harassed by intolerant fellow citizens. If the harassment gets to the point where it becomes dangerous or criminal in some way, the police should step in. The fact that this group has been harassed before, and now feel the need for additional undercover security officers, is cause for concern. To properly evaluate this argument, we would need to know what kind of harassment is going on (i.e., physical or verbal), and whether or not the police themselves are capable of handling the situation. This would obviate the need to resort to armed guards, who may or may not actually be necessary. It would help to determine whether or not the group's civil rights are being violated and whether the city would be within its legal obligations to grant such a request.

It is within the rights of private groups and citizens to hire private security officers. Celebrities, concert venues, and even high-powered business people hire security agents to maintain order when trouble is expected. Assuming there is some legal paperwork that must be filed, and this group completes it all correctly, there is no reason why they should not be allowed to hire outside help. But the outstanding factual and legal questions need to be cleared up before that conclusion is unequivocal. The group may feel it has been let down by the official police force and that they will not be safe without additional security measures.

Analysis

The author successfully identifies and analyzes this argument's contention: that the group in question should be allowed to have armed security guards at their event. In the opening paragraph, the author acknowledges that the group has the right to freedom of expression, and that this should not be infringed upon. However, she draws attention to the questions that need to be answered in order to hire private security guards at a public venue.

The author also cites these points, which must be determined before assessing the argument:

1. The nature of the harassment/threats being made against the group
2. Whether or not the police are capable of handling the situation and the legality of private security

The author makes judicious use of well-structured paragraphs—each starts with a strong assertion followed by supporting statements. Her ideas logically flow from one sentence to the next. She uses succinct, economical diction and intersperses complex and simple sentences. The essay concludes strongly by summarizing the conditions necessary for allowing the group to hire their guards, and, if these conditions are met, stating that they should be allowed to do so. The essay remains focused and clear throughout, earning a score of 6.

Argument 6:

The following memo appeared in the newsletter of the Happy Sun Happy Moon day-care center.

"Since the road construction on I-72 has begun, we've noticed that parents are picking up their children after the center is officially closed. Effective immediately, parents who pick up their children more than five minutes after closing will have to pay a $10 fee. Parents who pick up their children more than one hour after closing will be subject to an additional $30 fee. We predict this will encourage parents to leave earlier from work to pick up their children on time each day."

Write a response in which you discuss what questions would need to be answered to decide how likely the stated recommendation is to yield the predicted result. Be sure to explain how these answers would help to evaluate the recommendation.

Sample Response

If I were to put myself in the place of one of these parents, the first question I would have is, "How can you charge us, as parents, more if we are only a few minutes late? Traffic is always present, whether construction projects are taking place or not, so it does not seem fair to charge us extra for something that is out of our control." Six minutes late would, technically, mean a charge, and that seems a bit extreme. As such, I do not think that this recommendation would have the anticipated result. I think that some parents may leave work a bit earlier to try to get to their children earlier, but heavy traffic can begin before the standard five or six o'clock traffic, so to assume that if a parent leaves earlier they will arrive on time is false. I would imagine that some parents would arrive on time more frequently, as they would not want to be charged, but it could not be guaranteed. Without more information, the best one could say is that there's a chance that parents will always be on time. In fact, how could the daycare presume that parents could leave earlier, when some companies are quite stringent and do not allow their employees to leave before the very end of the day?

In the past, for example, I have had jobs where I could not leave early, unless I had a previously scheduled appointment. Certain tasks had to be completed by certain times, which tied me to my desk until the end of the day. Consequently, depending on traffic, sometimes I would have been late to pick up my child, and sometimes I would have been on time. I think that an hour late would warrant a fee, as the people who work at the daycare also have families to go home to, but merely a few minutes late, even up to 15 or 20 minutes late, should not be an issue.

To charge parents for being slightly late is unwarranted. Being too late is, of course, a problem, but slightly late should not be. The daycare should be more understanding and try to put themselves in the parents' shoes. Consequently, the final question that I would ask the daycare would be, "Could you only charge a fee at the end of the month to those parents who were consistently late, say, more than three times that month?" That, I think, would be a reasonable alternative. After all, if parents are dedicated to arriving on time, they will do their best to pick up their children at the appropriate hour. Naturally, they may get caught in traffic and arrive late sometimes, but if they are generally on time, I do not think that they should be penalized.

Analysis

The author begins with a provocative rhetorical question that grabs the reader's attention. He emphatically denies that the recommendation will have the predicted result. He notes that simply installing this policy will not make parents show up on time. The primary reason is that there are a number of circumstances beyond parents' control that affect their ability to arrive promptly. These include traffic and work restrictions, both of which cannot be solved simply by fining parents for being late.

Throughout the essay, the author uses well-organized paragraphs—each starts with a broad statement followed by supporting statements. He uses strong, emotional language to convey his point. The essay remains focused and clear throughout, earning a score of 6.

Argument 7:

In 1992, many farmers in Jalikistan began using a hormone designed to produce larger cows that would produce more milk. Since then, childhood obesity in Jalikistan has grown by 200 percent. The amount of milk and dairy consumed by children in this area has not increased or decreased. Children in the same area who are lactose intolerant, and who drink almond milk or soymilk, have not had the same increase in childhood obesity. The only clear explanation is that the introduction of the hormone is responsible for the increase in childhood obesity in that area.

Write a response in which you discuss one or more viable alternatives to the proposed explanation. Justify, with support, why the alternatives could rival the proposed explanation and explain how those explanation(s) can plausibly account for the facts presented in the argument.

Sample Response

While the hormone may well contribute to an increase in childhood obesity, it does not have to be the only problem. A 200 percent rise in obesity over a given period of time begs the question of whether other factors are at work. Obesity in all ages can be linked to many different factors: physical activity, increased consumption of solid food, or the type of food being ingested. A milk hormone—while being a potential source—is not the "only clear explanation." Other factors, from diet to physical activity, could be at work.

The argument concludes that the hormone is causing obesity in children. This is an assumption that is not necessarily true. This scenario says nothing about the activity level of the children; this is a large gap in the reasoning that could help the reader further understand the role that the hormone played in the children's obesity. If the hormone usage in 1992 converged with a decline in physical activity, then either factor, or both, could have caused the uptick in obesity rates. The fact that the use of the hormone coincided with the start of a period in which, due to the availability of automotive transportation, people are more sedentary, is worth investigating. During the time in question, television and video games may have become more prevalent, furthering a sedentary lifestyle. Nothing is mentioned about the levels of physical activity among these two groups of children.

The argument states that the children's dairy consumption hasn't changed, but says nothing else about their dietary habits. It is possible that the children who eat dairy products also have, since 1992, taken to eating richer foods, fewer vegetables, or more carbohydrates. Such a change in diet could account for the obesity rates within the population. It is also possible that, during the time in question, lactose-tolerant children have been eating more fattening food products that, while not dairy products themselves, employ milk, cheese, or butter in their preparation. This could cause the increase in obesity rates, and the lactose-intolerant children would be unaffected.

Given that we do not know the answers to these questions, the argument goes beyond the available data in asserting that it must be the hormone that is to blame for the obesity rates among the children who are lactose tolerant.

Analysis

The author of this essay recognizes that the argument depends on two unqualified assumptions and that simply stopping the use of the hormone may or may not have the desired effect. The author argues throughout the essay that the only difference between the two groups of children that we are made aware of is the type of milk they drink (or do not drink). We do not know:

1. The effect of diet (aside from dairy products)
2. Level of physical activity

Because we don't know the facts pertinent to environmental and behavioral factors affecting the two groups of children, both diet and exercise can be considered as potential alternative explanations. The argument in the prompt simply assumes that both groups are otherwise identical, and that assumption stretches beyond the known information.

Throughout the essay, the author uses well-organized paragraphs—each starts with a broad statement followed by supporting statements—and his ideas logically flow from one sentence to the next. He uses succinct, economical diction and rotates complex and simple sentences. The essay remains focused and clear throughout, earning a score of 6.

Argument 8:

The following appeared in a memo from an advertisement by Pest Protection, Inc.:

"Gardens along the coast are already being infested by the mill bug, a slimy purple pest that can decimate a vegetable garden in seconds flat. If you live within 100 miles of the coast, you need the Pest Protection cure today. Thousands of satisfied customers who have used our chemical-free treatments have never had mill bug problems. One treatment per year will ensure that you never have to lose your valuable crops to this pest."

Write a response in which you examine the underlying assumptions of the argument. Be sure to explain how the argument hinges on these assumptions and what the implications are for the argument if the assumptions prove unfounded.

Sample Response

At first glance, the argument proffered by the advertisement seems to make sense. Those who use Pest Protection will not suffer an infestation of mill bugs. The author makes claims that seem to meet the needs of someone living in the region. However, the author relies on several unproven assumptions. First, the argument mistakenly assumes that because the mill bug "can" decimate a garden, that it will in fact do so. There's no way to assess the extent of the current infestation. Nor is there anything that states which types of vegetables or flowers the bug devours. In order to assess the validity of the advertisement, it would valuable to know the true extent of the threat that the bug poses. If it's the case that the mill bug eats only root vegetables or only flowering plants, it's unlikely that everyone within 100 miles of the coast needs Pest Protection. If "thousands of satisfied customers have never had mill bug problems," how can we even be sure that the bugs do in fact pose a serious threat?

The biggest flaw in the author's reasoning is that the author assumes, without providing proof, that there is a direct, causal relationship between using the Pest Protection cure and being free of mill bug problems. Even if both are true, that someone is using the Pest Protection cure and they do not have a mill bug problem, there is no proof that the former has caused the latter. There could be other factors at work, such as climate, migration patterns, lack of food supply, or other such extrinsic concerns.

Many who used the Pest Protection treatment may have done so unnecessarily. There is no information to suggest what the level of infestation would have been without the treatment. The advertisement's reasoning amounts to arguing that since a town began sending police officers on "Bear Patrol," no one in the town has been attacked by a bear. Depending on where the town is, there may never have been a bear attack to begin with.

Finally, the company's claim that a single, yearly treatment will ensure that customers will "never have to lose . . . valuable crops" is broad. In order to assess the argument, we need to know the price and process for this treatment. It may be price prohibitive to have annual treatments. Alternately, the treatments may have side effects. The advertisement does qualify its claim: you never have to lose crops to this pest. But, if the treatment makes it impossible to grow certain crops or depletes the soil over time, the user would lose crops in another way. Pest Protection offers no support for the claim that the treatment will last for such a long time. Many things, such as climate change and inclement weather, could mitigate or dilute the effect of such a treatment over the course of a year. Thus, from a sales and customer standpoint, this argument is persuasive but has too many gaps in its logic to be convincing without further evidence.

Analysis

The author successfully identifies and analyzes this argument's underlying assumptions. The author of this essay recognizes that the argument depends on assuming that the use of the product will result in getting rid of the mill bugs. Additionally, we do not know:

1. Whether one yearly treatment will be enough
2. Whether the treatment is effective or not
3. Whether there is a causal relationship between Pest Protection treatments and prevention of the mill bug

The advertisement also does not indicate whether mill bugs have been killed in the past by inclement weather or environmental factors, as opposed to the product. Because we do not know these pertinent environmental factors, it is impossible to predict whether using the product will have the desired result.

Throughout the essay, the author uses well-organized paragraphs—each is taut and incisive, and the main point is quickly followed by supporting statements—and his ideas logically flow from one sentence to the next. He uses succinct, economical diction and rotates complex and simple sentences. The essay remains focused and clear throughout, earning a score of 6.

PART FIVE

Analytical Writing Content Review

CHAPTER 9

Writing Foundations

OVERVIEW

The focus of the GRE writing sample is on not only how well you write, but also the thought processes you employ to formulate and articulate a position. There are two GRE Analytical Writing sections, each 30 minutes long.

You'll write essays on two different types of prompts:

- The Issue essay task provides a brief quotation on an issue of general interest and instructions on how to respond to the issue. You can discuss the issue from any perspective, making use of your own educational and personal background, examples from current or historical events, things you've read, or even relevant hypothetical situations. In this task, you will develop your own argument.
- The Argument essay task contains a short argument that may or may not be complete, and specific instructions on how to evaluate the argument's strength. You will assess the argument's cogency, analyze the author's reasoning, and evaluate her use (or lack) of evidence. In this task, you critique the argument presented in the prompt.

The Analytical Writing section allows schools to evaluate your ability to plan and compose a logical, well-reasoned essay under timed conditions. You'll write the essays on the computer, using a simple word processing program.

This section of the book will review Kaplan's 22 principles for effective writing. Numbers 1–10 relate to writing style, 11–17 to grammar, and 18–22 to mechanics. Study these principles to refine your writing skills and score well on the GRE Analytical Writing essays.

WRITING STYLE

Remember, the GRE essay is a formal writing assignment. Here are a few elements of style to keep in mind while you're writing:

Concision

- Omit words, phrases, and sentences that do not add to your argument or support your position. An experienced GRE essay grader can spot such "padding" a mile away. Make every word count.
- Avoid redundant phrases such as *refer back*, *serious crisis*, and *general consensus*, which weaken your writing.

Structure

- Use transition words and phrases to show the relationship between your ideas.
- Start a new paragraph for every new topic or example.

Formal and Forceful

- Don't use slang or text-message abbreviations, and don't use an ampersand (&) in place of the word *and*. This is a formal assignment—treat it as such.
- Avoid weak sentence openings, such as *There is* or *There are*.
- Avoid the passive voice: *I finished my essay* is stronger and more concise than *The essay was finished by me*.
- Avoid clichés and overused terms or phrases. Remember, the graders are reading a lot of these; try to make your essays memorable.
- Use precise wording and avoid generalizations ("many people") and abstractions. Make your meaning clear.
- Avoid referring to your own opinion with constructions like "I think," "I feel," or "I believe." Also avoid retelling personal anecdotes or sharing your own philosophy.
- Vary sentence length and style.

WRITING STYLE EXERCISES

1st Principle of Effective Writing: Streamlining Wordy Phrases

1. An essential element of our consideration of the problem was finding the means to identify the more dubious aspects of the plan.

2. Foremost in their thinking was the capacity of the vehicle to traverse various kinds of terrain.

3. Anthony engaged a professional interior decorator to undertake the refurbishment of his apartment.

2nd Principle of Effective Writing: Eliminating Redundancy

4. At this point in time the scout experienced a serious setback.

---

5. None of her fellow classmates was at the party.

---

6. The leader had a special reputation for being calm in a crisis situation.

3rd Principle of Effective Writing: Avoiding Excessive Qualification

7. In a fairly rare moment of frustration, Toni pretty much lost her temper.

---

8. Lee's actions at Gettysburg seemed relatively uncharacteristic for someone whose qualities as a commander were usually sound for the most part.

---

9. I have to say that, as an employer, Helen showed a certain amount of boldness in providing what most would regard as generous benefits to her workers.

4th Principle of Effective Writing: Removing Unnecessary Sentences

10. This city's transportation system is a model for urban infrastructure elsewhere. Our bus and light-rail lines are second to none.

---

11. Where would this company be without the vision of someone like Carlo? Our success as a company owes everything to his belief in the future.

---

12. The builders of medieval cathedrals were not primitive laborers who had little idea of what they were doing. They were often highly skilled masons, carpenters, and workers in stained glass who were guided by a detailed plan drawn up by a master builder.

5th Principle of Effective Writing: Avoiding Needless Self-Reference

13. I am of the opinion that we can design cars that are much more fuel-efficient.

---

14. From my point of view, the pottery could increase its output simply by using a different glaze.

---

15. I feel it would be a mistake to take part in such a demonstration without a clear sense of purpose.

6th Principle of Effective Writing: Using Active Rather than Passive Voice

16. As the prisoner was brought into court by the guards, he glared at his accuser.

---

17. The question of who is to inherit the estate has never been asked.

---

18. When do you think the problem will have been solved by them?

7th Principle of Effective Writing: Including Strong Openings

19. There is every possibility that the police have found your lost dog.

---

20. It is to be hoped that officials can resolve this crisis before it gets out of hand.

---

21. There is a proverb that says, "Half a loaf is better than none."

_____

8th Principle of Effective Writing: Avoiding Needlessly Vague Language

22. To really demonstrate our obligation to some valued customer, we will forego the standard admission fee.

_____

23. All our employees are content here.

_____

24. Both kind of indigent and without much accommodation, she is indeed a sad spectacle.

_____

9th Principle of Effective Writing: Rewording Clichés

25. That man sleeping on the bench looks a bit over the hill.

_____

26. She always seemed to me to have ice water in her veins.

_____

27. With this win, the team looks like it's on a roll.

_____

10th Principle of Effective Writing: Avoiding Jargon

28. The consultant said that, if a company is going to downsize, it should go for the low-hanging fruit first.

_____

29. Let's connect ear-to-ear on this one.

_____

30. Just give me a ballpark figure so I can consider the offer.

_____

ANSWERS TO WRITING STYLE EXERCISES

1. Finding the plan's weaknesses was essential to evaluating it.

2. Their main interest was the vehicle's cross-country capability.

3. Anthony hired a professional interior decorator to redecorate his apartment.

4. The scout experienced a setback.

5. None of her classmates was at the party.

6. The leader was known to be calm in a crisis.

7. In a rare moment of frustration, Toni lost her temper.

8. Lee's actions at Gettysburg were uncharacteristic of someone who was usually a sound commander.

9. As an employer, Helen showed boldness by providing generous benefits to her workers.

10. The city's transportation system, with bus and light-rail systems that are second to none, is a model for other cities.

11. The success of our company owes everything to Carlo's belief in the future.

12. The builders of medieval cathedrals were not primitive laborers, but often highly skilled masons, carpenters, and workers in stained glass, guided by a detailed plan drawn up by a master builder.

13. We can design cars that are much more fuel-efficient.

14. The pottery could increase its output simply by using a different glaze.

15. It would be a mistake to take part in such a demonstration without a clear sense of purpose.

16. As the guards brought the prisoner into court, he glared at his accuser.

17. No one has ever asked who will inherit the estate.

18. When do you think they will have solved the problem?

19. The police have quite possibly found your lost dog.

20. Hopefully, officials can resolve this crisis before it gets out of hand.

21. "Half a loaf is better than none," as the proverb says.

22. Since we value you as a customer, you may enter free of charge.

23. All our employees have said they are satisfied with working conditions and benefits here.

24. Poor and homeless, she is sad to see.

25. That man sleeping on the bench looks old.

26. She always seemed unemotional to me.

27. With this win, the team looks like it's having a successful season.

28. The consultant said that, if a company is going to lay off workers, it should go for the easy targets first.

20. Let's discuss the details of this on the phone.

30. Just give me a cost estimate so I can consider the offer.

GRAMMAR

On the GRE, your control of language is important. Writing that is grammatical, concise, direct, and persuasive displays the "superior facility with the conventions of standard written English" (as the Test Makers term it) that earns top GRE essay scores. If your writing style isn't clear, your ideas won't come across, no matter how brilliant they are. Good GRE English is not only grammatical but also clear and concise, and by using some basic principles, you'll be able to express your ideas clearly and effectively in both of your essays. To display effective writing style in your essays, your writing must follow the rules of standard written English. If you're not confident of your mastery of grammar, brush up before the test using the exercises below.

GRAMMAR EXERCISES

11th Principle of Effective Writing: Ensuring Subject-Verb Agreement

31. If you or a member of your family have this problem, contact a doctor right away.

_____

32. The training given to car mechanics, particularly those who work in modern dealerships on cars with the latest electronic gadgets, are more complicated than ever.

_____

33. Each of the times you spoke about overcoming troubles were inspirational to me.

_____

34. Our staff are discussing this proposal in our monthly meeting on Friday.

_____

35. A range of options are open to businesses hoping to expand.

_____

12th Principle of Effective Writing: Avoiding Faulty Modification

36. Pleading innocent to all the charges, the jury was very sympathetic to the accused.

_____

37. A portrait artist would probably not be successful painting sitters without a deep appreciation of personal character.

_____

38. Lost when the ship sank, the rescued passengers had no possessions when they reached shore.

_____

39. Cynthia found the credit card she had misplaced when she looked under the bed.

_____

40. Usually never at a loss for words, the unresponsive audience left the comedian speechless.

_____

13th Principle of Effective Writing: Avoiding Unclear Pronoun Reference

41. Marie told her mother that it was time for her to leave home.

_____

42. Because of heavy snow on the roads, car drivers moved at a snail's pace until they were salted.

_____

43. Bob was generous in his praise of Gil because of his pleasant nature.

_____

44. Whenever the sergeant and the captain met, he saluted smartly.

_____

14th Principle of Effective Writing: Including Parallelism

45. The food you buy at the WonderKing Supermarket is less expensive than the Bislet Hypermarket.

_____

46. Helicopter pilots use one hand to control up-and-down motion, the other hand to control motion forward, backward, and sideways, while the feet control the turns.

_____

47. A good teacher knows her subject, her students, and has a good sense of humor.

_____

48. Students commonly preferred the teaching of Dr. Wolf to Professor Smith.

_____

15th Principle of Effective Writing: Using a Consistent Narrative Voice

49. If one is genuinely serious about helping the homeless, you must become familiar with their living conditions.

_____

50. From my perspective, you have to be truthful all the time. I don't see how we can claim to have integrity if we do anything less.

_____

51. When we vote, we take part in an extraordinary process. One chooses not a ruler but a representative for all of us.

_____

52. Each of you has a special responsibility to yourself and to others. We all have our own talents that we should develop for our own benefit and for the good of our families, our friends, and everyone we meet.

_____

16th Principle of Effective Writing: Avoiding Slang and Colloquialisms

53. It was agreed that, if James wanted to get to the theater on time, he had better get on the stick.

_____

54. When the city councilwoman tried to cover up her mistakes with lies, she just jumped from the frying pan into the fire.

_____

55. The city high-school football team creamed their opponents 35 to nothing.

_____

56. According to fund-raising gurus, you should concentrate on people with deep pockets.

_____

17th Principle of Effective Writing: Avoiding Sentence Fragments and Run-Ons

57. Bad drivers seem to be on the road in large numbers, many never signal what they intend to do.

_____

58. High-speed trains are once again a popular topic. Especially among businesspeople.

_____

59. Ever since our earliest ancestors discovered fire. We have needed to live near reasonable sources of fuel.

_____

60. In England, lawyers are usually either solicitors or barristers, in the past, solicitors gave advice to clients and practiced in lower courts, while barristers practiced before the "bar" in the higher courts.

_____

ANSWERS TO GRAMMAR EXERCISES

31. If you or a member of your family has this problem, contact a doctor right away.

32. The training given to car mechanics, particularly those who work in modern dealerships on cars with the latest electronic gadgets, is more complicated than ever.

33. Each of the times you spoke about overcoming troubles was inspirational to me.

34. Our staff is discussing this proposal in our monthly meeting on Friday.

35. A range of options is open to businesses hoping to expand.

36. Pleading innocent to all the charges, the accused received much sympathy from the jury.

37. A portrait artist without a deep appreciation of personal character would probably not be successful painting sitters.

38. Lost when the ship sank, the rescued passengers' possessions were gone when the passengers reached shore.

39. When she looked under the bed, Cynthia found the credit card she had misplaced.

40. Usually never at a loss for words, the comedian was speechless before the unresponsive audience.

41. Marie decided it was time for her to leave home, and she told her mother so.

42. Because of heavy snow, car drivers moved at a snail's pace until the roads were salted.

43. Bob was generous in his praise of Gil's pleasant nature.

44. The sergeant saluted the captain smartly whenever they met.

45. The food you buy at the WonderKing Supermarket is less expensive than the food at the Bislet Hypermarket.

46. Helicopter pilots use one hand to control up-and-down motion, the other hand to control forward, backward, and sideways motion, and the feet to control the turns.

47. A good teacher has a good sense of humor, and she knows her subject and students.

48. Students commonly preferred the teaching of Dr. Wolf to that of Professor Smith.

49. If you are genuinely serious about helping the homeless, you must become familiar with their living conditions.

50. It is important to be truthful all the time. We cannot claim to have integrity if we do anything less.

51. When we vote, we take part in an extraordinary process. We choose not a ruler but a representative for all of us.

52. Each of you has a special responsibility to yourself and to others. You all have your own talents that you should develop for your own benefit and for the good of your families, your friends, and everyone you meet.

53. It was agreed that, if James wanted to get to the theater on time, he would have to hurry.

54. When the city councilwoman tried to cover up her mistakes with lies, she went from a bad situation to a worse one.

55. The city high-school football team overwhelmed their opponents by a score of 35 to 0.

56. According to fund-raising experts, you should concentrate on people with plenty of money.

57. Bad drivers seem to be on the road in large numbers. Many never signal what they intend to do.

58. High-speed trains are once again a popular topic, especially among businesspeople.

59. Ever since our earliest ancestors discovered fire, we have needed to live near reasonable sources of fuel.

60. In England, lawyers are usually either solicitors or barristers. In the past, solicitors gave advice to clients and practiced in lower courts, while barristers practiced before the "bar" in the higher courts.

MECHANICS

Mechanics are more technical in nature than grammatical issues. They are the established conventions of punctuation, capitalization, pronouns, and so on. Remember, minor grammatical errors will not ruin your score. Many test takers mistakenly believe that they'll lose points because of a few mechanical missteps such as misplaced commas, spelling errors, or other minor mistakes. In fact, the Test Makers' description of a top-scoring essay acknowledges that there may be minor grammatical flaws. The graders understand that you are writing first-draft essays under timed conditions. However, if your errors obscure your meaning or make your essay difficult to follow, this will most likely be reflected in your scores.

To write an effective essay, you must be concise, forceful, and correct. An effective essay wastes no words, makes its point in a clear, direct way, and conforms to the generally accepted rules of grammar and form.

MECHANICS EXERCISES

18th Principle of Effective Writing: Correctly Using Commas

61. By federal law, interstate drivers of heavy trucks may be on duty for 14 straight hours, but must then take a 10-hour break.

_____

62. Monica, who was normally a conscientious agreeable colleague shocked her coworkers with her angry outburst.

_____

63. Spectators argued that the motorcycle stunt was an example of, sheer bravado, enormous courage, or arrant stupidity.

_____

64. Historically mounting a horse from the left side, dates back to the time when knights wore their swords on their left hip and could swing their right leg onto the horse's back without the sword getting in the way.

_____

65. Seeing the opportunity to make a quick breakthrough against her chess opponent she risked her queen by moving her remaining bishop well ahead of her pawns.

_____

66. During the American Civil War, doctors regularly treated ill soldiers with "blue mass," a concoction made up of ingredients such as mercury, honey, glycerol and, licorice.

_____

19th Principle of Effective Writing: Correctly Using Semicolons

67. We try to watch as little television as possible in our house, moreover we encourage reading by buying each other books as presents.

_____

68. We did not know what to do, we could either run, stay, or hide.

_____

69. Bringing a book to publication has often taken years, today, however, a book can appear on the Internet in a matter of weeks or even less.

_____

70. The success of the operation was particularly due to the efforts of Dr. Williams, a heart specialist with an innovative approach to surgery, Dr. Mallory, the anesthesiologist, who first noted the patient's breathing problems, and Dr. Thurman, the blood specialist, who overcame dangerous clotting that could have traveled to the patient's lungs.

_____

71. In recent weeks, Jake skimped on his training, therefore, his weak performance kept him from entering the tennis finals.

---

72. The 19th-century scholar Thomas Malthus wrote that limited food supplies would ultimately halt world population growth through starvation, this observation, highly influential at the time, may have prompted the historian Thomas Carlyle to describe economics as "the dismal science."

20th Principle of Effective Writing: Correctly Using Colons

73. A tragic hero may be: a powerful individual, a monarch, or, in modern tragedy, an ordinary person.

---

74. In recent years, Canada has produced a large number of world-class artists: including the following, the author Margaret Atwood, comedian Jim Carrey, singer Celine Dion, musician Neil Young, and actor Donald Sutherland.

---

75. The Navajo code talkers of World War II created special terms for wartime topics such as the following, submarine (iron fish), Britain (between waters), Germany (iron hat), dive bomber (chicken hawk), and August (big harvest).

---

76. I have one goal I really want to accomplish in my life, and that is: to scuba dive off the Great Barrier Reef.

---

77. The Empire State Building's special lighting system has been used: to commemorate only two non-Americans, Queen Elizabeth II of England and South Africa's Nelson Mandela.

---

78. Among the most sought-after qualities in a leader are the following character, enthusiasm, determination, confidence, cool-headedness, and decisiveness.

21st Principle of Effective Writing: Correctly Using Hyphens and Dashes

79. The company upgraded its technology system to what it called "a 21st century standard."

---

80. In a soon to be released statement, the chairman of the local soccer club reveals details of the club's new strip.

---

81. Only a few of the original members signed up for the forty seventh reunion of the class.

---

82. My objection—insignificant as it may seem, is the product of a lot of careful thought.

---

83. Almost certain ruin, the collapse of everything we have striven for, awaits us, such is the inevitable result of this change of policy.

---

84. It is to this extraordinary woman, and to her alone—that the credit for the reversal of this unjust law must go.

22nd Principle of Effective Writing: Correctly Using Apostrophes

85. You do know, I trust, that your no longer just the assistant manager.

---

86. The dealership was selling tire's and rim's at less than list price.

_____

87. The passengers confidence faded every time their bus broke down.

_____

88. Youd be surprised how many childrens books are now collectors items.

_____

89. Its easy for some people to say, "Go out and get a job," but they dont know how few jobs are open to you if you dont have a car.

_____

90. The veterinarian has no idea why the cat has lost most of it's fur.

_____

ANSWERS TO MECHANICS EXERCISES

61. By federal law, interstate drivers of heavy trucks may be on duty for 14 straight hours but must then take a 10-hour break.

62. Monica, who was normally a conscientious, agreeable colleague, shocked her coworkers with her angry outburst.

63. Spectators argued that the motorcycle stunt was an example of sheer bravado, enormous courage, or arrant stupidity.

64. Historically, mounting a horse from the left side dates back to the time when knights wore their swords on their left hip and could swing their right leg onto the horse's back without the sword getting in the way.

65. Seeing the opportunity to make a quick breakthrough against her chess opponent, she risked her queen by moving her remaining bishop well ahead of her pawns.

66. During the American Civil War, doctors regularly treated ill soldiers with "blue mass," a concoction made up of ingredients such as mercury, honey, glycerol, and licorice.

67. We try to watch as little television as possible in our house; moreover, we encourage reading by buying each other books as presents.

68. We did not know what to do; we could either run, stay, or hide.

69. Bringing a book to publication has often taken years; today, however, a book can appear on the Internet in a matter of weeks or even less.

70. The success of the operation was particularly due to the efforts of Dr. Williams, a heart specialist with an innovative approach to surgery; Dr. Mallory, the anesthesiologist, who first noted the patient's breathing problems; and Dr. Thurman, the blood specialist, who overcame dangerous clotting that could have traveled to the patient's lungs.

71. In recent weeks, Jake skimped on his training; therefore, his weak performance kept him from entering the tennis finals.

72. The 19th-century scholar Thomas Malthus wrote that limited food supplies would ultimately halt world population growth through starvation; this observation, highly influential at the time, may have prompted the historian Thomas Carlyle to describe economics as "the dismal science."

73. A tragic hero may be a powerful individual, a monarch, or, in modern tragedy, an ordinary person.

74. In recent years, Canada has produced a large number of world-class artists, including: the author Margaret Atwood, comedian Jim Carrey, singer Celine Dion, musician Neil Young, and actor Donald Sutherland.

75. The Navajo code talkers of World War II created special terms for wartime topics such as the following: submarine (iron fish), Britain (between waters), Germany (iron hat), dive bomber (chicken hawk), and August (big harvest).

76. I have one goal I really want to accomplish in my life, and that is to scuba dive off the Great Barrier Reef.

77. The Empire State Building's special lighting system has been used to commemorate only two non-Americans: Queen Elizabeth II of England and South Africa's Nelson Mandela.

78. Among the most sought-after qualities in a leader are the following: character, enthusiasm, determination, confidence, cool-headedness, and decisiveness.

79. The company upgraded its technology system to what it called "a 21st-century standard."

80. In a soon-to-be released statement, the chairman of the local soccer club will reveal details of the club's new strip.

81. Only a few of the original members signed up for the forty-seventh reunion of the class.

82. My objection—insignificant as it may seem—is the product of a lot of careful thought.

83. Almost certain ruin, the collapse of everything we have striven for, awaits us—such is the inevitable result of this change of policy.

84. It is to this extraordinary woman—and to her alone—that the credit for the reversal of this unjust law must go.

85. You do know, I trust, that you're no longer just the assistant manager.

86. The dealership was selling tires and rims at less than list price.

87. The passengers' confidence faded every time their bus broke down.

88. You'd be surprised how many children's books are now collectors' items.

89. It's easy for some people to say, "Go out and get a job," but they don't know how few jobs are open to you if you don't have a car.

90. The veterinarian has no idea why the cat has lost most of its fur.

PART SIX

GRE Resources

Kaplan's Word Groups

The following lists contain a lot of common GRE words grouped together by meaning. Make flashcards from these lists and look over your cards a few times a week from now until the day of the test. Look over the word group lists once or twice a week for 30 seconds every week until the test. If you don't have much time until the exam date, look over your lists more frequently. Then, by the day of the test, you should have a rough idea of what most of the words on your lists mean.

Note: The categories in which these words are listed are *general* and should *not* be interpreted as the exact definitions of the words.

Abbreviated Communication

abridge

compendium

cursory

curtail

syllabus

synopsis

terse

Act Quickly

abrupt

apace

headlong

impetuous

precipitate

Assist

abet

advocate

ancillary

bolster

corroborate

countenance

espouse

mainstay

munificent

proponent

stalwart

sustenance

Bad Mood

bilious

dudgeon

irascible

pettish

petulant

pique

querulous

umbrage

waspish

Beginner/Amateur

dilettante

fledgling

neophyte

novitiate

proselyte

tyro

Beginning/Young

burgeoning

callow

engender

inchoate

incipient

nascent

Biting (as in wit or temperament)

acerbic

acidulous

acrimonious

asperity

caustic

mordacious

mordant

trenchant

Bold

audacious

courageous

dauntless

Boring

banal

fatuous

hackneyed

insipid

mundane

pedestrian

platitude

prosaic

quotidian

trite

Carousal

bacchanalian

debauchery

depraved

dissipated

iniquity

libertine

libidinous

licentious

reprobate

ribald

salacious

sordid

turpitude

Changing Quickly

capricious

mercurial

volatile

Copy

counterpart

emulate

facsimile

factitious

paradigm

precursor

quintessence

simulated

vicarious

Criticize/Criticism

aspersion

belittle

berate

calumny

castigate

decry

defamation

denounce

deride/derisive

diatribe

disparage

excoriate

gainsay

harangue
impugn
inveigh
lambaste
objurgate
obloquy
opprobrium
pillory
rebuke
remonstrate
reprehend
reprove
revile
tirade
vituperate

Death/Mourning
bereave
cadaver
defunct
demise
dolorous
elegy
knell
lament
macabre
moribund
obsequies
sepulchral
wraith

Denying of Self
abnegate
abstain
ascetic
spartan
stoic
temperate

Dictatorial
authoritarian
despotic
dogmatic

hegemonic (hegemony)
imperious
peremptory
tyrannical

Difficult to Understand
abstruse
ambiguous
arcane
bemusing
cryptic
enigmatic
esoteric
inscrutable
obscure
opaque
paradoxical
perplexing
recondite
turbid

Disgusting/Offensive
defile
fetid
invidious
noisome
odious
putrid
rebarbative

Easy to Understand
articulate
cogent
eloquent
evident
limpid
lucid
pellucid

Eccentric/Dissimilar
aberrant
anachronism

anomalous
discrete
eclectic
esoteric
iconoclast

Embarrass
abash
chagrin
compunction
contrition
diffidence
expiate
foible
gaucherie
rue

Equal
equitable
equity
tantamount

Falsehood
apocryphal
canard
chicanery
dissemble
duplicity
equivocate
erroneous
ersatz
fallacious
feigned
guile
mendacious/mendacity
perfidy
prevaricate
specious
spurious

Family
conjugal
consanguine

distaff
endogamous
filial
fratricide
progenitor
scion

Favoring/not Impartial
ardor/ardent
doctrinaire
fervid
partisan
tendentious
zealot

Forgive
absolve
acquit
exculpate
exonerate
expiate
palliate
redress
vindicate

Funny
chortle
droll
facetious
flippant
gibe
jocular
levity
ludicrous
raillery
riposte
simper

Gaps/Openings
abatement
aperture
fissure
hiatus

interregnum
interstice
lull
orifice
rent
respite
rift

Generous/Kind
altruistic
beneficent
clement
largess
magnanimous
munificent
philanthropic
unstinting

Greedy
avaricious
covetous
mercenary
miserly
penurious
rapacious
venal

Hard-hearted
asperity
baleful
dour
fell
malevolent
mordant
sardonic
scathing
truculent
vitriolic
vituperation

Harmful
baleful
baneful

deleterious
inimical
injurious
insidious
minatory
perfidious
pernicious

harsh-sounding
cacophony
din
dissonant
raucous
strident

Hatred
abhorrence
anathema
antagonism
antipathy
detestation
enmity
loathing
malice
odium
rancor

Healthy
beneficial
salubrious
salutary

Hesitate
dither
oscillate
teeter
vacillate
waver

Hostile
antithetic
churlish
curmudgeon

irascible
malevolent
misanthropic
truculent
vindictive

Innocent/Inexperienced
credulous
gullible
ingenuous
naive
novitiate
tyro

Insincere
disingenuous
dissemble
fulsome
ostensible
unctuous

Investigate
appraise
ascertain
assay
descry
peruse

Lazy/Sluggish
indolent
inert
lackadaisical
languid
lassitude
lethargic
phlegmatic
quiescent
slothful
torpid

luck
adventitious
amulet
auspicious
fortuitous
kismet
optimum
portentous
propitiate
propitious
providential
talisman

Nag
admonish
belabor
cavil
enjoin
exhort
harangue
hector
martinet
remonstrate
reproof

Nasty
fetid
noisome
noxious

Not a Straight Line
askance
awry
careen
carom
circuitous
circumvent
gyrate
labyrinth
meander
oblique
serrated
sidle

sinuous
undulating
vortex

Overblown/Wordy
bombastic
circumlocution
garrulous
grandiloquent
loquacious
periphrastic
prolix
rhetoric
turgid
verbose

Pacify/Satisfy
ameliorate
appease
assuage
defer
mitigate
mollify
placate
propitiate
satiate
slake
soothe

Pleasant-Sounding
euphonious
harmonious
melodious
sonorous

Poor
destitute
esurient
impecunious
indigent

Praise
acclaim

accolade

aggrandize

encomium

eulogize

extol

fawn

laud/laudatory

venerate/veneration

Predict

augur

auspice

fey

harbinger

portentous

presage

prescient

prognosticate

Prevent/Obstruct

discomfort

encumber

fetter

forfend

hinder

impede

inhibit

occlude

Smart/Learned

astute

canny

erudite

perspicacious

Sorrow

disconsolate

doleful

dolor

elegiac

forlorn

lament

lugubrious

melancholy

morose

plaintive

threnody

Stubborn

implacable

inexorable

intractable

intransigent

obdurate

obstinate

recalcitrant

refractory

renitent

untoward

vexing

Terse

compendious

curt

laconic

pithy

succinct

taciturn

Time/Order/Duration

anachronism

antecede

antedate

anterior

archaic

diurnal

eon

ephemeral

epoch

fortnight

millennium

penultimate

synchronous

temporal

Timid/Timidity

craven

diffident

pusillanimous

recreant

timorous

trepidation

Truth

candor/candid

fealty

frankness

indisputable

indubitable

legitimate

probity

sincere

veracious

verity

Unusual

aberration

anomaly

iconoclast

idiosyncrasy

Walking About

ambulatory

itinerant

peripatetic

Wandering

discursive

expatiate

forage

itinerant

peregrination

peripatetic

sojourn

Weaken

adulterate

enervate

exacerbate
inhibit
obviate
stultify
undermine
vitiate

Wisdom
adage
aphorism
apothegm
axiom

bromide
dictum
epigram
platitude
sententious
truism

Withdrawal/Retreat
abeyance
abjure
abnegation
abortive

abrogate
decamp
demur
recant
recidivism
remission
renege
rescind
retrograde

Kaplan's Root List

Kaplan's Root List can boost your knowledge of GRE-level words, and that can help you get more questions right. No one can predict exactly which words will show up on your test, but there are certain words that the test makers favor. The Root List gives you the component parts of many typical GRE words. Knowing these words can help you because you may run across them on your GRE. Also, becoming comfortable with the types of words that pop up will reduce your anxiety about the test.

Knowing roots can help you in two more ways. First, instead of learning one word at a time, you can learn a whole group of words that contain a certain root. They'll be related in meaning, so if you remember one, it will be easier for you to remember others. Second, roots can often help you decode an unknown GRE word. If you recognize a familiar root, you could get a good enough grasp of the word to answer the question.

A: without

amoral: neither moral nor immoral

atheist: one who does not believe in God

atypical: not typical

anonymous: of unknown authorship or origin

apathy: lack of interest or emotion

atrophy: the wasting away of body tissue

anomaly: an irregularity

agnostic: one who questions the existence of God

AB/ABS: off, away from, apart, down

abduct: to take by force

abhor: to hate, detest

abolish: to do away with, make void

abstract: conceived apart from concrete realities, specific objects, or actual instances

abnormal: deviating from a standard

abdicate: to renounce or relinquish a throne

abstinence: forbearance from any indulgence of appetite

abstruse: hard to understand; secret, hidden

AC/ACR: sharp, bitter

acid: something that is sharp, sour, or ill-natured

acute: sharp at the end; ending in a point

acerbic: sour or astringent in taste; harsh in temper

acrid: sharp or biting to the taste or smell

acrimonious: caustic, stinging, or bitter in nature

exacerbate: to increase bitterness or violence; aggravate

ACT/AG: to do; to drive; to force; to lead

agile: quick and well-coordinated in movement; active, lively

agitate: to move or force into violent, irregular action

litigate: to make the subject of a lawsuit

prodigal: wastefully or recklessly extravagant

pedagogue: a teacher

synagogue: a gathering or congregation of Jews for the purpose of religious worship

AD/AL: to, toward, near

adapt: adjust or modify fittingly

adjacent: near, close, or contiguous; adjoining

addict: to give oneself over, as to a habit or pursuit

admire: to regard with wonder, pleasure, and approval

address: to direct a speech or written statement to

adhere: to stick fast; cleave; cling

adjoin: to be close or in contact with

advocate: to plead in favor of

AL/ALI/ALTER: other, another

alternative: a possible choice

alias: an assumed name; another name

alibi: the defense by an accused person that he or she was verifiably elsewhere at the time of the crime with which he or she is charged

alien: one born in another country; a foreigner

alter ego: the second self; a substitute or deputy

altruist: a person unselfishly concerned for the welfare of others

allegory: figurative treatment of one subject under the guise of another

AM: love

amateur: a person who engages in an activity for pleasure rather than financial or professional gain

amatory: of or pertaining to lovers or lovemaking

amenity: agreeable ways or manners

amorous: inclined to love, esp. sexual love

enamored: inflamed with love; charmed; captivated

amity: friendship; peaceful harmony

inamorata: a female lover

amiable: having or showing agreeable personal qualities

amicable: characterized by exhibiting good will

AMB: to go; to walk

ambient: moving freely; circulating

ambitious: desirous of achieving or obtaining power

preamble: an introductory statement

ambassador: an authorized messenger or representative

ambulance: a wheeled vehicle equipped for carrying sick people, usually to a hospital

ambulatory: of, pertaining to, or capable of walking

ambush: the act of lying concealed so as to attack by surprise

perambulator: one who makes a tour of inspection on foot

AMBI/AMPH: both, more than one, around

ambiguous: open to various interpretations

amphibian: any cold-blooded vertebrate, the larva of which is aquatic and the adult of which is terrestrial; a person or thing having a twofold nature

ambidextrous: able to use both hands equally well

ANIM: of the life, mind, soul, spirit

unanimous: in complete accord

animosity: a feeling of ill will or enmity

animus: hostile feeling or attitude

equanimity: mental or emotional stability, especially under tension

magnanimous: generous in forgiving an insult or injury

ANNUI/ENNI: year

annual: of, for, or pertaining to a year; yearly

anniversary: the yearly recurrence of the date of a past event

annuity: a specified income payable at stated intervals

perennial: lasting for an indefinite amount of time

annals: a record of events, esp. a yearly record

ANTE: before

anterior: placed before

antecedent: existing, being, or going before

antedate: precede in time

antebellum: before the war (especially the American Civil War)

antediluvian: belonging to the period before the biblical flood; very old or old-fashioned

ANTHRO/ANDR: man, human

anthropology: the science that deals with the origins of humankind

android: robot; mechanical man

misanthrope: one who hates humans or humanity

philanderer: one who carries on flirtations

androgynous: being both male and female

androgen: any substance that promotes masculine characteristics

anthropocentric: regarding humanity as the central fact of the universe

ANTI: against

antibody: a protein naturally existing in blood serum that reacts to overcome the toxic effects of an antigen

antidote: a remedy for counteracting the effects of poison, disease, etc.

antiseptic: free from germs; particularly clean or neat

antipathy: aversion

antipodal: on the opposite side of the globe

APO: away

apology: an expression of one's regret or sorrow for having wronged another

apostle: one of the 12 disciples sent forth by Jesus to preach the gospel

apocalypse: revelation; discovery; disclosure

apogee: the highest or most distant point

apocryphal: of doubtful authorship or authenticity

apostasy: a total desertion of one's religion, principles, party, cause, etc.

ARCH/ARCHI/ARCHY: chief, principal, ruler

architect: the devisor, maker, or planner of anything

archenemy: chief enemy

monarchy: a government in which the supreme power is lodged in a sovereign

anarchy: a state or society without government or law

oligarchy: a state or society ruled by a select group

AUTO: self

automatic: self-moving or self-acting

autocrat: an absolute ruler

autonomy: independence or freedom

BE: to be; to have a particular quality; to exist

belittle: to regard something as less impressive than it apparently is

bemoan: to express pity for

bewilder: to confuse or puzzle completely

belie: to misrepresent; to contradict

BEL/BEL: war

antebellum: before the war

rebel: a person who resists authority, control, or tradition

belligerent: warlike, given to waging war

BEN/BON: good

benefit: anything advantageous to a person or thing

benign: having a kindly disposition

benediction: act of uttering a blessing

benevolent: desiring to do good to others

bonus: something given over and above what is due

bona fide: in good faith; without fraud

BI: twice, double

binocular: involving two eyes

biennial: happening every two years

bilateral: pertaining to or affecting two or both sides

bilingual: able to speak one's native language and another with equal facility

bipartisan: representing two parties

CAD/CID: to fall; to happen by chance

accident: happening by chance; unexpected

coincidence: a striking occurrence of two or more events at one time, apparently by chance

decadent: decaying; deteriorating

cascade: a waterfall descending over a steep surface

recidivist: one who repeatedly relapses, as into crime

CANT/CENT/CHANT: to sing

accent: prominence of a syllable in terms of pronunciation

chant: a song; singing

enchant: to subject to magical influence; bewitch

recant: to withdraw or disavow a statement

incantation: the chanting of words purporting to have magical power

incentive: that which incites action

CAP/CIP/CEPT: to take; to get

capture: to take by force or stratagem

anticipate: to realize beforehand; foretaste or foresee

susceptible: capable of receiving, admitting, undergoing, or being affected by something

emancipate: to free from restraint

percipient: having perception; discerning; discriminating

precept: a commandment or direction given as a rule of conduct

CAP/CAPIT/CIPIT: head, headlong

capital: the city or town that is the official seat of government

disciple: one who is a pupil of the doctrines of another

precipitate: to hasten the occurrence of; to bring about prematurely

precipice: a cliff with a vertical face

capitulate: to surrender unconditionally or on stipulated terms

caption: a heading or title

CARD/CORD/COUR: heart

cardiac: pertaining to the heart

encourage: to inspire with spirit or confidence

concord: agreement; peace, amity

discord: lack of harmony between persons or things

concordance: agreement, concord, harmony

CARN: flesh

carnivorous: eating flesh

carnage: the slaughter of a great number of people

carnival: a traveling amusement show

reincarnation: rebirth of a soul in a new body

incarnation: a being invested with a bodily form

CAST/CHAST: cut

cast: to throw or hurl; fling

caste: a hereditary social group, limited to people of the same rank

castigate: to punish in order to correct

chastise: to discipline, esp. by corporal punishment

chaste: free from obscenity; decent

CED/CEED/CESS: to go; to yield; to stop

antecedent: existing, being, or going before

concede: to acknowledge as true, just, or proper; admit

predecessor: one who comes before another in an office, position, etc.

cessation: a temporary or complete discontinuance

incessant: without stop

CENTR: center

concentrate: to bring to a common center; to converge, to direct toward one point

eccentric: off-center

concentric: having a common center, as in circles or spheres

centrifuge: an apparatus that rotates at high speed that separates substances of different densities using centrifugal force

centrist: of or pertaining to moderate political or social ideas

CERN/CERT/CRET/CRIM/CRIT: to separate; to judge; to distinguish; to decide

discrete: detached from others, separate

ascertain: to make sure of; to determine

certitude: freedom from doubt

discreet: judicious in one's conduct of speech, esp. with regard to maintaining silence about something of a delicate nature

hypocrite: a person who pretends to have beliefs that she does not

criterion: a standard of judgment or criticism

CHRON: time

synchronize: to occur at the same time or agree in time

chronology: the sequential order in which past events occurred

anachronism: an obsolete or archaic form

chronic: constant, habitual

chronometer: a time piece with a mechanism to adjust for accuracy

CIRCU: around, on all sides

circumference: the outer boundary of a circular area

circumstances: the existing conditions or state of affairs surrounding and affecting an agent

circuit: the act of going or moving around

circumambulate: to walk about or around

circuitous: roundabout, indirect

CIS: to cut

scissors: cutting instrument for paper

precise: definitely stated or defined

exorcise: to seek to expel an evil spirit by ceremony

incision: a cut, gash, or notch

incisive: penetrating, cutting

CLA/CLO/CLU: shut, close

conclude: to bring to an end; finish; to terminate

claustrophobia: an abnormal fear of enclosed places

disclose: to make known, reveal, or uncover

exclusive: not admitting of something else; shutting out others

cloister: a courtyard bordered with covered walks, esp. in a religious institution

preclude: to prevent the presence, existence, or occurrence of

CLAIM/CLAM: to shout; to cry out

exclaim: to cry out or speak suddenly and vehemently

proclaim: to announce or declare in an official way

clamor: a loud uproar

disclaim: to deny interest in or connection with

reclaim: to claim or demand the return of a right or possession

CLI: to lean toward

decline: to cause to slope or incline downward

recline: to lean back

climax: the most intense point in the development of something

proclivity: inclination, bias

disinclination: aversion, distaste

CO/COL/COM/CON: with, together

connect: to bind or fasten together

coerce: to compel by force, intimidation, or authority

compatible: capable of existing together in harmony

collide: to strike one another with a forceful impact

collaborate: to work with another, cooperate

conciliate: to placate, win over

commensurate: suitable in measure, proportionate

COUR/CUR: running; a course

recur: to happen again

curriculum: the regular course of study

courier: a messenger traveling in haste who bears news

excursion: a short journey or trip

cursive: handwriting in flowing strokes with the letters joined together

concur: to accord in opinion; agree

incursion: a hostile entrance into a place, esp. suddenly

cursory: going rapidly over something; hasty; superficial

CRE/CRESC/CRET: to grow

accrue: to be added as a matter of periodic gain

creation: the act of producing or causing to exist

increase: to make greater in any respect

increment: something added or gained; an addition or increase

accretion: an increase by natural growth

CRED: to believe; to trust

incredible: unbelievable

credentials: anything that provides the basis for belief

credo: any formula of belief

credulity: willingness to believe or trust too readily

credit: trustworthiness

CRYP: hidden

crypt: a subterranean chamber or vault

apocryphal: of doubtful authorship or authenticity

cryptology: the science of interpreting secret writings, codes, ciphers, and the like

cryptography: procedures of making and using secret writing

CUB/CUMB: to lie down

cubicle: any small space or compartment that is partitioned off

succumb: to give away to superior force; yield

incubate: to sit upon for the purpose of hatching

incumbent: holding an indicated position

recumbent: lying down; reclining; leaning

CULP: blame

culprit: a person guilty for an offense

culpable: deserving blame or censure

inculpate: to charge with fault

mea culpa: through my fault; my fault

DAC/DOC: to teach

doctor: someone licensed to practice medicine; a learned person

doctrine: a particular principle advocated, as of a government or religion

indoctrinate: to imbue a person with learning

docile: easily managed or handled; tractable

didactic: intended for instruction

DE: away, off, down, completely, reversal

descend: to move from a higher to a lower place

decipher: to make out the meaning; to interpret

defile: to make foul, dirty, or unclean

defame: to attack the good name or reputation of

deferential: respectful; to yield to judgment

delineate: to trace the outline of; sketch or trace in outline

DEM: people

democracy: government by the people

epidemic: affecting at the same time a large number of people, and spreading from person to person

endemic: peculiar to a particular people or locality

pandemic: general, universal

demographics: vital and social statistics of populations

DI/DIA: apart, through

dialogue: conversation between two or more persons

diagnose: to determine the identity of something from the symptoms

dilate: to make wider or larger; to cause to expand

dilatory: inclined to delay or procrastinate

dichotomy: division into two parts, kinds, etc.

DIC/DICT/DIT: to say; to tell; to use words

dictionary: a book containing a selection of the words of a language

predict: to tell in advance

verdict: judgment, decree

interdict: to forbid; prohibit

DIGN: worth

dignity: nobility or elevation of character; worthiness

dignitary: a person who holds a high rank or office

deign: to think fit or in accordance with one's dignity

condign: well deserved; fitting; adequate

disdain: to look upon or treat with contempt

DIS/DIF: away from, apart, reversal, not

disperse: to drive or send off in various directions

disseminate: to scatter or spread widely; promulgate

dissipate: to scatter wastefully

dissuade: to deter by advice or persuasion

diffuse: to pour out and spread, as in a fluid

DOG/DOX: opinion

orthodox: sound or correct in opinion or doctrine

paradox: an opinion or statement contrary to accepted opinion

dogma: a system of tenets, as of a church

DOL: suffer, pain

condolence: expression of sympathy with one who is suffering

indolence: a state of being lazy or slothful

doleful: sorrowful, mournful

dolorous: full of pain or sorrow, grievous

DON/DOT/DOW: to give

donate: to present as a gift or contribution

pardon: kind indulgence, forgiveness

antidote: something that prevents or counteracts ill effects

anecdote: a short narrative about an interesting event

endow: to provide with a permanent fund

DUB: doubt

dubious: doubtful

dubiety: doubtfulness

indubitable: unquestionable

DUC/DUCT: to lead

abduct: to carry off or lead away

conduct: personal behavior, way of acting

conducive: contributive, helpful

induce: to lead or move by influence

induct: to install in a position with formal ceremonies

produce: to bring into existence; give cause to

DUR: hard

endure: to hold out against; to sustain without yielding

durable: able to resist decay

duress: compulsion by threat, coercion

dour: sullen, gloomy

duration: the length of time something exists

DYS: faulty, abnormal

dystrophy: faulty or inadequate nutrition or development

dyspepsia: impaired digestion

dyslexia: an impairment of the ability to read due to a brain defect

dysfunctional: poorly functioning

E/EF/EX: out, out of, from, former, completely

evade: to escape from, avoid

exclude: to shut out; to leave out

extricate: to disentangle, release

exonerate: to free or declare free from blame

expire: to come to an end, cease to be valid

efface: to rub or wipe out; surpass, eclipse

EPI: upon

epidemic: affecting a large number of people at the same time and spreading from person to person

epilogue: a concluding part added to a literary work

epidermis: the outer layer of the skin

epigram: a witty or pointed saying tersely expressed

epithet: a word or phrase, used invectively as a term of abuse

EQU: equal, even

equation: the act of making equal

adequate: equal to the requirement or occasion

equidistant: equally distant

iniquity: gross injustice; wickedness

ERR: to wander

err: to go astray in thought or belief, to be mistaken

error: a deviation from accuracy or correctness

erratic: deviating from the proper or usual course in conduct

arrant: downright, thorough, notorious

ESCE: becoming

adolescent: between childhood and adulthood

obsolescent: becoming obsolete

incandescent: glowing with heat, shining

convalescent: recovering from illness

reminiscent: reminding or suggestive of

EU: good, well

euphemism: pleasant-sounding term for something unpleasant

eulogy: speech or writing in praise or commendation

eugenics: improvement of qualities of race by control of inherited characteristics

euthanasia: killing a person painlessly, usually one who has an incurable, painful disease

euphony: pleasantness of sound

EXTRA: outside, beyond

extraordinary: beyond the ordinary

extract: to take out, obtain against a person's will

extradite: to hand over (person accused of crime) to state where crime was committed

extrasensory: derived by means other than known senses

extrapolate: to estimate (unknown facts or values) from known data

FAB/FAM: speak

fable: fictional tale, esp. legendary

affable: friendly, courteous

ineffable: too great for description in words; that which must not be uttered

famous: well known, celebrated

defame: attack good name of

FAC/FIC/FIG/FAIT/FEIT/FY: to do; to make

factory: building for manufacture of goods

faction: small dissenting group within larger one, esp. in politics deficient: incomplete or insufficient

prolific: producing many offspring or much output

configuration: manner of arrangement, shape

ratify: to confirm or accept by formal consent

effigy: sculpture or model of person

counterfeit: imitation, forgery

FER: to bring; to carry; to bear

offer: to present for acceptance, refusal, or consideration

confer: to grant, bestow

referendum: to vote on political question open to the entire electorate

proffer: to offer

proliferate: to reproduce; produce rapidly

FERV: to boil; to bubble

fervor: passion, zeal

fervid: ardent, intense

effervescent: with the quality of giving off bubbles of gas

FID: faith, trust

confide: to entrust with a secret

affidavit: written statement on oath

fidelity: faithfulness, loyalty

fiduciary: of a trust; held or given in trust

infidel: disbeliever in the supposed true religion

FIN: end

final: at the end; coming last

confine: to keep or restrict within certain limits; imprison

definitive: decisive, unconditional, final

infinite: boundless; endless

infinitesimal: infinitely or very small

FLAG/FLAM: to burn

flammable: easily set on fire

flambeau: a lighted torch

flagrant: blatant, scandalous

conflagration: a large destructive fire

FLECT/FLEX: to bend

deflect: to bend or turn aside from a purpose

flexible: able to bend without breaking

inflect: to change or vary pitch of

reflect: to throw back

genuflect: to bend knee, esp. in worship

FLU/FLUX: to flow

fluid: substance, esp. gas or liquid, capable of flowing freely

fluctuation: something that varies, rising and falling

effluence: flowing out of (light, electricity, etc.)

confluence: merging into one

mellifluous: pleasing, musical

FORE: before

foresight: care or provision for future

foreshadow: be warning or indication of (future event)

forestall: to prevent by advance action

forthright: straightforward, outspoken, decisive

FORT: chance

fortune: chance or luck in human affairs

fortunate: lucky, auspicious

fortuitous: happening by luck

FORT: strength

fortify: to provide with fortifications; strengthen

fortissimo: very loud

forte: strong point; something a person does well

FRA/FRAC/FRAG/FRING: to break

fracture: breakage, esp. of a bone

fragment: a part broken off

fractious: irritable, peevish

refractory: stubborn, unmanageable, rebellious

infringe: to break or violate (a law, etc.)

FUS: to pour

profuse: lavish, extravagant, copious

fusillade: continuous discharge of firearms or outburst of criticism suffuse: to spread throughout or over from within

diffuse: to spread widely or thinly

infusion: infusing; liquid extract so obtained

GEN: birth, creation, race, kind

generous: giving or given freely

genetics: study of heredity and variation among animals and plants

gender: classification roughly corresponding to the two sexes and sexlessness

carcinogenic: producing cancer

congenital: existing or as such from birth

progeny: offspring, descendants

miscegenation: interbreeding of races

GN/GNO: know

agnostic: person who believes that the existence of God is not provable

ignore: to refuse to take notice of

ignoramus: a person lacking knowledge, uninformed

recognize: to identify as already known

incognito: with one's name or identity concealed

prognosis: to forecast, especially of disease

diagnose: to make an identification of disease or fault from symptoms

GRAD/GRESS: to step

progress: forward movement

aggressive: given to hostile act or feeling

degrade: to humiliate, dishonor, reduce to lower rank

digress: to depart from main subject

egress: going out; way out

regress: to move backward, revert to an earlier state

GRAT: pleasing

grateful: thankful

ingratiate: to bring oneself into favor

gratuity: money given for good service

gracious: kindly, esp. to inferiors; merciful

HER/HES: to stick

coherent: logically consistent; having waves in phase and of one wavelength

adhesive: tending to remain in memory; sticky; an adhesive substance

inherent: involved in the constitution or essential character of something

adherent: able to adhere; believer or advocate of a particular thing

heredity: the qualities genetically derived from one's ancestors and the transmission of those qualities

(H)ETERO: different

heterosexual: of or pertaining to sexual orientation toward members of the opposite sex; relating to different sexes

heterogeneous: of other origin: not originating in the body

heterodox: different from acknowledged standard; holding unorthodox opinions or doctrines

(H)OM: same

homogeneous: of the same or a similar kind of nature; of uniform structure of composition throughout

homonym: one of two or more words spelled and pronounced alike but different in meaning

homosexual: of, relating to, or exhibiting sexual desire toward a member of one's own sex

anomaly: deviation from the common rule

homeostasis: a relatively stable state of equilibrium

HYPER: over, excessive

hyperactive: excessively active

hyperbole: purposeful exaggeration for effect

hyperglycemia: an abnormally high concentration of sugar in the blood

HYPO: under, beneath, less than

hypodermic: relating to the parts beneath the skin

hypochondriac: one affected by extreme depression of mind or spirits often centered on imaginary physical ailments hypocritical: affecting virtues or qualities one does not have

hypothesis: assumption subject to proof

IDIO: one's own

idiot: an utterly stupid person

idiom: a language, dialect, or style of speaking particular to a people

idiosyncrasy: peculiarity of temperament; eccentricity

IM/IN/EM/EN: in, into

embrace: to clasp in the arms; to include or contain

enclose: to close in on all sides

intrinsic: belonging to a thing by its very nature

influx: the act of flowing in; inflow

implicit: not expressly stated; implied

incarnate: given a bodily, esp. a human, form

indigenous: native; innate, natural

IM/IN: not, without

inactive: not active

innocuous: not harmful or injurious

indolence: showing a disposition to avoid exertion; slothful

impartial: not partial or biased; just

indigent: deficient in what is requisite

INTER: between, among

interstate: connecting or jointly involving states

interim: a temporary or provisional arrangement; meantime

interloper: one who intrudes in the domain of others

intermittent: stopping or ceasing for a time

intersperse: to scatter here and there

JECT: to throw; to throw down

inject: to place (quality, etc.) where needed in something

dejected: sad, depressed

eject: to throw out, expel

conjecture: formation of opinion on incomplete information

abject: utterly hopeless, humiliating, or wretched

JOIN/JUNCT: to meet; to join

junction: the act of joining; combining

adjoin: to be next to and joined with

subjugate: to conquer

rejoinder: to reply, retort

junta: (usually military) clique taking power after a coup d'état

JUR: to swear

perjury: willful lying while on oath

abjure: to renounce on oath

adjure: to beg or command

LAV/LUT/LUV: to wash

lavatory: a room with equipment for washing hands and face

dilute: to make thinner or weaker by the addition of water

pollute: to make foul or unclean

deluge: a great flood of water

antediluvian: before the biblical flood; extremely old

ablution: act of cleansing

LECT/LEG: to select, to choose

collect: to gather together or assemble

elect: to choose; to decide

select: to choose with care

eclectic: selecting ideas, etc. from various sources

predilection: preference, liking

LEV: lift, light, rise

relieve: to mitigate; to free from a burden

alleviate: to make easier to endure, lessen

relevant: bearing on or pertinent to information at hand

levee: embankment against river flooding

levitate: to rise in the air or cause to rise

levity: humor, frivolity, gaiety

LOC/LOG/LOQU: word, speech

dialogue: conversation, esp. in a literary work

elocution: art of clear and expressive speaking

prologue: introduction to poem, play, etc.

eulogy: speech or writing in praise of someone

colloquial: of ordinary or familiar conversation

grandiloquent: pompous or inflated in language

loquacious: talkative

LUC/LUM/LUS: light

illustrate: to make intelligible with examples or analogies

illuminate: to supply or brighten with light

illustrious: highly distinguished

translucent: permitting light to pass through

lackluster: lacking brilliance or radiance

lucid: easily understood, intelligible

luminous: bright, brilliant, glowing

LUD/LUS: to play

allude: to refer casually or indirectly

illusion: something that deceives by producing a false impression of reality

ludicrous: ridiculous, laughable

delude: to mislead the mind or judgment of, deceive

elude: to avoid capture or escape defection by

prelude: a preliminary to an action, event, etc.

MAG/MAJ/MAX: big

magnify: to increase the apparent size of

magnitude: greatness of size, extent, or dimensions

maximum: the highest amount, value, or degree attained

magnate: a powerful or influential person

magnanimous: generous in forgiving an insult or injury

maxim: an expression of general truth or principle

MAL/MALE: bad, ill, evil, wrong

malfunction: failure to function properly

malicious: full of or showing malice

malign: to speak harmful untruths about, to slander

malady: a disorder or disease of the body

maladroit: clumsy, tactless

malapropism: humorous misuse of a word

malfeasance: misconduct or wrongdoing often committed by a public official

malediction: a curse

MAN: hand

manual: operated by hand

manufacture: to make by hand or machinery

emancipate: to free from bondage

manifest: readily perceived by the eye or the understanding

mandate: an authoritative order or command

MIN: small

minute: a unit of time equal to one-sixtieth of an hour, or sixty seconds

minutiae: small or trivial details

miniature: a copy or model that represents something in greatly reduced size

diminish: to lessen

diminution: the act or process of diminishing

MIN: to project, to hang over

eminent: towering above others; projecting

imminent: about to occur; impending

prominent: projecting outward

preeminent: superior to or notable above all others

minatory: menacing, threatening

MIS/MIT: to send

transmit: to send from one person, thing, or place to another

emissary: a messenger or agent sent to represent the interests of another

intermittent: stopping and starting at intervals

remit: to send money

remission: a lessening of intensity or degree

MISC: mixed

miscellaneous: made up of a variety of parts or ingredients

miscegenation: the interbreeding of races, esp. marriage between white and nonwhite persons promiscuous: consisting of diverse and unrelated parts or individuals

MON/MONIT: to remind; to warn

monument: a structure, such as a building, tower, or sculpture, erected as a memorial

monitor: one that admonishes, cautions, or reminds

summon: to call together; convene

admonish: to counsel against something; caution

remonstrate: to say or plead in protect, objection, or reproof

premonition: forewarning, presentiment

MORPH: shape

amorphous: without definite form; lacking a specific shape

metamorphosis: a transformation, as by magic or sorcery

anthropomorphism: attribution of human characteristics to inanimate objects, animals, or natural phenomena

MORT: death

immortal: not subject to death

morbid: susceptible to preoccupation with unwholesome matters

moribund: dying, decaying

MUT: change

commute: to substitute; exchange; interchange

mutation: the process of being changed

transmutation: the act of changing from one form into another

permutation: a complete change; transformation

immutable: unchangeable, invariable

NAT/NAS/NAI: to be born

natural: present due to nature, not to artificial or man-made means

native: belonging to one by nature; inborn; innate

naive: lacking worldliness and sophistication; artless

cognate: related by blood; having a common ancestor

renaissance: rebirth, esp. referring to culture

nascent: starting to develop

NIC/NOC/NOX: harm

innocent: uncorrupted by evil, malice, or wrongdoing

noxious: injurious or harmful to health or morals

obnoxious: highly disagreeable or offensive

innocuous: having no adverse effect; harmless

NOM: rule, order

astronomy: the scientific study of the universe beyond the earth

economy: the careful or thrifty use of resources, as of income, materials, or labor

gastronomy: the art or science of good eating

taxonomy: the science, laws, or principles of classification

autonomy: independence, self-governance

NOM/NYM/NOUN/NOWN: name

synonym: a word having a meaning similar to that of another word of the same language

anonymous: having an unknown or unacknowledged name

nominal: existing in name only; negligible

nominate: to propose by name as a candidate

nomenclature: a system of names; systematic naming

acronym: a word formed from the initial letters of a name

NOUNC/NUNC: to announce

announce: to proclaim

pronounce: to articulate

renounce: to give up, especially by formal announcement

NOV/NEO/NOU: new

novice: a person new to any field or activity

renovate: to restore to an earlier condition

innovate: to begin or introduce something new

neologism: a newly coined word, phrase, or expression

neophyte: a recent convert

nouveau riche: one who has lately become rich

OB/OC/OF/OP: toward, to, against, over

obese: extremely fat, corpulent

obstinate: stubbornly adhering to an idea, inflexible

obstruct: to block or fill with obstacles

oblique: having a slanting or sloping direction

obstreperous: noisily defiant, unruly

obtuse: not sharp, pointed, or acute in any form

obfuscate: to render indistinct or dim; darken

obsequious: overly submissive

OMNI: all

omnibus: an anthology of the works of one author or of writings on related subjects

omnipresent: everywhere at one time

omnipotent: all powerful

omniscient: having infinite knowledge

PAC/PEAC: peace

appease: to bring peace to

pacify: to ease the anger or agitation of

pacifier: something or someone that eases the anger or agitation of

pact: a formal agreement, as between nations

PAN: all, everyone

panorama: an unobstructed and wide view of an extensive area

panegyric: formal or elaborate praise at an assembly

panoply: a wide-ranging and impressive array or display

pantheon: a public building containing tombs or memorials of the illustrious dead of a nation

pandemic: widespread, general, universal

PAR: equal

par: an equality in value or standing

parity: equally, as in amount, status, or character

apartheid: any system or caste that separates people according to race, etc.

disparage: to belittle, speak disrespectfully about

disparate: essentially different

PARA: next to, beside

parallel: extending in the same direction

parasite: an organism that lives on or within a plant or animal of another species, from which it obtains nutrients

parody: to imitate for purposes of satire

parable: a short, allegorical story designed to illustrate a moral lesson or religious principle

paragon: a model of excellence

paranoid: suffering from a baseless distrust of others

PAS/PAT/ PATH: feeling, suffering, disease

sympathy: harmony or agreement in feeling

empathy: the identification with the feelings or thoughts of others

compassion: a feeling of deep sympathy for someone struck by misfortune, accompanied by a desire to alleviate suffering

dispassionate: devoid of personal feeling or bias

impassive: showing or feeling no emotion

sociopath: a person whose behavior is antisocial and who lacks a sense of moral responsibility

pathogenic: causing disease

PAU/PO/POV/PU: few, little, poor

poverty: the condition of being poor

paucity: smallness of quantity; scarcity; scantiness

pauper: a person without any personal means of support

impoverish: to deplete

pusillanimous: lacking courage or resolution

puerile: childish, immature

PED: child, education

pedagogue: a teacher

pediatrician: a doctor who primarily has children as patients

pedant: one who displays learning ostentatiously

encyclopedia: book or set of books containing articles on various topics, covering all branches of knowledge or of one particular subject

PED/POD: foot

pedal: a foot-operated lever or part used to control

pedestrian: a person who travels on foot

expedite: to speed up the progress of

impede: to retard progress by means of obstacles or hindrances

podium: a small platform for an orchestra conductor, speaker, etc.

antipodes: places diametrically opposite each other on the globe

PEN/PUN: to pay; to compensate

penal: of or pertaining to punishment, as for crimes

penalty: a punishment imposed for a violation of law or rule

punitive: serving for, concerned with, or inflicting punishment

penance: a punishment undergone to express regret for a sin

penitent: contrite

PEND/PENS: to hang; to weight; to pay

depend: to rely; to place trust in

stipend: a periodic payment; fixed or regular pay

compensate: to counterbalance, offset

indispensable: absolutely necessary, essential, or requisite

appendix: supplementary material at the end of a text

appendage: a limb or other subsidiary part that diverges from the central structure

PER: completely

persistent: lasting or enduring tenaciously

perforate: to make a way through or into something

perplex: to cause to be puzzled or bewildered over what is not understood

peruse: to read with thoroughness or care

perfunctory: performed merely as routine duty

pertinacious: resolute

perspicacious: shrewd, astute

PERI: around

perimeter: the border or outer boundary of a two-dimensional figure

periscope: an optical instrument for seeing objects in an obstructed field of vision

peripatetic: walking or traveling about; itinerant

PET/PIT: to go; to seek; to strive

appetite: a desire for food or drink

compete: to strive to outdo another for acknowledgment

petition: a formally drawn request soliciting some benefit

centripetal: moving toward the center

impetuous: characterized by sudden or rash action or emotion

petulant: showing sudden irritation, esp. over some annoyance

PHIL: love

philosophy: the rational investigation of the truths and principles of being, knowledge, or conduct

philatelist: one who loves or collects postage stamps

philology: the study of literary texts to establish their authenticity and determine their meaning

bibliophile: one who loves or collects books

PLAC: to please

placid: pleasantly calm or peaceful

placebo: a substance with no pharmacological effect which acts to placate a patient who believes it to be a medicine

implacable: unable to be pleased

complacent: self-satisfied, unconcerned

complaisant: inclined or disposed to please

PLE: to fill

complete: having all parts or elements

deplete: to decrease seriously or exhaust the supply of

supplement: something added to supply a deficiency

implement: an instrument, tool, or utensil for accomplishing work

replete: abundantly supplied

plethora: excess, overabundance

PLEX/PLIC/PLY: to fold, twist, tangle, or bend

complex: composed of many interconnected parts

replica: any close copy or reproduction

implicit: not expressly stated, implied

implicate: to show to be involved, usually in an incriminating manner

duplicity: deceitfulness in speech or conduct, double-dealing

supplicate: to make humble and earnest entreaty

PON/POS/POUND: to put; to place

component: a constituent part, elemental ingredient

expose: to lay open to danger, attack, or harm

expound: to set forth in detail

juxtapose: to place close together or side by side, esp. for contract

repository: a receptacle or place where things are deposited

PORT: to carry

import: to bring in from a foreign country

export: to transmit abroad

portable: easily carried

deportment: conduct, behavior

disport: to divert or amuse oneself

importune: to urge or press with excessive persistence

POST: after

posthumous: after death

posterior: situated at the rear

posterity: succeeding in future generations collectively

post facto: after the fact

PRE: before

precarious: dependent on circumstances beyond one's control

precocious: unusually advanced or mature in mental development or talent

premonition: a feeling of anticipation over a future event

presentiment: foreboding

precedent: an act that serves as an example for subsequent situations

precept: a commandment given as a rule of action or conduct

PREHEND/PRISE: to take; to get; to seize

surprise: to strike with an unexpected feeling of wonder or astonishment

enterprise: a project undertaken

reprehensible: deserving rebuke or censure

comprise: to include or contain

reprisals: retaliation against an enemy

apprehend: to take into custody

PRO: much, for, a lot

prolific: highly fruitful

profuse: spending or giving freely

prodigal: wastefully or recklessly extravagant

prodigious: extraordinary in size, amount, or extent

proselytize: to convert or attempt to recruit

propound: to set forth for consideration

provident: having or showing foresight

PROB: to prove; to test

probe: to search or examine thoroughly

approbation: praise, consideration

opprobrium: the disgrace incurred by shameful conduct

reprobate: a depraved or wicked person

problematic: questionable

probity: honesty, high-mindedness

PUG: to fight

pugnacious: to quarrel or fight readily

impugn: to challenge as false

repugnant: objectionable or offensive

pugilist: a fighter or boxer

PUNC/PUNG/POIGN: to point; to prick

point: a sharp or tapering end

puncture: the act of piercing

pungent: caustic or sharply expressive

compunction: a feeling of uneasiness for doing wrong

punctilious: strict or exact in the observance of formalities

expunge: to erase, eliminate completely

QUE/QUIS: to seek

acquire: to come into possession of

exquisite: of special beauty or charm

conquest: vanquishment

inquisitive: given to research, eager for knowledge

query: a question, inquiry

querulous: full of complaints

perquisite: a gratuity, tip

QUI: quiet

quiet: making little or no sound

disquiet: lack of calm or peace

tranquil: free from commotion or tumult

acquiesce: to comply, give in

quiescence: the condition of being at rest, still, inactive

RID/RIS: to laugh

riddle: a conundrum

derision: the act of mockery

risible: causing laughter

ROG: to ask

interrogate: to ask questions of, esp. formally

arrogant: making claims to superior importance or rights

abrogate: to abolish by formal means

surrogate: a person appointed to act for another

derogatory: belittling, disparaging

arrogate: to claim unwarrantably or presumptuously

SACR/SANCT/SECR: sacred

sacred: devoted or dedicated to a deity or religious purpose

sacrifice: the offering of some living or inanimate thing to a deity in homage

sanctify: to make holy

sanction: authoritative permission or approval

execrable: abominable

sacrament: something regarded as possessing sacred character

sacrilege: the violation of anything sacred

SAL/SIL/SAULT/SULT: to leap, to jump

insult: to treat with contemptuous rudeness

assault: a sudden or violent attack

somersault: to roll the body end over end, making a complete revolution

salient: prominent or conspicuous

resilient: able to spring back to an original form after compression

insolent: boldly rude or disrespectful

exult: to show or feel triumphant joy

desultory: at random, unmethodical

SCI: to know

conscious: aware of one's own existence

conscience: the inner sense of what is right or wrong, impelling one toward right action

unconscionable: unscrupulous

omniscient: knowing everything

prescient: having knowledge of things before they happen

SCRIBE/SCRIP: to write

scribble: to write hastily or carelessly

describe: to tell or depict in words

script: handwriting

postscript: any addition or supplement

proscribe: to condemn as harmful or odious

ascribe: to credit or assign, as to a cause or course

conscription: draft

transcript: a written or typed copy

circumscribe: to draw a line around

SE: apart

select: to choose in preference to another

separate: to keep apart, divide

seduce: to lead astray

segregate: to separate or set apart from others

secede: to withdraw formally from an association

sequester: to remove or withdraw into solitude or retirement

sedition: incitement of discontent or rebellion against a government

SEC/SEQU: to follow

second: next after the first

prosecute: to seek to enforce by legal process

sequence: the following of one thing after another

obsequious: fawning

non sequitur: an inference or a conclusion that does not follow from the premises

SED/SESS/SID: to sit; to be still; to plan; to plot

preside: to exercise management or control

resident: a person who lives in a place

sediment: the matter that settles to the bottom of a liquid

dissident: disagreeing, as in opinion or attitude

residual: remaining, leftover

subsidiary: serving to assist or supplement

insidious: intended to entrap or beguile

assiduous: diligent, persistent, hardworking

SENS/SENT: to feel; to be aware

sense: any of the faculties by which humans and animals perceive stimuli originating outside the body

sensory: of or pertaining to the senses or sensation

sentiment: an attitude or feeling toward something

presentiment: a feeling that something is about to happen

dissent: to differ in opinion, esp. from the majority

resent: to feel or show displeasure

sentinel: a person or thing that stands watch

insensate: without feeling or sensitivity

SOL: to loosen; to free

dissolve: to make a solution of, as by mixing in a liquid

soluble: capable of being dissolved or liquefied

resolution: a formal expression of opinion or intention made

dissolution: the act or process of dissolving into parts or elements

dissolute: indifferent to moral restraints

absolution: forgiveness for wrongdoing

SPEC/SPIC/SPIT: to look; to see

perspective: one's mental view of facts, ideas, and their interrelationships

speculation: the contemplation or consideration of some subject

suspicious: inclined to suspect

spectrum: a broad range of related things that form a continuous series

retrospective: contemplative of past situations

circumspect: watchful and discreet, cautious

perspicacious: having keen mental perception and understanding

conspicuous: easily seen or noticed; readily observable

specious: deceptively attractive

STA/STI: to stand; to be in place

static: of bodies or forces at rest or in equilibrium

destitute: without means of subsistence

obstinate: stubbornly adhering to a purpose, opinion, or course of action

constitute: to make up

stasis: the state of equilibrium or inactivity caused by opposing equal forces

apostasy: renunciation of an object of one's previous loyalty

SUA: smooth

suave: smoothly agreeable or polite

persuade: to encourage; to convince

dissuade: to deter

assuage: to make less severe, ease, relieve

SUB/SUP: below

submissive: inclined or ready to submit

subsidiary: serving to assist or supplement

subliminal: existing or operating below the threshold of confidence

subtle: thin, tenuous, or rarefied

subterfuge: an artifice or expedient used to evade a rule

supposition: the act of assuming

SUPER/SUR: above

surpass: to go beyond in amount, extent, or degree

superlative: the highest kind or order

supersede: to replace in power, as by another person or thing

supercilious: arrogant, haughty, condescending

superfluous: extra, more than necessary

surmount: to get over or across, to prevail

surveillance: a watch kept over someone or something

TAC/TIC: to be silent

reticent: disposed to be silent or not to speak freely

tacit: unspoken understanding

taciturn: uncommunicative

TAIN/TEN/TENT/TIN: to hold

detain: to keep from proceeding

pertain: to have reference or relation

tenacious: holding fast

abstention: the act of refraining voluntarily

tenure: the holding or possessing of anything

tenable: capable of being held, maintained, or defended

sustenance: nourishment, means of livelihood

pertinacious: persistent, stubborn

TEND/TENS/TENT/TENU: to stretch; to thin

tension: the act of stretching or straining

tentative: of the nature of, or done as a trial, attempt

tendentious: having a predisposition towards a point of view

distend: to expand by stretching

attenuate: to weaken or reduce in force

extenuating: making less serious by offering excuses

contentious: quarrelsome, disagreeable, belligerent

THEO: god

atheist: one who does not believe in a deity or divine system

theocracy: a form of government in which a deity is recognized as the supreme ruler

theology: the study of divine things and the divine faith

apotheosis: glorification, glorified ideal

TRACT: to drag; to pull; to draw

tractor: a powerful vehicle used to pull farm machinery

attract: to draw either by physical force or by an appeal to emotions or senses

contract: a legally binding document

detract: to take away from, esp. a positive thing

abstract: to draw or pull away, remove

tractable: easily managed or controlled

protract: to prolong, draw out, extend

TRANS: across

transaction: the act of carrying on or conduct to a conclusion or settlement

transparent: easily seen through, recognized, or detected

transition: a change from one way of being to another

transgress: to violate a law, command, or moral code

transcendent: going beyond ordinary limits

intransigent: refusing to agree or compromise

US/UT: to use

abuse: to use wrongly or improperly

usage: a customary way of doing something

usurp: to seize and hold

utilitarian: efficient, functional, useful

VEN/VENT: to come or to move toward

convene: to assemble for some public purpose

venturesome: showing a disposition to undertake risks

intervene: to come between disputing factions, mediate

contravene: to come into conflict with

adventitious: accidental

VER: truth

verdict: any judgment or decision

veracious: habitually truthful

verity: truthfulness

verisimilitude: the appearance or semblance of truth

aver: to affirm, to declare to be true

VERD: green

verdant: green with vegetation; inexperienced

verdure: fresh, rich vegetation

VERS/VERT: to turn

controversy: a public dispute involving a matter of opinion

revert: to return to a former habit

diverse: of a different kind, form, character

aversion: dislike

introvert: a person concerned primarily with inner thoughts and feelings

extrovert: an outgoing person

inadvertent: unintentional

covert: hidden, clandestine

avert: to turn away from

VI: life

vivid: strikingly bright or intense

vicarious: performed, exercised, received, or suffered in place of another

viable: capable of living

vivacity: the quality of being lively, animated, spirited

joie de vivre: joy of life (French expression)

convivial: sociable

VID/VIS: to see

evident: plain or clear to the sight or understanding

video: the elements of television pertaining to the transmission or reception of the image

adviser: one who gives counsel

survey: to view in a general or comprehensive way

vista: a view or prospect

VIL: base, mean

vilify: to slander, to defame

revile: to criticize with harsh language

vile: loathsome, unpleasant

VOC/VOK: to call

vocabulary: the stock of words used by or known to a particular person or group

advocate: to support or urge by argument

equivocate: to use ambiguous or unclear expressions

vocation: a particular occupation

avocation: something one does in addition to a principle occupation

vociferous: crying out noisily

convoke: to call together

invoke: to call on a deity

VOL: to wish

voluntary: undertaken of one's own accord or by free choice

malevolent: characterized by or expressing bad will

benevolent: characterized by or expressing good-will

volition: free choice, free will; act of choosing

VOR: to eat

voracious: having a great appetite

carnivorous: meat-eating

omnivorous: eating or absorbing everything

Top GRE Words in Context

The GRE tests the same kinds of words over and over again. Here you will find the most popular GRE words with their definitions in context to help you to remember them. If you see a word that's unfamiliar to you, take a moment to study the definition and, most importantly, reread the sentence with the word's definition in mind.

Remember: Learning vocabulary words in context is one of the best ways for your brain to retain the words' meanings. A broader vocabulary will serve you well on all four GRE Verbal question types and will also be extremely helpful in the Analytical Writing section.

ABATE: to reduce in amount, degree, or severity

As the hurricane's force ABATED, the winds dropped and the sea became calm.

ABSCOND: to leave secretly

The patron ABSCONDED from the restaurant without paying his bill by sneaking out the back door.

ABSTAIN: to choose not to do something

She ABSTAINED from choosing a mouthwatering dessert from the tray.

ABYSS: an extremely deep hole

The submarine dove into the ABYSS to chart the previously unseen depths.

ADULTERATE: to make impure

The chef made his ketchup last longer by ADULTERATING it with water.

ADVOCATE: to speak in favor of

The vegetarian ADVOCATED a diet containing no meat.

AESTHETIC: concerning the appreciation of beauty

Followers of the AESTHETIC Movement regarded the pursuit of beauty as the only true purpose of art.

AGGRANDIZE: to increase in power, influence, and reputation

The supervisor sought to AGGRANDIZE herself by claiming that the achievements of her staff were actually her own.

ALLEVIATE: to make more bearable

Taking aspirin helps to ALLEVIATE a headache.

AMALGAMATE: to combine; to mix together

Giant Industries AMALGAMATED with Mega Products to form Giant-Mega Products Incorporated.

AMBIGUOUS: doubtful or uncertain; able to be interpreted several ways

The directions she gave were so AMBIGUOUS that we disagreed on which way to turn.

AMELIORATE: to make better; to improve

The doctor was able to AMELIORATE the patient's suffering using painkillers.

ANACHRONISM: something out of place in time

The aged hippie used ANACHRONISTIC phrases like *groovy* and *far out* that had not been popular for years.

ANALOGOUS: similar or alike in some way; equivalent to

In the Newtonian construct for explaining the existence of God, the universe is ANALOGOUS to a mechanical timepiece, the creation of a divinely intelligent "clockmaker."

ANOMALY: deviation from what is normal

Albino animals may display too great an ANOMALY in their coloring to attract normally colored mates.

ANTAGONIZE: to annoy or provoke to anger

The child discovered that he could ANTAGONIZE the cat by pulling its tail.

ANTIPATHY: extreme dislike

The ANTIPATHY between the French and the English regularly erupted into open warfare.

APATHY: lack of interest or emotion

The APATHY of voters is so great that less than half the people who are eligible to vote actually bother to do so.

ARBITRATE: to judge a dispute between two opposing parties

Since the couple could not come to agreement, a judge was forced to ARBITRATE their divorce proceedings.

ARCHAIC: ancient, old-fashioned

Her ARCHAIC Commodore computer could not run the latest software.

ARDOR: intense and passionate feeling

Bishop's ARDOR for the landscape was evident when he passionately described the beauty of the scenic Hudson Valley.

ARTICULATE: able to speak clearly and expressively

She is such an ARTICULATE defender of labor that unions are among her strongest supporters.

ASSUAGE: to make something unpleasant less severe

Serena used aspirin to ASSUAGE her pounding headache.

ATTENUATE: to reduce in force or degree; to weaken

The Bill of Rights ATTENUATED the traditional power of governments to change laws at will.

AUDACIOUS: fearless and daring

Her AUDACIOUS nature allowed her to fulfill her dream of skydiving.

AUSTERE: severe or stern in appearance; undecorated

The lack of decoration makes military barracks seem AUSTERE to the civilian eye.

BANAL: predictable, clichéd, boring

He used BANAL phrases like *Have a nice day*, or *Another day, another dollar.*

BOLSTER: to support; to prop up

The presence of giant footprints BOLSTERED the argument that Sasquatch was in the area.

BOMBASTIC: pompous in speech and manner

The ranting of the radio talk-show host was mostly BOMBASTIC; his boasting and outrageous claims had no basis in fact.

CACOPHONY: harsh, jarring noise

The junior high orchestra created an almost unbearable CACOPHONY as they tried to tune their instruments.

CANDID: impartial and honest in speech

The observations of a child can be charming since they are CANDID and unpretentious.

CAPRICIOUS: changing one's mind quickly and often

Queen Elizabeth I was quite CAPRICIOUS; her courtiers could never be sure which of their number would catch her fancy.

CASTIGATE: to punish or criticize harshly

Many Americans are amazed at how harshly the authorities in Singapore CASTIGATE perpetrators of what would be considered minor crimes in the United States.

CATALYST: something that brings about a change in something else

The imposition of harsh taxes was the CATALYST that finally brought on the revolution.

CAUSTIC: biting in wit

Dorothy Parker gained her reputation for CAUSTIC wit from her cutting, yet clever, insults.

CHAOS: great disorder or confusion

In many religious traditions, God created an ordered universe from CHAOS.

CHAUVINIST: someone prejudiced in favor of a group to which he or she belongs

The attitude that men are inherently superior to women and therefore must be obeyed is common among male CHAUVINISTS.

CHICANERY: deception by means of craft or guile

Dishonest used car sales people often use CHICANERY to sell their beat-up old cars.

COGENT: convincing and well reasoned

Swayed by the COGENT argument of the defense, the jury had no choice but to acquit the defendant.

CONDONE: to overlook, pardon, or disregard

Some theorists believe that failing to prosecute minor crimes is the same as CONDONING an air of lawlessness.

CONVOLUTED: intricate and complicated

Although many people bought *A Brief History of Time*, few could follow its CONVOLUTED ideas and theories.

CORROBORATE: to provide supporting evidence

Fingerprints CORROBORATED the witness's testimony that he saw the defendant in the victim's apartment.

CREDULOUS: too trusting; gullible

Although some four-year-olds believe in the Easter Bunny, only the most CREDULOUS nine-year-olds also believe in him.

CRESCENDO: steadily increasing volume or force

The CRESCENDO of tension became unbearable as Evel Knievel prepared to jump his motorcycle over the school buses.

DECORUM: appropriateness of behavior or conduct; propriety

The countess complained that the vulgar peasants lacked the DECORUM appropriate for a visit to the palace.

DEFERENCE: respect, courtesy

The respectful young law clerk treated the Supreme Court justice with the utmost DEFERENCE.

DERIDE: to speak of or treat with contempt; to mock

The awkward child was often DERIDED by his "cooler" peers.

DESICCATE: to dry out thoroughly

After a few weeks of lying on the desert's baking sands, the cow's carcass became completely DESICCATED.

DESULTORY: jumping from one thing to another; disconnected

Diane had a DESULTORY academic record; she had changed majors 12 times in three years.

DIATRIBE: an abusive, condemnatory speech

The trucker bellowed a DIATRIBE at the driver who had cut him off.

DIFFIDENT: lacking self-confidence

Steve's DIFFIDENT manner during the job interview stemmed from his nervous nature and lack of experience in the field.

DILATE: to make larger; to expand

When you enter a darkened room, the pupils of your eyes DILATE to let in more light.

DILATORY: intended to delay

The congressman used DILATORY measures to delay the passage of the bill.

DILETTANTE: someone with an amateurish and superficial interest in a topic

Jerry's friends were such DILETTANTES that they seemed to have new jobs and hobbies every week.

DIRGE: a funeral hymn or mournful speech

Melville wrote the poem "A DIRGE for James McPherson" for the funeral of a Union general who was killed in 1864.

DISABUSE: to set right; to free from error

Galileo's observations DISABUSED scholars of the notion that the sun revolved around the earth.

DISCERN: to perceive; to recognize

It is easy to DISCERN the difference between butter and butter-flavored topping.

DISPARATE: fundamentally different; entirely unlike

Although the twins appear to be identical physically, their personalities are DISPARATE.

DISSEMBLE: to present a false appearance; to disguise one's real intentions or character

The villain could DISSEMBLE to the police no longer—he admitted the deed and tore up the floor to reveal the body of the old man.

DISSONANCE: a harsh and disagreeable combination, often of sounds

Cognitive DISSONANCE is the inner conflict produced when long-standing beliefs are contradicted by new evidence.

DOGMA: a firmly held opinion, often a religious belief

Linus's central DOGMA was that children who believed in the Great Pumpkin would be rewarded.

DOGMATIC: dictatorial in one's opinions

The dictator was DOGMATIC—he, and only he, was right.

DUPE: to deceive; a person who is easily deceived

Bugs Bunny was able to DUPE Elmer Fudd by dressing up as a lady rabbit.

ECLECTIC: selecting from or made up from a variety of sources

Budapest's architecture is an ECLECTIC mix of Eastern and Western styles.

EFFICACY: effectiveness

The EFFICACY of penicillin was unsurpassed when it was first introduced; the drug completely eliminated almost all bacterial infections for which it was administered.

ELEGY: a sorrowful poem or speech

Although Thomas Gray's "ELEGY Written in a Country Churchyard" is about death and loss, it urges its readers to endure this life and to trust in spirituality.

ELOQUENT: persuasive and moving, especially in speech

The Gettysburg Address is moving not only because of its lofty sentiments but also because of its ELOQUENT words.

EMULATE: to copy; to try to equal or excel

The graduate student sought to EMULATE his professor in every way, copying not only how she taught but also how she conducted herself outside of class.

ENERVATE: to reduce in strength

The guerrillas hoped that a series of surprise attacks would ENERVATE the regular army.

ENGENDER: to produce, cause, or bring about

His fear and hatred of clowns was ENGENDERED when he witnessed the death of his father at the hands of a clown.

ENIGMA: a puzzle; a mystery

Speaking in riddles and dressed in old robes, the artist gained a reputation as something of an ENIGMA.

ENUMERATE: to count, list, or itemize

Moses returned from the mountain with tablets on which the commandments were ENUMERATED.

EPHEMERAL: lasting a short time

The lives of mayflies seem EPHEMERAL to us, since the flies' average life span is a matter of hours.

EQUIVOCATE: to use expressions of double meaning in order to mislead

When faced with criticism of her policies, the politician EQUIVOCATED and left all parties thinking she agreed with them.

ERRATIC: wandering and unpredictable

The plot seemed predictable until it suddenly took a series of ERRATIC turns that surprised the audience.

ERUDITE: learned, scholarly, bookish

The annual meeting of philosophy professors was a gathering of the most ERUDITE, well-published individuals in the field.

ESOTERIC: known or understood by only a few

Only a handful of experts are knowledgeable about the ESOTERIC world of particle physics.

ESTIMABLE: admirable

Most people consider it ESTIMABLE that Mother Teresa spent her life helping the poor of India.

EULOGY: speech in praise of someone

His best friend gave the EULOGY, outlining his many achievements and talents.

EUPHEMISM: use of an inoffensive word or phrase in place of a more distasteful one

The funeral director preferred to use the EUPHEMISM *sleeping* instead of the word *dead*.

EXACERBATE: to make worse

It is unwise to take aspirin to try to relieve heartburn; instead of providing relief, the drug will only EXACERBATE the problem.

EXCULPATE: to clear from blame; prove innocent

The adversarial legal system is intended to convict those who are guilty and to EXCULPATE those who are innocent.

EXIGENT: urgent; requiring immediate action

The patient was losing blood so rapidly that it was EXIGENT to stop the source of the bleeding.

EXONERATE: to clear of blame

The fugitive was EXONERATED when another criminal confessed to committing the crime.

EXPLICIT: clearly stated or shown; forthright in expression

The owners of the house left a list of EXPLICIT instructions detailing their house-sitter's duties, including a schedule for watering the house plants.

FANATICAL: acting excessively enthusiastic; filled with extreme, unquestioned devotion

The stormtroopers were FANATICAL in their devotion to the emperor, readily sacrificing their lives for him.

FAWN: to grovel *eager to please*

The understudy FAWNED over the director in hopes of being cast in the part on a permanent basis.

FERVID: intensely emotional; feverish

The fans of Maria Callas were unusually FERVID, doing anything to catch a glimpse of the great opera singer.

FLORID: excessively decorated or embellished

The palace had been decorated in a FLORID style; every surface had been carved and gilded.

FOMENT: to arouse or incite

The protesters tried to FOMENT feeling against the war through their speeches and demonstrations.

FRUGALITY: a tendency to be thrifty or cheap

Scrooge McDuck's FRUGALITY was so great that he accumulated enough wealth to fill a giant storehouse with money.

GARRULOUS: tending to talk a lot

The GARRULOUS parakeet distracted its owner with its continuous talking.

GREGARIOUS: outgoing, sociable

She was so GREGARIOUS that when she found herself alone, she felt quite sad.

GUILE: deceit or trickery

Since he was not fast enough to catch the roadrunner on foot, the coyote resorted to GUILE in an effort to trap his enemy.

GULLIBLE: easily deceived

The con man pretended to be a bank officer so as to fool GULLIBLE bank customers into giving him their account information.

HOMOGENOUS: of a similar kind

The class was fairly HOMOGENOUS, since almost all of the students were senior journalism majors.

ICONOCLAST: one who opposes established beliefs, customs, and institutions

His lack of regard for traditional beliefs soon established him as an ICONOCLAST.

IMPERTURBABLE: not capable of being disturbed

The counselor had so much experience dealing with distraught children that she seemed IMPERTURBABLE, even when faced with the wildest tantrums.

IMPERVIOUS: impossible to penetrate; incapable of being affected

A good raincoat will be IMPERVIOUS to moisture.

IMPETUOUS: quick to act without thinking

It is not good for an investment broker to be IMPETUOUS, since much thought should be given to all the possible options.

IMPLACABLE: unable to be calmed down or made peaceful

His rage at the betrayal was so great that he remained IMPLACABLE for weeks.

INCHOATE: not fully formed; disorganized

The ideas expressed in Nietzsche's mature work also appear in an INCHOATE form in his earliest writing.

INGENUOUS: showing innocence or childlike simplicity

She was so INGENUOUS that her friends feared that her innocence and trustfulness would be exploited when she visited the big city.

INIMICAL: hostile, unfriendly

Even though the children had grown up together, they were INIMICAL to each other at school.

INNOCUOUS: harmless

Some snakes are poisonous, but most species are INNOCUOUS and pose no danger to humans.

INSIPID: lacking interest or flavor

The critic claimed that the painting was INSIPID, containing no interesting qualities at all.

INTRANSIGENT: uncompromising; refusing to be reconciled

The professor was INTRANSIGENT on the deadline, insisting that everyone turn the assignment in at the same time.

INUNDATE: to overwhelm; to cover with water

The tidal wave INUNDATED Atlantis, which was lost beneath the water.

IRASCIBLE: easily made angry

Attila the Hun's IRASCIBLE and violent nature made all who dealt with him fear for their lives.

LACONIC: using few words

She was a LACONIC poet who built her reputation on using words as sparingly as possible.

LAMENT: to express sorrow; to grieve

The children continued to LAMENT the death of the goldfish weeks after its demise.

LAUD: to give praise; to glorify

Parades and fireworks were staged to LAUD the success of the rebels.

LAVISH: to give unsparingly (v.); extremely generous or extravagant (adj.)

She LAVISHED the puppy with so many treats that it soon became overweight and spoiled.

LETHARGIC: acting in an indifferent or slow, sluggish manner

The clerk was so LETHARGIC that, even when the store was slow, he always had a long line in front of him.

LOQUACIOUS: talkative

She was naturally LOQUACIOUS, which was a problem in situations in which listening was more important than talking.

LUCID: clear and easily understood

The explanations were written in a simple and LUCID manner so that students were immediately able to apply what they learned.

LUMINOUS: bright, brilliant, glowing

The park was bathed in LUMINOUS sunshine, which warmed the bodies and the souls of the visitors.

MALINGER: to evade responsibility by pretending to be ill

A common way to avoid the draft was by MALINGERING—pretending to be mentally or physically ill so as to avoid being taken by the Army.

MALLEABLE: capable of being shaped

Gold is the most MALLEABLE of precious metals; it can easily be formed into almost any shape.

METAPHOR: a figure of speech comparing two different things; a symbol

The METAPHOR "a sea of troubles" suggests a lot of troubles by comparing their number to the vastness of the sea.

METICULOUS: extremely careful about details

To find all the clues at the crime scene, the investigators METICULOUSLY examined every inch of the area.

MISANTHROPE: a person who dislikes others

The character Scrooge in *A Christmas Carol* is such a MISANTHROPE that even the sight of children singing makes him angry.

MITIGATE: to soften; to lessen

A judge may MITIGATE a sentence if she decides that a person committed a crime out of need.

MOLLIFY: to calm or make less severe

Their argument was so intense that is was difficult to believe any compromise would MOLLIFY them.

MONOTONY: lack of variation

The MONOTONY of the sound of the dripping faucet almost drove the research assistant crazy.

NAIVE: lacking sophistication or experience

Having never traveled before, the elementary school students were more NAIVE than their high school counterparts on the field trip.

OBDURATE: hardened in feeling; resistant to persuasion

The president was completely OBDURATE on the issue, and no amount of persuasion would change his mind.

OBSEQUIOUS: overly submissive and eager to please

The OBSEQUIOUS new associate made sure to compliment her supervisor's tie and agree with him on every issue.

OBSTINATE: stubborn, unyielding

The OBSTINATE child could not be made to eat any food that he disliked.

OBVIATE: to prevent; to make unnecessary

The river was shallow enough to wade across at many points, which OBVIATED the need for a bridge.

OCCLUDE: to stop up; to prevent the passage of

A shadow is thrown across the earth's surface during a solar eclipse, when the light from the sun is OCCLUDED by the moon.

ONEROUS: troublesome and oppressive; burdensome

The assignment was so extensive and difficult to manage that it proved ONEROUS to the team in charge of it.

OPAQUE: impossible to see through; preventing the passage of light

The heavy buildup of dirt and grime on the windows almost made them OPAQUE.

OPPROBRIUM: public disgrace

After the scheme to embezzle the elderly was made public, the treasurer resigned in utter OPPROBRIUM.

OSTENTATION: excessive showiness

The OSTENTATION of the Sun King's court is evident in the lavish decoration and luxuriousness of his palace at Versailles.

PARADOX: a contradiction or dilemma

It is a PARADOX that those most in need of medical attention are often those least able to obtain it.

PARAGON: model of excellence or perfection

She is the PARAGON of what a judge should be: honest, intelligent, hardworking, and just.

PEDANT: someone who shows off learning

The graduate instructor's tedious and excessive commentary on the subject soon gained her a reputation as a PEDANT.

PERFIDIOUS: willing to betray one's trust

The actress's PERFIDIOUS companion revealed all of her intimate secrets to the gossip columnist.

PERFUNCTORY: done in a routine way; indifferent

The machinelike bank teller processed the transaction and gave the waiting customer a PERFUNCTORY smile.

PERMEATE: to penetrate

This miraculous new cleaning fluid is able to PERMEATE stains and dissolve them in minutes!

PHILANTHROPY: charity; a desire or effort to promote goodness

New York's Metropolitan Museum of Art owes much of its collection to the PHILANTHROPY of private collectors who willed their estates to the museum.

PLACATE: to soothe or pacify

The burglar tried to PLACATE the snarling dog by saying "Nice doggy," and offering it a treat.

PLASTIC: able to be molded, altered, or bent

The new material was very PLASTIC and could be formed into products of vastly different shapes.

PLETHORA: excess

Assuming that more was better, the defendant offered the judge a PLETHORA of excuses.

PRAGMATIC: practical as opposed to idealistic

While daydreaming gamblers think they can get rich by frequenting casinos, PRAGMATIC gamblers realize that the odds are heavily stacked against them.

PRECIPITATE: to throw violently or bring about abruptly; lacking deliberation

Upon learning that the couple married after knowing each other only two months, friends and family members expected such a PRECIPITATE marriage to end in divorce.

PREVARICATE: to lie or deviate from the truth

Rather than admit that he had overslept again, the employee PREVARICATED and claimed that heavy traffic had prevented him from arriving at work on time.

PRISTINE: fresh and clean; uncorrupted

Since concerted measures had been taken to prevent looting, the archeological site was still PRISTINE when researchers arrived.

PRODIGAL: lavish, wasteful

The PRODIGAL son quickly wasted all of his inheritance on a lavish lifestyle devoted to pleasure.

PROLIFERATE: to increase in number quickly

Although she only kept two guinea pigs initially, they PROLIFERATED to such an extent that she soon had dozens.

PROPITIATE: to conciliate; to appease

The management PROPITIATED the irate union by agreeing to raise wages for its members.

PROPRIETY: correct behavior; obedience to rules and customs

The aristocracy maintained a high level of PROPRIETY, adhering to even the most minor social rules.

PRUDENCE: wisdom, caution, or restraint

The college student exhibited PRUDENCE by obtaining practical experience along with her studies, which greatly strengthened her résumé.

PUNGENT: sharp and irritating to the senses

The smoke from the burning tires was extremely PUNGENT.

QUIESCENT: motionless

Many animals are QUIESCENT over the winter months, minimizing activity in order to conserve energy.

RAREFY: to make thinner or sparser

Since the atmosphere RAREFIES as altitudes increase, the air at the top of very tall mountains is too thin to breathe.

REPUDIATE: to reject the validity of

The old woman's claim that she was Russian royalty was REPUDIATED when DNA tests showed she was of no relation to them.

RETICENT: silent, reserved

Physically small and RETICENT in her speech, Joan Didion often went unnoticed by those upon whom she was reporting.

RHETORIC: effective writing or speaking

Lincoln's talent for RHETORIC was evident in his beautifully expressed Gettysburg Address.

SATIATE: to satisfy fully or overindulge

His desire for power was so great that nothing less than complete control of the country could SATIATE it.

SOPORIFIC: causing sleep or lethargy

The movie proved to be so SOPORIFIC that soon loud snores were heard throughout the theater.

SPECIOUS: deceptively attractive; seemingly plausible but fallacious

The student's SPECIOUS excuse for being late sounded legitimate but was proved otherwise when her teacher called her home.

STIGMA: a mark of shame or discredit

In *The Scarlet Letter*, Hester Prynne was required to wear the letter *A* on her clothes as a public STIGMA for her adultery.

STOLID: unemotional; lacking sensitivity

The prisoner appeared STOLID and unaffected by the judge's harsh sentence.

SUBLIME: lofty or grand

The music was so SUBLIME that it transformed the rude surroundings into a special place.

TACIT: done without using words

Although not a word had been said, everyone in the room knew that a TACIT agreement had been made about which course of action to take.

TACITURN: silent, not talkative

The clerk's TACITURN nature earned him the nickname "Silent Bob."

TIRADE: long, harsh speech or verbal attack

Observers were shocked at the manager's TIRADE over such a minor mistake.

TORPOR: extreme mental and physical sluggishness

After surgery, the patient experienced TORPOR until the anesthesia wore off.

TRANSITORY: temporary, lasting a brief time

The reporter lived a TRANSITORY life, staying in one place only long enough to cover the current story.

VACILLATE: to sway physically; to be indecisive

The customer held up the line as he VACILLATED between ordering chocolate chip or rocky road ice cream.

VENERATE: to respect deeply

In a traditional Confucian society, the young VENERATE their elders, deferring to the elders' wisdom and experience.

VERACITY: filled with truth and accuracy

She had a reputation for VERACITY, so everyone trusted her description of events.

VERBOSE: wordy

The professor's answer was so VERBOSE that his student forgot what the original question had been.

VEX: to annoy

The old man who loved his peace and quiet was VEXED by his neighbor's loud music.

VOLATILE: easily aroused or changeable; lively or explosive

His VOLATILE personality made it difficult to predict his reaction to anything.

WAVER: to fluctuate between choices

If you WAVER too long before making a decision about which testing site to register for, you may not get your first choice.

WHIMSICAL: acting in a fanciful or capricious manner; unpredictable

The ballet was WHIMSICAL, delighting the children with its imaginative characters and unpredictable sets.

ZEAL: passion, excitement

She brought her typical ZEAL to the project, sparking enthusiasm in the other team members.

COMMONLY CONFUSED WORDS

Already—by this or that time, previously
He already completed his work.

All ready—completely prepared
The students were all ready to take their exam.

Altogether—entirely, completely
I am altogether certain that I turned in my homework.

All together—in the same place
She kept the figurines all together on her mantle.

Capital—a city containing the seat of government, the wealth or funds owned by a business or individual, resources
Atlanta is the capital of Georgia.
The company's capital gains have diminished in recent years.

Capitol—the building in which a legislative body meets
Our trip included a visit to the Capitol building in Washington, D.C.

Coarse—rough, not smooth; lacking refinement
The truck's large wheels enabled it to navigate the coarse, rough terrain.
His coarse language prevented him from getting hired for the job.

Course—path, series of classes or studies
James's favorite course is biology.
The doctor suggested that Amy rest and let the disease run its course.

Here—in this location
George Washington used to live here.

Hear—to listen to or to perceive by the ear
Did you hear the question?

Its—a personal pronoun that shows possession
Please put the book back in its place.

It's—the contraction of it is or it has
It's snowing outside.
It's been too long.

Lead—to act as a leader, to go first, or to take a superior position
The guide will lead us through the forest.

Led—past tense of lead
The guide led us through the forest.

Lead—a metal
It is dangerous to inhale fumes from paint containing lead.

Loose—free, to set free, not tight
She always wears loose clothing when she does yoga.

Lose—to become without
Use a bookmark so you don't lose your place in your book.

Passed—the past tense of pass, an euphemism for someone dying
We passed by her house on Sunday.

Past—that which has gone by or elapsed in time
In the past, Abby never used to study.
We drove past her house.

Principal—the head of a school, main or important
The quarterback's injury is the principal reason the team lost.
The principal of the school meets with parents regularly.

Principle—a fundamental law or truth
The laws of motion are among the most important principles in physics.

Stationary—fixed, not moving
Thomas rode a stationary bicycle at the gym.

Stationery—paper used for letter writing
The principal's stationery has the school's logo on the top.

Their—possessive of they
Paul and Ben studied for their test together.

There—a place, in that matter or respect
There are several question types on the GRE.
Please hang up your jacket over there.

They're—contraction of they are
Be careful of the bushes as they're filled with thorns.